"Clark Terry is an American Master. I love to listen to him, particularly 'Mumbles.' I was so delighted when we received degrees together, along with Edward Kennedy, at the New England Conservatory in 1997."
—ARETHA FRANKLIN

"I've always been a great admirer of Clark Terry's work on the trumpet and flugelhorn, and now I have become a big admirer of his work as an author—you will love this book."
—CLINT EASTWOOD

"I met Clark when I was sixteen years old. He saw something in me and without hesitation planted me in the most fertile soil any aspiring artist could hope to be in . . . his heart. I am eternally grateful for his generous spirit, love, encouragement, storytelling, and above all laughter throughout the years! Clark . . . I love you madly."
—DIANNE REEVES

"I've come to know Clark as undoubtedly the greatest teacher in the history of jazz. From the mentoring of Miles Davis and Quincy Jones, to the millions of young musicians touched by the Thelonious Monk Institute of Jazz all over the globe, Clark and his incredible music stand as a symbol of intellect and spirituality of the highest order to all of us. Thank God for Clark Terry!"
—THELONIOUS MONK, III

"Thank you, Clark, for a lifetime of your incredible talents, and for filling this world with so much love. All of us at the Jazz Foundation of America are sincerely thankful for your compassion and involvement in our efforts to help musicians in need. You are an inspiration and a classic role model truly beyond category!"
—WENDY OXENHORN

"His style, his sound, his look, his voice, his heart, his soul. That's what inspires Snoop Dogg about Mr. Terry. If I could only do half of what he did in the music business, my life would be complete. I had the honor and pleasure of spending a few days with Mr. Terry. He's the greatest to ever do it. Thank you, Uncle Quincy, for introducing me to Mr. Mumbles!!!"
—SNOOP DOGG

"Clark and I have been friends for many decades, and I've always enjoyed his music. Recently, on a long, three-hundred-mile drive to our gig, we listened to Clark's wonderful *Porgy and Bess* album. This was the second or third time that we'd done that. It sure was some great playing on your part, Clark! We enjoyed those Chicago Jazz Orchestra brass players, too. Congratulations on your book."

—DAVE BRUBECK

"Whenever I see Clark Terry, I always look forward to talking to him and reminiscing about the early bebop years. There's an expression coined by Lester Young that succinctly says it all about Clark Terry: 'chandelier,' a raconteur par excellence, 'Mumbles'-brilliant, original musical brilliance. It has been a privilege."

—BILLY DEE WILLIAMS

"When I saw Clark performing at the Blue Note in New York, I thought to myself, 'Could this be what all of us instrumentalists are really trying to do?' Before my eyes and ears, the legend/man/craftsman went *there*. As I saw it, *there* was straight to the source of personal expression. Through 'Mumbles' or through the flugelhorn, the man spoke to me that night, and I'll remember that always as a larger than life experience."

—ESPERANZA SPALDING

"Clark Terry is a jazz superstar and one of the most extraordinary individuals I have ever encountered. He's a world-class musician, educator, composer, jazz pioneer, and a cofounder of the Thelonious Monk Institute of Jazz. He has inspired people of all ages with his humor, courage, passion, and vision. Thanks for your friendship, Clark, and for always being there for the Institute."

—TOM CARTER

"The one I admire without restriction is Clark Terry, whose pronunciation at the trumpet or bugle is a model of sharpness, clearness, and authority. A model which is given with generosity to all of those who want to play this instrument . . . the way it should be played."

—MAURICE ANDRÉ

THE GEORGE GUND FOUNDATION
IMPRINT IN AFRICAN AMERICAN STUDIES

The George Gund Foundation has endowed
this imprint to advance understanding of
the history, culture, and current issues
of African Americans.

The publisher gratefully acknowledges the generous support of the African American Studies Endowment Fund of the University of California Press Foundation, which was established by a major gift from the George Gund Foundation.

Clark

Clark

The Autobiography of Clark Terry

WITH GWEN TERRY

Preface by Quincy Jones
Foreword by Bill Cosby
Introduction by David Demsey

University of California Press

BERKELEY   LOS ANGELES   LONDON

University of California Press, one of the most distinguished university presses in the
United States, enriches lives around the world by advancing scholarship in the humanities,
social sciences, and natural sciences. Its activities are supported by the UC Press Foundation
and by philanthropic contributions from individuals and institutions. For more information,
visit www.ucpress.edu.

University of California Press
Berkeley and Los Angeles, California

University of California Press, Ltd.
London, England

Library of Congress Cataloging-in-Publication Data

Terry, Clark.
  Clark / the autobiography of Clark Terry, with Gwen Terry ; with a
preface by Quincy Jones, a foreword by Bill Cosby, and an introduction
by David Demsey.
    p.   cm.
  Includes index.
  ISBN 978-0-520-26846-3 (cloth : alk. paper)
  1. Terry, Clark.   2. Jazz musicians—United States—Biography.
3. Trumpet players—United States—Biography.   I. Terry, Gwen.
II. Title.
  ML419.T375A3   2011
  788.9'2165092—dc22
  [B]   2011007956

Manufactured in the United States of America

20 19 18 17 16 15 14 13 12 11
10 9 8 7 6 5 4 3 2 1

This book is printed on Cascades Enviro 100, a 100% post consumer
waste, recycled, de-inked fiber. FSC recycled certified and processed
chlorine free. It is acid free, Ecologo certified, and manufactured by
BioGas energy.

To my beautiful wife, Gwen,
and to the past, present, and
future creators of jazz

Contents

Preface by Quincy Jones   xi

Foreword by Bill Cosby   xiii

Introduction by David Demsey   xv

1. Big Dreams   1

2. First Instruments   2

3. Kicked Out   8

4. The Vashon High Swingsters   11

5. First Road Gig   22

6. Nigga   28

7. Ida Cox   33

8. Stranded   39

9. Lincoln Inn   42

10. On the Road Again   48

11. Tennis Shoe Pimp   56

12. Jailed   58

13. Len Bowden   62

14. Navy Days   64

15. Gray Clouds   69

16. The Big Apple   73

17. George Hudson   75

18. The Club Plantation   80

19. Galloping Dominoes   85

20. Tempting Offers   87

21. Lionel Hampton   90

22. Road Lessons   94

23. Pauline   96

24. Charlie Barnet   102

25. Count Basie   110

26. Big Debt   115

27. Duke Ellington   122

28. Leaving Basie   126

29. The University of Ellingtonia   128

30. Working with Duke   132

31. Duke's Team   136

32. Duke's Management Arts   142

33. Miles and Bird   143

34. Billy Strayhorn   146

35. Endurances   148

36. Flugelhorn   152

37. Europe   155

38. Norman Granz   158

39. Norman's Battles   160

40. Q   165

41. NBC   170

42. Jim and Andy's   173

43. Johnny and Ed   174

44. Mumbles   176

45. First House   179

46. Big Bad Band   182

47. Carnegie Hall   187

48. Etoile   188

49. Jazz Education Arena   191

50. Those NBC Years   198

51. Storms   202

52. Black Clouds   205

53. Keep on Keepin' On   212

54. New Love   220

55. Whirlwinds   224

56. Through the Storm   230

57. Second Chance   239

58. The Biggest Surprise   250

      Acknowledgments   259
      Honors and Awards   269
      Original Compositions   279
      Selected Discography   283
      Index   303

Photographs follow page 186

Preface

Clark Terry is a dear, dear friend of mine. He is a giant, as a musician and as a human being. He's also a great storyteller, so I give big-time props to his autobiography. He wrote the sixth chapter of mine.

Our friendship goes way, way back. Like he says, "Backer than that!" It began when I was a young teenager in Seattle, where he was performing with Count Basie. In the late '40s, they worked at the Palomar Theater each night, and even though the early morning was Clark's sleep time, eventually he graciously offered to give me trumpet lessons before I went to school.

One of the greatest joys of my *life* was when he left Duke Ellington's Orchestra to join my band in Belgium when I was music director for the musical *Free and Easy* in 1959. Man, when he did that, I was the happiest cat on the planet!

Over the years, we've always kept in touch and been there for each other. He's never been afraid to get wet when it rains. Believe me, I'll love him until the day I die.

On the night when he received his 2010 Grammy Lifetime Achievement Award, I was sitting next to him in the audience. I left a recording session with fifty people to be there, and I wouldn't trade those moments with Clark for anything.

He has always been loving and encouraging, and he has helped countless aspiring musicians. Even at ninety years old, he's still making dreams come true for young hopefuls who want to learn from a true master. Still making time to share his wisdom.

Now, after twenty years of working on this book with his lovely wife, Gwen, I'm thrilled to see *his* dream come true.

Quincy Jones

Foreword

No matter where you see Clark Terry, or what physical condition or mental condition he's in, he's always ready to give anybody helpful instructions on how to play better or to find their answer to their playing better. No matter what they play.

You can come up to him and say, "Mr. Terry." And he'll say, "Yes." You could say, "I play the zither." And he would say, "Oh, that's wonderful." Then you could say, "But I'm having a problem with the zither. I want to play like Milt Jackson." And he would say, "On the zither? Well, let me hear you play." And you could play, and then at the end of your playing, Clark Terry would clean up all the problems you have by telling you what is wrong. I don't care if it's a zither or a zipper; it doesn't make any difference because this man is Clark Terry.

When Clark was a young boy, he had a dream of playing the trumpet, but he had no trumpet, so he went to the junkyard and he made one. He also helped his friends to make their instruments, and then he created his street-corner band.

Oddly, there's a similarity between Clark Terry's street-corner band and "Fat Albert and the Cosby Kids" in their junkyard band. When you see these animated characters playing music in the junkyard and singing along with their playing, I have to point to Clark Terry's opening paragraph to certify my story, because Clark made his first horn from pieces of what people didn't want anymore. Now that I think about it, he even used somebody's chewed chewing gum to make his valve tips. That's right.

You could look at it this way—that Clark could have bought some chewing gum and chewed it himself so he could make his valve tips, but he didn't. He found some gum in that junkyard that had already been chewed. So maybe it was the aging of the gum, I don't know. One thing that I do know is that Clark was determined to make his dream come true.

There's an old saying, I don't know what color the person was—green or purple. Lots of green people are at sea, usually bending over the railing of the ship. Anyway, there's a saying, "He who invents his own horn will live to hear himself play a real horn." The people who heard the early invented horn said, "Thank God!" when they heard the real horn.

Another old saying is, "He who played around on the horn that he invented, and later became a master, is a happier person, and so is the audience."

Clark is a master musician, a great storyteller, and an international treasure. Indeed, his music is played in the languages reflecting his worldwide admirers, and he is deeply respected.

Bill Cosby

Introduction

The singular life that Clark Terry chronicles within these pages is not just the story of one of the major pioneers in American and African American culture—a groundbreaking jazz trumpeter and flugelhornist, not to mention one of the original rappers via his infamous alter ego, Mumbles. It is also the life story of one of the original creators of jazz education. His vision, as well as his endless energy and steadfast determination, helped spread jazz from clubs and concert halls to other generations in school band rooms and summer youth camps across the United States and around the world.

Without Clark's efforts, the Jazz Studies Program that I co-lead at William Paterson University (home of the Clark Terry Archive) would not exist, nor would the similar programs at the University of New Hampshire, where Clark has long been associated, or at any one of the hundreds of colleges and universities that teach jazz as an academic area of study. Or, for that matter, at the thousands of public schools across the country where young students learn to play the music of Ellington, Basie, and others. Without the vast jazz education network that Clark helped to create, we might never have heard the generations of fiery young players that continue to break onto the scene. Without Clark's own brand of audience-building, jazz might have been relegated to the museum by now, instead of flourishing in jazz clubs worldwide.

I represent thousands of musicians and audience members whose lives have been touched by Clark Terry. Clark was one of the first jazz voices introduced to me by one of my early mentors, trumpeter/educator Don Stratton, who was in turn mentored by Clark. Later, as a young professional, I was fortunate enough to be in the saxophone section of several big bands that featured Clark as a guest artist.

My life changed in 1985 when, as a jazz faculty member at the University of Maine Augusta, I performed a full concert with Clark and a rhythm section. A few hours prior to the gig, Clark held a long and detailed rehearsal . . . and we did not play a *single one* of those tunes in the concert! Clark had sized us all up, knew precisely our strengths and weaknesses, had figured out what we knew and needed to know—and then he warmly, lovingly kicked our tails all over the stage, putting on an amazing show at the same time. I had never played better. On that day, I became not just Clark's fan and admirer, but his student as well, joining the seemingly endless ranks, among whom stand such legends as Quincy Jones and Miles Davis, whose lives have been changed by his presence and work.

In 2004, Clark and his wife, Gwen, announced that he had chosen the William Paterson campus to be the site of the Clark Terry Archive. The experience of working with Clark to assemble that collection has been a true joy. After Clark's announcement, I spent every Monday at his Haworth, New Jersey, home, arriving after my class ended at 1:00 in time to have a second breakfast with Clark and Gwen. Then Clark and I would explore his museum-like house. I crawled through his closets and basement with my laptop, cataloging his collections; it was like some sort of surreal jazz archaeology expedition, and I was giddy with excitement just to touch all of that history. I've lost count of the times Clark exulted, "Oh, Dr. D. D., I've been looking for that for thirty years!" And to learn about each artifact from Clark himself, the stories at turns moving and hilarious, was priceless. That process continues today as I make my way to Clark and Gwen's new home in Pine Bluff, Arkansas. On my last visit we unearthed a long-forgotten box of Clark's handwritten parts and scores, perhaps the rarest of his treasures.

Most rewarding has been witnessing Clark's relationship with our students at William Paterson University. In addition to holding regular classes and rehearsals in our music building, he hosted jam sessions as well as storytelling and joke marathons at his nearby home, which we came to call the William Paterson U. Eastern Campus. Most people feel lucky to experience a one- or two-day residency with Clark; our faculty and students got to interact with him almost daily—Prof. Clark Terry, obsessive educator! To be with Clark—whether it's in a classroom, backstage, or driving in a car—is to take a lesson. Our students quickly realized that his octogenarian status had absolutely no effect on his stamina or the amount of hours he would spend to perfect a tune. Although his departure for Arkansas left a huge void, Clark stays in touch with us at William Paterson, and he now brings his magic to the lucky students of the University of Arkansas Pine Bluff campus.

It has been my honor to help edit some of the more recent sections of this book. These pages, I find, have an effect similar to a Clark Terry Archive visit: in reading about the amazing life and pioneering career of this great gentleman, you gather in the personal magic that has so profoundly affected the people he knows and has taught.

David Demsey
Coordinator of Jazz Studies
Curator, The Clark Terry Archive
William Paterson University, Wayne, New Jersey

1. Big Dreams

I made my first trumpet with scraps from a junkyard. My friend Shitty helped me find the pieces on a blazing hot summer day in 1931. I coiled up an old garden hose into the shape of a trumpet and bound it in three places with wire to make it look like it had valves. Topped those with used chewing gum for valve tips. Stuck a piece of lead pipe in one end of the hose for a mouthpiece. And for the bell on the other end, I found a not-too-rusty kerosene funnel. I was a ten-year-old kid, blowing on that thing until my lips were bleeding, but I was trying to play *jazz!* It may have sounded like a honking goose, but it was music to my ears.

Jazz was everywhere in my hometown, St. Louis, Missouri. My brother-in-law played it in a band; I heard it on the radio, in parades, in the parks, in my neighborhood at block parties and the Friday night fish fries, and from the riverboats that I watched from the banks of the Mississippi River.

That junkyard trumpet, I made it right after I heard Duke Ellington's band play on a neighbor's graphophone (a predecessor to the gramophone) at a fish fry. I wanted to be involved with music like *that*.

Duke's band was different from any other band I'd ever heard! The sound. Those horns. That rhythm. It was powerful, like a freight train. Everybody knew about Duke's band. I had heard about him—heard that he was the most respected band leader anywhere. And that night, I heard *why*.

Nobody's band *moved* me like that. Nobody's. It blew my mind! Stopped me dead in my tracks. I couldn't do anything but listen to that music. It was like the whole world disappeared. Nobody was left but me and that band. I wanted to learn how Duke did it.

Twenty years later, I was fortunate enough to be hired by Duke. I was thirty years old. It was Armistice Day, November 11, 1951, at the Kiel Auditorium in St. Louis. Huge place. All the latest sound and lighting.

Believe me, I'd paid a lot of dues before then. Lots of acid tests, situations that seemed impossible—but nothing like the changes I had to go through that night in Duke's band. Back in '47, when I first joined Charlie Barnet's band, what he came up with for an acid test didn't compare. The way that Basie made me prove myself in front of his band in '48 was hard as hell! But even *that* couldn't touch what Duke whipped on me. That was the lay of the land: put the new kid on the spot. You either passed the test or got the ax!

Many of my dreams have come true, but what I've learned is that dreams change. New dreams come into play. What I thought I wanted most of my life changed, too.

I'd always thought that the most important thing was to play my horn—to get into this band or that band or Duke's band, to have my own band, to perform, record. And I did enjoy these things. Worked hard to achieve them. But later on, I had a new dream: helping young musicians to make their dreams come true. That became my supreme joy and my greatest aspiration.

2. First Instruments

The only person I knew who didn't love jazz was my old man. He liked country music. He was a short man, just over five feet tall—"Five foot two," he always said, smoking or chewing on a handmade Hauptmann cigar. He was a strong man. Didn't take crap from anybody! I remember when his union was trying to get the workers to go on strike at his job. He worked for Laclede Gas and Light Company, and the union wanted better wages, but Pop wouldn't cooperate. He said, "I got too many mouths to feed to play a white man's game." So some white union guys came to our flat after work. They were shouting from the street up to our front window. Calling him by the name he hated.

"Shorty! Come on down!"

Pop sent my sisters down the back stairs, so they could slip out to our Aunt Gert's place next door to the flat below ours. Then he armed my brothers with pistols, knocked out our window pane, aimed his shotgun, and let his bullets do his talking. The men below were armed with pistols, baseball bats, crowbars, and chains. When they heard Pop's shotgun blasts, they took off like chickens running from a cook.

Everybody respected him. He wore nice clothes and hats. His name was Clark Virgil Terry, and we called him Pop, but everybody else called him Mr. Son, because his nickname was Son Terry. All my friends were scared of him, and I was, too. He'd beat me at the drop of a dime. None of my brothers and sisters. Just me. Except one time he beat my oldest sister, Ada Mae, when she stood up for me and *begged* him not to whip me after I broke the limb off a neighbor's tree while I was swinging on a rope.

When I told him that I wanted to play a trumpet, he said, "Rotten on that shit, Boy!" He had a weird way of cussing, but I knew what it meant. He said, "Remember your cousin Otis Berry? Always walking up and down the streets on his paper route, playing that damn horn! He got consumption and died! So, I'd better not hear tell of you playing no damn trumpet, or I'll beat your ass till you won't see the light of day again!"

That wasn't gonna stop me. I didn't believe that I'd get consumption. (That's what they called tuberculosis.) I'd wanted to play a trumpet in the worst way ever since I was five and watching those trumpets in the neighborhood parades. I *loved* the trumpet, because it was the loudest and it led the melody. And after I'd heard Duke's band at that fish fry, I *had* to play some jazz on a trumpet and I had to have a band, too. No matter what Pop said.

I was born on December 14, 1920, in St. Louis, the seventh of eleven children. Eight girls and three boys. Ada Mae, Margueritte, Virgil Otto (we called him "Bus"), Charles Edward (we called him Ed), Lillian, Mable (her nickname was "Sugar Lump," and they told me that she only lived for six months). Then there was me, Juanita, Marie and Mattie—the twins— and my baby sister, Odessa. All my sisters looked like little brown dolls. Ed was about my father's height, Bus was tall, and I was medium height.

Before I was born, my brothers and sisters said they begged Pop to name me John. He named me Clark Terry with no middle name. But everybody called me John, including Pop.

My mother's name was Mary. She died when I was around six or seven. I don't remember too much about her because she was always gone. Working, they said. Ada Mae told me that Momma was from Crystal City, Missouri, and Pop was from Fort Scott, Kansas. They were both born in 1888. I don't know how they met, and I don't know anything about my grandparents.

As far as I was concerned, Ada Mae was my mother. When she married Sy McField and moved out, my next-oldest sister, Margueritte, became my mother. When Margueritte married Johnny Pops and moved out I tried to be happy for her, but I missed her. My mother's sister, Aunt Gert, was kind of like a mother after Margueritte left. But I always wondered why she wouldn't take up for me, knowing how Pop *beat* me. She was a short, dark-skinned woman who loved to cook special things for me. Still, whenever I played "Sometimes I Feel Like a Motherless Child" later on in my career, I felt every note.

We lived in a neighborhood called Carondelet, about a half mile from the Mississippi River, where trains went back and forth all day. *Clack*alacka, *Clack*alacka. *Whoo! Whoo!* And kids wore Buster Brown shoes with a knife pocket on the side. My knife was in my pants pocket because I couldn't afford Buster Browns. From our backyard, St. Louis seemed like it was way up high on a big mound and we lived down low near the river bottom. I dreamed of growing up and getting away from there. Away from the chickens in the backyard, the rats running around, the roaches, and the bedbugs that my brothers and I used to burn off of the bedsprings each Saturday.

Our pastor, Reverend Sommerville, instilled a lot of hope inside me. I loved him and admired the way he spoke—very clearly and with a lot of authority. He said, "The only way to get out of this ghetto is to get your education. And remember, in this enigma called life, we must hold on to God's unchanging hand!" He was a short, robust man with thick curly hair. Always dressed to the nines—double-breasted suits, fancy ties. And he had an impressive vocabulary. I wanted to learn some fancy words like he used.

He was the pastor of our small church, Corinthian Baptist. Each Sunday, my brother Ed, a few of my sisters, and I would head out to church dressed in our "Sunday-go-to-meeting-clothes." The best we had. We'd walk for a few miles west up Bowen Street from our flat to the "hinkty" people's neighborhood, where our church was located. We'd say, "They think they're better than us. Bourgeois. With their hot water and electricity." Still, there was a lot of love there at Corinthian. Lots of friends and pretty girls.

After church at Corinthian, on Sunday afternoon, I'd meet up with a few friends and sneak over to the Church of God and Christ at Broadway and Iron Street. Now, I knew Pop would beat me if he knew that I went over there, but I didn't care. I dug the polyrhythms of that church. Those powerful beats, the tambourines, the foot-stomping and the hand-clapping. The way they sang—multiple harmonies. Lots of spirit. We were too scared to go inside, since we had peeked through the window many times and seen the folks shouting and running and jumping and talking strange. "Speaking in tongues" is what they called it. So we sat on a nearby corner, within earshot.

But the love of my life was jazz! On Friday nights, I heard it echoing off the waters of the Mississippi. From our front window facing the river, I could see the corner of Broadway and Bowen. Men who were the lamp-lighters used to come walking with a long pole to light a small pilot inside the lantern on that corner. They called it a streetlight, but it was pitiful. Barely lit the area in front of the long two-story corner building that was jammed next to ours.

Our neighborhood looked like a row of two-story buildings with a few walkways here and there. We called them "gangways." Not much grass anywhere, just a few trees and mostly dirt in the front, back, and between. Eight of us kids and Pop lived in a three-room flat upstairs at 6207-A South Broadway, with no electricity and no hot water. We had one front window and a solid wood back door. Everything was heated and cooked with kindling and coal, which meant a lot of ashes for me to take down to the ash pit out back. There were some extremely uncomfortable moments in our little flat because we ate a lot of beans. The saying was, "Everybody knows you can't eat beans and keep it a secret."

Lots of families lived in those two-story buildings, with the doors and stairs to all flats in the back where the water pumps, woodsheds, and chicken coops were. There was a big, dusty vacant lot nearby where most of the kids hung out and played games like tin-can soccer. We didn't have a ball, but we had just as much fun with that can. I played goalie, and I had scars all up and down my legs. I guess the reason we didn't play football was that Carondelet had a lot of Germans living there, and they were into soccer.

There was an alley lined with ash pits that separated us from our white neighbors. That was the line that divided us from them. They were an alley away from the ghetto, but they were cool. My brothers and I used to make money hauling ashes for them.

Miss Liza was our next-door neighbor. She was a short, dark-brown-skinned woman who usually sucked on a chicken bone and spied on us through a hole in her window shade. I didn't like her. She caused me to get an ass-whipping when she told Pop about me kicking a soccer can through Mr. Butt's window a few doors down. (His name was Mr. Robinson, but I nicknamed him that after our gang peeked inside his window one night and saw him screwing his old lady, and all we could see was his big black butt moving around.)

My friend Shitty lived right below us. It was his grandmother's flat, and she took care of him and his sister, Elnora—a foxy, brown-skinned cutie. I had played "stink finger" with her a few times. Shitty was the color of molasses, with sleepy eyes and dark pointed lips. His real name was Robbie Pyles, but since he was always taking dumps in his pants, I nicknamed him "Shitty." He was cool with that.

When Pop went to work, he told me to stay at home. I didn't listen to *that*. I'd sneak about four blocks away to Didley's house with Shitty so we could listen to jazz on Didley's crystal radio. It had terrible sound. We strained to hear the music. But when we put that radio inside of one of his mother's mixing bowls, the sound was a little better.

Didley was a smiling cat with two big buckteeth. He walked with a little limp because he'd been hit by a car when he was a little kid. We listened to broadcasts by the Coon-Sanders Original Nighthawks Orchestra and Jan Savitt—all-white bands. But Jan had a black singer, a rare thing during that time. The singer was a scat singer named Bon Bon Tunnell. Then there was Larry Clinton's band, playing things like "The Dipsy Doodle":

> Dipsy Doodle is a thing to beware,
> Dipsy Doodle will get in yo' hair.

But no matter who I heard, I just couldn't get Duke Ellington's band out of my head. I wanted a band like that. Had to have one. So I talked some of the gang into getting a little street band together. I told them, "Don't worry about Pop, because he goes to his girlfriend's house all day on Saturday. So we can play on a corner right after the parade and make a little money."

We made some instruments from some scraps at the local junkyard, about a block away. I made a kazoo, which was actually a comb wrapped in tissue paper left over from gift-wrappings.

My brother Ed played drums, which we made with a worn-out ice pan turned upside down on top of a tall bushel basket. His sticks were rungs from a chair. I had another friend, Charlie Jones—we called him "Bones." He played "tuba," which I made with a big tin beer cup for the bell, stuck in one end of a vacuum hose that was wrapped around his neck. Charlie was a cool dude who was known for writing "Merry Christmas" in the snow with pee. Bones' chubby little brother, Pig, held the kitty, which was a cardboard cigar box tacked shut. It had a small slit in the top for donations.

Shitty played "bass," which was a broomstick with a taut rope tied to the top of the stick and attached to an old galvanized washtub turned upside down. He also agreed to be our "buck dancer," which was a kind of tap dance.

After the Labor Day Parade in '31, we hurried up and started playing on a corner before the folks walked away. I was blowing *hard* on that thing, and moving that paper around when the spit got it wet, while we played our version of "Tiger Rag."

Shitty was already prepared to do his buck dance because he had stomped on two Pet Milk cans—one for each foot—which he'd curled around the heels of his shoes. They had a great sound on the brick sidewalk. *Clack, CLACK, Clack!* At one point we were really wailing on "Tiger Rag." I mean we were getting down! Shitty jumped out front and went to work, clomping and stomping up a storm, doing his buck dance. Elbows flying up and down. Folks watching were eating it *up*. Cheering in spite of the smells coming from his pants.

We did pretty well doing our thing with the little crowd that gathered around us. About fifty cents for the musicians, and a few pennies for Pig. We were all proud!

But that kazoo just wasn't cutting it for me. So Shitty and I went back to the junkyard with the sun beating down hard. He and I were wiping sweat a mile a minute. He said, "Ok-kay, John. What sh-should we l-look for?"

I said, "Stuff that we can make a trumpet with."

We walked all over that funky junkyard. Over old tires, broken bottles, rusty car parts, dirty rags, used clothes, broken wheels, crushed dishes, furniture parts, newspapers, rusted sinks, cracked toilets, burned curtains, and a bunch of other crap until we found the parts that I thought would make a hip trumpet.

When we did our next performance, after the Thanksgiving Day Parade, I blew that junkyard trumpet so hard that the lead-pipe mouthpiece made a black ring on my lips. Even though we made a few more pennies than before, the gang wasn't digging all the practice time I was asking from them. They said they could make more money doing other things. Shitty said, "Grandma is s-sick, and I g-got plans." They all chimed in with reasons why they were quitting. I was speechless. Totally disgusted. But I wasn't going to give up on my dreams.

Mr. Butt walked up to me one day while I was blowing hard out by the chicken coop, and he was carrying a big brown paper bag. Pig, Shitty, Ed, and Bones were hanging out with me. Mr. Butt smelled like he'd just had a swig of home-brew and his eyes were bloodshot. We were snickering at his tight pants that hung down under his belly. He said, "Johnny Boy, we're tired of seeing and hearing you scuffling on that piece of garbage." He held the big bag up high then started shaking it in my face.

Beanie Roach came up to see what was going on. He looked like a roach with black beans for hair. Then my chubby cousin, Billy, joined us. He had just moved in with Aunt Gert. Mr. Butt glanced at everybody, and then he opened the sack. He said, "Let's see what you can do with this!" He pulled out a raggedy splintered horn case that looked like it had come from a haunted house movie. We all "oohed" as he handed it to me.

He said, "A few of us neighbors got together, and we bought this for $12.50 at the hock shop down on Kraus Street."

When I opened the case, there was a CG Conn Trumpet with no valve tips, and the mouthpiece looked and smelled like it had just been retrieved from an outhouse. But I was thrilled! And I couldn't wait to scrub it out with steel wool and O.K. laundry soap.

3. Kicked Out

Nobody told Pop about my trumpet. Not even Miss Liza. She helped to buy it, which surprised the hell out of me. That's when I learned that everything isn't always what it seems to be. Here I was, mad at her and making fun of her and Mr. Robinson with the gang, and here they were, giving money to help me have a trumpet. I felt smaller than an ant!

Everybody was encouraging me. That made me feel good. My brother-in-law, Sy, came by and gave me lessons while Pop was at work. He played tuba in a local jazz band named Dewey Jackson and His Musical Ambassadors.

Sy was always good to me. He was a short, medium-build man with a friendly brown face and a pointed head that looked like a steeple. He showed me some fingering and how to bend some notes to make them have flatter or sharper tails without using the valves, just my embouchure and breath. I practiced that horn whenever I could. A lot!

Things were going pretty good until I was twelve. That's when I really messed up with Pop.

Now, I had never liked for anybody to tell me what to do. And if I wanted to do something against Pop's orders, I just made plans and waited until I had a chance to do it. Everything I did was justified and reasonable, at least to me. I only did things that I thought were right. And they all seemed foolproof. Like when I sneaked out to buy some clothes from the secondhand store. I was making some pretty decent change hauling ashes for our neighbors with my brothers, plus I had a little money from a newspaper route. Pop knew about those jobs. I was using the money to buy him socks, like he told me to do. But I wasn't spending all of my money on him, and here's why.

My classmates teased me while I was at Delaney Elementary School, because I ripped my pants one day trying to climb over a fence during lunchtime, and all the kids saw that I was wearing my sister's paisley underpants. Everybody except my gang said, "Clarkie's wearing bloomers! Clarkie's wearing bloomers!" That was totally embarrassing. But I couldn't tell them that Pop didn't have enough money to buy me some decent stuff to wear, and that he demanded that I wear hand-me-downs, and that my brothers were five years older than I was and nothing of theirs was left by the time I came along, which is why I had to wear my sister's old clothes. They didn't care about all of that. They just laughed at me. So, I decided to buy myself some decent clothes, underpants, and shoes at the secondhand store. I hid them so Pop wouldn't find out. And he never did. Never found out that I changed clothes when I got to school.

Then there was the time that I started taking boxing lessons at Kid Carter's Gym in Carondelet, after Ed showed me how to beat up a cat named Squatty who was making me give him my bean sandwiches every day at school. I used newspaper to wrap my sandwiches, and I wished Squatty would choke from the ink that rubbed off on the bread. Squatty was a short, stocky cat with a gold tooth. I never found out how he got that gold tooth. He was a real mean kid. A "tush hog" is what I called him behind his back because that's what everybody called bullies in private company. He teased me for misspelling *cabbage*. I'd said, "c-a-b-b-i-t-c-h," and we'd lost the spelling bee. And he teased me about wearing my sister's shoes, which were too big.

When I told Ed what was happening, he said, "If you don't kick Squatty's ass after school tomorrow, then I'm gonna kick yours!" Ed tightened his doo-rag, and he showed me a few punches and gave me some tips on how I could kick Squatty's ass. Then Ed came to my school to make sure that I won. Well, I knocked Squatty out cold! From then on, I got respect from everybody. I loved my new "macho" image, and I wanted to learn more about fighting. So it made sense to me that I needed to go over to Kid's gym and learn from a pro. Didley went with me a few times, but he just couldn't dig it.

When I got good enough to start boxing, I won a few fights, and I noticed how the girls were flirting with me more and more. I dug that. And the thrill of kicking ass gave me a real *rush*. My muscles got tight, and I gained a reputation for being a winner. I started loving boxing almost as much as playing my horn, and I thought about becoming a professional. But I had to make a decision between my horn and fighting. I realized that I couldn't enjoy kissing the girls with a fat lip. My horn won, hands down.

Pop never said anything about the fat lips that I came home with, so I assumed that things were cool. As far as girls went, he said, "Don't bring no babies up in here or I'll kill you!" Now, I certainly couldn't tell him how tired I was of my solo stroking sessions with "Minnie Five." And I sure couldn't tell him about Cookie. She was one of the older neighborhood cuties. I was scared of the dark, so I was glad when Cookie walked up to me one night. I explained that I had to find Pop's dog, Sport. She agreed to help me find him. Then she encouraged me to stand on a crate so I'd be tall enough to kiss her while leaning against the chicken coop, and she didn't mind showing me a few "other things." I couldn't turn her offer down. Especially since my cousin Otis had told me that I was too young to get anybody pregnant because I could only make "glad water," and that wasn't as strong as real ejaculation.

Thank God that Pop never found out about me and Cookie. I had gotten away with that and a bunch of crap, so I didn't ever think that things would come to a screeching halt. But when Pop found out that I had a trumpet and that I had played it while riding on the back of a truck in a political fund-raiser for a local politician named Jimmy McIntire, he beat me damn near to death. While he was beating me, he was yelling, "Didn't I tell you that you would get consumption! Rotten on that damn horn! Now you take that damn horn and throw it in the trash, and I don't want to hear tell of you playing it again!"

I just hid my trumpet and recuperated. I shouldn't have listened to Margueritte's old man. Johnny Pops was his name. He had set that gig up with big promises of me making three dollars, but it turned into a bunch of lame excuses from him and a terrible ass-whipping from Pop. I didn't trust Johnny Pops in the first place, and neither did my younger sisters, especially since he'd asked us for some of Pop's home brew, which *everybody* knew was off limits. After that whipping, I learned that I needed to be more careful about following my instincts.

Then there was the *big* screwup. Other kids in the neighborhood had bikes, and I really wanted one, too. I knew Pop's rule: "No toys for anybody. If one of you crumb-snatchers has a toy, then everybody's gonna want something!" Even at Christmas, Pop didn't buy us anything. But I didn't see anything wrong with having a bike if *I* bought it.

So I made some plans. I put my new red and white Racer on layaway, paid a dollar on it each week, and figured that I'd hide it in the woodshed, because Pop never went out there. He always sent me or one of my brothers to get wood. Showing off was what got me into trouble. Instead of riding the bike home and hiding it, and then telling everybody about it, like I'd planned, I went by Odessa's school and picked her up. Just had to *style* on my new wheels.

I put her on the handlebars and took off, paying more attention to who was looking at me than watching where I was going. Flying down a hill, I hit a bump and *bam!* we crashed. Her foot was caught in the front spokes and she was crying. I was too scared to walk her home, because we both knew Pop was there that day. So since my front wheel was messed up, I thought it was a good idea to get it fixed. Give Pop a little time to cool down. We were only a few blocks away from home, and Odessa said she could make it. So she limped on down the road, and I prepared myself for an ass-whipping.

After I went back to the bike shop, which was only a block away, and I got my wheel straightened out, I rode toward home. I was still planning to hide the bike in the woodshed. But when I got close to our building, I saw the neighbors standing out front with scared faces. One of them told me, "Mr. Son said, 'If you see John on that bike, tell him to keep on riding!'"

I was shocked. I knew Pop never said anything that he didn't mean. I was twelve years old, and Pop was kicking me out. I went over to Didley's house, spent the night, sneaked back home the next day while Pop was at work, got my trumpet and my money that I had hidden in the coal bin, and said good-bye to my sisters and my friends.

I damn sure didn't want to live with Margueritte and her slick-talking husband, Johnny Pops. The only place I thought about was Ada Mae and Sy's new apartment across town at 2913 Lawton. I was wiping my tears and praying that they'd let me move in. I rode for miles and miles. When they said yes, I broke down crying.

4. The Vashon High Swingsters

The fall of '33 started out like a big drag, getting kicked out of Pop's house and all. I missed my old friends and Carondelet.

Sy and Ada Mae lived in a nice apartment. It was the only apartment on the third floor of their building. Nice neighborhood with grass instead of dirt yards. Three doors in the hallway and nice windows inside. A view of the tops of nearby stucco buildings like ours, backyards, and an alley. It was more spacious than Pop's flat by far. Had a big black gas stove in the kitchen—no need for kindling or hauling ashes outside. Electricity and hot water. Even had a real refrigerator instead of an icebox. Although I was glad that Sy and Ada Mae let me move in with them, I felt homesick. I was alone on my thirteenth birthday. No birthday celebration for me this year. No Christmas spirit like I'd had at Pop's house with my brothers and sisters.

Ada Mae and Sy worked late hours. She was a barmaid at a local bar, and he was gigging in and out of town. They were usually asleep when I was getting ready for school, and most of the time they were gone to work when I was at home.

By the time the second semester of my seventh grade year rolled around that January of '34, I had learned to enjoy my new digs. I had made some new friends in the neighborhood, and my trumpet playing was coming along pretty well. After I did my homework and chores, I kept the phonograph and radio hot. I was determined to learn some jazz tunes. Especially the big band stuff.

Ada Mae and Sy told me that as long as I kept my grades up in school and stayed out of trouble, I could pretty much do whatever I wanted to do. They trusted me, and I wasn't going to blow it. I'd gotten a paper route so I wouldn't be a burden, and I'd saved up and gotten some new duds.

When Sy had some spare time, he gave me some jazz lessons. I glanced at his pointed head as he told me all about the independent melodies of the different sections in big bands. Melodies that were being played at the same time. "Contrapuntal," he called it. I called it hip! The brass section was playing one thing, and the woodwinds were riffing something else. The bass was plucking different lines while the piano and drums were swinging with their own contribution. Man! I couldn't keep still.

Sy explained the concepts of horizontal components, vertical textures, temporal dimensions, and things like that. I couldn't have been in a better place. Personal jazz lessons, a comfortable couch to sleep on, and a whole lot of love.

I practiced my horn until my fingertips ached from playing with no valve tips, but I kept right on going. Got pretty good, too. Good enough for a few of the neighborhood kids to want to hear me play. Two girls, Flash and Marcella, and Marcella's brother, Mahew, and a few others, they'd come over, and the girls would do my chores for me—dusting, sweeping, washing dishes—while I played. Then we moved the furniture out of the way so we could dance. I'd slicked my hair down with lots of Vaseline so it would resemble the conks in the pictures of musicians that I'd seen in the

Sepia magazines on the coffee table. I'd copped some secondhand brown pants, a tan shirt, and shiny brown Friendly Fives.

One evening, I picked up my horn, winked at Flash, and started playing along with the Coon and Sanders big band on the radio like I was really a featured soloist. When "Tiger Rag" came on, I wailed up a storm because I *really* knew that song.

> Hold that Tiger!
> Hold that Tiger!

Notes were flying out of my horn that surprised *me*. I closed my eyes and gave it all I had. Whether I played along with the radio or a cappella, man, my friends were digging my sounds so hard that I felt like I was really blowing. All I could think about was that one day I'd be a professional jazz musician, and Pop would come hear me and be proud of me. My sisters and brothers, too. Sy and Ada Mae were already proud.

Even though nobody from Carondelet came over to hear me or visit me, I was too scared to ride over there, because I might run into Pop. At least I saw some of my friends from Carondelet at Lincoln Junior High School. Didley and my cousins Billy and Clyde were there. Clyde had moved in with Didley and Aunt Gert. We had all started out together at Lincoln. We used to ride the streetcar to Lincoln from Carondelet. It was a thirty-minute ride from Bowen and Broadway, a transfer to the Jefferson car for another fifteen minutes, and then a four-block walk. Now I lived about a half mile from Lincoln. Although I missed my friends, that was another good thing.

No band classes, no choir, no music of any kind was taught at Lincoln. It didn't bother me too much, because I knew that I only had one more year and then I could go to Vashon High. I knew they had band class, and I was hoping for some jazz activities. Clyde told me about a singing quartet at Lincoln that he was a member of, but I wasn't interested. I just wanted to play my horn.

Mr. Evans was the principal of Lincoln, and one day while I was sitting in history class, Mr. Evans' robust voice came over the loudspeaker. "Attention. Attention." Everybody got quiet. Then he said, "We're going to listen to our school quartet for a few minutes."

After a lot of static and some shuffling sounds, the singing started:

> Down by the old mill stream,
> Where I first met you,
> With your eyes so blue
> And your love so true.

I sat up in my seat. I was blown away by how good they sounded. I'd heard the Mills Brothers sing that song on Didley's radio, and I had no idea that Clyde's quartet could harmonize like that. Everybody knew who the Mills Brothers were, and it was just like having them at our school. I tapped out the rhythm with my pencil as they sang, and I tried to imagine what kind of trumpet riffs I could play behind them.

While we clapped when they finished the song, I was laughing to myself, wishing that Mr. Evans would let Clyde fart the scale over the loudspeaker. Clyde had always cracked us up farting the scale—do-re-mi-fa-so-la-ti-do—while we played marbles.

Every day, I kept practicing my horn and wishing Sy would ask me to go to one of the big band rehearsals. When I'd ask, he'd say, "When you're ready I'll ask *you*. In the meantime, keep blowin'."

In the fall of '34, I got wind of the Tom Powell Post #77 Drum and Bugle Corps. It was a community group of young boys and they were said to be really hot although they had never won the state championship. Even so, I auditioned and got accepted.

Pop Owens was the head of the Tom Powell Post #77 Drum and Bugle Corps. He was a short, slouchy brown-skinned man with false teeth that clicked uncontrollably when he talked. His eyes were stern with authority, although his face was kind, stroked from years of drinking liquor, which we could all smell a mile away. But we loved him.

For six months every Saturday and a whole lot of Sundays, we rehearsed under the instruction of Pop Owens. I talked with him a few times, and he eventually agreed to let us try some new rhythms and harmonies—a more swinging approach. That's when we filled the big beige brick Post #77 hall with resounding brass. Powerful drums. A jazzier sound.

Our marching field was a dusty vacant lot near the hall. That's where we executed our maneuvers and sharp turns to the whistle of our drum major, Russell Boone. Our bass drummer was John Fox, and our snare drummer was Charlie, who was his younger brother. John and Charlie had original, clever, and precise drum licks and they could really *swing*.

We created hip formations and serious steps up and down that dusty vacant lot. Nothing was the traditional stuff—the stiff postures, stone-faced expressions, short and choppy steps. When our corps played marches like "Semper Fidelis," we added intricate rhythmic patterns, syncopated harmony lines, and lots of pumping drum beats matched with hip dance steps, smiling faces, and a jazzy swing. So our hopes were sky high that we would win the championship and bring a huge trophy home. We couldn't wait to get there.

I loved the challenge of playing the G-bugle 'cause it didn't have any pistons. No valves at all. It was just a long horn. So my chops were stronger than ever from playing all notes by embouchure only—squeezing my lips together for higher tones or loosening them for the low tones. I also learned a lot about how the constriction of muscles in my jaw helped to make different notes, as well as the importance of breath control—taking in enough air to avoid fluffing notes or trying to play too many notes with one breath. I learned how to incorporate my jaw muscles and breath control to take some of the pressure off my chops so they wouldn't get too tired. It was a gas!

When the competition date was near, Pop Owens puffed on his stumpy cigar and told us that he couldn't go. He said he had some business to take care of. We all wanted to know what it was, but he didn't tell us. So Mr. Doug Cloud was our chaperone. He was a fat, light-complexioned man with a receding hairline that was funny to us, but we were all afraid to laugh. Mr. Cloud talked with threatening gestures. Squinted his eyes into tight slits. Pointed his finger quickly at anybody who dared to get out of line. So we whispered and snickered behind his back and tried hard to stay on his good side. We were a feisty bunch of kids, but we knew our boundaries.

Finally the day of the competition arrived. It was a warm day that April of '35. Air smelling like musty underarms, axle grease from the nearby trains. All of us corps boys were lined up as neatly as possible on Market Street at Union Station. What a sight we were. Twenty-five colored boys, all sizes, heights, and shades of brown. Teeth were flashing in the sunlight from the big smiles on everyone's face. We couldn't wait to board the big silver train for the statewide competition in Jefferson City, Missouri. Most of us, including me, had never ridden the train, and we were riled from excitement.

Finally, one by one we boarded in wide-eyed wonder through the silver door of the train with our instruments and brown-bag lunches (mine was a jack salmon sandwich with potato chips; fried chicken aromas wafted from others).

There was Ed Ledbetter, one of our drummers; his brother, "Little Ledbetter," a bugler; and then Carroll, Jr., a bugler who was really short but popular. He was always presented as a feature right behind our drum major, Russell, because Carroll could do some fancy footwork and really wow the audience just like Shitty used to do.

Another of our buglers was Arlington Grant. He always acted older than he was. Sort of a boastful personality with short brown hair and a honey complexion with a gate-mouthed smile and happy eyes. Though he could really sing, we didn't need that. I called him "Water Boy" 'cause he could belt out the words to that song so well:

> Water Boy,
> Where are you hiding?
> If you don't come now
> I'm gonna tell your mammy.

Then there was Vince, our real cut-up bugler. He was average-sized with an athlete's physique. He always defied authority, and he made us laugh and get into trouble with Mr. Cloud. But we curbed it when Mr. Cloud kicked and cussed.

Bola, who later became a protégé of mine, was a friendly, skinny kid about my height, and he knew just what to do with his bugle. He and I made fun of Mr. Cloud when he wasn't looking. We'd be busting at the seams.

The rest of the guys were friendly, but they weren't in my immediate circle of favorites.

Our excitement cooled during the long train ride, but when we got to Jefferson City we were revved up again. Several trucks and cars took us to an open field about thirty minutes away from the train station.

Hundreds of people were there. We all tried, according to Mr. Cloud's yells and threats, to stay together while pushing through the crowd up to a fence where we could watch the competition in the glare of the blazing sun. As we watched, we leaned close and discussed the other corps. They were good, but we still thought we could win, 'cause we felt like we had an edge. None of them were doing what we had rehearsed. Even so, we all admitted to having butterflies in our stomachs.

Soon our name was called: "The Tom Powell Post #77 Drum and Bugle Corps!"

We were dressed in white duck trousers, white shirts, and white shoes. We pranced out on that dusty field with our heads and hopes high.

Russell blew the whistle. "WheeeeeEEEEEEEE!" It seemed like he was almost seven feet tall. Very straight-faced and proper. He leaned so far back that it looked like he would fall over. Way, way back, holding that position, then rising verrrrr-ry slowly. He was a real showstopper.

Our drummers started with their swinging rhythms. Boomty-BOOM-baba-boomty-BOOM! Bam-bam-BOOMTY-*BOOM!* More pulsating than the Church of God and Christ. They were *hot.* From the corners of my eyes, I saw mouths in the audience drop wide open. Then our buglers hit some awesome syncopated riffs around the hip rhythms. Harmonies were flying high and tight.

"WheeeeeEEEEEE!" Russell blew his whistle. He loosened up, put on his happy face, and led us with his high-legged marching. Then he broke out with his half-march/half-dance steps. That's when the rest of us joined in and tore that field *up*. Showing off our fancy footwork, cutting sharp turns with abrupt hesitations, up and down the field rapidly, stopping, moving in zigzags, in waves, shoving our horn bells high and way down low, high notes screaming in tune, dust flying, sweat dropping, turning circles, syncopated steps and throbbing drums!

We cut the rug all the way up to the last drum lick. When we froze our last move with blank-faced expressions on our faces, cheers were everywhere. Some people were jumping up and down waving their hands or clapping hard while yelling and screaming for us. Oh, how I *loved* it.

A little while later, the announcer named third place, second place, and then he called our name for first place! We practically jumped out on the field, and Mr. Cloud accepted our big, shiny trophy. We were all overwhelmed. Fit to be tied. Mr. Cloud was laughing and smiling so much, it looked like he had fifty teeth in his mouth.

The only drag was that by the time the train pulled back up to Union Station in St. Louis, I was sick as a dog. I'd slept up in the drafty cargo rack most of the way home so I could stretch out. Man, I was coughing and sneezing, wiping my nose, shaking with chills. In my mind I heard Pop's voice yelling, "Didn't I tell you you'd get consumption from playing that damn horn?"

When Ada Mae found out how sick I was, she got me some cod liver oil, some Black Draught cough syrup, and some jimson weeds. She mixed those weeds with some garlic and herbs and made me an Asphidity bag, which was a little pouch that I had to wear around my neck. I wore that funky-smelling pouch and prayed hard. "Lord, don't let it be consumption. *Please* let me keep playing my horn."

Ada Mae took real good care of me and I made it through that storm. I'll never forget the loving way she talked to me, and how her smile gave me confidence not to worry—that I'd be okay. And when I felt better—first thing I did was grab my horn. I thanked God and Ada Mae.

That next September, it was finally time for Vashon High School! My hopes were sky high about playing jazz. Vashon was a dignified and stately building just like Delaney Elementary had been. I'd never liked Lincoln, but I loved the way Vashon looked. Brown brick, two-story. Bigger than Delaney or Lincoln.

On the first day of school, I was standing outside with a few friends, waiting on the bell to ring. A few hundred other students stood around, too. Flash looked at me with a scared face. She said, "Terry, one of my friends just told me that Fess Williams doesn't allow jazz at Vashon."

My eyes bucked, heart fell, like a brick falling to the river bottom. Fess Williams was the principal of Vashon. Sweat popped out on my face. I watched her mouth as she said, "This girl named Blanche just told me that Fess Williams said that jazz is the *devil's* music. Taboo! Absolutely taboo. He won't tolerate it at *all*."

The bell rang, and as I was walking, I kept thinking about how I was going to confront Fess Williams. How I was going to explain about how lo-o-o-ong I had waited to get to Vashon so I could play some jazz. One thing I knew for sure was that I was not about to give up on my dream.

I just couldn't believe that the principal of my high school could say those horrible things about jazz. If it was that bad, I thought, then why did white folks go to Sauter's Park to hear it? Or why did they play it on the radio and in the movies? And why did so many people love it? I thought, Maybe Fess Williams is just an old fuddy-duddy and he doesn't like anything hip, or maybe he never really felt the *power* of jazz and maybe he just needs for somebody to show him what he's been missing.

Going through the homeroom check-in system was a drag. A short, friendly lady handed me the schedule for my classes. The usual stuff— history, math, science, and English. Then she gave me a sheet of paper for choices of extracurricular classes. My eyes focused on two words: Band Class.

Wow! I felt like flying around the room, but I just smiled and played it cool and signed right up. I also signed up for French 'cause I figured that one day I would have to go to France with my trumpet. After all, Reverend Sommerville had said that if we studied hard that we could go places and see things. Studying hard and practicing my jazz were foremost in my mind.

I was sporting my newly acquired second-hand black pants and white shirt. My hair was slicked back with Murray's pomade. My teeth were brushed with Arm and Hammer baking soda, and I'd also put a little under my arms, which helped protect me from the stifling heat.

After hum-drum classes in rooms filled with mixed aromas of body funk, perfume, and sweat, and talkative students and disciplinarian teachers who talked over my head like my teachers had done at Lincoln, with a quick lunch in between, I eventually made it to Mr. Clarence Haydn Wilson's music class.

From my chair, I checked out the twenty or so other students and the huge band room with tubas hanging on the walls. The bass violins, tympani, and drums were stored on the opposite side of the room from the windows. The room smelled like sweaty students, oil, metal, and Mr. Wilson's English Leather cologne. Sunlight beamed through the wall of opened windows.

Music stands stood in front of each chair. They reminded me of Dewey Jackson's music stands in Sauter's Park. Only white folks were allowed at Sauter's Park, but I had talked my brothers, along with Beanie Roach, Pig, Bones, and Didley, into sneaking there with me. We'd hidden in an old rotunda there so no one could see us.

Now I had my very own black music stand right in front of me, and I couldn't wait to see some real sheet music sitting there.

Mr. Wilson was a light-brown-skinned, very suave, fastidious man with a small moustache. He had thick eyebrows and a full head of gray hair. He looked like a colored version of a typical orchestra conductor that I had seen in the movies. He seemed like a real nice man.

I noticed that as he issued out the instruments, he called everybody "Oscar." I didn't know why, but I guessed that he didn't have to remember anybody's name that way.

Minutes passed as I waited for him to call me "Oscar" so I could get a trumpet. When I told him what I wanted, six horrible words came out of his mouth: "I don't have any trumpets left."

I jeered at him and he stared through me like he had a thousand other things to do rather than look at my angry face. He pointed across the room and said, "Take that valve trombone over there. It's got the same three valves and you can use the same fingering as the trumpet."

I wanted to cuss out loud. No trumpet! Just an ugly-ass valve trombone? I cleared my throat and then I said, "Are you sure there aren't any trumpets, Mr. Wilson? 'Cause I've been playing the trumpet and that's what I was looking forward to for a long time."

He wiped the sweat from his brow, stared at me, and smoothed his hair back. Then he squinted his eyes and he said, "Go and get that valve trombone! You'll make more noise with it than you would with a trumpet anyhow!"

It was just a raggedy old dented brass valve trombone. It didn't even have a case! I tried to console myself while he talked to the other students. I dragged my feet across the room and picked up the valve trombone. I wiped off the mouthpiece with my shirt, placed it up to my lips, and I tried to see what kind of sound I could make with it. Nothing like the sound of a trumpet. And the mouthpiece was too big.

"Take your seat, Oscar! You can play it later!" Mr. Wilson shouted at me.

I felt completely disgusted. I shuffled back to my seat and plopped down. Then I raised my hand and said, "Mr. Wilson, I have a trumpet at home that I can bring to class, since you don't have any trumpets here, because the trumpet is what I've been playing for a long time, and . . ."

He rolled his eyes at me and said, "Look. You can't bring an instrument from home because the school cannot be responsible for your personal belongings. So it's the valve trombone or nothing!"

For the rest of the class period I didn't hear a word he said, and when the bell rang I put the raggedy valve trombone under my arm, picked up my books, and left. I knew I'd get a trumpet somehow. Wasn't going to stop until Mr. Wilson gave me one.

After lunch, I sparred a little with some of the guys near the athletic field to let off some steam and show off my skills. Nothing too serious that would give me a fat lip.

In the meantime, I blended in with the rave of football season and school spirit. I definitely didn't want to be in the marching band because I just couldn't dig their traditional John Philip Sousa routines. So I went to the games for the fun of it and because I loved the smell of popcorn and hot dogs. The raves from the crowd reminded me of winning the competition with the corps, and my old days after the parades in Carondelet when me and the guys did our first performances on the corner.

Between the hoorays for touchdowns, blocks, and passes, I asked lots of questions trying to find if there was anybody who might be interested in playing jazz. Since Fess Williams didn't allow jazz, I decided to solicit a few cats and form a secret jazz band. My plan was to get the band to the point where we'd be so good that the students would love us and join our crusade to convince Fess Williams to change his mind.

Soon somebody told me about James Barr, who could play a mean jazz guitar. He was a real smooth cat with a little round head, nutmeg complexion, sleepy eyes, long fingers, and a wide smile. He was easy to talk to, and he wasn't in the marching band either, so that gave me the chance to discuss jazz with him during the game. I was careful not to be too distracting, and I soon gained his confidence. We shared conversations about our desires to play the music we both loved.

Days later I met Walter Ray in the hall near my French class. He was a dainty kind of guy who was super intelligent, with the highest I.Q. in the state. He could play the hell out of the piano. Fats Waller was his favorite musician, and Walter said that he had learned Fats' library. Fats had one of the most popular small bands at the time, with Eugene Cedric on saxophone and Johnny "Bugs" Hamilton on trumpet. They played things like

> The joint is jumpin'.
> Who's that walkin' round with all that elephant patter?
> It must be Mable 'cause her feet's too big!

That same day, just before my last class, I met O. C. Reece out by the gym. He was a short, slick-looking cat. I'd heard that he could definitely play some jazz drums. He told me that jazz was a gift from God. That's all I needed to hear.

After school, Benny Nelson was watching some cats shooting marbles near the athletic field when I walked up to him. He was a dark-brown-skinned, lanky cat who rarely smiled even when laughing. Just kind of plain-faced all the time. I'd heard that he could play *up* some jazz on the clarinet. We spoke briefly and then he told me that jazz was an intellectual phenomenon. I just smiled and stayed cool. A few days later as I walked past the band room after school, I heard somebody plucking the strings of a bass with some hip jazz licks. I went in and checked this short cat out. When I had my chance, I introduced myself, and he told me that his name was William Wallick Dean. He was friendly but a little hinkty. His flashing white teeth contrasted with his mahogany complexion and he was dressed in a tan shirt, some tan pants, and some really shiny brown Fives. He ran his hand over his neat, short-cut hair, and he kept his eyes on his bass strings. He said, "I prefer to be called Wallick."

We shot a cool breeze for a few minutes, then he told me that he absolutely loved jazz more than anything in the world. His idol was Jimmy Blanton—the guy who revolutionized bass fiddle playing years later in Duke Ellington's band. Wallick was good, and he knew it. If you didn't believe it, you could ask *him*. We hit it off right away.

It didn't take me long to persuade James, Walter, O. C., Benny, and Wallick to take a chance with me and form a secret jazz band. We decided to get together the following semester. I named us the Vashon High School Swingsters.

Best of all, I kept bugging Mr. Wilson until he gave me a gray Wurlitzer trumpet that next semester! Complete with valve tips and a case. I named it the Gray Ghost, because I knew it would haunt me until I learned everything I could about playing it.

5. First Road Gig

A few years later—it was June of '39—my life had taken a serious dive. Just two months before my high school graduation, I was looking forward to marching across the stage at commencement as salutatorian of my class, with two scholarships in track, but I was kicked out of school. I had gotten a girl named Sissy pregnant, and both of us were expelled.

Today, no one is expelled for this reason, but back then it was a definite no-no! You might as well have committed murder.

Before Sissy, things were fine as far as sex was concerned. I was meeting up with a hooker named May, and because she was a pro there was no worry about her getting pregnant. An older dude in my neighborhood introduced her to me. She was a stone fox! Color of honey, skin-tight dress, and a bouncing bosom. Smelled like roses. When she asked me, "You ever felt heaven?" believe me, I let her show me exactly what that meant. We had a ball "twirling."

Sissy was a different story. It all started one night when I had just finished playing a scab gig with a guy named Emmett. "Scab" was a nickname we gave to gigs where we had no union card, were underage and resented by the veterans yet tolerated because of our talent. I can't remember Emmett's last name, but he was a popular guy—intelligent, a great jazz bassist, charismatic, and, according to rumors, very hip on chicks.

It was rainy that night and I was cold and soaking wet. I was planning to make it to the streetcar a few blocks ahead when Emmett stopped dead in his tracks and said, "Man, you oughta come go with me. I got a fine lady I'm gonna see and maybe I can knock her sister down to you." That was his way of saying he wanted me to meet her.

Before long, we were climbing up to the second floor of a poorly lit apartment row, very long with no gangways. Emmett's pretty girlfriend opened the door, and we went in and sat down in the warm living room. He said, "Baby, I brought my chum along to meet your sister."

Out comes this younger and smaller version of Emmett's girl. She walks right up to me, shakes my hand firmly, and says, "How do you do?"

I was taken with her boldness, and even though she didn't flip my heartstrings and make me feel like carving her name in a tree, she was pretty and I liked her.

One thing led to another for a few months, and before long, she told me, "I missed my cycle." In my mind, I could hear Pop laughing his ass off and saying, "See! I told you. Hooooooo weeeeeeee!"

A few days later, according to the lay of the land at that time, I was forced to marry her at City Hall. Ada Mae was there—just Ada Mae and Sissy's growling father. Sy was out of town on a gig. There were no smiles, no friends, no kiss; just a pitiful "I do."

Fess Williams called me into his office the next day and said, "Well, when a boy wrongs a girl, he should be made to pay for it. You're out of here!"

Rumors were flying that I wasn't really the father of Sissy's baby, that there was another cat across town. But she swore I was the culprit. There was no DNA testing back then, so if you were the one the girl pointed to, then that was your ass.

When Sy came home, he tried to help me out by getting me an audition with the Jeter-Pillars Orchestra. But I blew it. Wasn't ready for *those* charts. So Sy introduced me to a friend of his named Turk. His real name was Willie Austin. Tall dude with long sideburns that went down below the corners of his mouth and touched his wide, long goatee. Fair-skinned. Shifty eyes like Johnny Pops. But what really caught my attention was his long fingernails. Almost *two inches* long.

Turk had a band gig with the Reuben and Cherry Carnival traveling company, and after I'd auditioned for him, he hired me to play. I didn't know how much the gig would pay per week, and when I asked Turk, he said, "Don't worry 'bout that, kid. Depends on who comes to the carnival. Depends on the weather." All I really had was Sy's assurance that, since he and Turk were friends, Turk would take care of me.

So come a couple of weeks later, there I stood milling with the other band members at Union Station on Market Street in St. Louis. On the platform, I checked out the potpourri of characters—foxy women, midgets, muscular cats, plain folks, and the fattest woman I'd ever seen. Colored people stood in one area and whites a little distance away. Nobody was too friendly, so I strolled the length of the train, hoping things would work out. When I looked at the train cars, I thought about Aunt Gert and the times that we used to sit in her front room and count the white goats painted on the freight cars that used to pass in front of her window. There weren't any goats on the carnival train, just a lot of cars and a big silver engine.

I walked through the crowd and stood next to Shorty Mac, the other trumpet man in Turk's band. He was holding a half-smoked cigar. He said, "You all right, kid?" He was a few inches shorter than me, and the smile on his mahogany face was comforting. I checked out his hip brown double-breasted suit, shiny brown Fives, and the sweat beading his forehead. I said, "Yeah, thanks." His short, slick conk was shining in the sunlight. I lit a cigarette and said, "When are we pullin' out?"

He puffed his stogie and said, "Won't be long. Lighten up."

I wished Pop could have seen me dressed in my hip black double-breasted suit and my shiny black McAns, all grown up and ready to travel with Turk's band. But I hadn't seen Pop since he'd kicked me out back in '33.

I eyed some of the other cats in the band, but there were no welcomes. Shorty Mac said, "Don't worry 'bout the cats. They don't like young whippersnappers. But they'll get used to you 'cause everybody loves a winner and *you're* a winner." He spat on the ground and said, "And you gotta learn a few jokes. Laughin' makes life more fun."

I looked at his gold wristwatch and matching pinky ring, trying to think of something to say. He tossed his cigar butt and said, "You look like a centipede with fallen arches."

I said, "Do I?" Then I smiled.

He laughed and said, "That's better, kid. You lucky to be picked. We ain't got no time for long faces. We gonna be busier than one-legged midgets in a butt-kickin' contest." We cracked up, then he leaned close and said, "Watch yo' shit 'cause we got some sticky-fingered folk that go shopping when the stores ain't open."

When the crowd started moving toward the train, I followed Shorty Mac, but not too close 'cause he'd said that he didn't need a shadow.

I sat by a window. I don't remember who sat next to me. When the train departed, I watched St. Louis disappear. I kept to myself, humming tunes quietly and wondering how things would work out.

Later I settled into my berth, which was a small compartment with a thin, hard mattress. A dingy curtain hung for privacy from the aisle. I had the upper berth and I had to breathe musty body odor, smoke, cheap perfume, bad breath, farts, funk of midnight cohabitations, and the fumes from the non-flushing toilet at the end of our car. My belongings hung over my head in a net and there was no room to sit up, but I didn't care 'cause I couldn't wait to play and make some money.

As we rode down the tracks, I thought about things that had happened in my life that led up to this gig. Getting kicked out of Vashon just months before my senior graduation. Salutatorian of my class. How I had been so happy with the Vashon High School Swingsters, and how much fun we'd had. How I'd talked Mr. Mosely into letting us play at our junior class spring dance back in '37. He was the new assistant principal, and he loved jazz. Thank God! We played pretty good. Had a lot of work to do. Mr. Mosely had promised us that we could play at the senior dance. But that never happened.

I thought about Clarence Haydn Wilson, my band teacher at Vashon.

How I had to clean his apartment all summer long after my ninth-grade year, just so he'd go against the school rules and let me keep the Gray Ghost until the next semester. I'd bugged him so much that he finally got an upper classman to give me some fingering lessons. Leonard Small was his name.

I thought about all the hard work I'd done to be "well rounded" like Reverend Sommerville had urged. So I joined the glee club, the debate team, and I was a reporter for the school paper.

Those were the good old days, back at Vashon. The good old days with the Swingsters. All the talking I'd done to get the cats together, and now it was history. How I had to convince them to let me rehearse with the rival high school band, the Sumner High School Swingsters, so I could learn to read jazz charts with annotations that were new to me. That band's leader was real friendly. Ernie Wilkins. Such a nice cat. His brother, Jimmy, too. Ernie wrote and arranged original jazz. It was so hip! Then I taught the Swingsters everything I'd learned about those manuscripts. They dug it.

My two college scholarships in track—gone. All that running and hurdling I had done, wasted.

I thought about the cheap gigs I'd played when I was seventeen, trying to build my reputation. Scab gigs. Like the time when I played with Dollar Bill. I'd heard him play before at a block party. Neighborhoods would get permission from the city, and on hot nights they would close an area off from one end of a street to the next block. They'd hire a band to sit in the middle of the street and play. Ice up a bunch of cold beer and soft drinks and make hamburgers and other junk. People would come out to drink and dance in the street and have fun.

Sy had told me that when Dollar played at block parties, his side men didn't wear uniforms, since *he* wanted to be the center of attraction. Sy said cats had labeled Dollar an "E-flat player," which meant that they thought he was just average.

Dollar played piano. A very charismatic person. Very talkative and quite demonstrative when he spoke. He said, "Just in case you don't know who I am—I'm Dollar. Dollar Bill. I never worked and I never will. I come from a place called Compton Hill. Dollar Bill!"

He usually had a long ash on the end of his cigar, and he was a wild-dressing type of cat. Very colorful socks, and pant legs that were too short. When I first saw him, I was thinking that his shoes should give a party and invite his pant legs down.

He told me that I was fortunate to become a member of his band, Dollar Bill and His Small Change, and that I would be one of his "Pennies." I didn't like that title, but I played anyway. Happy to have a gig. Low pay and all.

While I was with Dollar's band, I played at several block parties and a few of the "knock-down, drag-out" greasy spoon joints and bars on the waterfront. His small band was okay. I played for tips and that was fine with me. At least I was playing *jazz*. Not carnival music.

I thought about some of my friends in Sy and Ada Mae's neighborhood. My high school buddies, Flash, Marcella, and Mahew. They used to do my chores just to hear me play. I had it made, and then I blew it!

This was my second train ride, only now I wasn't with the Tom Powell Post #77 Drum and Bugle Corps. I lay there wondering if I'd ever see those cats again. Them and Pop Owens. Eventually I fell asleep listening to the rhythms of the train—*Clickety, clack, clack, clunk. Clickety, clack, clack, clunk.*

Days later we stopped in the hot middle of nowhere—our first gig. There were a few patches of dry brown grass and dusty wind. We were near a small town in Mississippi and I hoped that there was somewhere I could take a bath. There had been no bathing facilities on the train, where we slept—just a cheap wash pan and some cold water.

With my suitcase in one hand and the horn I had bought the week before from a pawn shop in the other (of course I couldn't take the Gray Ghost with me since it belonged to Vashon), I followed the walking crowd toward a grassless dusty field a few hundred yards from the train tracks. Turk, Shorty Mac, and the cats stopped under a huge oak tree, so I joined them. I sat on my trumpet case in the shade and I felt excited, since I'd never been to a carnival. Shorty Mac was laughing and telling jokes, while I sipped a warm beer and smoked a Lucky Strike.

I checked out the white people gathering under the other trees. Then I watched the crew roll the trucks from the flatbeds. Next they unloaded the carnival equipment off the train cars onto the big trucks. When they rode past us, clouds of dust flew up—way more dust than when I'd practiced maneuvers with the bugle corps.

I squinted my eyes and pretended that it wasn't bothering me while fingering a few coins in my pocket that I had earned from washing dishes in the colored dining car. All that dust made me remember how the ashes from the alley pits back in Carondelet used to blow up into my eyes, nose, and mouth.

Percy rode by on the back of one of the trucks. I waved, glad to see his smiling face. He was the cook for the colored personnel, and he had been friendly to me when I complimented him on his pinto beans and hot water cornbread in the dining car. A short, robust guy with a neat haircut.

He waved back quickly, then jumped off the truck while yelling at the crew and pointing to where I guessed he wanted the colored dining tent set up. He'd said I could keep my dishwashing job in our food tent during the carnival.

Soon the dancers walked up, smiling, switching. Smelling like roses and vanilla. They were all shapely and seductive, and blushed at the admiring whistles and compliments from the cats. I put my arm across my lap and redirected my focus to my growling stomach. I already had enough problems waiting for me back home and didn't need anybody else telling me that they missed their cycle. I wondered when the dining tent would be ready.

Ethel Hut waved to me as she approached the tree. Her show name was Big Fat Mamma, so folks called her Big Mamma. I'd met her in the dining car and she made me feel welcome. Bright smile and motherly ways— saving me a seat and encouraging me to ask Percy for the dishwashing gig. She stashed sandwiches for me on the train so I wouldn't go hungry at night.

She was jiggling and bouncing and she had a big wide smile on her face. After Big Mamma spoke to everybody, she said, "Hey, Pepper, let's go see what fussy old whiskey-drinkin' Percy is gonna cook." Pepper was the nickname folks gave to somebody who was young. She was the first one to call me that, and I didn't mind. Her cocoa-skinned face was as pretty as ever—heavy lashes and lots of eyebrow pencil. Red cheeks, red lipstick, and red-painted fingernails. Her dress was low-cut, as usual, revealing pounds of bosom. She was a riot and loved to laugh at the few jokes I'd learned. Her heartthrob was a man she called Mr. Moondust because he made her feel like walking on the moon. She said, "You'll meet him one day."

A few hours later, we sat in the colored dining tent sipping beer and watching as the carnival was set up. Percy was boiling some great-smelling chicken and white beans and my mouth was watering.

Dust was flying everywhere while I watched the carnival come to life. There were food stands and rides. A Ferris wheel and merry-go-round, bumper car rides, souvenir stands, and games—bingo, darts, bottle-tops, ring-the-bell-with-the-sledgehammer, squeeze-the-grips, win-the-stuffed-animal ring-toss, win-the-prize-with-the-crane, and guess-the-weight-of-the-patrons.

The carnival was set up in the shape of a horseshoe. My feathers flopped when I saw that the colored attractions were set up in the back in what was called the Midway, while all the white features were located in the front on either side. While I was walking around feeling pissed off, I overhead some of the white folks call our band's show "The Jig Show." That really made me hot!

To top it all, I heard other names for us colored people that I had never heard before—Boots, Zigaboos, Spooks, Skeebines, Hucks, Clinkertops, Splives, Dinges, Oxfordgrays, and Bozos. There were also names for the whites that were new to me—Honkies, Rednecks, Crackers, Pencil Dicks, Flat Asses, and Ofays. It saddened me to hear how color was such a dividing line among people.

6. Nigga

"Step right up, ladies and gentlemen!" That's what the barker shouted to the crowd walking by our show tent. He stood on the platform yelling, "Get your tickets! The show's about to start!"

Our sexy chorus girls were dressed in shiny bras and short skirts. They swayed and smiled and kicked high to the music from our band. We were sweltering, sweating, and playing fast, hot dance music.

We had a man who was called a shill. He pretended to be an excited customer; rushed up and bought a ticket, encouraging the people to follow. Folks called this whole process "ballying."

As soon as the barker gave us the cue, we dashed inside the tent and scrunched up behind the bally curtain while the people found seats and bought popcorn and peanuts. Since the main show never started until we got a pretty good crowd, we did the bally scene three or four more times. In order to calm the impatient patrons, our pre-show included some stalling acts—a man doing dangerous sword tricks and a female contortionist who could almost kiss her own ass!

When enough people were seated, we sparked them up with a fast overture while our vivacious cabaret dancers pranced out. They sang and sashayed up a blue streak, backed by our high-spirited tunes and accented drum licks for their chorus-line multilegged kicks and sassy bends. They winked and threw kisses to the cheers and raves from the crowd. It was a wild scene.

Then Big Fat Mamma strutted out to a strong blues introduction. She wowed the audience by jiggling each of her butt cheeks and shaking her bosom while she sang "I Want a Big Fat Mamma." Her soul-stirring, raspy voice penetrated the air as she delivered her captivating performance. Then she revved up and belted out the ballad "Blue Skies."

After her standing ovation, we spiced up the music for our shake dancer, Mozelle. *Man.* You talking about stacked! Curves everywhere. Real graceful. She wiggled, shook, and glided across the stage to "The Song of India." It was quiet like cotton while she danced. She *had* that audience. Then we shifted to "Black and Tan Fantasy" while Mozelle picked up her feathers and fluttered her arms like bird's wings. It took a lot for me to keep my mind on the music.

With a wave of Turk's baton, Mozelle bowed to a raving audience. Then we hit "Moonlight and Roses," and Jimmy Hitson came on stage, tapping his way front and center. Splits, jumps, hops, and slides. Effortlessly! I thought of Shitty back in Carondelet doing his buck dance with those Pet Milk cans crushed under his shoes so they'd sound like taps on the concrete. Sweat flew from Jimmy's face as he spun around and dropped down, jumped up, and tapped on every *inch* of that stage as we segued into "Tea for Two." The audience was raving!

Things slowed down when our comedian came out. I was glad because my chops definitely needed a break. Donald VanEpps was his name. He had the crowd howling with his big white eyes and fast lines. On cue, we accented his hard-hitting punch lines. He was a riot and they loved him.

For the finale, the entire entourage came back and made a few curtain calls while the band hit a few loud repetitious overtures. Then we went outside quickly for the next show's ballying.

With an average of seven shows a day, my chops ached and my clothes were soaked with sweat. We barely had time to rush over to the food tent and scarf down a few bites before dashing back to the bally stand. On rainy days sometimes we did *more* shows because people would hurry past the games and rides to get out of the weather. Tired wasn't even the word to define how I felt at the end of the day, but after a week I was looking forward to my first payday. When it came, I was disgusted! It was a measly two dollars and fifty cents!

Turk handed me the money with his long fingernails pinching the coins. He said, "Things will pick up, kid. Everybody gotta get paid. Lotta people in our show."

Town after town, week after week, things remained the same. To make matters worse, I wasn't digging the music at all! I wanted to play some *jazz.* But since I needed the bread, I kept going.

At one hot and crusty southern town I took a stroll between shows to check out some of the other acts, and I noticed a big crowd watching one of the other bands. So I eased up and saw a clarinet player who was dancing and sustaining a note while removing the bell of his horn.

He knew just how to keep the crowd captivated, bulging his eyes and making faces like he was going to pass out from holding that note so long. As he removed the lower sections of his horn, I noticed that instead of stopping the note to take a breath and fill his lungs like everybody else did, it looked like he inhaled quickly through his nose and filled his cheeks with reserve air and used *that* air to keep the note going. He never missed a step in his dance routine. Kept playing that same sustained note while taking those quick breaths through his nose.

I was standing there in shock! Like everybody else. We watched him dancing around frantically and contorting his face like he was having a heart attack while he continued blowing that same uninterrupted note as he dismantled that clarinet all the way up to the mouthpiece. Then he unscrewed the mouthpiece and played on the *reed*. It was amazing!

I stood there thinking how great it would be if I could learn how to play sustained notes like that on *my* horn. Not only could I hold notes longer, but I could play some difficult passages faster because I would eliminate the need to stop for breath.

I practiced and practiced until I figured out how to do it. I inflated my cheeks with air and used my fingers to slowly squeeze the air out of my mouth, then I took a quick breath through my nose while still pushing the air out of my mouth. After a while I could do it a little better by making sure that my tongue was blocking my throat when I took the quick inhalations through my nose. Finally I was able to do it without using my fingers. And when I kept trying it with my horn, I did it. Not much—but I did it. I wasn't going to stop until I learned how to do it right. That was my introduction to "circular breathing."

Rumors were flying about Meridian, Mississippi, and how much more money we'd make there. How we could rent rooms, take baths, check out the town, and party after the shows. When we finally rolled up there, I counted the little money I'd saved and rubbed my lucky rabbit's foot. Marvin and I had a couple of beers. He was our drummer and Mozelle's boyfriend. The three of us had developed a light-hearted friendship, and we looked forward to enjoying Meridian.

Marvin was a few years older than me and just a tad shorter. Slight-built cat with small eyes; short hair and a friendly smile. Reading was one of his favorite pastimes and we had fun challenging each other's vocabulary. I was pretty good with words, since I'd been on Vashon's debate team and a reporter for the school newspaper. I loved to study my dictionary and an English textbook that I'd found years ago in Carondelet in a trash can.

I'd always been impressed with the big words that Rev had used back when I was a boy at Corinthian Baptist Church. He'd get up in that pulpit, dressed to the nines, and spit out words I'd never heard. Made him sound so impressive. Well, I wanted to be like that. So I always beefed up my English by studying that little English book and that dictionary every chance I got. Took those books with me everywhere. Had them with me in my suitcase on the train.

The first night in Meridian, Marvin, Mozelle and I rented a cheap room, glad to finally have something better than that small berth and cold water. We cleaned up and washed our clothes and hung them on anything we could find—chairs, lines, hangers, nails, and lamps. For the next few nights we went to some greasy spoons and some dingy bars. Hit a couple of the popular night spots where local musicians played jazz. Drinks and flirty ladies! There was a buzz around town of a hip dance following our closing night at a nearby joint featuring Lucky Millinder and the Mill's Blue Rhythm Band. I couldn't wait!

The evening of our final show, a thunder shower rolled up. I prayed for it to stop because I didn't want any dampers on our party time and getting a chance to finally hear some jazz. Luckily, the clouds rolled away. The Midway was empty and our crew was packing up and getting ready for the next town. Mozelle had gone back to the train.

Marvin may have been Mozelle's boyfriend, but he was also a ladies' man. While he was in the tent breaking down his drums, I waited outside on the muddy grounds with one of his local pulls, a very fair-skinned, foxy girl named Twinkle. She could have passed for white. She was very friendly. Tight dress that dipped low in the front with a high split in the back. No one else was around and I was anxious to get to the dance while trying to keep Twinkle company.

One of the local white security cops strolled up. Eyed Twinkle's complexion. Shot hostile glances at me. He was tall and lanky. Wet blonde hair hanging down from under his wet black cowboy hat. He tapped his nightstick in his hand and then he said, "Whatchu doin' on this har Midway afta tha lights out, boy?"

I wanted to give him a Kid Carter punch. Knock out his brown teeth! But I stood calmly. I said, "Waiting for my friend Marvin to pack up his drums."

The cop spat a big wad of tobacco on the ground near me. He said, "You wit this har show, boy?"

I looked him straight in his eyes and put my trumpet down. I said, "Yes, I'm with the show."

He tapped his stick harder and sneered. He said, "What did you say, *boy?*"

I said, "Yes, I'm with the show. I play in the band."

He reared back, gripped his huge low-hanging silver belt buckle, spat again, and said, "Nigga, do you realize you said 'yes' to a white man?"

Now, I knew he wanted me to say, "Yes, sir." But I just wasn't going to do that. Wasn't going to dignify him, because he was a jackass!

Twinkle eased away. So I'm standing there looking in the red eyes of a rat-faced idiot! When I turned to see where she was going, he hit me hard against my temple with his night stick. POW! Everything went black.

I woke up with hazy vision in a strange berth, then I focused on a crowd standing in the aisle.

Big Mamma said, "Pepper, you okay?"

One of the white crew members whose name I'd never known said, "Pepper, man, I'm glad you're all right. I found you lying in the mud outside the tent."

As he talked, his face was full of fear. My head felt twice its normal size. Throbbing like hell! I couldn't say anything. All I could do was look at his scared eyes.

He said, "You were out cold, man. I yelled for Jim and we brought you here."

Big Mamma was crying. She said, "That's right. When I saw you like that I told them to put you here in my berth."

The crew guy said, "Yeah. Then when Jim and me went back to the tent to finish breakin' down, a whole buncha mean-looking white guys came up to us with chains, knives, bats, and all kindsa shit! And the creep they had for a leader asked us, 'Whar's that nigga I lef lyin' in the mud?'"

I tried to get up but I couldn't.

He kept telling the story. "So then I told 'em we had kicked your ass and you had ran up toward Main Street. Man! They took off like bats outta hell afta you, but we had already brought you here."

I took a deep breath and whispered, "I don't know what to say, man. Thanks." I was thinking, These white guys saved my life tonight! I'd never known their names. Never talked to them, just worked around them.

Big Mamma said, "Okay, that's enough." She waved her arms. Perfume smelling like wildflowers. Smiling down at me the way Ada Mae sometimes did, she said, "He needs some rest. Y'all leave him alone, now."

When I looked at all the worried faces of the folks from the carnival, all standing around me like I was dying, I reached out for the crew guy who had come to my rescue and we shook hands. Unforgettable handshake. Firm and warm. Indelibly etched in my mind.

7. Ida Cox

When the carnival ended we were in Wilkes-Barre, Pennsylvania, in the dead of winter. A few members of the show headed to their various homes nearby. Most of us stayed on the train, which was going to Jacksonville, Florida, where the show equipment would be stored until the spring tour. It was late November in '39, stone freezing cold, and I was more than ready for some Florida sunshine.

I decided to call Big Mamma just Hut, because she had told me that she was really sensitive about her weight. We had become the best of friends, and I felt sad to think that we'd have to say good-bye when we got to Jacksonville. She planned to go to St. Louis from there.

By that time, though, I had learned that people come and people go. So I swallowed my sadness, just like I'd done when Shitty disappeared on Christmas Day back in '32. I'd run downstairs to show him that I'd gotten some Tom Mix gloves. Tom was our favorite cowboy movie star. The gloves were in a big handout box from the Forrestels, a wealthy white family in St. Louis. Like a lot of other families, my brothers and I had pulled a sled for miles in the snow to wait in a crowd on the Forrestels' huge front lawn, hoping that we'd be selected to get a big box of gifts. Those were our only Christmas presents each year, since Pop had said, "I spend my money for food and needs and that's it!" When I ran downstairs to show Shitty my new gloves, he was *gone*. Elnora and their grandmother, too. Aunt Gert told me that the old lady had died the night before, and some folks had come for Shitty and Elnora. Gone! Just like that. And I never saw them again. Ever.

So instead of thinking about Hut going back to St. Louis, I focused on my empty pockets and what I was going to do to fatten them up. I hadn't earned enough money to go back home, so I talked to Turk. He fingered his goatee and he said, "When we get to Florida, maybe I can hook you up with another traveling show. Ida Cox and Her Dark Town Scandals."

I ran my hand through the small change in my pockets. Then I looked into his beady eyes and I said, "You think they pay about the same money I made with you?"

He looked down for a moment, then up at me. He said, "Ida's show don't have as many people as mine. So you can probably earn some pretty good money with her if I can get you on."

When we stopped in Jacksonville, I stepped down to the ground and I stretched under the hot Florida sun. Glad to get off that stuffy train. Hut walked up to me wiping her sweaty brow. She hugged me so tight, she almost choked me. I looked at her sad face. She said, "Pepper, now this ain't gonna be the last time I see you."

I smiled at her and gave her a quick kiss on her salty cheek. I said, "I'm sure we'll meet again one day."

She smiled back, then wiped her brow. She said, "Sure we will 'cause you gotta come home sometime, Pepper. So I'll see you in St. Louis. And when you get there, you can always stay in my rooming house next to the fire station at Vandeventer and Enright. 'Cross from the Hodiamont Tracks. I'll have a room there just for you."

She squeezed me again, then she dug around in her big purse and handed me two sandwiches. "Now, Pepper, you take these 'cause I know you gonna get hungry." She reached deep down into her brassiere and pulled out two dollars. She said, "I know Turk's gonna try to get you on with Ida's show. I hope he can. But either way you gonna need a couple of bucks to tide you over."

I hesitated, but she said, "This is just a little loan. You can pay me back in St. Louis. And if you get into a pinch, get in touch with me, okay?"

I said, "Thanks, Hut." I took the sweat-soaked bills and gave her another hug.

After she walked away, she turned around and waved a few times and I waved back. Including the deuce that Hut had given me, I had a total of four dollars to buy a few personal items and some toiletries.

A few seconds later, I caught up with Turk and a few cats. We carried our bags and instruments over to a local chitterling joint. After we downed a few servings and some drinks, I asked Turk if they would be there long enough to watch my stuff while I did a little shopping in the local five and dime.

He said, "Go 'head." He pointed at the door with his long fingernail, then said, "We'll be here for a couple of hours."

Our bass player, whose nickname was Fats, went with me. He was a jovial guy with a round face, small eyes, a wide nose, and thin lips. Color of pecans. He was dripping with sweat when we got close to the store. When I asked him about his nickname, he told me that it didn't bother him.

It was late in the afternoon as we shopped in the crowded store. Fats accidentally bumped into an old white lady on a cane. He said, "Excuse me."

That short, frail woman screamed to the top of her voice, "That nigga tried to knock me down! Kill him!"

Folks started murmuring, "Nigga, nigga, nigga!"

I looked around and I said, "Fats, let's get the hell out of here!"

We darted through the crowd and squeezed out the side door and ran uphill. My high school track experience kicked in and I was booking hard with Fats right behind me. I peered over my shoulder and he was hanging close. Huffing, puffing, and hauling much ass.

As we ran, we glanced over our shoulders at the growing number of angry faces that were chasing us. We had a slight edge on them, but they were gaining on us.

We turned a corner and dashed into a round building construction site. Our noisy shoes were a dead give-away as we sprinted across the wooden platforms. While we made the turns, we heard their footsteps getting closer.

Finally, we spotted an excavated area with debris and mud. I grabbed Fats and we jumped for cover. We burrowed down in that muddy hole and concealed ourselves with pieces of canopy and boxes just in time. A few seconds later we heard their footsteps run past.

Thank God there were no dogs, or they would have sniffed us. We waited for more than an hour, then crept out.

Looking like muddy hounds, we walked along the back streets in silence, heading toward the chitterling joint, watching from the corners of our eyes. I thanked God over and over, hoping that Turk and the cats were still drinking, shooting the breeze, and keeping up with our instruments and bags.

Finally we made it. When I opened the door, they looked at us with horror! We explained what had happened and eventually everybody calmed down. Fats and I changed our clothes, then we sat down and joined the cats for a few rounds of drinks. That's when I found out that Turk had made the connection with Ida for me. But I was *most* happy just to be alive!

Later that evening, I was sitting in a cramped seat on Ida's big ragged bus with a bunch of unfriendly strangers—except for VanEpps, the comedian from Turk's show. All the equipment and props for Ida's show were either inside the crowded bus or rope-tied on top. No heater and, of course, no toilet.

Ida was a massive dark-brown-skinned woman. Huge breasts and a robust butt. Dressed in a low-cut, tight, gaudy dress. Teeth pearly white. Stern shifty eyes. She was bossy and quite domineering—almost masculine. Cussed like a sailor.

My assigned seat was next to VanEpps, who wasn't much of a talker. We rode for hundreds of miles back up north into the freezing weather.

Our feet ached from the cold, so we wrapped them up with croker sacks (gunnysacks), rags, and blankets. By stuffing newspapers along the bottoms of the loose-fitting windows, we kept some of the icy air from whizzing through the bus. Not a great view in the daytime, but nobody cared.

At first I wondered why Ida had hired a white driver, but I soon found out when some mean-looking highway troopers stopped us with a roadblock near Paducah, Kentucky.

The trooper walked up to our driver with his hand on his gun. He said, "Where you takin' these niggas?"

Our driver said, "This is a blues show and they entertainahs. They all right." The trooper peered through the windows, spat on the ground, and looked back at his partners standing by their black cars with red lights on top. Then he said, "Okay, you *say* they all right. But you make sho you keep an eye on 'em!"

We made it through racist "checkpoints" like that with no major problems. Made it on to our gigs, which were in funky little theaters after the movies were over. Our show was called "The Midnight Ramble," because it started after twelve and it was very risqué.

There was no microphone, but Ida's strong voice easily traveled from the stage and could have knocked a fly off the back wall. She strutted front and center, bouncing here and there and singing:

> See that spider crawlin' down the wall—
> He's going down there to get his ashes hauled.

Next there was a peg-legged guy. Medium build. Color of coffee with a dash of cream. His slicked back conk was so oily that a flea would have broken his neck trying to land. He had a cordial expression. The ladies eyed his thin nose, small lips, and sparkling white teeth. He also had a great sense of humor. I nicknamed him "A Track and a Dot," because when he'd walk in the snow he'd made a footstep and a hole.

When I asked Track about his hair he said, "It might be greasy, but it combs so easy." We howled as he joked around, but I wanted my unruly hair to look like his.

Each night while I had been with Turk, I'd put Murray's pomade on my hair. It was slightly scented and as stiff as axle grease. The skull cap I'd use was a tight silk stocking tied in a knot on the end, called a peanut. It kept my hair slicked down for a while, but my hair never looked as good as Track's.

Our band played "Moonlight and Roses" as Track danced out onstage. I thought, One day I'm gonna get my hair gassed like his.

Track's performance was unbelievable! He moved all over the stage with style and grace, jumping and hopping to the drums and doing steps with his real foot shifting quickly under the peg leg. Even balancing on his peg leg then doing a version of a tap step called "Buck and Wing," where his elbows rose up high and his arms flapped simultaneously like a bird's wings; his foot did a front slide while he balanced on his peg leg, all to the beat of the bass and drums. The only other peg-leg dancers I saw later who could do that difficult step were Peg Leg Bates and Peg Leg Jefferson.

When Track finished, roaring cheers filled the room and he got a standing ovation.

No show was complete without a sexy shake dancer, and Ida's show was no exception. Our dancer was the color of roasted almonds. Tall, statuesque, and very well endowed in the right areas. Her face was sort of nondescript, but nobody cared a hoot with all of her sensual gyrating and the way she made her breasts look like they were slapping the air.

Following her ovations, VanEpps waltzed out front in blackface, which I didn't care for because I felt that it was demeaning. He would have been just as effective without that jet-black makeup, which was a pasty black mixture of burned cork and Vaseline. His eyes and lips were circled in white and he looked deranged, especially when he bulged his big eyes.

I thought of Sy when I glanced at VanEpps' steeple-shaped head, and he reminded me of Mr. Butt when I glanced at his great big belly. It was barely covered with a red plaid jacket that rose up in the back over his extra-large derriere, which had a big red patch on his right cheek. His stovepipe pants were huge and just high enough to reveal his big black scuffed shoes that looked like swimmer's fins.

At the edge of center stage he went into his rip-roaring "Signifying Monkey" routine, with flapping arms, flip-flopping feet, and jiggling belly all accented with drum rolls and cymbal bangs:

> As I walked through the forest
> I passed beneath the sycamore tree
> and a monkey tried his damnedest to shit on me.
> I knew he was gonna shit 'cause I heard him fart—
> the type of monkey who was pretty damn smart.
> I yelled to him, if you shit on me as I pass,
> I'll climb that tree and kick your ass!

The audience rocked back and forth in howling laughter, and after he bowed to their cheers and whistles, our midget, Prince, dashed onstage. A real novelty act. He could jump high, do splits, turn flips, and his voice was high pitched. After his energetic opening he toned down and sang "Only

God Can Make a Tree" while looking real serious and evoking all possible emotion from the crowd. Then he bowed deeply and rose slowly to roaring applause and a standing ovation.

After our finale we packed up and headed back to the bus. An ill-mannered patron walked up after the show to one of our dancers, trying to get a date. He was swaying drunk. Staring at her bosom. He said, "What are you doing later?"

She slapped the shit out of him and we died laughing.

There were just two crew members who traveled with us, so we all helped to lift, position, and tie the mountain of our belongings on top of the bus rack with thick ropes. It was a major undertaking that would become routine throughout our tour, as was riding all night long to the next gig so that we could get the "New Day" rates in the sleazebag motels we slept in. Those rates began at seven o'clock in the morning and avoided our having to pay for the previous night *and* the new day. Sometimes we'd circle the area of the motel for hours if we got in a town earlier than seven.

One cold night after we had been on the road half the night on our way through the hills of West Virginia, our bus just couldn't make it over one of the inclines. Our hopes died. So did the possibility of napping, because when the bus stopped Ida jumped up and shouted, "All right! All out! Let's push this motherfucker up the hill!"

Everybody wrapped up in blankets, sweaters, coats, hats, gloves, and whatever we could find to keep warm. The bone-throbbing icy wind howled around my head as Ida yelled, "Okay! Everybody get a place and when I say GO, y'all push!" We all got ready, but Ida walked toward the bus door and screamed, "Prince, get your narrow midget ass off the bus!"

He yelled from inside, "But I'm so little, Miss Cox!"

She yelled right back, "Well, we got a little bitty place just for you!"

Prince hobbled off and found a place at the side of the bus near me. When Ida yelled, "GO," we all gave our best, and after what seemed like forever we pushed the bus to the top of the hill.

For six months we played in remote theaters. Through the dirty windows of our bus I watched the scenery change from snow and ice up north to tall green trees and sprawling grassy fields in small farm towns down south. Sometimes we toured a few thriving cities. All and all, we brought smiles to thousands. Still, I didn't make much money and I felt disgusted!

At least we hadn't run into anymore roadblocks and our bus didn't give us too much trouble. But I was worn out and just about broke when we stopped in the outskirts of Hattiesburg, Mississippi. Ida told me that Turk's band was working a carnival gig nearby.

As I walked away from the bus I saw a pretty young girl. Big bright eyes and a round brown face. About the same size and height as Sissy. She was carrying a screaming little baby in her arms. I wondered about whether or not I was really the father of Sissy's baby and whether it would be a boy or a girl. Before then I'd tried to chase all thoughts of Sissy and the baby out of my mind by focusing on the challenges of life on the road. But standing there and watching the girl and the loud baby painted a picture that I couldn't ignore.

Remembering that Pop never deserted us and how he'd worked hard to provide a place for us to stay, I swallowed the lump in my throat and fingered through the change and few wadded dollar bills in my pockets.

Most of the little money I'd made from the show had been spent on food and drinks. With not much more than a couple of bucks to show for myself, I didn't want to go home broke. So I made it my business to find Turk, hoping that I could make enough money to get back home.

8. Stranded

After searching around town I found the old gang in Li'l Mama's Soul Food Restaurant, which was said to have the best chitterlings around. I knew Turk loved "wrinkles," which was a nickname for the delicacy. I'd figured he might be there because it wasn't too far from the Midway grounds.

When I walked up to Turk's table, he wiped a few drops of grease from the corners of his mouth and his well-groomed goatee with a napkin pinched between his long fingernails. He said, "Hey, Pepper!"

We shook hands and I greeted Shorty Mac, Lucy London, one of the chorus girls, Jimmy Hitson, and Turk's old lady, Mary Johnson.

I glanced at Turk's shifty eyes. I said, "Sure glad to see you guys and get off that iron lung!" That was the nickname I'd given Ida's bus.

Shorty Mac gave me one of his knuckle-crushing handshakes. Lucy played it cool so Jimmy wouldn't be jealous like he'd been before. He nodded, and she offered a thin smile. Her honey-colored curves were tempting. She said, "Aw, Pepper, you look like you thin enough to ride a rooster. Come on, eat somethin' with us."

I waited for an endorsement from Turk before I put my horn and suitcase down.

He stroked his goatee and said, "Come on, Pepper, sit down."

We ate and talked about the horrors of traveling in the winter by bus. But I let him know that I appreciated the hookup. Though I didn't make much money, it had been a great experience.

Turk looked me in the eyes and asked, "Wanna get off the road and stay put for a while?"

He didn't have to ask me twice. His newest connection was a small carnival that traveled in several trucks but was now stationary in Hattiesburg for a few months. This meant I could share a room, take a bath, and do laundry. Maybe even find a pretty girl. A professional, so I wouldn't have to worry about knocking her up.

We worked the small carnival for a few weeks with attendance dropping off steadily, then Turk came to me and said, "Well, Pepper, you know this show ain't gonna make it much longer."

I had already heard the rumors that money was tight and I thought, That's why they didn't fix the carnival ride with the turning box. My shoulders drooped. "Yeah, I know. What are we gonna do?"

His nails flashed in the sunlight as he stroked his goatee. He said, "Well, the only way I can see us getting back to St. Louis is in Mr. Suggs' truck. Me and Mary gonna ride up front in the cab, and the rest of you have to ride in the back with the monkeys."

I'd never spoken to Mr. Suggs before or seen his monkey show at the carnival, and I couldn't imagine traveling in the back of a truck with his monkeys for seven hundred and fifty miles, but my choices were limited. Starving in Mississippi with the possibility of getting killed by racists, or hopping on a freight train, or hitch-hiking. I looked at the ground and said, "Well, if that's the only way . . ."

He said, "It *is*."

The next day, Lucy, Jimmy, Shorty, and I walked up to the back of the rusty truck. Old man Suggs had put a box on the ground for us to step up to the tailgate and get in. Nobody moved. We just watched the monkeys. Nine monkeys playing, fighting, and chattering. It smelled like an outhouse.

Mr. Suggs' big handle-bar moustache was gray and stained with chewing tobacco, and his black hillbilly hat was pulled down over his forehead. With such a deep tan, he looked like a high-yellow colored man instead of white.

He saw our hesitation. He spat on the ground and he said, "Y'all ain't gotta worry 'bout my monkeys. Don't bother them and they ain't gon' bother you." His pants were secured with a belt *and* suspenders, and he'd pulled them up so high until it looked like he had a wide waistline only a few inches from his chest.

He pointed to the monkeys, then said, "'Sides, I got that there ride kinda partitionin' 'em off. It's a little crowded, but y'all squeeze on up in there." Another wad of brown spit hit the ground.

Lucy looked at the rolled-up tarp across the back of the open-ended truck. She glanced at us and then she said, "Hell, let's get on up in this motherfucker!" She stepped up in that truck with her suitcase and purse like she was getting on the *Abraham Lincoln*, a luxury-liner train that went from St. Louis to Chicago.

My heart was racing with fear as Shorty, Jimmy, and I followed. I swallowed hard and thought about my best roundhouse punch in the boxing ring just in case I had to *sock* one of those monkeys.

Lucy's dark eyes turned to slits. She said, "I'll knock the shit outta them damn monkeys if they mess with me!"

We made ourselves as comfortable as possible, using our baggage and gear for seats. I watched the monkeys' noses sniffing in our direction and I thought about the greasy chicken sandwiches in our pockets. I touched my lucky rabbit's foot and my horn case, then said a prayer when we took off.

As we traveled I began to notice the personalities of the monkeys. I named each one. The fidgety one was Twitchy. Chatty talked a lot. The one with a tooth missing was Snags. No-Tail was just that, and the old-looking one was Old Man Mose. The one with the big mouth was Lips, and the one with the protruding eyeballs was Bubble Eyes. Ribs was skinny, while the Warden fought a lot. They became tolerable after a few hours, and it seemed like they didn't want to be bothered with us any more than we wanted to be bothered with them. So the trip wasn't too bad, other than the smell and the noise. But we did have to turn our back and sneak bites from our food.

Finally we made it back to St. Louis at Grand and Laclede. Turk and Mary got out and started walking. Didn't even say good-bye.

We were surrounded by businesses, a movie theater, and a church. The rest of us got out hoping that nobody would see us climbing down from that funky truck. Luckily it was very early in the morning and no one was in sight.

Lucy straightened her wrinkled dress, fluffed her dark brown hair, and said, "Pepper, you take care of yourself. I'll see you at one of the clubs." Then she gave me a big hug.

"See you down the road apiece," Jimmy said while shuffling his feet like he was checking if he could still dance after that long, crampy ride.

I said, "Okay, see y'all soon."

9. Lincoln Inn

The Lincoln Inn was my first hope of being able to "put some duckets in my bucket." I was twenty years old and I needed money in the worst way! It was a small neighborhood bar on Market Street. Ada Mae worked there behind the bar. She was the bar maid, and she had worked there for a long time. The place smelled like old beer and stale cigarettes.

The bar was up front, near the door. A long bar. Mahogany with brass spittoons on the floor, flanking each end. Smack dab in the middle of the bar was a big jar of hard-boiled eggs. The shelves behind the bar were stocked with Seagram's Five Crown and Seven Crown, Johnnie Walker Red and Black, and good Gordon's Gin. I remembered Ada Mae's warning. She had said, "Don't drink that cheap house liquor 'cause I really don't know where it comes from. Always drink name brands."

I sat down at a table near the piano in the back and ordered a "Greasy Dick." That was the slang name for Griesedieck Brothers beer. Gus Perriman's long fingers were taking full advantage of that much-out-of-tune black upright with his back to the small dance floor. Gus was a cool dude. I'd met him before when he was playing with my brother-in-law, Sy, in Dewey Jackson's band. Gus was a short, friendly cat with medium brown complexion and obviously false white teeth.

I forgot about my troubles and disappeared into the tune he was playing—"Coquette." Since I didn't have my horn, I closed my eyes and hummed some harmonies and get-off riffs.

He had a real laid-back voice. He said, "Hey, Terry. Wanna go get your ax?"

I sat straight up and I said, "Yeah, man!"

I stood up quickly and he gave me a nod and a skimpy smile. Then he reached for his burning cigarette in a tin ashtray on top of the piano.

When I returned with my horn, I waved at Ada Mae, strolled up behind Gus, and sat down at the same table as before.

Gus hit "Nagasaki" and I joined in to the best of my ability. Afterward he turned his head slightly, nodded, and smiled. Then he said, "Don't pay much, but you can work here if you want to."

I said, "What's the line?" That was jive talk I'd learned on the road. The "line" was an imaginary divider that cut a salary in half. That way, the low wage sounded like more money than it actually was, and it made us musicians feel better about our meager earnings.

He turned his head toward me and said, "Line three." That meant $1.50

a night. "But you gotta work for it. We start at 8:30 and we go till 4:30 in the morning."

I said, "I'll be here! Thanks, Gus." I was thinking that this would be an easy gig compared to ballying and playing for seven shows a day with Turk's gig and only getting paid two dollars and fifty cents a week— maybe. And Gus' gig sounded a hell of a lot easier than riding all over God's creation on Ida's bus and playing midnight rambles, or enduring a seven hundred and fifty–mile ride home in the back of a sweltering truck with nine funky monkeys.

After Gus and I played a few more tunes, I left with a big smile on my face and walked up Lawton Street. I decided to stop by the Orange Front, which was a restaurant at Vandeventer and Finney, across the street from the musicians union. The outside stucco was painted bright orange and the inside was furnished with a few orange plastic booths. There was a big counter in the back where the kitchen was.

It was frequented by union and non-union musicians. One of Sy's old hangouts.

I'd been there back in '38, and I'd met the owner, Big Jim. At that time, I was looking for Sy because he and Ada Mae had broken up and he had just up and moved out. She had some new dude staying with her. Surprised the hell out of me when I came home from school after Sy left. Some cat named Red was walking around her apartment barefooted. I was fuming!

I knew that Sy and Ada Mae had argued a lot about her staying out late, working at the Lincoln Inn. And she wasn't having it! But I never thought that Sy would leave like that. It was a good thing that Turk had hired me to go on his carnival gig, because I would have made big waves in Ada Mae's new relationship with Red.

Back then, Big Jim had told me that Sy had moved to the *one* place that I wouldn't go. Carondelet! I never went back there. Too scared to face Pop.

It had been a few years since the last time I was at Big Jim's place. And I was seriously hoping, again, that I'd meet up with Sy there. I loved Sy and I missed him. As I walked, I thought about the days when I had lived with Ada Mae and Sy, and how he had taken me to rehearsals with him when he played with Dewey Jackson and His Musical Ambassadors.

I remembered the time at one of their rehearsals when one of their trumpet players asked me to watch his trumpet while they took a break. His name was Mr. Lattimore. When he came back in the room, I was blowing hard. Instead of being mad at me like I thought he'd be, he said, "Well. Looks like you gonna be a trumpet player when you grow up."

Then there was the time when I was hanging outside the Lincoln Inn one night wishing I was old enough to go in and play. Gus was playing with a trumpeter. I was digging the sounds!

A little while later the man who had been playing the trumpet walked outside. He was a thin, dark-skinned cat, not too much taller than me. He had red eyes and a little peanut head with a slick conk that reminded me of some of the cats in Dewey's band. He lit a cigarette, and I eased up next to him, being careful to stay away from the window 'cause I didn't want Ada Mae to see me. I said, "I wanna be a professional trumpet player one day and I was diggin' your sound, but I couldn't hear you too good from out here."

His eyes stayed on the ladies who were entering. He said, "Ain't you a li'l young to be hangin' 'round here, kid?" Then he flicked his ashes toward the street.

I stuck my chest out proudly and said, "I'm sixteen! I play trumpet and I want to ask you a question."

He took a long drag on his cigarette and blew the smoke high into the air, then looked at me and said, "What's the question?"

I said, "Well, I was just wondering if you could tell me how I could improve my tone in the lower register. 'Cause when I try to play low notes like you did, mine come out fluffy sometimes."

He reached into the inside pocket of his black double-breasted suit, pulled out a silver flask, and took a long swig. He put his dark brown lips around his cigarette and took another long drag. He said, "That's simple." Smoke followed his words. "You ever hung your trumpet from the ceiling?"

I said, "No."

He said, "Well, if you did that you'd know 'bout walkin' up to it like you kissing it and then you'd know 'bout playin' them low notes without using much pressure with yo' lips. You dig?"

I fumbled the small change in my pocket and said, "Well, I guess I could try it."

He said, "Naw. That might be too advanced for you. First you got to go home and sit in a chair in front of a mirror. Be sure you sittin' way back. Up straight in that chair." His eyes pierced into mine and then he said, "Understand?"

I swallowed hard. I said, "I understand."

He said, "Then you got to keep yo' arms relaxed and not too close to yo' body so the air ain't blocked. Hold yo' horn steady." He took another drag and he said, "Got it?"

I said, "Got it."

He said, "Make sure yo' feet are flat on the flo'. Then you gotta grit yo' teeth as hard as you can and wiggle yo' left ear while you play. Not the right one. The *left* one. You dig?"

He stared at me with eerie red eyes, but I didn't blink. I said, "I dig."

He flicked his cigarette butt into the street and then he said, "Go home and practice."

I said, "Okay." Then he walked back inside.

As soon as I got home, I took one of Ada Mae's make-up mirrors and propped it up with some books on the kitchen table in front of a chair. I tried for hours to grit my teeth and wiggle my left ear while playing. Finally I did it. But my low notes didn't sound better. So I stood on a chair and suspended my trumpet from the ceiling with a nail and some of Ada Mae's old stockings. When my lips touched the mouthpiece, I couldn't make a note. An hour later I stopped. Disgusted. I tried to console myself by remembering that the man had said this technique was advanced.

Well, later when I told Sy about what that trumpet player had said, he cracked up laughing! Finally he said, "That's some bullshit! I betcha that old fart told you those lies 'cause he was scared you might be a threat to him one day! All you gotta do is get a larger mouthpiece with a deeper cup if you wanna play better in the lower register."

He patted me on the back and said, "Next time you got a question, you just ask me, okay?"

I said, "Okay." I was trying to play it off, but inside I was fuming! Right then, I decided that when I learned enough about jazz, I would teach anybody who wanted to find out more about the music!

Finally, I got to the Orange Front. When I opened the door, I was met with the familiar smells of onions, burgers, bacon, beer, and smoke. I looked past the booths and a few happy patrons, then I walked up to the counter in the back. I sat down and lit a cigarette. I watched Big Jim giving orders and keeping an eye on the smoky kitchen behind him. When I caught his attention I asked him if he had seen Sy.

Jim was a robust guy with a dark coffee complexion. Long conked hair that was slicked back to his neck. He was draped in a greasy white apron. He smiled, threw a stained white towel over his shoulder, and walked up to me. His gray hair almost matched the color of his small eyes, which focused at me from behind his black horn-rimmed glasses. He snatched his dingy towel from his shoulder, popped it in mid-air, then wiped my area briskly.

He said, "Sy was here a few weeks ago. Told me he's giggin' on the boat."

Rumors had it that the Streckfus Steamboats paid at least twenty dollars a week or more to jazz musicians who were lucky enough to get hired. I'd heard that there wasn't much jazz, though. Mostly bouncy dance music for the all-white patrons. On Mondays, when Captain Streckfus allowed colored folks to ride, it was said that the jazz was jumping. Still, I was happy to think that Sy was making that kind of money!

After I ate a hamburger I said good-bye to Big Jim and left, heading back to Ada Mae's apartment. I thought about the time that Sy and I were sitting in the kitchen back in '36, when he was laughing and telling me about the trumpet players in St. Louis. He was always encouraging me. He said, "Just wanna make sure you know 'bout some of St. Louis' trumpeters from way back."

I leaned forward in my chair and I watched his mouth as he talked.

He said, "Ever heard of Charlie Creath?" He took a swig of beer.

I said, "No. Never heard of him."

He sat up straight and said, "Well, Charlie was known as the King of the Cornet! Played his *ass* off! And Levi Madison! Oooooh, man! He had the most beautiful tone of all the trumpet players you ever heard!"

I said, "I've heard of him. Didley and Billy and I sneaked over to Levi's apartment and listened to him practice. Some people said he was crazy 'cause he'd practice about ten minutes and then he would laugh out loud— 'Ah, ha, ha, ha, ha! Ah, ha, ha, ha!'—for twenty minutes to half an hour. Then he'd go back and play a short phrase that was even more beautiful than before."

Sy took another swallow of beer. Then he said, "But Ham Davis—he was the greatest! Like *you* gonna be one day."

Now, I had seen Ham Davis (Leonard "Ham" Davis) at one of the parades back in Carondelet when I was a boy. I'd heard whispers about how he played an octave higher than necessary with his right hand holding his trumpet and his left hand in his pocket. So for Sy to mention me and Ham in the same breath, I was bowled over! I didn't know what to say.

As I got close to Ada Mae's apartment, I also remembered when Sy took me on a New Year's gig with him when I was around seventeen. Sy and I rode the streetcar cross-town to a dingy-looking joint with dim lights, red and gold balloons, and Happy New Year banners. There were two other musicians, a drummer named Spareribs and a banjo player named Banjo Pete. We played for five hours in front of a sweaty crowd of rowdy people who laughed, cheered, danced, and toasted the night away. To me it seemed like they were so drunk that they could've cared less who was playing, what was being played, or how good or bad it was being played.

When the gig was over, Sy handed me my pay. Fifteen dollars! My eyes bulged! That was the most money I'd ever held in my hands!

That was then. Now, here I was twenty years old getting ready to play a scab gig at the Lincoln Inn. Another scab gig, like the ones I had played while I was at Vashon. Scab gigs—non-union, low-paying gigs. It was rough, being damn near broke and all, but I knew things had to get better.

That night at the Lincoln Inn I played with Gus to a dozen or so customers. It wasn't a real jazz setting like I wished it could have been. Nobody acted like they really knew a damn thing about the music. No one was sitting and listening to Gus and me, digging our intricate intervals, our creative articulation, our point and counterpoint harmonies, or the rapidly ascending and descending chromatic scales. They only wanted to drink their problems away and dance up close on that sawdust floor, breathing each other's breath. I felt like I could've been playing a washboard and nobody would've given a damn. But at least they were having a good time, because the sawdust was settling.

Late in the night when all the good liquor was gone and most of the house brands were low, smells of urine hovered in the air. Instead of people putting money in our kitty jar on the piano top, they mostly bought us beers. Gus drank most of them 'cause I couldn't handle that much. He'd had at least ten mugs and still he wasn't drunk.

Somebody shouted, "Lemme sang!" A man staggered up. He slurred over the words something terrible:

> Down by tha ole mih stree,
> Wah I fur meh chu.
> Wi' yo' eye so blue.
> Dah dah ooh ooh ooh.

I'd had a few rounds of beer and I was cracking up at the slurred lyrics. It was a gas! Then a woman got up and sang some blues.

> My baby lef me
> Don know whut I'm gon do.
> Yeah! My baby lef me
> Now I'm sang'n a blue
> If you see my baby
> Tell im I'm bad like two lef shoo.

I could hardly play for laughing! It was like each singer was trying to outdo the other and the only thing that mattered was their emotion. Nobody cared about the lyrics. They were singing their hearts out about some personal experience and using the club to vent their feelings. And they were all drunker than Cooter Brown—as the saying went, though I never knew who Cooter was.

When the night ended I trusted Gus to bust the kitty the way he wanted. I was glad when he counted out a couple of dollars and some change for me.

He smiled and said, "Ain't much, but it'll grow if you stick with me. We make a damn good duo." He went on to tell me that he'd gotten off the road because he'd gotten tired of traveling all the time. Leaving people he cared about. Having to deal with endless trials and tribulations.

As he'd predicted, over the next few weeks my tips picked up, and quite a few more jazz lovers began to come around. Sitting and listening up close. I enjoyed playing there and tried to stay out of the way of the occasional fights that broke out, which were usually over some sexy chick with one too many admirers.

One night a really sharp-dressed guy strutted through the door. All eyes followed him through the room. His black Fedora hat hid most of his fair-skinned face. He wore a flamboyant gray and white plaid jacket and high draped pants that hugged his ankles but flared from the waist down. I knew he was somebody important. The closer he got, the more I focused on the huge half-chewed cigar that hung out from the corner of his big lips.

After Gus finished his solo on "Cabin in the Cotton," I leaned over and asked him, "Who's that guy?"

He turned his head slightly, a cigarette hanging out of the corner of his mouth, and looked. He said, "That's Fate Marable! You don't know him?" Gus put his cigarette in the ashtray. "Fate's *big* time, man. Probably just got off the boat!"

Fate walked right up to me and said, "Whatcha doin' playin' here for peanuts, man, when you can come downtown with me and make Line Six?"

Gus said, "Go 'head," and then he mashed out his cigarette.

10. On the Road Again

Playing with Fate's band that May of '40 was very tough because his temper was horrendous! He had a highly respected name and was practically a household word as far as the jazz scene was concerned, but he'd been playing on the riverboat for a long time. Been replaced by the newest swinging bands like Dewey Jackson's and Fats Pichon's.

Fate had been reduced to playing at a club near the fashionable downtown riverfront. The joint was patronized by whites only who dressed up in fancy suits and sparkling dresses. They sat at white-linen-covered tables, danced on a highly waxed wooden floor. Even though the room was spacious and classy—high ceilings, shiny mirrors, twinkling lights, security guards—Fate was pissed.

The cats in Fate's band had no welcome for me. They were as cold as a December blizzard. But I laced up and waded on through, trying my best to play every note perfectly.

A few nights in, I mistakenly played a C major when I should have played C minor, and hit E-natural instead of E-flat. Before I knew it, Fate's big jingling ring of keys hit my music stand. BAM! He laughed, "Ahhh HAH huh hah hah! Huh HUH ooooooooooooh, hah HAH!"

I was so embarrassed. Wished I could disappear! I kept my cool and went right on playing. No more mistakes. No one even looked in my direction. They just kept on playing, too, smiling and nodding to the audience with high noses like nothing had happened.

During our break out back I stood by myself, smoking a cigarette and listening to the cats signifying about somebody who had pissed Fate off on the boat by getting drunk and playing too many wrong notes. They were holding their stomachs and bending over laughing. Passing bottles and firing joints. Saying that after that gig Fate told every member of the band, except the cat who had screwed up, to come to work a half hour earlier on the following night. Fate threatened to fire anybody who told the victim.

The next evening when the victim arrived, the whole band was already seated. Then Fate kicked off "There'll Be Some Changes Made," while the ousted cat stood staring at his chair where Fate had placed an ax.

They kept howling with this story, calling it "getting the ax" while shooting glances at me. I took their joking as a serious warning.

A few evenings later I stopped by the Lincoln Inn on my way to work. When I told Gus what had happened he gave me a small grin and said, "See. You just keep on and you're gonna learn that an easy gig like this is better than the headaches of those big gigs." But nothing he said could drown my hopes for playing professional jazz.

At the beginning of the following week, Fate busted my pay down to Line Five a night. He said, "Just to remind you, can't be bullshittin' with those notes!"

One bad note and he had the audacity to crack my pay! I didn't swallow that too easily. Besides, I wasn't the only one who hit a wrong note.

Gus had told me that Fate was required to pay everybody equally when he was playing on the boat—per Captain Streckfus. Now, since he wasn't on the boat, Fate could call the shots and be a real horse's ass. I felt like he was looking for a flimsy reason to pocket more pay for himself. Although I stayed on, my fuse was short!

I smiled and played it off as more and more white women came on to me, but I brushed them off like lint. I'd been warned by Fate that those women were strictly taboo. Socializing with them was a sure way to get fired—or killed.

Since Fate had hung out in New Orleans, he was pretty hip in jazz. Always kept up with the latest sounds. So I took full advantage of the situation, while making plans to move on soon. I stockpiled my money, and meanwhile I improved my sound and learned to play more tunes by heart, like "Basin Street" and "Struttin' with Some Barbecue." I also added a few Ellington tunes, like "Mood Indigo," "Take the A Train," "Perdido," and "In a Mellow Tone," to my repertoire. I practiced each day at home before going to work, mainly trying to improve my technique. Playing the show tunes over and over until my chops ached and sometimes blistered or bled.

I was relentless. I copped an Arban's Method Book, also a B-flat clarinet book because it was packed with a lot of new and challenging runs. I played those runs over and over until I could do them pretty fast, thinking that Fate would notice my accomplishments and give me a raise. But he didn't. Gus said, "It's probably a cheap tactic to keep down tension from the cats 'bout you being so young."

After three months of working with Fate, I had saved some good bread, giving some to Sissy for the baby, some to Ada Mae for food. I also paid a few bucks to the hock shop for "Honey Babe," Ada Mae's gold watch that she pawned on a regular basis.

I also hung out at the union, listening for any new opportunities because I was more than ready to get away from Fate. The union had moved from Vandeventer and Finney to the 4900 block of Delmar, close to a popular jazz supper club, Jordan Chambers' Riviera. As I walked through the union door one afternoon I spotted one of the regulars, who was a beer drinking buddy of mine. A cat named Elwood Buchanan, but everyone called him "Buke." He was a music teacher at Lincoln High School over in East St. Louis, and he was always trying to get me to come hear one of his students who played trumpet. After I spoke to some of the other cats here and there and I didn't hear about any new gigs, I sat down at Elwood's table.

He was jovial, as usual. Puffed on his cigarette. He said, "Man, when are you gonna come over to the school and hear this cat, li'l Dewey Davis? Man, you got to hear him! He's mean!"

The last thing on my mind was going to Buke's school, but since he'd been at me for so long, I said, "Okay, man. I'll come tomorrow around two, if that's a good time."

He said, "Yeah, man. Two is cool!"

Back outside the union, I saw Sy. My heart jumped for joy! We hugged and slapped backs and then he said, "I was hoping to run into you."

I said, "Yeah! I've been looking for you for a while! I was just heading over to the Orange Front to grab a bite. Wanna go? My treat."

As we walked, we caught up on old times. He was still gigging on the boat and he had a new lady. I hipped him to the changes that I was going through with Sissy and Hiawatha—how Sissy seemed to only care about getting money from me and the way she was always fussing about me being gone, talking about how I wasn't even there when he was born. I said, "What does she think I'm supposed to do? I'm a musician like you. I've got to go and play wherever I can make money." He just listened as I kept talking. "He's a cute kid and all," I said, "but I'm not even sure he's mine, even though he does kind of look like me." I didn't mention Ada Mae.

Over tripe sandwiches and R.C. Colas at the Orange Front, I told him about Fate, and he said, "Man, that's a bummer." Then he ran it down to me about Jerry Lynch, a sax player who had a gig in Champaign, Illinois, where Sy had been playing with Dewey Jackson's Band. He said, "I'll make a call to Jerry, see if I can get you in his band, and get back with you." We made plans to meet the next afternoon around five.

Around two the following day, I made it over to Buke's music class. He introduced me to Dewey, a dark-skinned kid who was very thin and timid. I listened to him play while Buke kept threatening to hit his knuckles with a ruler. He said, "Stop shaking those tones and play straight! You'll shake enough when you get old!"

The kid had a lot of potential, which I told him and Buke. But I didn't hang around too long because I didn't want to be late meeting Sy. Turns out that kid was Miles Dewey Davis.

A few hours later, Sy and I met up at the Orange Front. He said, "I set it up for you, Johnny Boy. All you got to do is meet Jerry at the bus station in Champaign and show him what you can do."

I knew that the protocol was to give two weeks' notice, but I didn't care. Fate hadn't been fair to me. So after the show that night, I took my mutes and derby and left without saying a word.

The next day, I boarded a Trailways Bus to Champaign. That September of '40 when Jerry met me, with his gold-toothed smile and fine black hair shining in the sun, we hit it off like biscuits and molasses. He seemed to have all the connections, including some of the finest ladies I'd ever seen. But the club where his combo played was nothing more than a dive in the woods for whites only.

No matter that the weekly pay was only Line Four, I loved playing with Jerry. His musicianship was superb and his sound was round and full. Hot jazz every night, nearly raising the roof off that dank shanty with sawdust on the floor. The small crowds loved us and we all had a good time.

Afterward we dug some local colored jam sessions and kept our horns smoking. We played Ellington tunes like "Sophisticated Lady," "Rain Check," and "Cottontail," and Lunceford tunes like "For Dancers Only," "River Saint Marie," and "Tain't What You Do It's the Way That You Do It." My repertoire was getting fatter than a liver-fed cat. I felt like I'd finally gotten closer to my dreams of having my own band, although my money was getting tight.

Jerry was more musically advanced than I was, composing and arranging his own tunes. He wrote our theme song, which one white guy at the gig often requested. That sneak stole Jerry's tune and made it a big hit. I won't mention the name or the tune because I know that God will take care of that creep.

With the small change I was making, between paying for my cheap hotel room and scrounging up food, hard times resurfaced. Jerry and I were so hungry one night, we got in his rusty Ford and ran over stray chickens in the countryside! We collected them, went to his tiny apartment, and fried them up in some well-used lard. For breakfast we met at the day-old bakery in town. Copped some really stale donuts, took them to Jerry's place, dunked them in water, put them in the oven, and ate what we called "stalies."

Sometimes he'd use his witty charm and good looks to talk one of his girlfriends into fixing us "a mess of greens and some shortenin' bread." With ten cents' worth of beans and a nickel piece of fatback, we farted the evenings away and funked up the bandstand something terrible. All the while laughing and swinging that jazz. Cheers and raves from admiring patrons.

Eventually I tied two sheets together and sneaked out my hotel window because I couldn't pay my bill. I ran down the railroad tracks in the stark black night. Made it over to Jerry's and explained my situation. Even though I'd dug him and his music, I needed to get something else going. He understood and said, "Hey, man. We'll meet again. Do what you gotta do."

That September of '41, our other sax player, Richard Outlaw, hitchhiked with me over to Danville. He was a tiny, dark-skinned cat who was a threat to most sax players around. We checked on a gig in an old restaurant owned by Gotch Pender, a white fellow with a big snaggle-toothed smile who used to be a wrestler and who loved to quote W. C. Fields. He only drank straight whiskey. Never water. He said, "Fish fuck in it."

Richard didn't get hired, but I did. So I helped him out with a few bucks for a while, and he eventually left after thanking me for seeing him through.

Pender's club was named the Paradise and he was paying Line Six. His band leader was Toby Dyer. So bowlegged that we called him "Hooks." Jim Hall played drums, Tim Jones on piano, John Cameron on tenor sax, and Toby played alto. I can't remember who played bass, but the band was pretty tight.

Jim was a big, slew-footed guy. Skin the color of raw peanuts. His teeth needed a serious overhaul and he had a big lower lip, but he looked dapper with his shiny conk. His hair was so smooth. Looked like it had been pressed with hot combs and slicked down with lots of grease.

One night on the bandstand, when we'd just finished playing "I Never Knew," he looked at me and said, "Man, you need to *fry*." Meaning he wanted me to get a conk like his. He said, "Yo' hair looks like sheep shit on shallow water." He started calling me "Brillo," which really irked me. Prompted me more than ever to get a conk.

I said, "Okay, okay. You win. Whip one on me."

Later that night, I agreed for him to gas my hair. We were staying in the Just-A-Mere Hotel, which had only one bathroom on each floor. Only one toilet for ten or fifteen rooms. Surprisingly, it was pretty clean. So he got all the stuff together, potatoes, lye, and Vaseline, and we met in the bathroom.

I sat on the toilet lid and he stood next to me in front of the face bowl. First he greased my head, neck, forehead, and ears with the Vaseline. I watched him mix the formula in a glass jar, and it didn't take me long to understand why they called it a "fry": when he mashed the raw potatoes with a wooden stick and mixed them with lye, the concoction sizzled. Sounded just like bacon frying. When the sizzling stopped, he stirred it up good.

Then he dug into the jar with a small wooden paddle and applied it to my hair. Combed the strands straight back repeatedly until my head felt real warm all over. As he continued to comb through my hair, my head got warmer and warmer, until I said, "Okay, wash this shit out!" I jumped up and leaned over the bathtub while he rushed to get the water going. After he washed the mix out of my hair, I used a bar of soap to make sure it was all out.

A few minutes later, when I looked in the mirror, I said, "Well, you can't call me Brillo anymore."

He smiled and beamed. Then he said, "Want me to wave it for you?"

I said, "Naw, that's enough."

The next evening, Hooks looked at me and laughed, but the chicks dug it, so it was cool with me. But I didn't really enjoy it until after the burns on my ears healed up.

A few weeks later, my hair needed another conk. I tried to do it myself and blew it because after I washed and dried it, I tried to comb through it and a lot of my hair came out. It left me with a big bald spot on the right front side of my head. Since I was getting ready for the gig that night, I decided to wear a cap on the bandstand. That wasn't very hip.

I went down to Jim's room and he said, "You didn't use enough grease."

When we got to the club, he told Hooks why I had the cap on and Hooks just died laughing.

We'd played there for about six months when I met Jimmy Raschel. Man, he had a *nice* big band there, and I'd go and listen to their rehearsals and gigs. Logs of good musicians on the scene in Danville, and we'd usually end up on gigs together. I played with a talented piano player—nice looking—named Bernice Hassell, who had a boyfriend named Squirt, a drummer.

Later I met Milt Buckner, a short, roly-poly guy who clicked his false teeth to keep rhythm while he played with Jimmy. Milt was a hell of a vibraphone player, and he was being solicited by Lionel Hampton. Milt was too afraid to leave his hometown of Danville, though, so we got him real drunk one night and led him to the train. It was good for him because he ended up making great recordings with Hamp like "Chew, Chew Your Gum" and "Hamp's Boogie."

My pockets weren't so flat anymore, and I was having a ball. I sent a little money to Sissy back home and bought a few new clothes for myself. Then I heard that Peoria was even more lucrative and if you could be lucky enough to pimp a prostitute, which a lot of cats were doing, then you could *really* make it. Since I wanted to go home with a pocket full of money and show Pop how good I was doing, the idea of Peoria caught my attention. When I learned that prostitution was legal there, my eyebrows raised. I thought that maybe I could make out good enough to get a place of my own back home. Cop a gig on the boat. Maybe get my own band. Jam at the after-hours joints. Throw a party in my new place and invite everybody from Lawton Street, other places in Carondelet, and even my friend Hut. Hadn't seen her in a while.

Pete Bridgewater wanted to go, too. He was my newest buddy, a disc jockey who played bass with his brother, Cecil, who played trumpet. (Cecil was the father of today's Cecil and Ron.) They were known as the Bridgewater Brothers. *Big* names in Champaign, Illinois, not too far away.

I'd done a couple of shows with them, and a radio show for the University of Illinois with Pete, which was actually a remote broadcast taped in the men's restroom. One time a dude came in there while we were broadcasting and he took a shit. Things were quiet until he flushed the commode. Never knew how loud a flush could be! That water was gurgling and running and hissing. So, to try and smooth things over, Pete said, "Folks, we've got to get that air conditioner fixed." We both cracked up silently.

A few days later Pete drove me in his convertible Ford over to Peoria. Richard Pryor's hometown. It was a cold day and I almost caught pneumonia because his car didn't have a top. We stopped on a corner not too far from the whore district, in front of Bris Collins' joint, the Grenada. The buzz was that it was the place for hot jazz.

Through the big front window I could see a dark atmosphere. A bar and a few tables. When I opened the door, familiar smells of smoke, old liquor, and piss met us. Pete and I walked straight through the loud talking and high-volume jazz from the jukebox, heading toward the back to gamble. A big, tall dark guy who was the bouncer met us at the private back door to the gambling room. Eyed us up and down. Then he waved us in. After mixing and mingling, I got into a serious craps game, trying to fit in with the crowd. I hit a lucky streak because I kept rolling and winning, my trumpet between my feet.

When my pockets were bulging, I went back up front to the bar and was met by a horde of prostitutes, including an alluring fox called Feather. She was accompanied by another lady named Priscilla, an attractive brown-skinned beauty not my type, who talked about her mother's rooming house on Monson Street. I needed a room, so I listened to her. The jukebox was distracting me. A Jimmy Lunceford tune was wailing, "Walking through Heaven with You."

But my main concentration was on *Feather*, even while I kept an eye on my horn case and strained to hear what Priscilla was saying. Feather was just over five feet and stacked. Pretty face. Coffee and cream color. Not dressed like a prostitute. She was classy, elegant and demure. I wanted to grab her boa and pull her toward me.

I bought rounds for us and a few strangers, trying to gain points with Feather. She was shooting me some very inviting looks. She said, "New in town? Haven't seen you here before."

I hated too much make-up on women. But she had just the right touch. Sexy eyes and pink lips. Low-cut dress. When she smiled, her perfect white teeth flashed in the lights.

I smiled back at her. I felt pretty confident because I was sporting my conk and my new suit. I said, "Just got here. I'm a trumpet player looking for a gig."

Checkers McTomson was a drummer—the bandleader at the club—who had been gambling with me in the back. He walked up to us. Dark-skinned guy with a scraggly moustache, dressed in a suit that barely covered his pot belly, fedora set low over his small eyes. He grinned at Feather. Then he looked at me and said, "Hey, Terry." He fumbled with a curl in her bangs and stuck out his AAA-width shiny black shoes with long pointed toes, which he referred to as "'ho kickers."

His antics pissed me off. Even though he was dressed sharp as a tack, his pants were much too short. I thought, He should save those for a wading party.

He patted his obviously pistol-packing waist. Then he looked at me and said, "I saw you hitting them licks in the do'." He was talking about my winnings in the back room. He said, "I was bettin' against ya, but maybe you're just a long rollin' son of a bitch!"

My eyes were on Feather's tempting cleavage as she adjusted the top of her dress. I said, "I guess Lady Luck was just with me." Then I looked straight at Checkers and said, "Any old blind pig would stumble up on an acorn sooner or later."

After he and I talked for a while he said, "Well, this is *really* yo' lucky night, 'cause I heard about you and we can use a trumpet player when we open here in a few nights. Pays pretty good." He put his hand back on the gun in his belt and then he said, "And if thangs go wrong, well . . . I'll burn ya!"

11. Tennis Shoe Pimp

Feather called me her "tennis shoe pimp" because I didn't beat her. But there was no reason I'd be mean to her; she was struggling to make it just like I was. We respected each other. She helped me set up my room in Priscilla's mother's house on Monson Street, and she kept me happy.

Each night after gigging at the Grenada, I walked five blocks over to the whorehouse and met Feather. All prostitutes in this house had to go and get tested for diseases each Tuesday. If they passed inspection, they got a clearance paper and kept doing business. Government-inspected prostitutes, clean and documented.

At the back door of the house, where the "working girls" came and went, I rang the bell. One of the ladies opened the door and then went to get Feather while I stood there straight and tall, proud of my muscular physique, which I'd kept up by shadow boxing.

A few minutes later, Feather came smiling and took my hand. With my trumpet in my other hand, I walked her down the dark alley toward the club. One of the first nights we spent together in a nearby hotel, I promised that nobody would mess with her while I was in town. I also told her I was married. I felt at ease with Feather because we both knew that what we had was just a temporary thing.

I admired her wit. She could tell some mean jokes, and she felt comfortable to crack up laughing, not feeling like she had to pose and tease. I shared my newest jokes that I'd learned from the cats at the club. We talked about her experiences and the hot jazz at the Grenada.

Sometimes while I was working, Feather spent evenings at the Inglaterra, which was a ritzy ballroom famous for dancing and big band music. It was patronized by rich white men who wore foxy women on their arms like accessories. It was the completion of a successful look—a fine chick holding on to you. Feather easily fit the bill. She was a real show-stopper.

She had some of the wealthiest clients from miles around, and she'd fill me in on all the details—their fancy cars and posh hotel rooms with velvet drapes, big soft beds, and room service of steak dinners, caviar, and champagne—while kissing my ear with her soft little lips. As we walked and talked, she would inconspicuously place a small wad of bills in my hand, still laughing and telling me about the soft carpet and high ceilings. Then she'd say how her "escort" for the night couldn't hold a light to the way I made her feel when her services were "on the house." We twirled up a storm on her satin sheets! "You can be my tennis shoe pimp as long as you want," she'd whisper.

The cats discounted anybody who fell for a chick. The saying was, "Down it and get from 'round it." But I didn't have any fear of falling for Feather because she knew where I was coming from.

A couple of weeks after I started gigging with Checkers' band—it was December of '41—I was walking out the door of the local shoe store with a package of new black Florsheims when I felt pandemonium in the air. People were running and crying and panicking. They were screaming, "The Japs just bombed Pearl Harbor!" I didn't have the slightest idea what they were talking about, but I knew it was something horrible. Fear zapped through my veins like a triple shot of Dixie Bell gin.

Later that day, I listened to radio appeals for volunteers to join the armed forces. I hoped it would die down, but it didn't. Headlines painted a gory picture of reality. War was declared.

At the gig that night everybody was riled, not knowing what was going to happen. Tension surrounded us. It was like a fog from hell. Cats were sweating and talking about which branch of the service they wanted to join.

But when we played "Blue Moon," the atmosphere calmed, almost being controlled by the music. That's when I realized the undeniable power of jazz. I loved it even more! As I licked my chops and placed my horn to my lips, I closed my eyes and played a solo from my soul. Deeper than ever before. I played for all the folks that were killed. Hurt. Maimed. For their families. Their children. Their friends.

When I finished, there wasn't a dry eye in the house. Including my own.

12. Jailed

Sooner or later I knew that I'd go back to St. Louis and join the service because the war was heavy. But I wanted to cop a few more dollars. So a few days later I said a fond farewell to Feather and Peoria and took a gig at the Southern Barbecue, a beautiful place just on the outskirts of Grand Rapids, Michigan. I was getting paid Line Forty-Two for the week, working with Tim Jones on piano, John Cameron on tenor, and a guy named Basie was on bass. It was Beaver Palmer's gig, and he was a great drummer.

Hot jazz and pretty ladies. It was good money—the most I'd ever made since that New Year's Eve gig with Sy back home—but the job only lasted two weeks. Not only that, but I'd gambled some of my money away, tried to win it back, and lost even more. I didn't have enough left to pay for my hotel room. So at the end of the gig, I was hoping for a miracle.

Beaver was a braggadocio cat with a pompous stance. Said he could get us another gig, this time in Flint, Michigan, but we needed a ride. He called a guy named Blue Belger. Blue was a thirty-five-year-old dark-brown-skinned cat with a big wide nose, graying temples, a gray moustache, and a receding hairline. We all met in the lobby of our hotel, which had a pool hall in the basement. Beaver had won and lost a few times, playing eight ball. He had told me that Blue was a retired trumpet player who was up on the jazz scene in Michigan. He'd said that Blue had been in Grand Rapids for years and used to play at the Grenada, but now he was waiting tables at a fabulous cabaret place because it paid more money than gigging.

When we went outside, I saw that Blue had a sharp-looking silver Packard. We all got in and headed toward Flint, where Blue said he knew somebody. While we were riding I thought, This is the finest car I've ever ridden in, and I remembered Feather and the cars she'd told me about.

I got a little nervous when none of Beaver's conversation was about a gig. Instead he was talking nonstop about his girlfriend in Flint. I flicked my cigarette butt out the window and said, "Is *that* why we're going to Flint, or do you really have a gig lined up?"

Beaver said, "Don't worry, Terry. Blue knows everybody. He just likes to have a little fun first, that's all."

Blue sat back in his seat and drove like he was the president of all jazz connections. He had a deep, raspy voice. He said, "I like to do favors for favors. A good time ain't never hurt nobody!" Then he rolled the window down, since he had farted and the whole car smelled worse than a chicken coop.

We got to Flint early that evening. Light snow was falling. We stopped at a pay phone so Beaver could call his lady. He said that she would meet us at a drinking house that was an after-hours joint.

We pulled up to a shack in the woods on the outskirts of town, with a few red lights on the outside. We were greeted at the door by a hefty, cantankerous white woman who looked us up and down then stared into our eyes.

Beaver's girl, Evelyn, sashayed up and around the woman. She smiled at Beaver and said, "Hey, baby." She smelled like cigarettes, wine, and honeysuckle. Real bony chick with heavy circles under her eyes.

I stood in shock because she was a white woman. She kissed him lightly on his cheek, then she pointed to a blonde-headed woman standing behind her. She said, "This is my friend, Marie."

Blue grinned at Marie like she was the steak at his last supper. I touched my rabbit's foot. He stuck out his big chest, reared back on his heels, and looked at the tight-lipped house lady. Winked at Marie. He said, "Run 'em around!"

The house madam watched the five of us sit down at one of the half-dozen wooden tables. She said, "Who's paying?"

Blue patted his pocket like he was king of the world. He said, "I'm paying."

I had only a little change in my pocket, so I was glad that Blue was gonna pay for the tab. Beaver had said that he didn't have much money either.

Evelyn whispered something into the ear of the robust madam. A few minutes later a tray of drinks arrived.

Evelyn smiled at Beaver and said, "Let's have some fun, honey."

I sat there trying to be patient. Glanced around the small, dimly lit room and hoped that Beaver's plan would turn out all right. Faded curtains hung over the two small front windows. I prayed that the possibility of Blue turning us on to a gig was for real.

We were all getting a little smashed, and it was getting late. Marie winked at Blue. She told us that she was a waitress and she had to go to work.

Evelyn touched up her flaming red lipstick and giggled at Beaver. She said, "You know my pimp will kick my ass if I come home broke. So do you want a date or what?"

Blue gave us a cheesy grin. He said, "I'll be back. I'm gonna take Marie to work."

Beaver whispered something in Evelyn's ear and she giggled while rubbing his thigh. He and I watched nervously as Blue left with Marie. We kept drinking, waiting on him to come back. Steadily running a higher tab.

The heavy-footed house matron cleared her throat real hard like Mr. Wilson used to do in band class when we'd gotten on his nerves. She walked over to the windows. I could feel her footsteps vibrating the dark wood floor.

She pulled the curtains aside and looked out. Then she walked over to our table. She said, "Well, it's getting kinda late and that weather is bad outside." She put her hands on wide hips, looked at *me*, and said, "Y'all better settle up now."

I looked at Beaver. "You got any money? I ain't got but fifteen cents."

He said, "You got more than I do."

The matron got mad but before she could speak, Beaver smiled. He said, "Blue is our manager and he has all our money. He'll be back to pay up."

I felt like this was a bold-faced lie, but I played along, praying that Blue would walk back through the door.

We waited and told more excuses to the woman who, by now, wanted to sock us.

Finally she said, "Well, it's three o'clock in the morning. Y'all gonna have to get the hell outta here!" She couldn't call the police because she was running an illegal joint.

Evelyn leaned over toward the matron and whispered loudly, "Don't worry, I'll make it right later."

The matron said, "Maybe so, but yo' asses got to go right now!"

The three of us coated up and opened the door to six inches of snow.

Evelyn looked down at her silver high-heeled shoes. She said "Shit!"

We all plodded our way for about twenty minutes. I was gripping my horn tight. Finally, we saw a cab and flagged it. I cussed Blue under my breath. But mostly, I was mad at myself for gambling all my money away and winding up in such a mess!

Evelyn approached the white cab driver, batting her eyes at his stone face. She said, "Take us down this road until the meter says eighty-five cents." It was all she had.

He looked at our snowy faces and grumbled something under his breath. Then he told us to get in. A few miles down the road when our money was used, he said, "Okay, get out."

Evelyn looked at me. Then she said, "He's got fifteen more cents. Can you take us a little further?"

Reluctantly, he drove a few more blocks, which put us, according to Evelyn, only about three blocks away from a cat who could help us. The more she talked about him, the more I thought I knew him. His nickname was St. Louis. Big, tall, fair-skinned cat with light-brown wavy hair. Used to live in the 3900 block of West Bell in St. Louis.

He opened the door, dressed in silk pajamas and a matching robe. He let us in, cutting his eyes at me like he knew me. He made us comfortable and warm in his small, tidy living room. Then he offered us some drinks.

Thirty minutes later, somebody was beating on the door. BAM, bam, BAM, bam, BAM! St. Louis peeked through the window drapes and whispered, "It's the cops."

When he opened the door, two white policemen entered. One of them said, "Hiya, St. Louis. Now, we don't want no trouble, but a cab driver told us that there was two cats that he just gave a ride to. Says they was walking from that after-hours joint and when they got outta his car, they came in here."

The cop looked past St. Louis to Beaver and me. He said, "Now, you folks ain't from 'round here. And you might not know, like St. Louis does, that we're cleaning Flint up. We want a clean town. So you boys gonna have to come with us."

They took Beaver and me to jail, but not before I ditched my knife in the crack of their backseat. For nine days and nights they roughed us up, trying to make us agree with their ridiculous assumption that we were new pimps on the scene, while we kept insisting that we were just musicians.

It was a horrible nightmare, but finally they let us out. I thanked God that I didn't have a fat lip. Only a few knots, a slightly swollen eye, and some bruises here and there. Beaver wasn't hurt too badly either. We were cold, hungry, and dirty, and we were anxious to get away from there. But we didn't have any money. At least they didn't decide to keep my trumpet.

One of the cops pointed to a nearby street with a thin layer of snow. He said, "Now, see that highway there? I want you to hitchhike or whatever you have to do, 'cause we don't need your faces 'round here. Y'understand?"

After he walked away, we figured that his demands were a setup. That we would probably get arrested again for vagrancy. So we begged some nearby strangers for money until we had a nickel. Enough to make a phone call.

Beaver called a sax player named Don Goins who lived there in Flint, and he came and picked us up, then he drove us back to Grand Rapids to our hotel.

When we asked the desk clerk about our suitcases, which we'd left in our rooms, he scratched the side of his sullen face. He told us that they had been set out in the hall and that nobody was responsible for anything missing.

Don gave Beaver a couple of bucks and split. Then, after some searching, Beaver and I located our stuff near the trash in the basement, by the pool room. The locks had been picked and somebody had ransacked everything, but somehow the thieves had overlooked my nice electric shaver. So Beaver and I went into the pool hall. He put the shaver on the table as collateral for betting on a game and chalked up a cue stick. He sharked his way to enough money for his ride back to Nashville and for me to wire my sister Margueritte for some money so I could get a cheap meal somewhere and ride the bus back home.

13. Len Bowden

The war raged and everybody was scared. I imagined Pop saying, "See, now you gonna get drafted! You dead broke from foolin' around with that damn jazz! You ain't even got a rotten dime!"

I moved in again with Ada Mae. I didn't want to, but with no money to pay for a room, I had no choice. I rubbed my lucky rabbit's foot and hoped for some kind of miracle to get some money.

When I got to the union building, I walked through the dank atmosphere and glanced at the cats who were hanging out, eating, drinking, smoking, and shooting pool. Fear of the draft crept through the room like the Grim Reaper. But they weren't talking about the war. Instead, they were talking about Len Bowden's band, which was playing around town.

I'd met Len once before at the union. He was a veteran player, played trombone. Mostly led the band, a pretty good one. Well respected on the scene. Just when I was about to ask where I might contact him, he walked in, dressed to kill. He came straight up to me. He said, "Hey, Terry. I got a gig for you."

Inside, I felt like I'd hit my mark in a craps game. I glanced at his receding hairline and his peanut-shaped head, which reminded me of Sy. His small, neat hair waves looked like he'd slept in a tight doo-rag like my brother Bus did.

I smiled and said, "Really? Sure glad to hear that, 'cause I could use it."

He looked at me through his wire-rimmed glasses. He said, "The gig starts on Friday at the Castle Ballroom. Rehearsal is there Thursday at six. Okay?"

I smoothed my conk and said, "I'll be there."

Two days drug by like crippled snails. But Thursday finally rolled around, and I headed over to the rehearsal, which was a few blocks away.

My hands were sweaty. I gripped my Buescher trumpet, refusing to allow Pop's words to break me. Instead, I concentrated on my faith in jazz. I knew it wouldn't let me down. I was determined to make it, come hell or high water! I thought, God will take care of the war, and the day will come when Pop will hear me play and know that I made the right choice.

The Castle Ballroom was a fabulous place on the second floor of a hip building on Olive Street. Huge inside with a revolving chandelier of tiny mirrors that reflected a prism of colors all over the room. No tables. Just benches on the sides. The air was stuffy, but I was excited as I took my seat.

Thankfully, the cats were friendly, since they were some of my old cronies that I'd hung out with at the union, and we'd shared a few scab gigs.

Most of Len's book of stock charts was quite familiar. The ones that I didn't know were easy to read, and he was pretty easy to work with. Nothing like that crazy Fate Marable! When the rehearsal was over, he was happy, and I was relieved.

That night, I felt like I could face Sissy and the boy that she said was mine. I'd seen him a few times before, but I never could tell if he looked like me or not. But this time when I went to her small flat and the kid walked into the living room, I looked at him and it seemed like he had a nose like mine. Maybe even my hands. We were both about the same color. A weird feeling came all over me. I didn't know what to believe.

I did know that Sissy and Hiawatha needed money, though. So that gig with Len was right on time.

The following night we kicked off with our pumping swing-dance tunes. It was Friday night and folks were obviously there to have a good time. The dance floor was crowded. Fancy dancers gathered in the center to showcase their hip moves. I had never seen white folks cut the rug like that! I had to snap out of staring. Sweat flew and smiles flashed under the sparkling lights.

When we played "Franklin D. Roosevelt Jones," the floor filled up quickly, with dresses twirling and couples moving flawlessly to the syncopated rhythms in a counterclockwise motion. It was truly a sight to see! White folks swinging and bouncing to the sounds of an all colored band. "Len Bowden and His Melody Masters."

While I blew my heart out, I checked out the few colored couples who joined with a hot jitterbug. They really ripped it up! Flipping the girls up in the air, throwing them and catching them. The other couples checked their moves and came back with strong competition. The whole thing was a total gas!

When the gig ended, I couldn't wait to get paid. Nobody was talking "line" pay anymore. They said the exact figure. For Len it was five dollars a night. We had played from nine till one-thirty in the morning. I was too glad to get those dollars.

14. Navy Days

A few weeks later, Len talked about how soon we all might be drafted. He said, "A naval recruiting officer ran it down to me. They have the best plan for coloreds. A new phase of naval service for us. But they need volunteers."

I wanted to say, "Volunteers for what?" Still, I was intrigued because

I knew that the navy, like the other armed forces, only had openings for Negroes in the kitchen. The "galley," as they called it. Chefs, cooks, and bottle washers—our slang for dishwashers.

I said, "What do you mean by 'a new phase'?"

We were standing outside the union building in the hot August sun, dressed to a "T"—conks, hip suits, crisp white shirts sticking to our sweaty bodies, shining gators on our feet. It was 1942.

Len flicked the ashes from his cigarette, which was in a classy long black cigarette holder. Smoke trailed his words. He said, "Well, till now, colored sailors only had a 'C' on their uniforms: they could only be cooks or chefs." His eyes penetrated mine and his pupils constricted. He said, "You know that, right?"

I said, "Yeah." I looked him in the eye like Kid Carter had told me to do when you're searching a man's soul.

He took the smoldering butt from his long holder and dropped it on the ground. Then he looked me square in the eyes and he said, "They've got some brand new ratings for musicians. Really sharp." He stepped on the butt and his shiny shoe flashed in the sunlight.

I said, "New ratings for musicians?"

He smiled and said, "Look, they want me to put together a naval band, and you're my first recruit." Then he squared his shoulders and said, "Now, you don't want to get *on* the ball, you want to get *in* the ball. 'Cause the handwriting is on the wall. A hint to the wise should be sufficient."

He went on to explain that we would all be "ship's company" and that we wouldn't leave the base. He said, "Recruits in this particular branch of the navy, for the first time, will be signed up as musicians. We'll have a handsome new rating, an insignia of a G clef instead of a 'C' on the cuffs."

He was talking a mile a minute about a navy big band playing jazz! I was thinking, If I have to go in, this sounds like the right choice. For a moment I hesitated, but he wasn't the type of cat to con you.

I was listening hard. Navy big band. Playing jazz. All of us dressed sharp with new prestigious ratings. Going into Chicago on weekends. Performing for special political events. Weekly radio broadcasts. Training recruits for big bands. Jazz for all United States naval bases.

I stood there chain-smoking, trying to keep my cool.

He said, "They know that jazz is powerful . . . Good for our troops . . . Important for the morale of our men and our nation . . ."

I took short breaths. It felt real. I kept listening attentively as Len's perfectly enunciated words filled my head with dreams of jazz.

A few days later, on August 19, 1942, I signed up for the navy. Then we recruited the Wilkins brothers, Ernie on clarinet and tenor, and Jimmy on trombone. They were cats from my rival high school. I'd met them before, rehearsed with their band "The Sumner High School Swingsters."

Next was Russell Boone. He played sousaphone and was our choice for drum major based on his reputation when we were with the Tom Powell Post #77 Drum and Bugle Corps.

For trumpets, we got Mason Prince, Gydner Paul Campbell, Merrell Tarrant, Stanley Thomas, and Leonard Small, the cat who taught me fingering in high school. Then we got John "Five-by-Five" Brooks on violin and baritone, and Roy Torain on trombone. David Kimball was our tuba and string bass man. And there were many other great cats who joined.

I was excited to see Ernie and Jimmy again, and Russell too. We all slapped backs and shot the breeze up a blue streak. "Long time, no see!"

Later, we lined up for our physicals. Cats of all sorts. Short, tall, fat, skinny, brown, charcoal, yellow—but all of us sweating. Engulfed with hopes of being more than just mess attendants. Believing that we would wear the new insignia on our sleeves, we held our heads high.

We were called Boots, because it was required to wear leggings that were referred to as boots in boot camp.

The medics looked up our noses, shone lights in our eyes, probed our ears. Then they said, "All right, Mac, say aah!"

They called all of us "Mac." Examined us from our heads, looking for lice, to toes, making sure we possessed all our extremities. Then came the most embarrassing exam, when a medic demanded, "All right, Mac, skin it back!" He was speaking of the foreskin on my family jewel, as the general nickname was.

I'd heard that gonorrhea would produce an ooze, but I knew I was clean, thank God. So I followed the instructions quickly, and even said, "Ninety-nine," like I was told. I didn't understand why I had to quote that number. But when the doctor squeezed my other jewels, which made me cough and shriek, I said it fast.

Following the violating physical, I walked over to the next line, where I discovered that I had to get a crew cut. No more conk. I thought, Back to Brillo. But I took it like a man, like the rest of the guys, as I watched my hair fall onto the floor.

I took a deep breath of relief when they said that the swim test wouldn't be until we got to boot camp at Great Lakes Naval Training Center, Illinois, a training camp that would go down in history as the "Great Lakes Experience," a springboard for thousands of colored musicians. When I admitted my lack of swimming talent—all I'd ever had was those few swimming lessons at the neighborhood YMCA pool near Ada Mae's apartment—the recruiter said, "That's okay. If you pass the physical, they'll teach you how to swim when you get there."

When I had cleared all medical tests, I was ready! Ready to play some jazz for the navy. I felt happier than a toddler in a sandbox!

Soon I found myself back at Union Station, the same train station I'd left from two years ago with Turk's band and the Reuben and Cherry Carnival. Only now, I stood in line with the rest of the navy recruits. Even though I was disappointed that no one was there to see me off on that dreary day, not even Ada Mae, I smiled and waved to families and other people, holding my trumpet case with a death grip. In my other hand I held my small suitcase, which was packed with enough clothes for three days, as instructed.

Thirty miles north of Chicago and an equal distance south of Milwaukee on Lake Michigan, we reached our station. Then we rode in trucks until we reached the camp. The Great Lakes Naval Training Center, a massive spread of facilities along the waterfront. It was one of the major boot camps for basic training of naval recruits, an impressive setting with breezes carrying smells of munitions and oil.

As I got off the truck, I noticed that all of the colored recruits were being corralled in one area. Camp Robert Smalls. That really pissed me off. I felt like there was a white navy and a colored navy. My excitement died like a wrong note in a mellow solo.

It was explained to us that we were not allowed to openly visit the white camps, that a pass was required. Even for the administrative office area, which was called "Main Side."

My jaws were tight as Len explained the layout. We were all lined up. Standing straight. But my spirit had slumped. I thought, What a slap!

Len was put in charge of the new musician recruits—similar to a drill sergeant. He walked back and forth, up and down the line, as the sun beamed down with no mercy. He said, "Each camp is self-sufficient—a mess hall, church, outdoor drill field, known as 'The Grinder.' There's a drill hall, infirmary, movie theater, and several barracks."

He told us that all of us colored musicians were relegated to live together in a two-story barracks known as 1812. He had the upstairs office with a few bunks.

I gritted my teeth as he talked. He walked up to my face and looked into my angry eyes. After taking a deep breath, he shouted, "All right, you gasher! What did you expect?"

I said, "Nothing, sir!" I knew he wanted me to help ease the tension, but I was mad enough to spit bullets. I said, "Sir! I went to an all colored elementary, middle and high school. So this is more of the same to me, sir!" I ran my hand over my short hair, looked past Len toward the white camps. Then I glanced into the grim faces of the rest of my colleagues and I thought, Well, fuck it! Here we are. Let's get it on.

Our responsibilities were to train recruits for other naval bases. Initially, all new recruits were in the same category, which was generally referred to as "FFT," which meant "For Further Transfer." But we had our own version, "FFL," which to us meant "Fucked for life."

Each day we had a jam session, to get to know each other and to check out each other's styles. These moments were pure *joy* for me because these were all serious musicians. We loved those jam sessions, where we could vent our feelings and show off our skills.

As the days passed, Len supervised dozens of bands, which were to be trained as units and shipped out to other bases. At other times during the day, Boone and a few others showed the new recruits how to do the marching drills. New recruits constantly came through our camp—scared faces that turned into smiling faces during our daily jam sessions. Then frightened faces again when they packed up for assignments.

One of my duties was to show recruits how to lash hammocks. I taught them right and warned them about falling. But just like we all had done, they would fall out of their hammocks at night while trying to turn over. After a number of broken arms, cracked heads, and busted kneecaps, the navy replaced all of the hammocks with bunk beds and the snickering stopped.

Another one of my duties was to keep the head clean. The toilets and showers. I really hated it! But after reevaluating the situation, I decided that the latrine was an excellent place to play my trumpet. Being totally alone with those great acoustics. I sat on the shower room bench and practiced a lot after cleaning everything to a spit shine. I practiced for hours and hours and hours. One day I got creative and took one of my navy white hats, slit the dome and hung it over the bell of my horn. This was my version of softening the tone. Adding a sense of intimacy, like the sound of the flugelhorns in Jimmy Lunceford's Band. When I first heard those cats playing that sound, I flipped! It was so mellifluous. I knew that one day I'd have to master it.

During some of those lonesome times, I played a lot of blues that I had learned from the radio. I thought about Pop and wished he could have been different. Kinder. Ada Mae and Margueritte had written me and told me that he was sick. I prayed for him to get better. I missed my sisters and brothers. I played for them and my friends at home. When I finished, I put my horn back in the case, went to my bunk, and wrote a short letter home, wishing well for all.

A few weeks later, the swim test time arrived. I knew it wasn't the end of the world because the navy had spent a lot of money on me by then, and that doctor at the physical had told me that they would teach me if I flunked.

I was wearing my navy-blue trunks, trying to act like I wasn't scared. But I was petrified just thinking about the fact that half of the pool was over seven feet deep. My toes gripped the concrete. I couldn't even tread water. But I knew I had to jump into that huge, sparkling, Olympic-sized pool. Larger than life! I had to swim the length and come back. My heart was beating a fast cadence.

It was getting closer to my turn. Everybody ahead of me was swimming with no problems. I was mad at Pop. I thought, Why didn't you let us learn how to swim? At least I'd learned to swim underwater at the YMCA.

WheeeeEEEE! The whistle blew for my turn. I closed my eyes and asked God to please let me get through. I glanced at the instructors, who were to my right. Then I concentrated on the breath it took to play my horn. Breath was all that was on my mind.

I took a big one, held it, and dove in the water like the others had done. I stroked for dear life, thinking about what I'd been taught. "Relax and consider the water your friend." I did my underwater thing and made it to the other end. Then I turned around fast, came up for a quick breath, pushed off with my feet and made it back the best way I could.

I got out and walked away hoping that they had accepted what I'd done. When the instructor blew the whistle, I glanced back and saw the next guy jump in. No one called me back, so I walked away calmly, while my insides were jumping for joy.

A few weeks later I got an unwelcome letter from home.

15. Gray Clouds

"Dear John, Pop is real bad sick." The rest of Margueritte's words became a blur and my stomach dropped. I prayed hard that God would take care of him. I remembered how sick I was after that train trip to Jefferson City with the Drum and Bugle Corps. Since I had gotten well, I felt like Pop would be okay.

To ease my mind, I dove into my duties and the jam sessions every day. On the weekends, I enjoyed the liberties, which meant sporting my new tailored navy blues—G-clef insignia and all. Decked down and sharp. I'd get my pass and head to Chicago or Milwaukee, where there were always huge smiles from throngs of colored people who were proud to see us sporting something other than "C's" on our sleeves. If my crap winnings were slim or if I had crapped out, I'd head for Waukegan, Illinois. We'd nicknamed it "Boogie Bear Town" because it wasn't endowed with pretty girls like Milwaukee or Chicago.

But wherever I went, jazz was there. Women flocked to sailors like bees to honeysuckle. I made a beeline to the music scenes, then I went to check out the chicks.

One weekend I went to Waukegan. Some of the guys from 1812 had put together a group called the Funky Five. They were playing at the Club Afrique. I sat in and had a ball. Their leader was a tenor sax player named Alonzo Stack Walton. They had Julius Wright on piano and Paul Campbell on trumpet. Paul had played with Lester Young and Les Hite. David Kimball on bass. Woodie White was on drums. Years later, Woodie was Duke Ellington's tailor.

The next weekend I went to Chicago. First I checked in at the USO on 39th and Wabash. It was a moderately sized place that used to be called Bacon's Casino—Joe Louis' former training site. My next targets were the night spots. On my way out the door I saw Charles Allen, whose nickname was Chuck. He was tall and lean with a thin moustache. Man! He could wail on the oboe, bassoon, and clarinet. I loved his articulate speech, which kept me on my toes. We'd jam a little, then I'd move on, hoping to run into Bennie Green, an awesome trombone player. He was stationed at an army camp close to Chicago. Somehow, we'd always manage to meet up with each other. People would say, "Look out! Here comes that wild gruesome twosome!"

With a few drinks under our belts we made all the hot joints in Chicago on the Southside. Not the big clubs, but the swinging sets with smoking jam sessions, serious patrons, and winking chicks. Gold's on 58th Street, the Propeller Club on Cottage Grove, the Subway Lounge on South Parkway, and the DuSable on 39th Street, which was a hotel and bar. We'd play awhile then head to the bar.

They had a disc jockey at the DuSable named Daddy-O Daylie and he was all the rage. Average sized, dark skin, thin hair, thick glasses, and a deep voice. His favorite saying was, "Jazz. For people who live it and love it and make a living of it. Daddy-O."

He had great jazz connections and a hip radio show called "Daddy-O's Patio" that was broadcast from the club. When he invited me on his show, he didn't have to ask twice. He ended up promoting one of my records, which was produced by the Chess Brothers—"Out on a Limb."

The weeks of boot camp zipped by and I hadn't received any bad news from home. So I felt like Pop was okay.

When the weather got cooler, we heated up the concert halls with live broadcasts. It was incredible! Sometimes I played with the navy big band or else with one of our combos. Our orchestra had a hell of a string section. During my solos, I occasionally used the slit hat over the bell of my trumpet. Still trying to get that mellifluous sound of the flugelhorns in Lunceford's band.

As the days passed, I played my heart out with my friends—Ernie, Jimmy, Sykes, Batch, Chops, Cam, Mines, Perk, Pillars, Casey, Woody, Merle, Reese, Jacquet, Kimball, Boone, Gerald, Mason, Stanley, Skrippy, Skylark, Barnett, Sax, Chuck, Trombone Smitty, Willie, Little Red, Jerome, Jam, Jones, Stack, Epps, Mack, Donald, Bridge, and Five, to name a few. Believe me, we lit up those jam sessions with some of the *hottest* solos I'd heard.

Even so, the ever-present darkness of war surrounded us. I was thankful that I was at Great Lakes, and I prayed for all the men whose lives had been lost. I wished the war would end. But it kept going.

While bombs were dropping, we played our hearts out to keep up the morale of our troops. We made appearances in Chicago at the ballparks, the football fields, and the lakefront. Even at blocked-off intersections like 55th and Michigan, where they held fund-raisers for the government. The Bud Billiken Parade; CBS radio broadcasts from the base; entertainment for the troops each Wednesday for happy hour. Rehearsals and playing the music for visiting stars like Lena Horne, Dorothy Donegan, Lionel Hampton, and Hazel Scott. The hippest music with the hottest stars. I couldn't have asked for more!

The concerts we did for the Sunday-afternoon socials were cool because we had civilian visitors from neighboring cities. And the ladies—ooooh wee! Dozens. Smiling and congenial.

One Sunday after we'd finished, I found myself enamored with a girl named Annette. A real bombshell. Graceful, classy, articulate, intelligent, and demure. As she lowered her long lashes, I was struggling for savoir-faire.

Mattie Chapel, a distinguished-looking matron and local dress shop owner in Chicago, introduced the girl to me. She said, "Terry, this is Annette Singleton. She's a model in my shop."

I wanted to say, "Well, Annette, just *model* your way on into my life." Instead, I smiled and struck up my best conversation.

Later on, I used the pointers I'd learned from May and Feather to lay my best on Annette. After a while, we grew to expect each other's company. One weekend we went to the S & S Hotel on South Parkway in Chicago. I didn't know if the initials stood for Sailors and Soldiers, but whatever it stood for, it was a place where we could drink our rum, smoke our cigarettes, and "do the vonce"—a nickname for making love.

I always made it back to the base on time, except for once. I must have fallen asleep because when I opened my eyes, the morning sun was blazing through the window. I panicked. The time to return to the base had long passed. I was AOL—Absent Over Leave. My ass was in trouble for sure!

As quickly as possible, I returned to camp and faced Len. With a somber face, I said, "I blew it. I'm sorry, but I blew it."

He flicked his ashes harshly and went into his regular lecture. "You're supposed to be *in* the ball not *on* the ball. A hint to the wise should have been sufficient! Extra duty! Police the grounds and clean the back ladder! Dog watch for three nights!"

I cleaned the back ladder—all of the stairs from the back part of the barracks down to the ground floor. The dog watch was guard duty from midnight till six in the morning. I tried to distract myself from being afraid of the dark, so I hummed some jazz tunes. It didn't help much. Nobody wanted to do the dog watch because it was lonely and long, but *that* encouraged me to get my ass back on time from that point forward.

The months passed and things were going great. Then we heard about how a lot of cats who had come through our camp had gotten killed at the munitions dump in California. Fear was all over the place like a damp chill. I wondered if we would be bombed, too.

When Christmas was getting close, nobody was feeling the spirit. Just emptiness and loneliness. Everybody missed home. A telegram came for me from Ada Mae. "John, Pop is delirious. He keeps saying, 'I got to go to court. But I can't go till John gets here.' He keeps getting worse, John."

I just played my horn and kept my dream alive that he'd get well and hear me play one day. A few weeks after the holidays, though, I got another telegram: "January 17, 1943. Dear John, Pop died today. Come home. Love, Margueritte."

Everything faded to gray. I knew I was walking, but I couldn't feel my feet. Knew I was talking to somebody, but I didn't know who it was or what I was saying.

The cats took up a collection for me to go home, but I didn't. I just couldn't.

16. The Big Apple

Pop's voice was *still* in my head. All the time. Telling me what to do and what not to do. Sometimes I ignored him. Sometimes I listened.

Jazz saved my sanity. Which made me love it even more.

As the weeks passed, I became more and more determined to get a divorce from Sissy. Between jamming, performing, and hanging out, I made a few contacts with some attorneys and got the ball rolling.

During the next year, thousands of troops came through our camp. We helped Len form fifteen- and eighteen-piece bands, sometimes twenty-five-piece bands. They were all shipped out to naval bases. Guantánamo Bay (Cuba), Tulsa (Oklahoma), Memphis (Tennessee), Fort Pierce (Florida), Quonset Point in Detroit (Michigan), Pier 92 (New York), Chapel Hill (North Carolina), Corpus Christi (Texas), Newport News (Virginia), Banana Creek (Florida), Olatha (Kansas), Seattle (Washington), Pensacola (Florida), Earl (New Jersey), New Orleans (Louisiana), Boston (Massachusetts), Treasure Island (California), Honolulu (Hawaii), and my home town of St. Louis. Heavily talented cats came through—cats like Al Grey, Gerald Wilson, Lou Donaldson, Rocks McConnell, Major Holley, and Willie Smith who was one of the best-known alto saxophone players around.

At first Willie went to one of the other camps, a white camp because he was so fair-skinned. When we found out that he was on base, we got together with him and brought him over to our camp. Main Side offered him an officer's rating to stay with them and pass for white, but he said, "No, I'm gonna stay over here for no rating at all with my kind, and if I earn a rating or if I don't, it's okay."

Racism was strong, but I dealt with it, as usual. I wanted to master my craft, so I got my clarinet method book out, because the exercises were more intricate, challenging, and melodic. I kept practicing and practicing, determined to make my dream come true and to be true to my dream.

Rumors of New York caught my attention. All about the hot clubs there and the legendary talent. I wanted to go. I *had* to go. So I saved my money and backed off the crap games. All the while, I kept in touch with several attorneys about my divorce.

As far as Hiawatha was concerned, just in case he *was* mine—even though I'd heard that there were some other cats who could have been his father—I decided to include getting custody of Hiawatha in my papers because I didn't want Sissy to have the right to keep him away from me or dictate my time with him. I knew she didn't have the money to fight it. Plus, I had grown to love him, if the day ever came when I really knew he was my son, I could take him and be the kind of father that I'd never had. Even if he'd have to stay with Sissy for a while.

I got those papers on February 15, 1944. Divorced with custody of Hiawatha.

A year later, I was getting ready to check out New York! The Big Apple. Bright Lights, Big City. With a two-week pass and money in my pocket, I caught the train. My cousin Billy, who used to live in Carondelet, now lived in Harlem and he said I could stay with him.

Billy met me at Grand Central Station. I was overwhelmed by all the people. All colors, foreign accents, moving, pushing, talking. Billy was grinning like crazy, telling me all about the things he had planned for us. I didn't hear much of what he was saying while we were walking to the subway, 'cause I was totally wowed! Tall buildings, a sea of yellow taxi cabs, restaurants, stores, and honking horns.

Billy said, "Don't look up. They'll know you're a mark."

I held tight to my horn and suitcase and tried not to look like a hick. Tried not to look at the dogs, the bicycles, the busses, and the crowds.

Fifty-second Street! Clubs on both sides. I bought a bottle of beer in the Onyx, where Billie Holiday was singing. Billie Holiday! *Live!* Hypnotizing the audience and me with her incredible style.

After half of her set, Billy grabbed my arm and pointed toward the door. He said, "Come on, let's go check out who's over there!"

I left my drink on the bar, then Billy and I darted across the street to catch a little bit of Ben Webster. After that, we scurried next door to catch Coleman Hawkins. They were playing some jazz like I *loved*. Masters, both of them. I was excited and bright-eyed, like a kid playing in snow for the first time. When we made it back to the Onyx before Billie finished her set, my beer was still sitting on the bar where I'd left it.

There I was listening to the best live jazz I'd ever heard. There on "The Street"—the nickname for 52nd Street—we were surrounded by legends. Stuff Smith's trio had John Levy and Jimmy Jones wailing. There was the

Spotlite, the Three Deuces. All tiny joints. Real crowded, standing room only. People reaching all across each other to buy drinks at the bar. I didn't have enough money for reservations, so the bar was most accessible. Smoke filled the air. Drinks were a dollar a swallow.

At one of those tiny clubs there was an Italian jazz clarinetist playing with a small group. His name was Tony Scott. He spotted me holding my trumpet case and said, "Hey, sailor! You, out there at the bar with the trumpet. Come on up here."

I was nervous, but I joined in. I did my best, and later he got me a gig at the 845 Club in the Bronx with his band—a rhythm section and him and me. He had a swinging little group. My first gig in New York! I don't remember who else was in the group or what we played, but I do remember that I had a ball.

When we rode the A train to Harlem, it was incredible. Hot jam sessions, Cadillacs, pretty ladies, brownstones, storefront churches, hustlers and pimps, and more black people than I'd ever seen in my life. A two-week leave filled with more excitement than I'd *ever* had. Smoking jazz, fun, and Tony Scott's one-night gig. Subway rides: twenty-one miles for a nickel. Orange Julius—"A Devilish drink"; ice cream and hot waffles; ham and eggs served on the long counter in the same skillet they were fried in. Street vendors selling roasted chestnuts. Chinese food, Italian food, soul food restaurants galore. Collard greens, cornbread, neck bones, chitterlings, and hot sauce; fried chicken, smothered pork chops, hot buttered grits and eggs. Cats on the corners selling watches and rings.

New York was an electric place, and that was the fastest two weeks of my life. I knew then, without a shadow of a doubt, that I had to *live* in New York.

On my train ride back, I heard the news: President Roosevelt had died. It was April 12, 1945. People were running, screaming, and crying. I closed my eyes and prayed.

17. George Hudson

"Germany Capitulates!" That was the newspaper headline. Celebrations began that day in May of '45. I joined the big crap game at the barracks back at Great Lakes. I knew I'd be discharged and heading back to St. Louis in less than a month. When my turn came, I rolled the dice hoping for fat pockets. When the game ended, I was busted. Lost every cent I had.

In spite of the temptation of gambling during the next few weeks, I didn't play any of my twenty-four dollars of weekly pay. I wasn't going home broke *this* time. By the time June 29th crept up, I was more than glad to get the hundred dollars mustering-out pay and the $46.74 travel allowance to get back to St. Louis. Though I kept my cool as I signed my discharge papers, I was highly pissed when I zeroed in on my stats: Height 5 feet, 8 and ¼ inches; Weight 150 pounds; Eyes—Negro, Hair—Negro, Complexion—Negro. I wanted to scream, "My eyes are brown! My hair is dark brown! My complexion is brown!" I knew that if I acted a fool, I'd only get into trouble. So I cooperated and moved through the procedural lines like everybody else. But on the inside I was more determined than ever to get respect through jazz.

When my feet hit the St. Louis dirt, I made it over to the Hodiamont streetcar tracks, looking for Hut's house. I was hoping hard that she still had that room she'd promised when we last saw each other in Jacksonville after Turk's show.

When I reached Vandeventer and Enright, there it was, just like she'd described it: a gray two-story house trimmed with bright red paint. Crab grass in the front yard, and a few small wild-looking bushes huddled under the big window next to the front door.

I smelled fried chicken as I climbed the steps to the porch. When Hut saw me all dressed up in my navy whites, she grabbed me and gave me a smothering hug. She grabbed my suitcase and pulled me inside. She said, "Ain't you a sight for sore eyes! Come on in, Pepper. I *knew* I'd see you again."

She led me past her small living room to a chair in the kitchen. Steam was rising fast from a big black skillet. She said, "Let me turn this bird over." She wiped her forehead with her red apron and then she took the lid off the skillet. Crackling grease muffled her words. She said, "When did you get back? You got a place to stay? I got a room. You hungry?"

I watched her turn down the gas fires underneath the skillet and the other two pots on the stove. One smelled like greens. I couldn't tell about the other one.

I lit a smoke. Then I said, "Just got in. I'm starving and I'm tired. How much is the room?"

She plopped a glass in front of me and filled it with tea. Then she poured one for herself and she sat down. She looked just like I'd remembered. Friendly, loving, and smiling.

She said, "Don't worry 'bout the price. I can work with you."

I pulled out a ten and put it next to her glass. I said, "I need a gig, Hut. Got any leads?"

She buried the ten in her bosom, then said, "Well, George Hudson's getting ready for the Club Plantation. Maybe you can check him out."

She showed me to my room, which was down the hall from the kitchen.

She pointed to the door next to mine and said, "There's the bathroom. My room's across from yours. The other two are upstairs."

A bed, a dresser, a chiffarobe, and a chair. That's all I needed. I said, "Thanks, Hut."

She said, "Come to the kitchen when you finish settling in."

I divided my money into three sections. After I looked around the room, I put my expense money under the rug in the closet. My most sacred money, which I called my "don't go money," I placed under the rug where the big wide foot of the bed touched the wall. The rest of the bills went into my pocket.

After I sucked on the last chicken bone back in the kitchen, I headed to Uncle Ben's Pawn Shop down on Franklin Avenue because I needed some clothes in case I got a gig.

Zoot suits were the rage. Wide shoulders—much wider than your actual shoulders. A long jacket that came almost halfway between your hip and knee. The double-breasted ones were called "One Button Roll." Wide lapels that bowed across your body, instead of being flat. Pants with thirty-inch-wide knees and sixteen-inch-wide bottoms—real skinny bottoms. It was hard to get the hem of the pants over your feet. You definitely couldn't do it with shoes on. Then there was the long chain from the watch pocket that drooped down to your knees and back up to your right front pants pocket.

Shoes had to be AAA, which made my feet look extra long. Pointed toes. I had to get a couple of sizes longer than I usually wore in order to compensate for the sharp points and excessive narrowness. Cramped toes, and eventually lots of corns. But I had to be hip, even though I ended up with more corns than a farmer.

A good zoot suit from Fox Brothers mail order catalog cost sixteen dollars, and the big apple hat was two to three dollars. But at Uncle Ben's I copped a nice suit for five dollars. Thom McAn shoes were only three bucks. Friendly Fives—just five bills.

And then there were "Mr. B." shirts, supposedly nicknamed after the style that Billy Eckstine wore. Long, long collars with two buttons under the front dips. A small piece of elastic was hooked onto the collar buttons, which held the collar tightly closed. You couldn't see how the collar was fastened, and it looked really neat. To top everything off, a nice narrow tie.

Now I felt confident enough to check out the scene at the union. I figured that Ada Mae was probably at the Lincoln Inn and I planned to catch up with her later that night as a surprise.

When I reached the union building, I played a little tonk (a card game) and drank a few beers. Talked with some of the cats. I found out that not much was happening. Just small talk about a couple of low-paying "scab gigs" in some after-hours joints or local bars. There was a buzz about George Hudson's Band, but rumor had it that it wasn't easy to get in.

George's book was fat. Lots of cats had given him charts—Stan Kenton, Tiny Bradshaw, Buddy Johnson, Count Basie. He also had stock arrangements of all the popular tunes because his band played hit tunes from the radio. When the patrons came to dance at the Club Plantation after hearing some new pop tune earlier that *day*, George's band was known for being able to play it that night. All the hippest selections. "Tea for Two" with a cha-cha-cha beat. Tommy Dorsey's theme song, "Getting Sentimental over You." Lunceford tunes like "Marie" and "For Dancers Only." George's band was the hippest, and everybody knew it. His charts were serious. And he didn't have much patience.

I went across the street to the Orange Front. As I headed toward the counter, I spotted Big Jim, a big white apron hoisted high above his waistline, flipping hamburgers. He turned around and saw me.

He was squeezing the grease from the burgers with a spatula. He said "Hey, Terry, I heard you were back. I was hoping you'd come by."

I sat down, lit a Lucky Strike, and said, "It's good to be back, Jim. I missed your tripe sandwiches."

He smiled and said, "Coming right up. I know you want one, so I got one in the works for you. RC Cola as usual?"

I flicked my ashes into the tin ashtray and said, "You know it."

A hush came over the room. I turned around and saw George Hudson at the door. I had met him while working at the Castle Ballroom; he was nicknamed "Dapper Dan." Conked hair, hip togs, medium brown skinned, about five and a half feet tall.

Ladies turned and flashed smiles. He glanced back and forth with a debonair flair, headed to the counter, took the stool next to me, and ordered a cup of coffee. He said, "Hey, Terry."

I took a sip of RC and said, "How you doing, George?"

His big white teeth sparkled as he talked. He said, "I heard from Len that you were blowing your ass off in the navy."

I was admiring his conk and wishing I still had mine. I put my cigarette out and said, "I learned a lot from all those great musicians who came through."

As Big Jim set my sandwich in front of me, George said, "Oh, yeah, like who?" He lit a cigarette.

I was looking at my steaming sandwich and wanting to take a bite. Instead, I turned toward him and said, "Big George Matthews, Rocks McConnell, Stack Walton, Lou Donaldson, Ernie and Marshal Royal, Willie Smith. Lots of cats."

I took a bite and my tongue was swimming in pleasure. Big Jim eased over and nodded at my sandwich. "Bet you didn't have nothing like *that* in the navy."

I laughed and said, "The food was pretty good. But nothing could beat your tripe sandwich."

We all laughed, and then Big Jim walked over to another customer.

George took another sip of coffee. He said, "What're you doing later this evening?"

With a mouthful, I said, "Nothing. Why?"

He said, "I'm having a trumpet section rehearsal at the union tonight. Eight o'clock." He smoothed his conk and said, "If you want to, you can sit in."

I shook his hand and said, "I'll be there. Thanks, man."

Now, I knew that George's music was very difficult. The Club Plantation was the hottest scene around; every major act in show business played there. While I was in the navy, we'd had a whole week to rehearse for one major act like Lionel Hampton, but with George's band the acts came and went quickly, and the music had to be perfect for each star. So I was concerned whether I could handle all those charts on the spur of the moment.

That night at the union hall, I greeted the cats, sat down, and warmed up my horn, then rubbed my lucky rabbit's foot. Although the band comprised my friends—guys I had scabbed with, gigged with, and hung out with in and out of town—there was still a thick tension in the air. I knew that friendship didn't have anything to do with the audition. They were all excellent musicians who could read their asses off, and they even took their music home to practice. Each one had mastered a good sound and superior interpretation of jazz. In other words, they *all* swung. There were no cornies.

I was strictly on my own and would have to earn these guys' confidence. The books were passed out and I fingered through some of the four hundred or so arrangements. I had never seen so much music in my entire life! I wiped my forehead with my handkerchief, then I ran it across my hands. Taking short, deep breaths, I concentrated on thoughts of victory. At least I didn't have any lead parts; I was definitely glad about that.

Through the first few pieces, I did all right. Then George called "A String of Pearls." When I saw that the solo part had been given to *me*, it took my breath away. This was a very popular Glenn Miller recording on which Bobby Hackett had played the cornet solo. A very difficult solo, embellished with intricate intervals and fast runs. It had serious chord structures and changes and elaborate rhythmic patterns.

Even though I was a pretty good sight reader, there was no way on God's green earth that I could breeze through the hundreds of notes in that manuscript. But the cats were seriously checking me out, so I tried to remain as calm as possible.

What they didn't know was that I had practiced that solo dozens of times in the latrine while I was in the navy. I'd learned the ins and outs of each measure, played it forward and backward, like I'd done for many other pieces. But I'd never mastered it.

When the time came for the solo, I played it while looking at the music, when in fact I played mostly from memory.

After I finished, George said, "That was a bitch, Terry!"

18. The Club Plantation

In George Hudson's Band, we played with the hottest acts in show business—the Mills Brothers, Patterson and Jackson, Peg Leg Bates, Ella Fitzgerald, Sarah Vaughan, Nat King Cole, Savannah Churchill, the Ink Spots, Austin Wright, Pete "Public Tapper #1" Nugent, the Dyerettes, Derby Wilson, Holmes and Jean, and Joe "Ziggy" Johnson's Revue. I was sitting up there with all those top musicians, under all those sparkling lights, playing solos, pinching myself to see if it was real. We were swinging like there was no tomorrow, backing all those sizzling acts.

They loved working with our band because we delivered. Satisfaction guaranteed. Not to mention how the patrons cheered and cut the rugs to our smoking renditions of the latest hit tunes. And when that spotlight hit me. Man! I played my solos with all the fervor that I could muster. Mixing in comedic overtones that made the cats laugh, then closing my eyes and taking off with technical phrasing that shocked everybody—even me.

We looked sharp, too, in our uniforms from the Fox Brothers catalog. Suits like tan plaid jackets with brown trousers, tan jackets and beige pants, and a spiffy rust-toned number. Black or brown shoes, white or tan shirts, hip ties or dapper bow ties, enough for three changes each night.

We were a gas! We had Cliff Batchman, Gishard, William Rollins, Irv Williams, Kimball Dial, and Willie "Weasel" Parker on reeds; John Orange, William Seals, Robert Horn, and two cats I remember only as Fernando and Blott on trombone; and on trumpet, Cyrus Stoner, Basil Stone, Gydner Paul Campbell, and me. Bunky Parker on piano, Singleton "Cocky" Palmer on bass, Earl "Siam" Martin on drums. Jimmy Britton was our singer for a year or so, then we had Jimmy Grissom. Both dapper, devilish, and smooth ladies' men.

We played several dance sets every night and two or three shows with the stars. And man, we were the gossip of the industry because they all said that we played their music better than it had ever been played before. We were so serious about our music, not only did we take our music home to practice, but we even had section rehearsals so that we could keep our great reputation going. It was just unbelievable.

Now, I knew that the Big Boys from the mob owned the club. I saw them every night, dressed to kill—literally. I also knew that anything could happen at any moment. But I just played my way right on through it all. Especially at times when the Purple Gang came to St. Louis. Or when Owney Madden walked in, decked out in a sharp suit, escorted by his bodyguards. His signature style was a white cap and a real pigeon roosting on his shoulder.

At times, the bodyguards came in handy. For instance, one of the acts was a short little piano player named Peanuts. He rolled the piano from table to table while a sexy girl named Mary Calendar sang and did risqué dancing. It was customary for her to do little private dances at a particular table. After her dance, she'd pick up any coins given to her with her "other set of lips." On one occasion a rowdy patron heated the coins, and when Mary burned herself, she screamed. Immediately, the Big Boys visited that table and rough-housed the villain out and down the back iron stairs. Meanwhile, the band played on; didn't miss a beat.

After the show, the hub of all activity was our dressing room. Sometimes the bodyguards hung out with us in there. It was a huge room in the back where big money changed hands every night. Everything under the moon went on in that big room. And I do mean *everything*. Peddlers selling the latest rage in clothes and jewelry; sex and gambling—flowing liquor, smoky air, card games of tonk and blackjack, and "galloping dominoes," better known as craps.

It was an electric atmosphere and we all blended pretty well together—the wait staff, band members, singers, comedians, showgirls, and the wise guys. Believe me when I tell you that we had some hold-your-breath-fine dancers back there. Bronze and tan beauties from troupes like the Claudia Oliver and Hortense Allen Dancers. All curves, seductive costumes with low cuts, small waistlines, shapely legs, grace, and smiles.

Everybody had fun except when one of the wise guys would flirt too much with a tempting dancer who was the girlfriend of one of the cats. A hush would fill the room; the dice would freeze. A gun was pulled and there would be a standoff. But it always worked out and nobody was wasted in there. Thank God!

When the night ended, we all exited out the back door—the only door colored folks could use. All except Whitesides. He was the maître d' of the joint. Big, muscular cat, color of mahogany. Real articulate dude who dressed dapper, of course, since it was a big-time all-white club. No colored people allowed except working behind the bar, in the kitchen, or in the band.

One night in particular, a cat named Green was taking a break from working in the kitchen and bar. He was sitting back in the dressing room, smoking a cigarette. Huge guy, color of nutmeg. He had loose teeth that moved when he talked. They weren't false, just loose. One of the two Scarapelli Brothers walked up to him and said, "Hey Green. Come on go down to the basement and let me shoot the fire off your cigarette." The Scarapelli Brothers were patrons of the club.

Green ran his hand over his gray conk, which receded from his hairline, and said, "Yeah, okay."

Most of the band, including me, glanced at the Scarapellis. They were both great big muscular guys. One was a tad bigger than the other. We followed them and Green downstairs to witness this madness. After we all piled into the basement, Green stuck his chin out with the cigarette in his mouth. The gun went off and half the cigarette fell on the floor.

I swallowed hard and hoped that they wouldn't ask me to do that stupid shit because I'd have said flat *no*.

We all went back to the dressing room. After I'd changed from the band uniform into my regular clothes, Shorty Ralph walked up to me. He was one of the Big Boys. Shorty stood around five feet tall, had a head full of thick brown hair. Real easygoing dude—pleasant looking with the air of a Sunday school teacher.

George was standing nearby. Shorty checked me and George out for a few seconds, then he flicked his ashes and said, "You's need some better threads. You and George here oughta let me take you down to Holland and McGloshen and get you's some tailor-made suits like mine."

I looked at his fine dark gray pin-striped double-breasted wool suit. Then I glanced at the threads that George and I were sporting, which definitely paled in comparison. George gave me a nod and then I smiled at Shorty. I said, "Sure, man. Just let me know when you want to go."

The next day George and I met up with Shorty at the H&M store, and a while later we walked out of there with some of the finest clothes I'd ever seen. Pin-striped fine navy wool, soft black silks, dark gray linens. All double breasted. Altered on the spot to fit perfectly. Shorty was all right with me, even though he was a known hit man. I made sure that I never crossed him.

I was making as much each week as school teachers made in one month. I also loved winning at craps. When I lost, I'd try to win it back. Sometimes I did and sometimes I didn't.

By that time, Sissy understood why I had filed for custody. She was boiling mad at first, but I cooled her down. I told her that I wasn't going to take Hiawatha from her, there was no way I could do that, playing gigs and all and having to be ready to go on the road if I got the chance. He did look more like me than before. In my gut, I felt like he was mine. Still, there was no way for me to be absolutely sure.

I spent a little time with him. Let him call me "Daddy." Bought him the latest clothes like mine, had some pictures taken of us dressed in sailor suits. Bought him some toys and a puppy, Downbeat. Even bought him a trumpet and set some lessons up for him with a cat named Ferrente. He was so happy. He said, "Wait till I tell Odell!" referring to Odell McGowan, my nephew and his friend. I laid some bread on Sissy for incidentals and kept stepping.

Each night I joined the fun in the dressing room. The cats had given me the initial sobriquet of "Newboy," but it didn't stick. Our bass player, Singleton Palmer, labeled me "Dixie Bell," after my favorite gin. "Cocky" was his nickname, since he was cross-eyed. Cock-eyed. Then Kimball Dial, our tenor man, started calling me "Reet Pleat"—words from the song "Zoot Suit"—because I loved those zoot suits. Kimball's nickname was "Cabbage," 'cause his head looked like a cabbage. The nickname "Bell

Bottoms" also came up for me, since that was the style of pants I'd worn in the navy.

I was just glad they didn't call me "Brillo." My hair hadn't grown enough for a good conk, but I loaded it with pomade each day and at night I did the doo-rag thing. I thought they would tease me about my hair, but instead they had sour faces when George began letting me have more say in the molding of our band. He welcomed my ideas and announced my input as easily as blowing smoke from his cigarette. The guys swallowed it like lumpy oatmeal at first, but they eventually dug my suggestions.

More and more, George was impressed with my talent, my ambition, and my ideas. He gave me the opportunity to rehearse the band and incorporate my systems of phrasing.

Now, I didn't want to piss off the guys, but I was thrilled to have a chance to try out my techniques. While we were going through a number, in spite of the walling eyes from some of the cats, I'd say something like, "Hey, George. When we get to Section B, the fifth and sixth measures, let's try doing that first eighth note long, the second one short, the third one long, then make the last eighth note a long fall-off with a shake and a growl."

He'd look at me with a suspicious eye, then say, "Well, let's try it and see what happens."

Nobody came out and said anything negative because they all respected George's authority, but I was cautious not to offer too much too fast.

George and the guys smiled real big when we played my ideas and they worked. He'd flick the ashes from his cigarette and say, "Mark that and keep it in," then he'd smile at me and say, "I'm glad *I* thought of that."

Not only was I in the hottest band, but George made me feel that everything I'd done in order to get there was worth it. He made himself totally open to try things that had built up in my mind over the years about jazz. A lot of them were based on sounds from Carondelet—like the train rhythms I'd heard while helping Aunt Gert count her goats; the rhythm of the clip-clops from the milkman's horse; the romping-stomping taps of Shitty's shoes with the PET Milk can bottoms hitting the brick sidewalk when he did his buck dances; licks that Ed hit on that old worn ice pan in our street corner band; raindrops on the coal shed in the old chicken yard and the way the roosters crowed. I also used techniques I'd gained while on the road and in the navy.

The only problem was that I was hooked on those dice!

19. Galloping Dominoes

The weeks zipped by and I found myself rolling the dice one night in a hot dressing room game. At first I raked it in. Then the tables turned and I was busted. I hurried home, raised up the closet carpet and that heavy brass-bedpost carpet, and I got my "don't go money." Then I dashed back, about a five-minute run, and I got back into the game.

> The dice jump into my hands. I roll. "Lick in the doh!"
> Seven. I win. I stuff most of the money in my pocket.
> I roll again. "Bird nuts!" Two aces—Craps. I lose.
> My money's down. I shake 'em up hard and blow over my hand.
> "Finney fucked a fox in a forest and got a pheasant!"
> Deuce and trey. Five. My point. I light a smoke fast and roll again.
> "Sea sick and water bound!" Five and ace. Six.
> I'm wiping my sweat and praying to get my five.
> Money is piling up on the table.
> Some cats are betting on me. Some against me.
> I take a draw off my Lucky Strike, up the ante, and roll again.
> "Big Dick from Boston!" Two fives. I'm feeling lucky.
> I bet the rest of my wad.
> I pick up the dice and whisper to them to win for me.
> Shake, rattle, and roll again. "Fordyce!
> Between Pine Bluff and Little Rock." Double deuces. Four.
> I can feel it in my bones. I'm gonna win.
> I pick up the dice and shake so long, till somebody yells,
> "Roll, motherfucker!" I let 'em go. "Ada Ross and the pootin' hoss!"
> Five and trey. Eight. I'm smiling now, 'cause I know the *five* is next.
> I take a quick breath, close my eyes, and let her rip.
> Hog Mouth got me! Damn! Craps! I'm flat broke.
> Winner's teeth flash and losers' eyes sneer.
> I reach for my Dixie Bell, take the last sip, and leave.

When that chilly air hit my face outside, I told myself that that was the last time I'd ever shoot craps. Those galloping dominoes. I headed over to the Spoon, a little greasy-spoon, soul food restaurant not far away. There was a waitress there whom I'd nicknamed "Chippie." She and I had a little thing going on. I liked her curves and she liked my generous tips and my jokes. This time I only had jokes. We made each other smile a lot and she reminded me of Feather—sensuous, intelligent, and easy to talk to.

Chippie's hair was always styled and shiny. Her sexy, tight uniform covered her "abundant tempting endowments." She must have sensed that I'd crapped out because she said, "Hi, Clarkie. Tonight's on me. What would you like?"

When I smiled and opened my mouth to answer, she winked and walked away. Before I could take the second draw from my Lucky, she brought me a half pint of cold milk. She knew just what I wanted. I loved cold milk after a hot night.

After she closed out, we headed a few blocks over to Birdlong's which was a speakeasy. Dingily lit joint where you couldn't even see who was sitting next to you. Illegal drinks in coffee cups. Lots of smoke. She sponsored and we cuddled awhile. Then we headed over to the Elks Club, an all-colored place where there was usually a spillover of celebrities who had appeared at the Club Plantation, the Riviera, and Jordan Chambers' Club. Eddie Randle's band was playing at the Elks on this particular night.

As we made it up the long flight of stairs, I heard this *fantastic* trumpet playing. It was really wailing. I knew it was somebody I'd never heard around St. Louis before. I ran up the rest of the stairs, and there was this little timid-looking, dark-skinned cat up on stage, blowing some smoking notes!

A few minutes later I walked up to him and I said, "Man, that was mean!"

He sneered at me and he said, "Yeah, motherfucker! You come here to hear me play *now*. But you fluffed me off when I met you in Carbondale! Remember?"

I looked at him, and it all came back to me. Buke's student. Skinny little kid. Dewey. I remembered him being in Carbondale, Illinois, back in '40. I was between gigs with Jerry Lynch. I was playing in Benny Reed's band for a few nights at a little roadhouse gig. Sawdust on the floor. Benny Reed—a peg-legged piano player.

I remembered that Dewey had come down to play in an affair with different high schools. He was in a band that had come down from East St. Louis. Benny Reed and I were playing for the dancers at an event in the park. I was watching all those pretty girls dancing around the maypole, and Dewey came up to me and he asked me, "Mister, can you show me something about trumpet playing?" I interrupted him and I said, "Man, I don't want to talk about trumpet playing *now*, with all these pretty girls around here."

So now we were at the Elks Club. I looked at him again and then I said, "Yeah, I remember. You're Buke's student, right? Dewey. Right?"

He said, "Yeah, I'm Miles *Dewey* Davis, motherfucker!"

I said, "Okay, Miles. It's cool."

That was the beginning of a lifelong friendship, which had some high mountains and low valleys yet to come. It was also the beginning of my vow to never fluff anybody off again.

Chippie and I left after a while and we went over to the jam session at the Hawaiian Club, a ground floor joint on the corner a few minutes away. It was jumping too! Great musicians. Jimmy Forrest was working there. He was an unbelievable sax player. Charlie "Sluggo" Fox was tickling the keys on the piano as only he could do. Different bass players were taking turns. Emmett and Cocky.

Brer Koon was there, too. His real name was Joe Smith and he could play some mean drums. Called himself the sepia Chick Webb. Chick was the most notorious drummer of that era. And I never understood why Joe called himself that because "sepia" had a connotation of being dark brown, but Chick and Joe were both about the same medium brown color.

While the band played, Ella Fitzgerald walked in and they invited her up to the bandstand. She blew everybody's mind. Rocked the house! Her voice was amazing, like flowing gold. She could *swing*. Her range was awesome and her pitch and intonation were impeccable.

Then they asked me up, and I ended up jamming all night long. George Simon was there. He was a reporter for the *Metronome* magazine. He was writing an article on me, but I didn't know it. All I knew was that I was having the time of my life.

Everything was great until I got ready to go and I discovered that some snake had walked with my brand-new powder-blue, wraparound Ragland topcoat. I was mad enough to fight a tiger!

20. Tempting Offers

Eddie "Cleanhead" Vinson was in St. Louis in '46 with his band. Volley Bastine, Cleanhead's cousin, called me and said, "We'll be recording in the morning. Why don't you come on by and bring your horn? Eddie might want you to sit in."

I was flabbergasted. I fumbled for a smoke, then I said, "Okay."

Where the place was, I don't remember. But I know I showed up early. I was excited! That was my first recording session; plus, Cleanhead had always been one of my favorite singers and players. We made a tune called "Kidney Stew," with Cleanhead singing and playing alto:

> Goin' back home to get my old gal Sue.
> Goin' back home to get my old gal Sue.
> She's not the caviar type, just plain old kidney stew!

On that same day, we did a few other tunes, like "Railroad Porter's Blues." Lee Pope was on tenor, Volley was on cornet, Ves Payne was on drums, Leon Comegys was on trombone. I can't remember who was on bass and piano, or who else was in the band. It was a wild scene, real exciting. When I left there I couldn't wait to tell all the cats at the union.

Then Louis Jordan scouted me for his band. He sent me a telegram: "APRIL 7, 1946 WOULD YOU LIKE JOB IF SO HOW SOON CAN YOU JOIN BAND WIRE LOUIS JORDAN PARADISE THEATRE DETROIT MICH." The next day he sent me another one: "CALL ME AFTER 12 EST TONIGHT AT GOTHAM HOTEL TEMPLE 10600 ROOM 805 LOUIS JORDAN."

Louie offered me this big-time bread. He had a famous band, with a renowned reputation. For a small band, some folks said that it was the greatest band of the century. Played stuff like "Caldonia, Caldonia! What makes your big head so hard?" You know, tunes like that. Hit tunes. Lots of hit tunes. Hard-hitting tunes. Aaron Eisenhall was with that band, but he'd gotten sick, so Louie wanted me.

A few nights later at the Club Plantation, just before the show, George came up to me in the dressing room and said, "A little bird told me about Louis Jordan's offer." I don't know how he got wind of it. And I felt guilty just thinking of leaving him, since he practically let me run his band. Trusted me totally.

Everybody was getting ready for the show and there was a lot of joking around as usual. Loud talking. Smoke and laughter.

I stopped dressing for a moment and looked straight into George's sad eyes. He said, "That was some mighty big bread he was gonna mash on you. But I told him, I said, 'Louie, if you take Clark, I'd be lost. He rehearses the band, stylizes the band, he's my lead player, he's my soloist, he's a role model and everybody respects him.'" George lit a smoke and looked straight into my eyes. Then he said, "So, Clark, I told him I'd be ruined without you."

His piercing look made me antsy. I took a sip of Dixie Bell and I said, "Well, that's the end of that."

We both smiled, but in my heart I knew that sooner or later I'd have to move on.

Not long after that, I got a telegram from Jimmy Lunceford asking me to join his band. Talk about decisions. I had always wanted to play in that band. They had such mellow sounds on those flugelhorns. Mellifluous. The type of sound I wanted to perfect. I'd fallen in love with that sound a long time ago, tried to duplicate it all kinds of ways, with felt over the bell of my horn, hats, anything I could find that could make that smooth, rich sound.

Lunceford's band also had a real strong marching sound. Very precise band. Snooky Young and Gerald Wilson, my old navy buddies, were once sidekicks in that band. Now Jimmy had Peewee Jackson and a little cat that had a great big beautiful sound—Freddie Webster. They also had Paul Webster, and Steve . . . I can't remember Steve's last name. Russell Bowles, Trummie Young, Joe Thomas, and another navy buddy—a tenor player—Willie Smith.

Before I could think about joining Jimmy's band, George came to me really excited before the show. He said, "Hey, Clark. We finally got the go for the tour with Illinois. The TOBA circuit, Man!"

I'd heard about the TOBA circuit—Philadelphia, Baltimore, Washington, New York. TOBA stood for Theater Owners Booking Association, but cats had a nickname for it—"Tough on Black Asses." I didn't care what they called it. I was gassed!

Illinois Jacquet had a really hot band on the scene. He had recorded a solo on a song titled "Flyin' Home" with Lionel Hampton. Because it had been such a hit, Illinois now had his own band and they were all the rage. But he needed a strong opening act for his show. Based on our hot reputation, Illinois wanted George's band.

So much for Lunceford. I couldn't run out on George when I knew he needed me.

A few days later, Jeter Pillars' Band replaced us at the club. I was itching to go on the tour, but George said, "It'll be a few weeks. No more than a month."

Man, I couldn't wait! George got us a few local gigs, but he didn't get much work for the band. So I took some local gigs here and there in between.

Shortly after that, Lionel Hampton offered me an opportunity to go on the TOBA circuit with him for a few weeks. I really wanted to go, so I had to find a way to tell George.

Now, it wasn't particularly that I wanted to play with Hamp. It wouldn't have mattered to me if it had been Shithouse Shorty and His Fart Busters. Joe Banana and His Musical Appeal. Bob Grape and His Bunch. It didn't matter. I was just ready to get away from St. Louis so I could make more money, get more exposure, and breathe new air. I wanted to go somewhere with somebody, and soon.

George's thing of going on the road with Illinois wasn't for a month or so, *if* it worked out. And George's band wasn't working that much. A few gigs here and there but nothing steady.

I sat down with George at the Orange Front over coffee and I explained how I felt. I said, "George, I'll come back in time to do the tour with you and Illinois. But until then I want to go with Hamp."

We both took drags from our cigarettes and nobody said anything. I was staring outside as George took a sip of coffee. Then he said, "Well, now, let me get this straight. You're gonna come back after this brief thing with Hamp. Right?"

I said, "Right. Then I'm coming back to go on the tour with you."

21. Lionel Hampton

Ada Mae stood in front of me in her kitchen with a black eye, crying her heart out. Now, I had gone over there to relax and to share the good news about joining Hamp's band. I'm sitting at her table, looking up at my pretty sister with a big swollen eye holding a towel up to her face. Telling me that she and Red had gotten back together and they had a fight. Man! I wanted to kill that big son-of-a-bitch.

She said, "John, Red is so mean. Threatening me, saying I need to quit my job and stay home. You know I need my own money."

This was the same argument that I'd heard her and Sy having a hundred times. Sy didn't want her working late at that bar either, but at least he'd never hit her.

I got up and left in a huff. Half-running, half-stumbling, and cussing for the whole two miles over to Cocky's house. That's where I had stashed my gun.

I told Cocky—my friend who played bass in George's band—what had happened. I ignored him telling me to calm down. Got my "Five Brothers," which was the nickname for my gun with five bullets in the chamber. Hoofing back over to Ada Mae's, I happened to glance in the window of the restaurant near her apartment. I came to a screeching halt. There they were, Red and Ada Mae. All hugged up. Goo-goo eyed and grinning at each other. Sitting at a table, eating a jack salmon sandwich. With sunglasses covering her black eye and all.

I just stood there and watched them kissing. All I could do was spit! I felt real stupid looking at them with my gun in my pocket. That taught me a lesson: "Never put your shovel where there ain't no shit!" Better known as staying out of other people's business.

Later on, I made a beeline for Hamp's band bus. As we left St. Louis, I blended in with the jokes and camaraderie—especially with my old friend Milt Buckner. We laughed about the time in Danville when the cats and I had to get him drunk and make him get on the train because he was nervous about joining Hamp. My old navy buddy Mitchell "Booty" Woods was there, too. He and I talked about old times and caught up on what some of the Great Lakes cats were into.

Wish we had known then that Great Lakes would be so historic. Getting jazz bands together all over the States to treat our troops for all the hell they had to go through. Rewarding them with jazz. But more than anything, it was the first time that black musicians were given a special rating that was higher than cooking and bottle-washing. More than fifty years after we left that scene, the navy gave us a big reunion and flags and all kinds of stuff. Fifty years later!

But when I joined Hamp's band, when Booty and I were just jiving around and passing the time, all I was looking forward to was a chance for the big times.

It was fun playing with those guys. I felt like I'd really made it because I was playing with very well known musicians who had savored the life I wanted to taste. They had played all around. Not like the cats in George's band, who were hometown cats playing for scale in St. Louis. The cats in Hamp's band had played with the *best*—Benny Carter, Lucky Millander, Tiny Bradshaw, Buddy Johnson.

And man, Hamp was a *gas!* He gave a whole new meaning to the word "swing." Maybe it was because he'd originally been a drummer, but he never missed a beat. His rhythmic patterns, speed, dexterity, harmonic structure, and humor blew my mind. He was a fantastic musician, whether he played the piano, the drums, or the vibes. And he was so animated. A great band leader too. The energy of his band was riveting. I *loved* it.

Trumpets were Joe "Chop Chop" Morris, Duke Garrett, Dave Page, Lamar Wright, Jr., and Skeeter Evans. On 'bones we had Booty, Buster Scott, and Harpo. I never knew Harpo's whole name. Saxes were Johnny Griffin, Bobby Plater, Johnny Board, Charlie Fowlkes, and Herbie Fields. The rhythm section was George Jenkins on drums, Milt on piano, Superman on bass—I can't remember anything but his nickname—and I think it was Eric Miller on guitar. All remarkable cats.

We played things like "Hey Bop-a-Ree-Bop," "Flyin' Home," "Air Mail Special," which Hamp had done with Benny Goodman, "Chew, Chew, Chew Your Gum," and "Hamp's Boogie Woogie." All hot tunes.

On top of all that sweat-poppin' music, Hamp had Dinah Washington with the show. Man, what a vivacious chick! She could belt a tune like Kid Carter could throw a punch—precise and right on target. She had that deep home gospel sound. Such perfection. She could sing the blues like a true champ. Made the goose bumps rise.

Then there was Madeline Green. Cocoa curves that would make your mouth water, and a face to match. She had that Nancy Wilson kind of flair. For the ladies there was Rubel Blakey, a handsome balladeer. Color of creamy coffee. Made the ladies swoon and cry.

After a few weeks with Hamp, I knew I wanted to keep playing with him. Great music and, at twenty-three dollars a night, great bread.

The bus was real comfortable and the pee stops along the roadsides were frequent enough. Plus, we had all the help we needed with our luggage because we had a valet named Leroy who could pick up a trunk with one hand. Big, burly caramel-skinned cat. Almost six feet tall, with a weight-lifter's physique. George Hart was our road manager. A shrewd, no-nonsense cat. He loved to gamble. Milt Buckner did the arrangements, and his charts were smoking hot. So everything was great.

It was a northern tour at first—the Royal in Baltimore, the Earl Theatre in Newark, the Apollo in New York, the Howard in D.C., and the Regal in Chicago. We didn't have a lot of time to visit other clubs and jam—it was all about play, pack, and travel.

When the southern dates came, we rode the train, heading to Louisville, Kentucky. The train made better time, and it was much safer than the bus—racially speaking.

Buster Scott had been telling us about his Muslim studies. By this time he had changed his name to Abdul Hameed. We didn't think much of it until the time when we were nearing the Mason-Dixon Line on the train. Normally this meant that all colored passengers had to get up from their regular seats and relocate to the back of the train in the "Jim Crow" car.

Abdul told everybody in the band that he was not going to ride in the Jim Crow car; he was going to stay right where he was. As he put a fez on his head, which was a big thimble-looking hat like what the Shriners wore, bets were laid. Next Abdul pulled out a newspaper that was written in Arabic; then he pulled out his Koran, also written in Arabic.

We were cracking up at him and betting against him totally. When we reached the Mason-Dixon Line, the white conductor said, "Okay, now all you coloreds go in the back to the colored car." Including Herbie Fields, who was Jewish. But Abdul didn't move.

We all piled up around the window of the back car trying to see how soon we'd win our money. The conductor gestured for Abdul to move, but nothing happened. The first conductor went and got his buddy, the other white conductor, and they both tried to get Abdul to move. We couldn't hear anything because we were too far away, but we were watching like hawks.

Abdul gave both of them a sarcastic look and continued reading his Arabic paper. Finally he reached into his pocket and handed them a card, which we later found out was also written in Arabic. The conductors looked at the card like two monkeys looking at a Swiss watch movement. They glanced at each other, shrugged their shoulders, and then they walked away.

I never bet against anything else that Abdul said he could do, and neither did anybody else.

Our next gig was in a little town near Louisville, Kentucky. After we'd finished performing, Dave, Hamp, and I ventured to a house of ill repute and gambling. A few hours later, all three of us had run out of money.

Hamp had a standing rule that anybody who wasn't there when the bus was ready to depart would simply get left. Well, by the time we made it to the pick-up point, the bus was gone.

So Hamp got on the pay phone and made a collect call to Gladys. Not only was she his wife, but she ran his business with an *iron* hand. She was in Detroit, where we were supposed to be going with the rest of the cats on the bus.

Dave and I huddled close to Hamp, trying to hear what Gladys was saying. We backed up a few steps because she was yelling. She said, "Where are you, Lionel? Give me the exact address!"

He swallowed hard, then said, "Uh, we're here at the hotel where we were staying, and, and, uh, we went to a restaurant. And uh, when we finished eating and everything, uh, the bus was gone. So, so, can you wire us some money so we can catch the plane to get to Detroit? We gotta get to Detroit."

Our band was a headliner at the big jazz festival and I felt pretty confident that she would help us out, since the show couldn't go on without Hamp. Or so I hoped.

She yelled, "Stay right there, Lionel! Till you hear from me!"

We kept asking the hotel folks if a telegram had arrived from Gladys. Several hours later, a little wispy dude showed up. Color of dark honey. He was Gladys' personal valet.

Now, when I'd first heard the word "plane" come out of Hamp's mouth, I'd started taking big swigs from my cup because I was terrified of flying. I'd never flown before in my life! And I don't remember the flight at all. But I know we made it to Detroit and I played the gig.

When Hamp's tour ended and we were back in St. Louis, he asked if I could leave George and join him for an extended tour. I told him I'd talk it over with George. Hamp and I planned that if things worked out, I'd meet him in two weeks at a nearby bus stop.

When I hipped George to my plans, he said, "Well, Clark, you know I'll miss you. But, hell! If Hamp offered me a gig, I might take it myself. And besides, if you ever want to come back, you know you can."

So I told all the cats in George's band about my plans, and we toasted to my success.

Two weeks later I stood on the corner with my suitcase and my trumpet. I waited and waited and waited. No bus. No Hamp.

22. Road Lessons

When spring of '46 came, I *still* hadn't heard from Hamp. I had been in and out of the Club Plantation with George's band, and my pockets were thinner than my old shoe soles in Carondelet. I was barely making ends meet. Trying to turn five into ten, craps still ate most of my pay. Then I got a big chance to sit in with Lucky Millander at the Castle Ballroom. Bright lights and big bread!

The tree bark that Lucky had "blessed" was selling like hotcakes. It was just a gimmick to fatten his pockets, but everybody thought they'd be lucky playing the numbers if they had a piece—even my brother Ed. When I visited Carondelet, Ed's wife, Mamie, was raving about it. She stood around four foot eight. Color of bittersweet chocolate. Her bottom lip was stuffed with Skeetin' Garret snuff, as usual. She said, "Yeah, John. Now you talkin'! Lucky Mil'ner 'bout the best thang you came 'cross. I got my piece of lucky bark, too!"

Margueritte was busy raising her thirteen-year-old daughter, Murlene, and dealing with Johnny Pops' antics. Bus and his wife, Dimples, were faring okay, as were my other sisters. Marie was pregnant and happy. Still, none of them came to hear me play, even though colored folks were allowed at the Castle. I thought it was because Pop had embedded the taboo about jazz in their minds and they couldn't shake it. It hurt me, but I just let it alone and kept playing.

Lucky's music was very difficult. But with a piece of his "blessed bark" in my pocket, I made it through those strange, handwritten arrangements and enjoyed his showmanship. The manuscripts were marked where he'd jump down off a high pedestal onto a gigantic galloping domino—a big die. Then at another point he'd jump down and spin around onto the next die. With those two oversized dice for props, he milked the show to the last drop. The audience went wild, and I got paid. But his show didn't twang my heartstrings.

Before long, George told me that Illinois was ready with his tour and that we'd be leaving in a few days. While I was packing the next day, I heard Ada Mae say that I was in *Metronome* magazine. So I dashed out and bought a copy. It had a great article that George Simon had written about me one night while I was gigging with George's band, and it even had a picture.

It was a full-page article about my career—my high school band, the Vashon Swingsters; my idols—Roy Eldridge and Charlie Shavers; the Reuben and Cherry Carnival; the V-discs I'd made in the navy. And it ended with, "You'll be hearing a great, modern trumpeter who plays with a beat, with feeling, with facility, and, above all, he plays like nobody else!"

Man! I pasted that article in my scrapbook right next to my first publicity shots with George's band and a solo shot of me dressed in the expensive threads that Shorty Ralph had arranged for me to buy—an awesome navy blue suit with thin white pinstripes. Autographing those photos had been all the rage. But still, I couldn't wait to get out of St. Louis.

That evening I boarded the bus with George and the cats. We were joking about the conflicting meanings of TOBA—the newest one was Theater Owners Benevolence Association. Whatever the latest definition might be, it was still Tough on Black Asses for me. Miles of travel, bad food, no sleep, living out of a suitcase. Slick talkers like Johnny Pops. But it was still worth all the hardships, because when I put my trumpet up to my chops and played, I loved it. I knew that one day jazz would be respected by the world just like classical music. I wanted to teach jazz and be right there when it got its due reward.

I also wanted to be respected, in spite of the fact that I hadn't finished high school—which bothered me a lot. But I kept studying the dictionary and my English books, so that my grammar and vocabulary would be up to par.

When we played the Apollo, I looked at the intricate architecture, the domed ceiling, the velvet seats and the carved balconies. I felt the beat of Harlem, the soul of black, brown, and beige America. It was deep! An appreciation of our music with roots from Africa. A pulse. I knew then that I'd have to go to our "Mother Country" one day.

We played a few hot, swinging tunes that night at the Apollo, then we rushed to change clothes. The audience was on their feet! I felt that applause all over. We were dressed sharper that Gillette razors. Then we hit "Body and Soul"—an arrangement by Bugs Roberts out of St. Louis. The lights went down and the spotlight came on. Zap, right on Weasel, a little bitty cat whose tenor was almost as big as him. He played this awesome solo. I was staring along with all the cats, and the audience was roaring. He played some shit I'd never heard him do before. He started out in one tempo and then went into double time. Then Weasel just *flew*, notes jumping out of his horn a mile a minute. He was so animated, bobbing and weaving. Man! Unbelievable. He blew everybody's mind. Maybe even his own.

After all the ovations—and the applause went on for a while—we went backstage in an uproar. But Illinois was pissed! He screamed at George, "I don't want that shit! Take that number out!"

That's when I learned, more than ever: everybody ain't gonna be glad for you.

23. Pauline

Even though I appreciated everything that George had done for me, the bread just wasn't hitting the mark. I wanted a house, a smooth ride, and a nice lady waiting for me. That cost more money than I could cop working with George. Even though he was a great cat.

But more than that, I was getting that old empty feeling inside. That kind of loneliness that used to wait for me each day after school when I first moved in with Ada Mae and Sy. All the short-term chippies were nice, but there was no *root* in that.

And craps was definitely not helping me to build a bank roll. So I made up excuses for not rolling. Things like "I'm saving up for a house." Or, "I'm gonna learn how to drive and get me a car." Or, "Go ahead. I'll just watch."

When we got back to St. Louis, I decided that if I wanted to meet a home-minded lady, I'd better start going to some different kinds of places between gigs, like ice cream parlors. I even went to the Veiled Prophet Parade, since I'd always loved parades.

No one knew who the Veiled Prophet was. Just a mysterious person, all dressed in costume. It was a silly thing in a way; still, it drew the attention of thousands. There were lots of bands like Vashon High, Sumner High, the Tom Powell Post #77 Drum and Bugle Corps, and many white bands, elementary through college.

I was standing in the crowd, watching the embouchures of the Masonic band as I had done years ago, just before the debut of my little street corner band. It felt like déjà-vu. When the trumpets from each band passed by me, I cheered them on.

Then I saw her. She wasn't flashy like the foxy dancers I'd seen in the shows. But she was just as shapely. And pretty. What caught my attention the most, though, was the way she blushed at my glance.

I cocked my Stetson hat and fingered the change in my pockets. She was the perfect height for me. Seemed like she was made to fit in my arms. My palms got sweaty.

When I made it through the people to where she was standing, I introduced myself. Then I said, "What's your name?"

I reached for her hand, which she extended. Soft. She said, "Pauline. My name is Pauline." She was real shy.

I said, "I'd like to call you sometime. May I have your number?"

An average-looking chick was with her, and she said, "Come on, girl, let's go." But Pauline told me her number before they left and I clocked it into my memory. I didn't call her that night because I didn't want to seem too eager.

The next day, I went by the Homer G. Phillips Hospital to visit my sister Marie, who was ready to have her baby. When I went up to the information desk to find out Marie's room number, Pauline was working at the switchboard. Man! She took my breath away.

After we fumbled through our greetings, I went on to see Marie and her new baby daughter, Barbara Jean. But my mind was on Pauline.

For the next few days we talked on the phone and I saw her when I visited my sister at the hospital. Pauline loved my jokes, and I dug her sweet voice. She had great diction, too. I liked that. And a whole lot more.

Instead of letting me take her out, she invited me to dinner at her home. She lived with her parents in a small white wooden house at 4273 W. Garfield. Not too far from where I was staying with Hut.

When she opened the door, I smelled good food. Smelled like fried chicken, greens, and cornbread. Some nice seasonings. Herbs. I wanted to grab her and kiss her. Run my hands through her dark brown hair. But I played it cool.

I was digging her tight skirt as she walked me to the table where her folks were sitting. Henry and Fannie Mae. They were real warm. Friendly. Seemed like a nice couple.

Henry was a tall, dark-skinned cat. Slight-built. Dressed in a plaid flannel shirt and corduroy pants. Fannie Mae was the color of honey, like Pauline. A nice-looking woman, robust with big smiles that reminded me of Hut. It felt like home.

As we ate dinner together, I checked out Henry's protective eye and Fannie Mae's open-armed welcome.

I must have been staring too much at Pauline, because Henry cleared his throat real loud like Mr. Wilson used to do. He said, "So, you're a jazz musician. Usually they a feisty bunch. But I know my baby girl got mo' sense than to pick trouble." He squinted his eyes at me. He said, "'Course, 'Trouble' *can* be my middle name." That was his way of warning me to do right by Pauline.

Fannie Mae cut her eyes at him, dabbed her thin lips, then smiled at me. She said, "I like jazz. Listen to it on the radio whenever I get a notion."

Pauline smiled at me.

When dinner was over, I helped her with the dishes. While the water was running, she looked down. She said, "I remember you from Vashon High. I thought you were real nice, but you never looked my way."

I swallowed hard. I said, "Well, I must have been blind!"

She smiled.

I said, "Why don't you come hang out with me at the after-hours clubs after I finish working? I wish you could come and see the show at the Club Plantation, but, you know, it's whites only." She blushed and then she said, "I don't really go to clubs that much, raising Rudy and all. But maybe I could go sometime."

She told me all about her six-year-old son. I told her about my divorce from Sissy and all about Hiawatha. He was eight then. She explained that Rudy was visiting his father, and how their marriage ended, and that she had divorced her second husband, since he couldn't handle being a stepfather.

I liked her honesty. She was easy to talk to. After a while, she put her finger to my lips to stop me from talking. I drew her close and kissed her. Really nice. I knew right then that I wanted to marry her.

George's band was back at the Club Plantation, and I usually headed straight to Pauline each night after the gig. No more hanging out in the dressing room with those galloping dominoes. No, no. And no more craps. I wanted to save my money.

One night after work, I went over to the Hawaiian Club to check out the set. Dizzy Gillespie walked up to me. He was in town for a gig at the Club Riviera with his big band. We had a few drinks and then he said, "A lot of folks in the music education scene have a problem with the way I puff my cheeks when I play. You know Harry James stopped puffing his cheeks?"

I said, "No, man, I didn't know that."

He said, "Yeah. Well, these education folks don't want the kids copying me because they say that's the wrong way to play."

I sat there in shock and kept listening.

He said, "So, I heard about this cat named Gusto. And I want you to take me over and introduce me to him. Maybe he can give me some new ideas."

The next afternoon, I introduced Dizzy to Gustat. I'd seen him a few times in the St. Louis Band and Instrument Company where he worked, but I'd never met him formally. He was the principal trumpet player in the St. Louis Symphony Orchestra. An average-sized white guy with no distinguishing features. My only contact with him was through Batch's proxy lessons in high school years ago. He was the one who gave Batch those lessons that Batch used to brag about.

The store was filled with music, instruments, and all kinds of interesting accessories. I introduced Dizzy and myself and told him why we were there. He looked at Dizzy with a stern, intimidating face.

Then he said, "Take out your horn and play something."

So Dizzy took his horn out and played some "snakes" and sort of startled Gustat.

Gustat looked quizzical. He said, "Play some more."

He watched Diz this time real closely. Diz's jaws puffing—bling, bling, bling—like a huge bladder. Then Gustat said, "Do that again."

So Dizzy did something even more fantastic this time, playing in octaves and fast notes.

Gustat wrinkled his eyebrows. He said, "How long have you been doing that?"

Dizzy answered reluctantly, "Well, I've been doing this all my life."

Gustat said, "You just keep on doing it and get the hell out of here!"

That weekend, I hired a car and went over and got Pauline. She looked so beautiful in her dainty dress. I just wanted to put my arms around her small waistline and draw her to me. But I kept my cool.

We went to the Elks Club and the Hawaiian Club, where I jammed and showed her what I could do. I introduced her to some of the cats and bought us some drinks, although she couldn't finish her Dixie Bell. Then we left. I didn't want to keep her out too late.

When we got outside under the moonlight, I walked her over to a quiet place near a tree. I kissed her and then I said, "Pauline, I've been dreaming of a woman like you for a long time. I don't know if you can handle my lifestyle—being on the road sometimes. And I don't want you to rush your decision, but if you feel the same as I do, well, I can't think of anyone else in the world that I'd want to marry but you."

She looked at me with very serious eyes. She said, "Clark, the way I feel right now I'd say, 'Yes.' But I want to give us a little more time, if you don't mind. Okay?"

I said, "Okay, baby."

That Monday, Pauline brought Rudy over after school to visit me at Hut's. He was a friendly kid. Big front teeth and just a bit shy. He favored Fannie Mae—light-complexion and keen features. He was dressed in his Cub Scout uniform, and he showed off his Cub Scout badges. When I gave him a jar full of pennies, he thought I was the greatest cat in the world.

A few days later, I went and got Hiawatha and introduced him to Pauline and her family. Hiawatha was decked down in a sharp suit and a tilted stingy-brimmed hat. He wasn't too friendly, and I said, "We haven't spent as much time together as I'd like, since I've been on the road and all. But that's all going to change."

He and Rudy got along okay, but I could see that I had a lot of work to do in order to get Hiawatha to warm up. So I took everybody with me on Saturday afternoons to a few of the softball games that I played with some of the cats from our band and Gerald Wilson's band. Gerald was one of my old navy cronies, and his band was playing at Jordan Chambers' Riviera Club. Joe Williams was singing there too, and we had developed quite a friendship.

Ella Fitzgerald was working again at the Club Plantation, and she played ball with us. Each morning after our gigs and jam sessions, we'd get together at a park. It was nice and cool and we'd get down to business. It was a lot of fun. And man, Ella could hit and run just like one of the cats. She could really hit that ball, and she could run up a storm. So alive and active. What a beautiful girl!

Joe came to bat and swung hard, but he must have twisted something wrong or pulled something out of joint because he slumped at the base. Plop! I ran over to him and picked him up and I carried him to George's car.

We took him to the hospital and he was eventually all right. He teased me later. He said, "How in the world did your little midget ass pick me up and carry me to the car?"

We laughed it off and I said, "You ain't *that* much bigger than me."

But he was about six inches taller and a bit heavier. His voice was even larger. He had a deep, robust tone, and he could swing anybody's blues away. With his dark complexion, white teeth, and mastery of his craft, the ladies would swoon, 'cause when I tell you he could blow—you'd better know it!

I found myself spending more and more time with Pauline. When I went to dinners at their home, I lavished her and Fannie Mae with their hearts' desires—perfume, clothes, jewelry. Rudy got more pennies. And since Henry loved good pipe tobacco, we shared some of the best I could find. He'd stick out his chest, wearing his signature plaid flannel shirt and corduroy pants and one of his cardigan sweaters, and he'd tell me about the "good old days of struggle and guns" and how his smarts, his secret sage-sausage recipes, and his next-door grocery store had led the way to him being able to buy their house.

As I puffed with him, I told him about my having legal custody of Hiawatha, my trials on the road, and my dreams of buying a house so I could settle down. Then I said, "Henry, I want your permission to marry Pauline, but I want to make sure that she can deal with me being on the road sometimes."

He just smiled and kept puffing. Then he said, "Time'll tell."

Before long, I was helping him out in his grocery store, moving boxes, putting up advertising signs, and chatting between customers. And man, his sausage was mouth-watering. He could mix up some great seasonings. No wonder his sausage was bought by customers from miles around.

Two months later, Henry said, "Ain't no use in you stayin' over at Hut's since you over here most of your off time. Why don't you move in here?"

So I moved into the house on Garfield, and I felt a sense of family that I hadn't felt since living with my brothers and sisters. I wished Pop could have been like Henry—full of animated stories about how St. Louis evolved, and great advice about how to stay out of trouble on the road, like: "Craps ain't never gonna pay off. And much as folk brag 'bout what they won, they don't tell you what they spent for that win."

24. Charlie Barnet

I took Henry's advice to heart and stayed away from the tables. Then one morning, while we were all in the dining room eating a scrumptious breakfast of Henry's sage-flavored sausage, some hot buttered grits, fluffy scrambled eggs, and some syrup-sopping biscuits, the phone rang.

A few seconds later, Fannie Mae brought it to me. In those days all telephones were heavy and black. But theirs was covered with red plastic.

I swallowed a mouthful of sausage and said, "Hello."

"Hey, Clark. This is Charlie Barnet."

My sausage almost came back up. But I managed to say, "Who?"

He had a friendly voice and his enunciation was impeccable. He said, "Charlie Barnet, man. You know, the band leader. I'm calling you from California to see if you'd like to join my band."

Henry could sense the importance of the call, so he got up and headed for the living room door, pulling Rudy behind him. Pauline and Fannie Mae headed for the kitchen with their mouths hanging open.

I struggled for breath and then I said, "*The* Charlie Barnet?"

He chuckled, then told me about the conditions and monetary details of his offer. Finally he said, "So how would you like to travel? Plane, train, bus, or car?"

I was afraid of flying. After that flight with Hamp, I vowed that I'd never do it again. I hadn't learned to drive, and I'd had enough of the bus. So I agreed to ride out to California by train.

I'd heard that his deceased mother used to own the controlling stock in the New York Central Railroad. Her name was Charlotte. She had given him a million dollars to get his band together, and he had the best musicians that money could buy. I'd also heard that he gave Lincolns and Cadillacs for Christmas presents.

This was a huge break for me. Charlie was renowned—for movies, featurettes, live broadcasts, and dozens of recordings. I'd heard his recordings, and I liked his sound. I knew this was an offer that I couldn't refuse.

A week and a half later, after getting a warm good-bye hug from Ada Mae, I hired a car to take me over to Carondelet, where Marie was doing fine with her new baby. Margueritte and Murlene were doing all right, too, and my other brothers and sisters were faring well. Sy wasn't at home, and Aunt Gert was in New York, visiting our cousin, Billy. But I said good-bye to everybody I could.

When I got back to my side of town, I gave Sissy some bread and hugged Hiawatha good-bye. That time when Sissy slammed the door behind me, it didn't hurt so much because Pauline and her family were seeing me off for my trip. I'd never had that before. Even more, Pauline and Fannie Mae cried. I hugged Rudy and Henry, and we all said our good-byes. As the train pulled off heading west, I felt excited to see countryside I'd never been to before.

Three days later, Gerald Wilson met me at the train station in Los Angeles saying, "Hey, Clark!" He was about my same height, and he had a full head of salt-and-pepper hair, a matching moustache. Lots of moles on his medium-brown-skinned face, and a great big smile.

In the car heading to his house, we had a rip-roaring conversation about our old days at Great Lakes, our softball games in St. Louis, and how I'd picked Joe Williams up and carried him to George's car.

He said, "Man! I'm so *excited* about you joining Charlie's band"

I was trying to stay cool about it. I said, "I just hope I make it."

He said, "Aw, you don't have to worry 'bout that. I'm just glad I'm off the road for a while so I could pick you up and be a part of this. You know we trumpet players have to stick together."

On the way to his house, I admired the palm trees and exotic flowers. Pastel-colored stucco structures lined the streets. I'd never seen such beauty. And the weather was fantastic—mild and breezy.

As we rode, my heart was beating double-time. We talked about Charlie Barnet's hit tunes that we'd heard on the radio—"Red Skin Rumba," "Gal from Joe's," "Charleston Alley," "Pompton Turnpike," and "Cherokee," which was his theme song, but it was the only one of the tunes we talked about that Charlie didn't write. Ray Noble had written that one.

Eventually we pulled up into the driveway at 5612 Ascot, Gerald's house. His wife, Etta, greeted us at the door. She was much shorter than Gerald, plump but shapely and very accommodating. She hugged me tight, helped me get settled, and then fed us well. Though it didn't taste like Pauline's cooking.

That night, Gerald drove me out to where Charlie was working. It was at a beach in a dancehall named Aragon, on the outskirts of Los Angeles. The moment I walked into the room with Gerald, I eyed the huge all-white crowd. Then I glanced at Charlie Barnet with his band up on the bandstand.

Gerald pulled me close. He said, "He's broadcasting live from coast to coast."

When Charlie got to a point in their performance where he had an opportunity to walk away from the microphone, Gerald led me up and said, "Charlie, this is Clark, the trumpet player that you just sent for."

Charlie smiled at me and he said, "Oh, good! Get your horn out."

Shocked, I said, "Right now?"

"Yeah. Right now!"

So I hurried and took my cold horn out. I closed my eyes and said a fast prayer.

A few seconds later, Charlie went back to the mike and he said, "Right now, ladies and gentlemen, we'd like to feature a new trumpet player, Clark Terry. He's just in from St. Louis to join the band."

Then he kicked off a tune and whispered to me, "You got it!"

I had never heard the tune in my life! And here I am, on a live radio broadcast. A *coast-to-coast* live radio broadcast. On my debut with Charlie Barnet's Band. Talk about being on the *spot!* Luckily, although it was an unfamiliar tune, I could hear the changes. So I managed to get through it. That was a real acid test! And after that number, his smile of approval settled my stomach. A bit.

When the gig was over, he sent word for me to come backstage. I walked up to him, and he said, "Are you ready to go?"

I said, "Just say when." And we shook hands.

My first gig with Charlie was at Jantzen Beach in Portland, Oregon. His show was ritzy—a big-money production. "Ladies and Gentlemen! Tonight, get ready to swing and sweat with Charlie Barnet!" A mirrored chandelier cast prisms of light that were mixed with hot music all over the huge dancehall. Ocean-front view. Clinking glasses and the latest gossip. Big Boys grinning at money that's flowing like Niagara Falls. Sexy waitresses. All-white jubilant crowd.

Charlie laid down some heavy sounds with his horns—his tenor, his alto, and his soprano. The band members were wailing, dressed in showy gray tuxedo jackets and matching bow ties.

I was playing serious charts, written by some of the best in the business, like Neal Hefti, who wrote the Basie hit "Li'l Darlin'," and Andy Gibson, who wrote charts for Duke Ellington. Awesome music, swinging all over the room. I was wishing that some colored folks could walk in and join in on the fun.

Then the spotlight landed on Bunny Briggs. Zap! He was a brown-skinned featherweight dancer. He rushed out center-stage, dressed in a white tuxedo. Then he launched into difficult syncopated steps, tapping, splitting, and hoofing on every inch of that mirror-polished floor. Lightning-fast feet—slides, skips, hops; breath-taking jumps.

After that, the music segued to a smooth ballad, and Bunny sang it with a voice of velvet. Sweat was popping out of all his pores, and mine, and everyone's on stage. Charlie's eyes were closed tight. He was blowing blood-curdling melodies, featured in the midst of an eighteen-piece orchestra of men who have given up their homes, their families, their loved ones, all for the love of jazz.

When the show was over, I got my money, and then I got angry, dreading going to the colored accommodations. Abhorring racism. Trying to digest reality in my knotted stomach. Then I heard Rev's voice in my head—the preacher from my hometown church, First Corinthian Baptist. His voice screamed, "The race goes not to the swiftest, but to those who can endure to the end!"

I was enduring hard. Smiling in the faces of Charlie and the other cats. They talked about the show's success. How "good" things were. Then I hung around the other colored cats for a smoke. Briggs and Wilson, our valet. They told me about the other Negro musicians who used to be in the band, like Peanuts Holland and Al Killian, who both played trumpet, and how the racism scene was a big drag on everyone.

A little later, backstage, Doc Severinsen was introduced to us by a real excited dude that I'd never seen before. He was standing not far from me and Charlie, all smiles. Doc was looking anxious. So the cat said to Charlie, "We got a guy here who can really play!"

Charlie ran his hand through his hair and said, "Okay, well, let's hear him play something."

Doc was a real slight-built cat. Handsome face, chiseled features. He had a light tan and wavy blonde hair. You could tell he was nervous, facing an on-the-spot audition. He rushed and took out his horn and played "Hora Staccato." It was perfect, with ascending and descending intervals zipping fast.

Charlie looked unimpressed, cocked his head, and said, "Yeah, well, fuck that! Can he play the blues?"

Doc gave it his best and Charlie hired him right then.

While we played Jantzen for a few weeks, Doc and I became very, very good friends. He told me that his real name was Carl, but because his father was a dentist, his friends had nicknamed him "Doc."

His mother made me lots of cookies. She was a short and kind, rather timid blonde. I dug his family. They treated me like another son. His dad had some impressive dental equipment, including a big black leather chair with a foot pedal and pump at the bottom that controlled his drill. He had dark hair; medium height, average size.

One day he said, "Come on, Clark, let me have a look at those teeth."

This was the first time I'd been to a dentist since I was a kid. I swallowed hard and said, "Okay, but don't do anything too painful."

He gave me his word then pulled out his magnifying glasses. After examining my mouth, he said, "You've got the hardest damn teeth I've ever seen. But they could use a good cleaning." Then he laughed and said, "Got to take care of your teeth 'cause they're an integral part of your embouchure!"

When Charlie's band left Portland, Doc went with us. And my teeth looked better from the work his dad had done on them.

Sometimes we did one-nighters, but we played extended engagements often. Charlie would ride on the bus or he'd drive his car or be driven. Sometimes he'd fly in his private plane.

He shared his plane with the band by allowing one member at a time to "have the luxury of flying" with him. I'd always sell my chance to somebody else.

That December, the Christmas gifts from Charlie were fifths of whiskey. The days were gone when he'd give expensive cars, but I didn't care because I dug his style, his musicianship, and the fact that he let me have a *say* in his music. All the cats welcomed me. Everybody just wanted to play the best jazz.

Our show uniforms were hip and expensive. Gray or black silk tuxedos, bow ties. Stylish white jackets and tan trousers. Smooth leathers for our feet. The fact that he bought our threads allowed more money to stay in my pocket. And he laid some good bread on me—more than my stint with Hamp, and definitely more than I made with George.

For ten months, Charlie's band toured nonstop. From the West Coast to the East Coast. I kept in touch with Pauline by phone. She always sounded happy to hear from me. She made the trials I was facing worthwhile. Things like "No Coloreds" at the Chinese restaurant in Portland. Everywhere we went, I had to endure bigotry. But I just had to plow on through that, regarding places to sleep and eat.

Soon Jimmy Nottingham left Hamp's band and joined us, and I was thrilled to have another Negro musician. Nott was an awesome player. So much so that Charlie decided to feature our hot trumpet routines. So he bought the cats in the band some blue tuxedo jackets, and for Jimmy and me he bought these real hip duds—gray tux jackets. We really stood out. Jimmy and I *loved* it.

On trumpets we had Doc, Joe Graves, Jimmy Campbell—our lead trumpeter—and me. Our 'bones were Freddie Zito, Porky Cohen, and Red Benson. Along with Charlie on woodwinds, we had the Weidler Brothers, Jack Hennessey, Bob Dawes, and Curt Bloom, who was also the road manager. He was the fastest-eating cat in the world. He'd go into a place and gulp, gulp, gulp. Then he'd say, "Okay, guys, let's go."

Eventually, Bud Shank joined our sax section. Don Tosti played bass, Dick Shanahan was on drums, and Claude Williamson played piano. Bunny Briggs was our male singer and dancer. And we also had a girl singer whose name was Jean Louise Boggs.

It was really a fantastic band, and Wilson was a fun-loving valet. At that time there was a popular whiskey named Wilson, and its slogan was "Wilson, that's all." So whenever Charlie called Wilson to do something, Wilson would answer by saying, "That's all!"

During the hundreds of miles on the road, there were no crap games in the back of the bus and our trips were relatively short. No hops from Philadelphia to Chicago. Just a four- or six-hour trip between gigs. So I used some of that time to write some tunes.

Sometimes the guys' wives would join them, which made me miss Pauline even more. But I knew that she didn't want to travel with me because she wasn't too comfortable around white people. She'd told me how when she was a little girl, some white men dragged her cousin out of their house, strung him up to a tree, and hanged him right in front of the whole family. I could definitely understand, but I still missed her while watching the other cats enjoying their wives traveling with us.

As we went to and from our destinations, we listened to the radio, which was hot with the new bebop sounds of Dizzy Gillespie, Charlie Parker, and Thelonious Monk. We all marveled at the dramatic changes their music incorporated. I had heard something similar from Jabbo Smith's records, but Dizzy had taken it farther. It was amazing.

I occupied my time with intense familiarizing, improvising, and memorizing of this new technique of bebop. Plus I stockpiled some of my original tunes, looking for the right time to share them with Charlie. He dug my compositions, and we chatted about the possibility of recording them.

At times on the road, I joined the other cats joking around, including their water pistol antics. Water pistols broke the monotony, because just when you'd least expect it, you'd get squirted right between the eyes. Most of the time they were fun. Except the time that Don and Curt got more and more aggressive. They finally stopped squirting and laid the pistols down, heading for a real confrontation, until some of the cats separated them. After that day their friendship caught a draft.

Other than those two, everybody got along great and dug the music. Charlie had a great sound, a style similar to Johnny Hodges and Sidney

Bechet. A very booting style of tenor. A swinging and deep-rooted "boop-BAP" sound.

Charlie constantly told me how pleased he was with my work. Except the time when I missed my cue with the spotlight at the famous Strand Theatre in New York on Broadway.

The night before that, I'd hung out really late, partying and jamming around. So the next day I wasn't up to par, and I was nodding out on the bandstand.

There was a humongous prop of a huge saxophone with swirling notes behind us. We were sitting on this huge stage, dressed to the nines. Charlie and I had choreographed our performance with spotlights to add spark and highlight. But when that spotlight went "Zap!" I wasn't there.

After the performance that night, Charlie went straight to Jimmy Campbell and started yelling. "Why didn't you have that man down there on that mark!"

Jimmy looked quizzically at me, then at Charlie, then back at me. Then he said, "Ain't that a bitch!"

Charlie was never hostile to me. He always took it out on somebody else, and we'd all end up laughing it off.

One day I had time to burn, and I went to an audition with Basie at Nola Studios. I'd heard about it the night before, after the show. George Hudson had told me to reach for the stars, and that's what I intended to do.

Now, I'd listened to the style of Basie and I had it down pretty good. But no matter how many times I'd listened to his songs on the radio, or how many tunes of his I'd analyzed and memorized, I wasn't prepared for what I was to face.

Basie was real laid back. Slick conk, costly vines, shiny skins. The cats checked me from the corners of their eyes while shuffling some of the dozens of charts on the stands in front of their chairs. They were looking at me like they were thinking, "Who is this pipsqueak?"

Welcome was nowhere in the air. But I introduced myself and took a seat. Basie glanced at the cats and called "Hey Rube"—a number with a truckload of trumpet high C's. All shake. "DAH-ah-AH-ah-AH-ah."

I'd heard it before and I knew this was the real thing. While putting my trumpet together and warming it up fast, I called on every guardian spirit I had. My mother, Aunt Gert, and all my sisters and brothers; Shitty, Beanie Roach, Didley, and Billy; the Vashon Swingsters, Sy, Mr. Wilson, George, Hamp, and anybody else I could think of. Then I took a deep breath and played it like I'd die if I didn't. When it was over, I heard one of the cats say, "Well, shit! This little sucker can play. Let's whip 'South' on him!"

That's when I called on the spirit of Kid Carter from my teen-aged days in the boxing ring. I even reached deep for Pop's help. I imagined him saying, "Rotten on it, Boy! Play it or I'll beat your ass!"

Basie's band had recorded "South" years earlier with Snooky Young playing the solo, hollering that high A at the end. I had memorized the solo. But I'd never hit that high A before in my *life*.

After glancing at all the stone faces around me, I took a big breath and I played. When the time came for that high A, I tightened my embouchure and my ass and I hit it. From the looks on their faces, everybody was shocked. I even shocked myself. When it was over, I put my trumpet in my lap and saw Basie's first smile of the day.

By the time Charlie's band bus pulled out of New York, I had high hopes for joining Basie. As Charlie's tour continued, I was finding it extremely hard to accept that we colored musicians always had to stay in rooming houses or private homes, while the rest of the band stayed in nice hotels. They didn't like it either, but that was the lay of the land.

When we got to D.C., we played the Howard Theatre. It was a colored venue, and after the show some very angry patrons came backstage, objecting to the difference in color of our tuxedos. They were throwing names around like NAACP and the Urban League. They asked Charlie, "Why are the two colored musicians dressed differently than the rest of your band?"

Instead of seeing us as featured players, they labeled it racist. I was shocked, disgusted, then angry.

After they left, Charlie asked my opinion, and I said, "Well, since I've calmed down, I've thought about it. Maybe they have a point." After that, Charlie had our gray tux jackets dyed blue to match the rest of the band.

That night as usual, Wilson, Briggs, Nottingham, and I were relegated to staying around the corner in the 7th and T area at a rooming house. The standard E-flat type of joint where you could easily pick the lock with a hairpin. The rest of the cats stayed at the Congress Hotel.

Early the next morning, we "coloreds" took taxis and joined the rest of the band at their hotel where they were eating breakfast. Neither of the two colored waitresses came to take our order. Finally, I called one of them over and said, "Why is it that we have to wait so long?"

She walked away and had a little chat with the other waitress. Then she came back and said, "I'm sorry. But we don't serve colored people in here."

The rest of the band grabbed pies and cakes and everything and slammed them into the back wall mirror. As we all rushed to the door, Doc yelled, "And you can tell Bilbo to pay the bill!"

Bilbo was a notoriously racist senator who had said, "The streets will flow with blood before I'll allow mixed fraternization!"

We hurried onto the bus and headed to our next gig. I could tell that Charlie was tiring of the trials of racism and the one-nighters. He didn't have the same high spirit that he'd had at the beginning of the trip. So I wondered how much longer our tour would last.

Several recordings were made while I was with Charlie, and he featured me as he'd done on the bandstand. I had lots of solos on the album "Deep Purple/Jubilee Jump." The solo I played on "Deep Purple" became one of my favorite solos of all time. Great tunes on that album, including "Charleston Alley," "Gal from Joe's," and one of my tunes, "Phalanges."

That was the first time that one of my compositions was recorded! It was a gas. I was so excited. I couldn't *wait* to hear it. I was proud of the title, too, which referred to all the finger movement, since it was a swift bebop type of tune. I had run across the word "phalanges" while I was studying my dictionary, and I thought that it was the perfect title for that tune.

Putting one of my compositions down at a session was a turning point. Now I looked forward to recording more of my tunes. As it turned out, I wrote more than two hundred compositions during my career. There's even a book out with a lot of them in it, named *Terry Tunes*. Things like "The Snapper," "Hawg Jawz," "One Foot in the Gutter," "Joonji," and "Slop Jar," which I named for the overnight bucket that my father used, to keep from having to get up and go to the toilet. Out of all my brothers and sisters, I was the one who had to empty it every morning.

Back in '47 and into '48, things were going great with Charlie and me. We did several other recordings. At the Clique Club in Philadelphia we did a live thing, which we called "One Night Stand." Later, we did another live recording, "Town Hall Concert," in New York.

Still and all, I could feel that a change was coming, and I was ready for it.

25. Count Basie

When my feet hit the St. Louis dirt that October of '48, all I could think about was asking Pauline to marry me. When I got home, I ran upstairs, where she met me with open arms. Before I could say a word, she kissed me hard. Then she said, "I missed you."

I held her tight and said, "I missed you too, baby."

Then she started jumping up and down and she said, "Ooooh, and guess what?"

"What?"

"Basie called you!"

I said, "Well, that's great. I was hoping he would. But what I'd like to do first, I mean, if you're ready, because I've got to have you in my life, and I'm ready, so, will you . . ."

She said, "Yes, I'll marry you!"

I was happier than a pig in slop!

For the next two days the whole family celebrated our upcoming vows—Henry, Fannie Mae, and Rudy. Then Pauline and I packed to meet Basie in Detroit. We didn't have time to get married in St. Louis, because Basie needed me in Detroit right away. So we planned a small ceremony there. Weasel took off from playing with George Hudson and rode there with us because I wanted him to be my best man.

When Pauline and I checked into the Gotham Hotel in Detroit, she was so happy! It made me feel so proud to show her my world on a grand scale. Real nice rooms with mahogany furniture. Fancy carpets. Good food. It was a well-known place where all the greats stayed in Detroit—Duke, Cab Calloway, Billie Holiday. If you stayed at the Gotham, you were in *tall* cotton. All the musicians stayed at the Gotham.

After a while, I went and met with Basie to take care of business. I was on clouds nine *and* ten. Two dreams coming true at the same time

That evening, October 28, 1948, I stood beside Pauline in front of Weasel's brother, Reverend J. Allen Parker, at Margueritte's new residence in Detroit. She had moved there with Johnny Pops into the home of his brother, Carl, and sister-in-law, Rachel, in the Valley.

The house was nice. White wood, two-story. It had a big living room, which was great because Basie and a few of the cats from his band joined us for the ceremony. That was a great surprise. Basie alone would have been enough for me. But it wasn't just Basie; it was Basie and the cats. Now, that was a wedding gift.

Margueritte was there too, along with her daughter, Murlene.

When it came time for me to put a ring on Pauline's finger, Weasel couldn't find it. He fumbled around in his pockets, looking worried. Searching all over, for what seemed like an eternity. Then he shrugged his shoulders. I shot him a threatening look. He dug around his clothes again, and this time he found it. When he handed it to me, I wiped the sweat off my face. As I slid that band of gold on her finger, I thought, Now I have the right woman.

When it was over, we all made toasts with a little champagne, took some pictures, and shot the breeze for a while. But not too long, because we had to get to the hotel so I could freshen up for the club.

Pauline hung with me for a few days while I played the gig with Basie. I think it was at the Majestic Theater, but I'm not sure. The combination of marital bliss *and* playing with Basie was almost too much for me. Talk about ecstasy!

Basie was an *exceptional* musician and leader. I loved his theory of "space and time." Whether Basie played two notes or two measures, he packed in more power and said more than most cats who played two thousand notes or two thousand measures. His feel of time and the way he articulated was totally original and very effective. With a few basic chords, during which the bass walked, his sound permeated the entire band. With the simple drop of his finger, the band hit, "Zow!" It felt like we had knocked down the Great Wall of China.

Each time he stepped off the bandstand to socialize, the band kept the swing going, low key. I'd heard he'd developed his style during his early days in the clubs of Kansas City, like the Cherry Blossom. He had so many friends who would come to see his performances; he'd play a while, then get up and chat while the rhythm section was still swinging, return to his piano, hit a few notes, then walk over to another table for a drink and a few words. All night long!

I had listened to his mastery before on radio, records, and jukeboxes, but to actually be there and watch him was beyond my imagination.

On top of that, he had a built-in sense of tempo. Like mother wit. He was born with it, I guess. Being around so many years and playing with so many great musicians only made it stronger. If Basie contested a tempo, you could bet your life that he was right. It didn't matter if the tempo was fast or slow, if he felt it should be a certain tempo, then that's where it was.

And he had a way of getting that feeling through the whole band without having to use linebacker tactics—no show-biz antics of batons or jumping around, or dancing, or running back and forth. I caught on quickly to his laid-back method of directing. A nod, a smile, or a slight move of his shoulders—just pure connection. Jazz at its best. With some of the greatest arrangements ever. I loved it more than Aunt Gert's fatback and greens.

Playing with Basie, I felt and heard the music better than I ever had before. Man, his swing was powerful! Then sometimes it was elegantly dynamic. During his easygoing renditions, there was a soul-stirring feeling. His four-four rhythm swayed a head-nodding and ear-bending groove, an easy foot-tapping bounce. Then during his up-tempo renditions he created a finger-popping force that made you move. Unmistakable. Undeniable. And *very* signature.

His style of accompaniment—"comp," we called it—was unparalleled. He never overshadowed the soloist. He just pushed you to your best. Subtly, but you could feel his power. He'd make you rise until you were there, at the top of your craft. And all the time, he's looking cool. Smiling at the audience. Conk smooth and shiny. Hitting those keys just right. I tried to be cool too, but inside I was exploding.

Gigging with Count Basie. Man! I could see why everybody in the band dug him personally, because I loved him right away. He was fair, warm, humorous, gentle, understanding, and completely down to earth. He righteously deserved the cats' private nickname for him—"Holy." This was the sort of nickname that was endowed only on the most special thing in your life. Your most treasured blessing.

His band had their act together. Not only was everyone extraordinarily gifted, but we all worked together synchronously. It was like reading each other's minds.

The cats made me feel at home, and I forgave their hostility a few weeks before during my audition in New York. I knew that their attitude was simply the standard, and it had garnered the crème de la crème. They could all sight-read anybody's chart.

On trumpets there were Harry "Sweets" Edison, Emmett Berry, Ed Lewis, and me. Sizzling! Then on trombones were Dicky Wells, Ted "Muttonleg" Donnelly, Bill Johnson, and Big George Matthews. Powerhouses! Our reeds were Earl Warren, Jack Washington, and Buddy Tate. Awesome! Then we had Gus Johnson on drums, Freddie Green on guitar, and Basie on piano. I can't remember who was on bass.

It was pumping pure swing, way beyond the rhythms of that sanctified church in Carondelet, for sure. But there was more. Our vocalist, Jimmy Rushing, had an unusual set of pipes, whether he was singing a ballad or an up-tempo tune. Each night I had to wind down from the excitement.

Pauline went with me to the next gig in Chicago at the Regal Theater. And after hours we hung out at the Club DeLisa. We had a ball. But our time together was winding down because she had to get back to St. Louis for her job, while the band was getting ready for the next town's gig.

I loved playing with Basie, and that helped to ease my regrets of sending Pauline back home. I couldn't wait to get to New York, since Basie said we'd probably get an extended engagement there and Pauline could come and live at the hotel with me.

The Basie band traveled by bus on the TOBA circuit and a few clubs in between. All over the United States. Hundreds of miles between gigs—nothing near the short jumps I'd made on Charlie Barnet's tour.

For my initiation in the Basie band, I was assigned as Jimmy Rushing's seatmate. He was a huge cat, whose nickname was "Mr. Five by Five." Five feet tall and five feet wide. He didn't mind that nickname, but I didn't call him that. Still, his butt took up all of his seat and most of mine. The cats cracked up about it. But after a while, my trial period was over and I was allowed to move to a seat all by myself where I could spread out and relax.

There weren't many hotels like the Gotham, especially in the South. Sometimes we might luck up and get something halfway decent. But usually, in town after town, we stayed in rooming houses, family residences, and mediocre hotels. Even with pockets full of money, there was no welcome for coloreds. Many times our food was far below standard as well. Unless we were lucky enough to be invited to dinner by a friend of someone in the band or at one of the cats' latest ladies, we had to cook for ourselves. We cooked beans in a pot on a hotplate or on the back of an iron. Skillets filled with rice and chicken over sternos. Tiny stoves in small apartments with pans of unnamed concoctions. Or just plain crackers with sardines or potted meat.

Still, the music was fantastic and I loved every minute of it. And man, when we played the Howard in D.C., I hit the numbers big time! My favorites, 3-8-7, came in, and I had bet them "boxed, single action, and six-way combination." My pockets were *fat*. But after I paid off debts or loaned money to the cats, my winnings deflated quickly.

More than anything, though, I loved being with those guys, and our bus was a den of excitement. Jam sessions and hot craps. Risqué joke telling and playing the dozens until we'd double over with tears of laughter rolling down our faces. "Seen yo' momma on the railroad track, picking up shit in a paper sack." The dozens was a way to pass the time, a rip-roaring game where we made fun of each other's families or the cats in the band or anybody we knew. Nobody took it personally, and we had a ball playing it.

Basie cracked up, too. He wasn't the type of cat who said, "You cats go on ahead, I'll meet you later." He always rode on the bus with us. Even though he rode up front, as was apropos for a band leader, he let us have our fun and never tried to boss us around.

The only problem was that he loved betting on the horses. "Ponies," he called them. And he ran up huge gambling debts. Continuously. Soon everybody was worried.

26. Big Debt

Before long, our worst fears were confirmed. The cats and I were huddled backstage at the Howard Theatre staring at Basie's worried face. He looked at the floor and he said, "The agency said we have to disband for now till I get this thing over."

We all knew about Basie's monumental debts from losing on those damn ponies. And since *we'd* also been bitten with the sweet and sour sting of gambling, nobody said a word.

He went on to explain that our booking agent in New York, Willard Alexander, had given the ultimatum—an immediate plan to pay the Big Boys.

Basie said, "We have to cut expenses, let the orchestra go. We'll form a small group soon. I don't know who. Before long, we'll have it all back together."

As we stood silently, I glanced at the cats' long faces. Breaking up all that talent was a crying shame! Outstanding, individualistic musicians. All signature sounds. Not one was a copycat of anybody in the world. Each had mastered a sound that reflected his unique personality.

There was Harry "Sweets" Edison. Handsome, dark chocolate, a ladies' magnet. Svelte physique draped in expensive threads, dripping with accents of rich gold and pristine diamonds. The notes that floated through his trumpet made you feel his statements of "Cool Daddy. Laid-back." And like he always said, "I'm the One and the Only. The Alpha and the Omega!"

Dicky Wells was older than most of us, and I admired his neatly trimmed moustache. He was a master of the slide trombone, with his octave jumps, slurs, slurps and bends that sent notes swirling. His sound was gut-bucket raw and soul-stirring. One of his features was using a tin straight-mute. He'd hammered lots of nail holes in it. He held it reversed in the bell of his horn, and it made a very signature kazoo-like sound, like a magnified version of an old comb covered with tissue paper. The audience loved him.

George Matthews was a heavyweight. Well over six feet tall. A lightning-fast reader, he was the musical epitome of articulation perfection. We'd been in the navy together, and whenever he was around, if I'd run into a difficult passage, he'd walk up behind me with his trombone and transpose, "Bah-da-de-biggity-biggity-biggity." Flawlessly. Then in his deep bass, West Indian accent he'd say, "That's the way it goes, mon."

Then there was super-relaxed Ted Donnelly. "Muttonleg" was his nickname, bestowed by the ladies from his youth. Impeccable dynamics on his trombone and a hell of a tone to match. Plus, he was an extraordinary soloist. He'd zoom you above the moon, then float you back to earth like a feather.

Bill Johnson, or "Frog" as we called him because of his big frog eyes and his voice that sounded like a big fat croaking frog. He was the real slop house sound of the band. A down home, "Um-bah-du-BOW!" type of style. All sorts of guttural sounds and real funky.

Earl Warren—"Smiley." A superb lead player who influenced the style of the reed section. Serious but swinging. Easygoing yet powerful. Always smiling. A dangerous undercurrent in smooth waters.

Jack "Sergeant" Washington. His baritone sax was never cumbersome like most bottom horns. Active. Very, very active. Fluent and unmistakably articulate. And—you could depend on him for a good solo. Wailing! Always capable.

Buddy Tate. A real Texas sound. Big fat tone. Authoritative with a drawl. Friendly but not crossable. One of the creators of the Texas Tenor Titans. Rugged with an overtone of warmth.

Gus Johnson. A great big guy who knew how not to murder the bass drum. The right beat. Hitting solidly yet tenderly enough not to hurt the mood. He swung and made you feel it. Deep.

Freddie Green was purely at the top of the guitar scene. A master who put the right chords down with a soft one and three—"ching CHANG ching CHANG." He drove those strings like a Cadillac.

And whenever Jimmy Rushing sang, he penetrated the heart of everyone around. Perfect intonation in a hard-hitting voice that was backed by fortitude and conviction. He was one of my favorite blues vocalists by far.

As I stood there in the midst of these fantastic guys, not to mention Count Basie himself, I wished I had the money to pay his gambling debts so we could stay together. But my pockets were nowhere near that deep. So we all said our good-byes, hoping to reunite soon.

Now, more than anything, I wanted to be a part of the small group. I wanted to help put us all back together. So when Basie said, "Clark, I'll call you soon to help me form the small group," I wanted to shout!

When I got back to St. Louis, Pauline did her best to pacify me, but my heart was heavy while I waited to hear from Basie. Meanwhile, I got some local work.

A few nights later, I was hanging out, drinking and jamming in George Borders' club over in East St. Louis. Of all the cats there that night, I most enjoyed playing with a guy whose name was Duke Brooks. I learned later that his real name was Emmanuel St. Claire Brooks. I dug his swinging piano technique, which was copied from the sides of Duke Ellington. It was a real good set.

I drug home around six A.M. and plopped into a dead sleep. Around nine that morning, the phone rang and rang. Everybody was gone, so I struggled up and answered it.

"Hey, man," said the voice on the other end. "This is Duke."

I said, "Man, what in the hell are you doing calling me up? I just left your ass! Call me this evening. Bye."

That evening, just after Pauline had called to tell me she was on her way home, the phone rang again.

I said, "Hello."

He said, "Hi, this is Duke. I called you this morning and you said, uh, call you back later today. You didn't seem to be feeling too well."

Then it hit me! I felt like going under the table because now I recognized the voice. It was Duke *Ellington,* not Duke Brooks like I had thought. He talked about wanting me to sub.

In spite of my stuttering apologies and shock, I managed to accept his offer and get some sketchy details—just outside St. Louis, a dancehall, tomorrow night. My first time in Duke's band, and I had fluffed him off on the phone the first time he called me. But he called back! I was a nervous wreck. I made the gig, but I can't remember where it was, who was there, or what we played.

Same thing happened the second time he called me to sub. Can't remember a thing.

A few days later Basie called. He said, "I think we're ready." My heart jumped as he talked. He said, "You remember that cat in Louisville, Kentucky, on bass? Jimmy Lewis?"

I said, "Yeah."

He said, "Well, I got him. So I want you to look around town and see who's a good tenor player."

I was really excited. I said, "Well, there are two cats who are outstanding—one named Jimmy Forrest, who's a more established cat. Then there's a young Caucasian kid who plays real good by the name of Bob Graf."

Basie said, "Get the kid."

So I immediately called Bob and asked him if he wanted to come to Chicago and join Count Basie. At first he didn't believe me. Finally, when I convinced him that it was true, we made preparations to go.

So I left for Chicago with Bob. He was a blonde-headed, slightly built, braggadocio sort of fellow. But he could definitely play sax.

It was 1949 when we met up with the cats at the Southway Hotel on

South Park at 60th in Chicago. Gus Johnson, Freddie Green, Jimmy Lewis, and Basie. It was almost like old times. We were all glad to see each other.

Basie said, "The office put this Italian cat named Buddy DeFranco in the group. They say he's a hell of a clarinet player. So he'll be here for rehearsal, since we open at the Brass Rail tonight."

When Basie told me that Willard Alexander's booking office was paying Buddy DeFranco a higher salary than Basie, I was pissed! But I didn't say anything because I knew that Basie owed big. Plus, it wasn't my place to say anything.

When Buddy sauntered up, he seemed like an okay guy. Thick dark hair, clean shaven. Dressed hip.

That night, we opened at the Brass Rail, which was downtown in the Loop in Chicago. It was a unique place. Shaped like an "L" behind a corner building. Had entrances from the two intersecting streets. A nice cozy feel.

The group was very tight and Basie was remarkable as usual. Bob, Buddy, and I were the three horns. Gus pumped the drums, Freddie Green strummed that mean guitar, and I think Jimmy Lewis was on bass. And to my pleasant surprise, Buddy played some awesome clarinet.

When Basie told me that we'd probably work at the Brass Rail for a while, I moved in with one of my old navy buddies, Chuck, and his girl-friend, Mamelle, on 60th. His real name was Charles Allen, but it wasn't the Charlie Allen who was famous for mouthpieces. Chuck was just a plain kind of guy. We'd been real close ever since the navy days at Great Lakes. So with a few savings in my pocket, since Chuck wouldn't accept any rent from me, Pauline came to visit more often. She liked Melle and Chuck.

Well, we gigged at the Brass Rail for a few months, and things were going great. The patrons loved us. Everybody was happy and the band sounded great.

Carlos Gastel, the manager of the Woody Herman herd, came into the club regularly, trying to entice Bob Graf to leave our band and join them. Eventually Bob did leave us, and Wardell Gray replaced him.

Next, we went to California to do a film short for Snader Transcriptions. Right away we knew something was wrong when the head honcho frowned, pointed at Buddy, then screamed, "We can't do a film with the Basie band with this white guy sitting up there in this colored group! He's got to go!"

I felt bad for Buddy. I hated racism.

Basie got Marshal Royal to replace Buddy. Marshal had worked at the Crescendo Club with Basie's big band before, as a sub for Earl Warren. So Marshal was a shoo-in. And the band was as tight as ever.

When we left California, we went up and down, back and forth, zigzagging across the United States. Miles and miles and miles of travel, hot sounds and great camaraderie.

Months later, we were at Birdland in New York finishing the gig there. The High Hat in Boston was next, and in order to make the gig on time, Basie told us that we'd have to fly.

I didn't say anything about my fear of flying. Instead, I got up the next morning, got ready, and we all went to the airport. It took all I had to calm my nerves. I didn't want to be a drag, so I prayed and sat down with the cats.

When it was time for us to get on the plane, I was scared as hell. I said, "Holy, I'm not going to do it."

Basie said, "Aw, man. You've *got* to get on this plane. That's the only way you're going to make this gig tonight."

Now, I hadn't been on a plane since that night I was with Hamp, when we'd missed the bus messing around and gambling at the whorehouse a few years before. This time, I just couldn't do it. At all. Couldn't get on that plane. Too much metal up in the sky. All I could think about was falling through the clouds.

When Basie saw how scared I was, he said, "Come here with me."

I followed him into the men's room, where he pulled out a half pint of gin. He handed me the bottle and said, "Here, drink some of this."

I took a slug, then handed him the bottle, but he pushed it back to me. He said, "Drink some more."

So I took another slug, and he took a few. Before I knew it, we had killed the whole bottle.

Then he said, "Now come on and let's get on this plane and go on up to Boston and make some music."

I said, "Okay, let's go."

A few gigs later, we ended up in Wilkes-Barre, Pennsylvania, with no place to stay. So Basie and I scouted several houses and found places for everybody except ourselves. Finally, he knocked on the door of a house owned by a lady named Mrs. Jones.

She said, "I've got a couple of beds up in the attic. One is regular size and the other is a pull-down."

We paid her for the accommodations and settled in. Of course, I got the slab. There was a small dresser where Basie put the contents of his pockets. I put my stuff on the other side near his things.

There was one major problem with Basie and me being roommates: he couldn't sleep with the light off and I couldn't sleep with it on. So I thought, Ain't nothing for me to do but lie here and wait for him to read his comic book till it flops on his belly. Then I'll know he's asleep, and I'll sneak over and pull the light chain.

At first he was reading and laughing out loud, "Ha, ha, ha." After a few minutes I heard the book go "Plop" on his belly. I looked at him and he was snoring, "Zzzzzzzzzzzzzzzzzzzz."

I eased up and sneaked over to the dresser, and just as I was about to pull the chain, he sat straight up in the bed and said, "Put it back!"

By the time we played at Goody's Club in Toronto, Canada, our uniforms had gotten very, very ragged. So I went to Basie and I said, "We need some new uniforms, man. You can *see* that."

He said, "Aw, man, ain't nobody looking at those damn uniforms. You look all right."

That night after we got through with the gig, I talked Marshal into ripping up his uniform, while I did the same. Then we hung them on Basie's doorknob. I lit them with a match and knocked on his door and ran away.

He opened the door and saw all the smoke and fire. We were hiding while he fanned the flames until they were out. Then he stomped on the ashes. After the fire was out, we walked back up to the door of his room. He looked at us with a harsh scowl and then a sheepish grin. He said, "You motherfuckers weren't kidding!"

The next night Marshal and I went to the gig dressed as sharp as tacks. And shortly after that, the whole band got new uniforms.

From Toronto we had to take a long train ride to Vancouver—halfway across Canada. Henry Snodgrass was the road manager at the time, and Basie had arranged for us to ride on the train sitting up, but he had gotten himself and Snodgrass some berths where they could relax.

So I talked some of the cats into going with me to talk to Basie. We all stood around in front of Basie. At first, he didn't want to hear it. But I kept talking. I said, "Well, man. If you've got to open on the day after tomorrow, you're going to have to open by your damn self because we're not going to ride all the way across Canada sitting up while you're laying up sleeping in comfort."

He looked at our stern faces; then he said, "I think you guys mean it."

I said, "Yes, we do."

Snodgrass took our tickets back and changed them so that we could have berths too.

As time passed, we ended up at a gig in the Seville Theater in Seattle, Washington. A skinny young kid came up to the club every night. I guess he was maybe twelve or thirteen. He walked up to me with a determined look on his nutmeg-toned face, smiled real big, and said, "My name is Quincy Jones and I play trumpet. I'd like to take some lessons from you and study with you."

Although my schedule was pretty tight—we were working like gang-busters and I knew this would interrupt my sleeping schedule—I remembered Miles and my personal vow never to fluff off anybody else. And Quincy looked like a pretty serious kid. So I said, "Well, the only time we could do it would be early in the morning before you go to school, because late in the evening I'm usually getting ready to go to the gig."

He smiled and said, "Okay. Well, I can come up to your room at six or seven in the morning."

For two months, every morning around six, Quincy knocked on my door. I'd drag up and answer it. There he'd be. Standing straight. Bright-eyed and bushy-tailed. His voice was real perky. He'd say, "Good morning, Mr. Terry." Then we'd get down to work.

We got to be good friends, and when he brought his first arrangement to me, even though it wasn't the greatest thing in the world, I encouraged him and he was appreciative. I knew that he had great potential, because he was talented and determined.

When our engagement ended in Seattle, Quincy was more eager than ever. He thanked me for all the lessons and then he said, "Mr. Terry, I'm gonna make it. Just wait and see!"

We said our good-byes, and a few days later the band was gigging in San Francisco. After a rehearsal, I pulled Quincy's chart out and Basie agreed to run through it. The cats laughed at it. Said, "Where did you get this?" But I kept my hopes high for Q.

From there, we went back up to Seattle, where Q was waiting eagerly.

At our regular six o'clock lesson, he said, "What did you think about my arrangement, Mr. Terry?"

Now, I didn't want to hurt his feelings. I wanted to encourage him. So I said, "Well, it was pretty good for a beginner. Just keep at it and one day you'll make it for sure."

Soon I was at the airport trying to calm my nerves enough to board the plane for Chicago. Basie nodded at me as I took a few swigs of gin from my silver flask. The gin helped, of course, but the thing that motivated me most was what Basie told me. He walked over, put his arm around my shoulders, and said, "Well, Clark, I've talked to the office. They said the debts are almost paid off. So we'll put the big band back together soon."

I congratulated him and kept taking swigs. Then he said, "After Chicago, if things work out, we've got a pretty long stint at the Strand in New York, so you could send for that pretty young bride of yours like you've been waiting to do."

He patted my back and walked over to talk with some of the other cats. I sat there with dreams of Pauline dancing in my mind. Hoping that our marriage had stood the road test. She had sounded all right when I'd last talked to her. But I'd been gone a long, long time, and we still had to do the Brass Rail in Chicago.

27. Duke Ellington

Duke sent his wife, Evie, to scout me at the Brass Rail. I learned later that she was a former Cotton Club showgirl. Not a dancer but a pretty girl who decorated the stage during a show. Since I loved Basie and the cats, I didn't give her the time of day. She was very fair-skinned and I didn't know if she was colored or white. She was tall, shapely, elegant, and quite self-assured. But despite her determination, I wasn't budging.

A few days later, Duke sent John Celley, his road manager Al Celley's brother, to talk to me about joining the orchestra. John was an easy-spoken, slump-shouldered Italian guy with lots of hair. But I just wasn't interested; Basie and I were real close and I didn't want to leave a tight-knit situation to become a drop in the ocean. With Basie I had a say. With Duke I didn't feel that I would.

John bought me a drink during an intermission. We sat over in the corner and shot the breeze for a few minutes. Then he said, "So, would you like to be in Duke's band?"

I took a sip and said, "No. I'm really happy with Basie."

When Duke's publicity man, Joe Morgan, came up to me while I was on break a few nights later, I thought, Man, Duke is relentless! But I still wasn't leaving Basie.

Joe was a short, heavy-set Caucasian cat. He lit his smoke and I lit mine. We smiled and I checked out his sharp vines. He must have seen me eyeing his stingy-brim hat. He puffed his smoke and then he said, "If you join us, you might come by a hat like this and a whole lot more. You know Duke wears custom shoes, hats, suits, and ties. We all have nice things, too. He takes real good care of his people."

For a moment, I looked into the air and thought about it.

Joe leaned closer. He said, "And Duke will pay you a hell of a lot more than you're making with Basie."

I sat back and said, "Well, I like where I am, but let me think about it." I felt guilty even thinking about leaving Basie, especially now that he was about to get the big band back together. He'd been so excited about it.

The next afternoon when the phone rang in my room at the Southway Hotel, I recognized Duke's voice.

He said, "Hey, I'd like to talk to you. Sure would like to have you aboard."

I said, "Okay."

He said, "Can we talk?"

I said, "Yeah."

He said, "Well, I don't want to come up to your room, because somebody might come in there. So why don't we just happen to meet in the hall and have a quick discussion. I'll come up there tomorrow. But, uh, I don't want to, naturally, hang around in the lobby. So when I come, I'll just call you and, uh, we'll go from there."

I said, "Okay."

So he did. The next afternoon he called and I answered the phone.

He said, "Well, I'm in the lobby. So just let me know what floor you're on and meet me at the elevator and we'll have our conversation."

I said, "All right. I'll meet you at the elevator on the sixth floor."

When the elevator door opened, there was Duke. But when I turned around, I saw Freddie Green's door open. It was right in front of the elevator. He saw me and he saw Duke getting off.

Freddie had a shocked look on his face. He said, "Oh, shit!" Then he went back into his room and slammed the door.

Duke smiled and smoothed his silk suit. Without one word about Freddie, he said, "Now, I can't just take a player out of a buddy's band. That doesn't work nicely. What I think is that you'll need to fake illness. You just say you're sick and you just go home to St. Louis. Tell Basie that you're going to cool it for a while until you recover. We'll be coming through there on Armistice Day, November 11th. And when we do, you'll just happen to join us. It's only a few months away, and meanwhile, I'll put you on salary at two hundred fifty dollars a week, which will be your starting pay with us."

My head was spinning. I looked at the floor and thought, Wow! What a fantastic deal! Leave Basie and go with Duke and be on salary with Duke before I even join the band. I'd get a chance to go home and see Pauline and everybody *and* get paid.

I remembered when Hamp told me to wait for him and he didn't show. But I didn't get the feeling that Duke was jiving. I imagined having Duke's salary compared to the one-forty a week that Basie was paying me. Then I felt lousy, since Basie had just given me a raise. But when I looked into Duke's impatient eyes, I knew I had to make a decision right there.

Duke took a step closer and said, "Is there anything else?"

I said, "Just give me a little time to tell Basie."

He smiled and said, "But of course." He jingled some change in his pocket and he said, "Your salary starts with us as soon as you leave Basie. I'll have my people in touch with you. And we'll see you in St. Louis on November 11th?"

I said, "I'll be there."

That night at the gig, Freddie did his usual looking off with no eye contact routine when he talked to me. He said, "Shit, you're a fool if you don't!"

I didn't respond. Nobody else said anything, so I didn't either. In the back of my mind was a ball of guilt, but I was also excited.

Joe Williams joined us that night and we were all glad that he'd decided to join our group. He teased me after the first show about carrying him to George Hudson's car when he'd collapsed at the softball game back in St. Louis.

I laughed and talked, but in the back of my mind was a ball of guilt. Still, we all had fun. But the real spotlight was on the Joe Louis fight that night. We'd all bet on Joe Louis to win, except for Joe Williams. He'd bet on Ezzard Charles. And when Ezzard won the fight I asked Joe about his bet.

He had a pocket full of money. Just beaming and grinning. He shrugged his shoulders and said, "Well, when I went to Louis' training camp, I saw how sluggish he was and how his training partner was knocking him around. They were telling Joe to quit fighting. So I knew Joe wasn't gonna make it."

I sneered at him. He said, "I didn't really want to bet against Joe, man. But you know, I just wanted to make some extra bills. You understand. If I had told anybody what I knew, well, that might've jinxed the fight. Plus Joe might have won. I was still pulling for him."

After the Brass Rail gig ended a week later, we went on to New York for the Strand Theater job. I tried to find a way to tell Basie, but I just couldn't. I went back and forth with my decision to leave, but deep inside I knew I wanted to go with Duke.

Basie was getting more and more excited about getting the big band together. As I sat with him in his dressing room at the Strand, he said, "I need a trombone player and an alto saxophone player."

I said, "Okay, I've got them for you. Ernie Wilkins and his brother, Jimmy."

He looked at me quizzically. "Can they play?"

I said, "Does a bear shit in the woods? And besides, when Buster Harding and Jimmy Mundy get a little busy, Ernie can help them out with the writing."

He smiled his usual wide smile and said, "Okay. Tell them to come on."

While Basie was in the steam cabinet, I picked up the phone and called St. Louis. The steam was at full blast—"Ssssssssssssssssssssss"—and Basie couldn't hear me.

Ernie answered his phone. I said, "Hey, Ernie. You want to come and join Count Basie's band?"

He said, "Aw, man, don't be playing with me like that!"

I said, "Naw, man. I'm *serious*, and I can't talk long and I can't talk loud. Do you want to do it?"

He said, "Sure!"

I said, "Good. And get Jimmy."

His voice rose. He said, "Jimmy, too?"

I said, "Yes. But the only thing is that you've got to play alto."

He said, "Man, I don't play alto. I'm a tenor man. I never played alto in my *life*."

I knew from our navy days that he was a good reader and he had a good sound, and I knew that he could play alto if he wanted to. So I said, "Get an alto and come to New York. I'll make a reservation for both of you at the Hotel America. Not the Americana. We're in a little fleabag off 47th Street."

He said, "Okay. All right. I'll be there. We'll leave tomorrow and I'll be there day after tomorrow."

I said, "Make it for sure."

He said, "Okay."

They came to the hotel and checked in. The next morning bright and early, we went over to the Strand and I took them to meet Basie.

I said, "This is your new alto player and your new trombone player."

Ernie's borrowed alto was held together with rubber bands, chewing gum, and cigarette wrappers. When he pulled it out, everybody looked at him and said, "What? Where did this guy come from?"

But he passed the acid test, and Jimmy did too. Then Basie said to Ernie, "Well, we just got Joe Williams. Can you write something for him?"

Eventually Ernie came up with "Everyday, I Have the Blues." Joe Williams sang the shit out of that song. Much later, it became a mega hit, catapulting Basie into the mainstream. But that was yet to come. For now, we had to finish getting the orchestra together and hit the road again.

28. Leaving Basie

A lie is like a tick that sucks that joy out of your life. That lie I told Basie made me feel like shit. But I just didn't think he would understand. I knew that he depended on me, and that he'd feel I was betraying him even if I'd told him the truth.

Duke had told me that it wasn't proper to steal a man from a friend's band. I didn't want to lie to Basie. But I did want to join Duke's band. I figured that Duke didn't get to where he was by being dumb. So I thought about what he said I should use for an excuse—fake being sick and lie to Basie. I decided to do it.

On one hand, I was thrilled to be joining Duke's band. On the other, I felt bad that I hadn't been honest with Basie. Nevertheless, I had made my choice. At that moment, I decided that whenever I reached the point in my career where I had my own band, I'd always encourage my people to come to me and express their desires to move on. Even if somebody wanted someone in my band, all they'd have to do is ask. If my band member wanted to go, I'd wish them the best.

After the show one night at the Strand, I got my nerve up to tell Basie that I was leaving. I said, "Holy, I've got something to lay on you. I'm really tired and I think I need to go home and rest. So I'm gonna put in my two weeks' notice and go back to St. Louis and cool it till I get myself together."

He didn't seemed surprised and I wondered if Freddie Green had said something to him. Basie was real cool. He said, "Okay, well, just want you to know that when you're better, the door is open and the chair is always yours."

I felt like a small dot on a huge manuscript. To make matters worse, when Snodgrass paid me at the end of that week, my check was fifteen dollars short. Basie had taken back the raise that he'd given me a month before. I was busted down from a hundred and forty dollars to a yard and a quarter. But I didn't say anything because I felt lucky to have squeezed out without any commotion. And I knew I'd told that big-ass lie.

With a guilty conscience, I went back to St. Louis for a few months to wait for Duke's band.

Pauline and I were so glad to be together. I was home and things were cool. Not like some of the episodes I'd heard about when cats would get home only to hear gossip about their wife's new lover or, even worse, catch the clap from their wife after being faithful on the road, or, worst-case scenario, actually *walk in* on their old lady with some sleaze-ball. Pauline wasn't like that at all.

My new mom and pop, Fannie Mae and Henry, were cool with my being gone so much and they made me feel welcome. Rudy and I got along great, but Hiawatha's eyes had lost some of their gleam for me. Maybe because I had been gone so much—all ten years since he was born. So I bought him some hip clothes and laid some bread on him, but he seemed more distant than ever. My explanations of why I had to be gone so much were like pouring water into a bottomless can.

Margueritte was still living in Detroit, but my other sisters and brothers were all glad to see me back in St. Louis. I bought gifts and laid some bread on them, and they were ecstatic that I was joining Duke's band. We had grown up listening to his music on radio broadcasts, records, and jukeboxes. I just wished that Pop could have been there to share in all of the excitement.

One afternoon I went to Leon Dagg's house a few miles away from Carondelet, near Corinthian Baptist Church in the Valley, where I wanted to give a party for my ex-brother-in-law, Sy. He lived a block or two away from Leon, and I hadn't seen him in a long time. He'd been such a light in my life. Giving me lessons, taking me with him to rehearsals, pointing me in the right directions, and just being there for me. I treasured how much Sy had taught me about jazz, so I was hoping he and a few friends could come to the gathering.

I bought some barbeque ribs and chicken, beer, and a whole bunch of other stuff. We got the radio set up, tuned into some jazz. Then a lot of my old friends came by with smiling faces. We all had a great time eating and drinking and shooting the breeze about our younger days at Leon's shoe shine parlor and in Carondelet.

When Sy got there, we hugged each other tight. I reached in my pocket and handed him a hundred-dollar bill. His eyes got bigger than syrup-sopping biscuits! It made me feel good all over; it was the least I could do, since he'd done so much for me. He didn't want to take it at first, but I insisted. He said, "Thanks, John. I'm so proud of you!"

The party was a gas. Everybody told me the latest on their families and jobs, and I answered their questions.

Duke's checks came regularly through the mail, while I jammed around town and played scab gigs. Some of the local cats cut their eyes at me and I heard comments like, "Well, look who's doing scabs." But that didn't ruffle my feathers, since I knew that something better was just around the bend.

I thought about the no-show thing that Hamp had sent me through following the good-luck toasts that George and the cats had given me. But each time doubt crept into my mind, I thought, "Duke is paying me. Why should I worry? He'll be there."

A short time later, I joined Local 197 of the American Federation of Musicians—the colored union in St. Louis. The whites had theirs and we had ours, but we all read the same black notes on white manuscript.

Since everybody knew about my joining Duke's band, I was a little nervous with anticipation.

29. The University of Ellingtonia

Finally, it came: November 11, 1951—Armistice Day. I rushed to join Duke's band at the Keil Auditorium in St. Louis, praying that it was all true. The Keil was a brand-new facility with all the latest equipment, from sound to lighting. When I met up with the cats in the dressing room, the air was thick with smoke and with smells of cologne, coffee, and whiskey. I lit a cigarette too.

Subbing for Duke was one thing, but when he hired me to be a member of his band on a regular basis at the Keil in '51, and I saw those *penlights* being put on our music stands, I knew what that meant. The house lights would be so low we might as well have been in the damn dark. All that music in the dark. Not only Duke's music—five or six hundred charts—but the music of the celebrity acts, too.

This wasn't just a regular one-nighter like a dancehall thing. It was billed as "The Biggest Show of '51." Headliner celebrities, in addition to the Duke Ellington Orchestra. Other big-time acts like Nat King Cole, Sarah Vaughan, Stump and Stumpy, Peg Leg Bates, and Patterson and Jackson. I've still got the souvenir program. Saved it all these years.

It was a hot show. Everybody called it "The Big Show." A show that folks had looked forward to for a long time.

At least the first two times I'd subbed for Duke there was enough light. No penlights on music stands. But not this time. And the band had already gone through the rehearsals by the time I joined.

No rehearsal for me, and I had to play in the dark. I was as nervous as a rabbit running from an eagle.

The dressing room was filled with strange faces. Before when I'd subbed, I hadn't hung around much afterward, and most of the cats who were there that night I'd never seen before. They were preoccupied with their routines of dressing, getting their instruments together, drinking, and socializing. Only a few of them spoke to me, very casually. I had to prove myself. I knew that.

The same thing was happening again on my first night as a member of Duke's band. No friendly faces. So I put on my uniform—gray tuxedo jacket, black pants, white shirt, bow tie, and black shoes. I wished I could have a swig of Dixie Bell to settle my butterflies, but I knew I had to be totally alert.

The butterflies were multiplying, knowing that I was the new kid on the block and that this wasn't like joining semblances of family like with the other bands, Hudson, Barnet, or Basie, where I played with and traveled pretty much with the same cats. Instead, Duke always had a colossal team of cats in and out of the orchestra, *and* an awesome supply of premiere backups who were ready at a moment's notice to swoop right in and take your seat. Everybody knew how easy it was to be replaced. It was do or die.

Duke's band was nicknamed for the best baseball team at that time, the Yankees. Crème-de-la-crème musicians, top-shelf masters of their craft. Ready, willing and able. Sometimes he had cats on trumpet like Cootie Williams, Rex Stewart, Willie Cook, Fats Ford, Cat Anderson, Ray Nance, and a whole bunch more. Each section had a roster that would choke a mule.

On top of that, there was Shorty Baker. He was from St. Louis too, and we were both celebrated trumpet soloists, so there was uneasiness between us. Maybe I would have felt the same way if the situation had been reversed, I don't know. What I did know was that I had to stay calm and focused.

After I finished dressing, I took my seat on the bandstand before everybody else to make sure everything was in order. Including my little penlight that was attached to my music stand.

I knew that the rest of the band had pretty much *memorized* the book. I'd learned that from the first two times I'd subbed. But I had to sight-read the music, and keep up with the cue sheets and the list of who followed whom, when, and where in the damn dark. After some acts there were tacit sheets that indicated the breaks for the band, which would give me the chance to scan ahead for the next performance. Thank God!

I thumbed through the mammoth book of music and wondered how I was going to keep my eyes on Duke *and* all of the papers in front of me. I knew that I had to watch Duke's every move to catch the tempo changes and the crescendos and decrescendos.

After folks were seated, the lights went down. Way down! I took a deep breath and said more prayers. We were featured for a few numbers before the headliner acts came out on stage, so all eyes were on us. The place was packed. And it was in my hometown, which meant if I screwed up, there would definitely be gossip.

There was no way I knew what tunes Duke was going to call. He simply raised his hand and counted off, or he'd play an intro on the piano. Sometimes, like with "Caravan," he played a rhythmic pattern that indicated the tune. Or his clue might be the key and tempo, like when he was ready to play "Mood Indigo." Other times he used the nickname for a tune. Instead of saying "Sophisticated Lady," for example, he said, "*Sophla*."

Actually, I thought it was really hip that he didn't have to say, "We're going to play 'A Train' or 'Number 56.'" I admired how he had such command, how everyone had to pay complete attention to him. But I was as lost as a marble in a corn field, and nobody seemed to care.

Shorty Baker wasn't gonna tell me a damn thing, for sure. I couldn't depend on the other trumpet players because even though Ray Nance had been cordial in the dressing room, now he was busy doing his own thing, and Cat Anderson was too preoccupied with himself.

When Duke kicked off the first tune, I wracked my brain trying to figure out what tune it was. I was fumbling with the music, looking for the chart like a squirrel digging for nuts in the snow.

God answered my prayers because finally Quentin Jackson, down in the trombone section, had mercy and came to my rescue. His nickname was Butter because of his robust size. He mouthed a number for the tune, "467." But by the time I figured out what he was saying and I'd scuffled in the dark through all those charts, I was only able to play the ending. Each time.

It was a challenge, but I loved challenges. I was determined to catch on and keep the sweat out of my eyes.

Duke's way of conducting was entrancing, as he emphatically delivered the down beat with his right hand and body in sync, then, with the same hand, made a big sweeping motion across his body with the second beat. He knew exactly how to use each man's sound to create the most amazing voicings. The sounds of trains, whistles, birds, footsteps, climaxes, cries. Rhythms that vibrated the floor. Harmonies with ebbs and flows that almost lifted me right up out of my chair. The music was so great that I had to snap myself out of listening sometimes and get my mind back on playing.

The audience was spellbound, then standing and applauding or dancing in their seats while finger-popping, their heads moving while their eyes stayed glued on us like we were the fountain of life. The music was so powerful and electric, if I'd had a big plug I could have stuck it in the air and lit up the whole world.

Duke was sheer *genius.* The most admired conductor in the business. He was more than the cat's meow—he was the whole cat! He was the epitome of his name—Duke.

After our orchestra played a few numbers, Stump and Stumpy came on. Just the rhythm section played for them. I was too glad for that break. I caught my breath, adjusted that damn penlight, organized my music, and said some more prayers. After a while, I started watching the show along with the rest of the band.

Stump was tall and had a wide smile. Stumpy, who closely resembled Miles Davis, was short. They had a rip-roaring comedy routine, doing tap dances with fillers of puns, quotes, and quips. Little Stump said, "Remember, everything you say will be held against you." Big Stump said, "Sarah Vaughan!" Then there was a tussle on stage between them. Little Stump said, "Oh, gosh! Is my nose bleeding?" Big Stump examined him then said, "No. It's *snot!*" They were hilarious.

Peg Leg Bates danced out next. He was a middle-aged man, very dapper. Fine vines, white shirt, and tie. Big taps on the front, back, and middle of his very soft shoes. He did what was called a "crimp," which was a manipulative articulation that required great skill to keep rhythmically intact with the music and tempo. He was light brown skinned, had conked hair. He did the buck and wing step, splits, jumps, leaps, and even hops all the way across the stage on his peg leg while flailing the good leg back and forth with his body in a horizontal position. It was breathtaking.

The step that knocked everybody out was the one that looked like he was jumping through an imaginary hoop. He jumped with the peg leg while the other leg was extended behind him. Everybody gasped while he danced to the accompaniment of the piano, drums, and bass. Then he had one step that sounded like a machine gun, while at the same time he gyrated his body in sync with the beat and faked like he was holding a machine gun.

Pork Chop Paterson and Al Jackson followed. They were a great duo. One of the tunes they did was made famous by the Ink Spots—Bill Kenny, Deek Watson, Jerry Daniels, and Charlie Fuqua. Al sang a beautiful part like Bill Kenny, "If I didn't care for you." Then Pork Chop would mimic Deek's bass quotation, "If I didn't care." Each of them weighed more than three hundred pounds, and they stirred up some funk on stage. They said, "We may not have as many members as the Ink Spots, but we make it up in weight." Al was a great singer and Pork Chop was a wonderful comedian and dancer. Fat as he was, he could tap his ass off.

Paterson was notorious for his appetite off stage. I was with him in a barbeque joint later when he ordered two slabs of ribs and a half gallon of orange soda with a huge side order of french fries. As he watched somebody coming through the door, I reached for one of his fries; he immediately said, "Put that tater back!"

Sarah Vaughan came out next. I could see right away that she fit the nickname Dave Garroway had given her—the Classy Miss Sassy. She held the audience in the palms of her hands. Her voice was truly an instrument, very mellow. She was beautifully endowed with chord progressions. The cats used to say, "What great ears she has," because she could hear the next chord progression and determine the flavor. She also knew how to put together exciting rhythmic patterns, and her intonation was masterful.

There may have been other acts in the show, but I don't remember them. I do remember Nat King Cole. Definitely!

When Nat made his entrance, he walked out on stage and started singing a cappella, hitting the first phrase—"Funny, how I started loving you"—in perfect pitch. Amazing. I wondered if he'd had a pitch-pipe. His voice flowed like hot molasses, smooth and rich. The orchestra started in around the third measure. He was absolutely captivating and had impeccable diction. He was dressed to the nines and had such an elegant presentation.

When the show ended, I was so relieved, I felt like I'd pulled my D-width feet out of a brand new pair of AAA pointed-toed shoes!

Being with Basie had been like prep school. The University of Ellingtonia was a completeness of everything I needed to know about music, like establishing a rapport between the bandstand and the audience, and, more than anything, what I needed to know about life. Period.

There was so much that I wanted to learn. But I could tell that the challenges were going to be monumental. Even though I was up for it, the real test was whether or not I could endure it all and make the grade with Ellington.

30. Working with Duke

Duke was endowed with a supernatural magic that opened doors and carried him along highways and hallways, through cracks and crevices. He could cuss you out and rarely use a cuss word. He'd chastise you from the piano by hitting a discord and everybody knew what was going on.

A frequent utterance of his was simply "Aaaaaahhhhh!" It might mean something like, "You're not paying attention! You're not listening!" Or it might mean that what you played was beautiful to him. But whenever he made that sound, we all knew where he was coming from.

He was very firm about us listening to what we were playing. He'd say, "Listen!" When he got fed up, he'd say, "Listen, goddammit, listen!" At first I didn't understand and I was thinking, What is he talking about? Does he think we're deaf or we have cotton in our ears? But then I understood that he was telling us to listen to the *totality* of the music. The texture, the timbre. What each section meant to the total piece. Especially your section. And what your section was contributing contrapuntally to the other sections. Listen to the vibrato being used. Follow the lead man.

I especially loved his principles. He'd say, "There are two rules of life. Rule number one is 'Never quit.' And rule number two is 'Don't forget rule number one.'" And my favorite quote of his was "I'm easy to please. Just give me the *best*."

I was on the road again with Duke—TOBA circuit and more! East coast to west coast and all in between—clubs, ballrooms, and theaters. The Beehive, Blackhawk, Blue Note, DeLisa, Regal, Apollo, Trianon, Savoy, and many others that I'd never been to before.

It didn't take long to learn that Duke never allowed anybody in his business, nor did he get into anyone else's. He had this invisible wall around him that prevented any involvement with bullshit. I admired that quality. And I admired the way he dressed. Tailored shirts and suits. Fine fabrics and custom-made shoes. He was his own man, not following trends. Just doing things the way he liked. Since he didn't like cuffs in his trousers, he was one of the first to wear trousers with no cuffs. Then when cuffless trousers came into vogue, he started wearing three-inch cuffs!

He designed a lot of his clothes for personal comfort. He didn't like buttons, so his shirts had hooks, zippers, or only one button, which was hidden under his collar. His shirts draped nicely over his torso, and he usually wore designer cufflinks. He didn't wear hats often, I guess because he didn't want to cramp his hairstyle, which was conked and waved.

Coming from a childhood like mine of having to wear my older sister's hand-me-downs, it was a gas for me to be able to wear fine vines and hip shoes. I was in a world where dressing elegantly came with the program. It was a far cry from my old days in Carondelet, wearing shoes that were too big and flip-flopped when I walked. Jazz was truly providing a better way for me, and I loved it more and more.

Dreams of having my own big band stayed on my mind. I was always taking mental notes about Duke. It was amazing to watch his main ingredient for keeping the guys together. All these very different attitudes and egotudes. He'd just wow them with his music. His mind-blowing music. Music they loved, respected, and admired. Music they couldn't get anywhere else. It was uncanny—complex yet simple. He made a quote once about simplicity. He said, "Simplicity is a most complex form."

Sometimes he would make seemingly trite endings, like one-three-five. The tonic, the third, and the fifth. It was so simple, but when listening to the overtones of what else had happened before in the piece, it sounded complex. You could quiz it and question it and say, "What was that?" But in the end, it worked perfectly.

He would add unique ingredients, too. For instance, a B-flat major chord on the end, way down at the bottom of the piano. He would drop in the lowest note possible on the keyboard, a flatted fifth, adding it to the simple one-three-five. Then he'd let it resonate. Awesome.

During the eight years that I spent with Duke, he wrote such great music. It is said that those years were some of his most important as a composer because in addition to the incredible variety and number of his creations, he composed some renowned suites. I played the part of Puck in his suite "Such Sweet Thunder." Talked through my horn. A way of speaking and playing at the same time. I remember the phrase "What fools these mortals be." Duke knew just the right formula, and I was glad I could deliver.

We recorded many of our concerts, like the ones in '52 in Seattle and at Birdland in New York. Then there was the one in Pasadena in '53, and one in '54 in Los Angeles. Over the years there were other recorded concerts, like in Chicago, D.C., Newport, Paris, and more. We recorded albums all over the place, and I loved it more than ants love sugar!

That August of '54 while we were in Los Angeles, Dinah Washington was hanging out of the window of the Adams Hotel when we were getting out of our bus. She was yelling at somebody, then she saw us. She waved at me and said, "Hey, I didn't know that you were going to be in town! We've got a record date to do tonight."

I said, "Who's on it?"

"Maynard Ferguson, Clifford Brown, Max Roach, Richie Powell, Keter Betts, David Schildkraut," and she kept naming a whole bunch of people.

So I said, "And me, too."

She said, "Of *course!* Just come on and show up."

It was an unusual type of session; I'd never been to one where people were invited to sit in at the studio. Even though I was unadvertised and unexpected, it turned out to be a real fun date. When the album came out, it was titled, *Dinah Jams*.

Everybody called her the Queen. She was definitely on the ball at that recording session, as usual. Really taking care of business. I'd first met her when I joined Hamp's band, and she was a fabulous lady. Vivacious, lively. A marvelous person. I loved working with her because she was an absolutely incredible singer. Powerful and extremely articulate.

I played on almost all of her recordings, even if I had to play under the pseudonym of "Dobbie Hicks," which I used whenever I had to avoid the repercussions of breaking the BMI and ASCAP rules. They were competitive publishing houses that required us to make a signed commitment for one or the other. They didn't permit us to record with an artist unless it was someone who'd signed with their company.

Dinah was notorious for throwing parties. Like a pajama party she had once. The only thing I remember about that party was a picture that someone took of me. On the floor, totally drunk. Like Louis Jordan's song went, "Sho' had a wonderful time last night—least wise—they told me I did."

When Dinah got tired of all the people there and she was ready to enjoy her man privately, she said, "All right! Everybody out. The party's over. We all had fun but it's time to go home." She never minced her words. You could bet that whatever she said was exactly what she meant.

She'd told me about the time down south when she'd rolled up to a service station in her car. It was one of those lazy towns where things were slow but still dangerous for colored folks. After she'd filled her car with gas, she asked the attendant where the ladies' room was. He told her, "We ain't got no ladies room for no niggas!"

She said she pulled a pistol out of her glove box and said, "Oh, yeah? Well, since you don't, then you just take your gas out of my car because I'm not paying for it!" Long story short, she left with the gas and eased on down the road.

Being on the road was a tough business, and ladies had to be tough, too. Dinah surely was, and so was Billie Holiday. Billie told me about the time when she was singing in a club and there was a drunk white patron who kept talking throughout her performance. Just swaying and lip-flapping and disrupting things. Billie said that when the show was over, she walked over to the bar where the guy was standing, and she laid some money on the bar. She told the bartender, "Give this man a drink on me." When the guy walked up to her, she socked him right between the eyes. Pow! He dropped down right there on the floor. Then she sashayed off. Smiling and talking to her fans.

I did a few shows with Billie. She was an awesome vocalist, too. A great singer with inflections in her voice that weren't like anyone else's. Just absolutely fantastic and very signature. And her phrasing was so unique. She could penetrate your soul and make you *feel* the pain she was singing about. Pain from her addiction and her personal life.

She and Lester Young were great buddies and to see the two of them perform together was totally unforgettable. Her voice was like a superb instrument. Such a great talent she had. And she was feisty to boot.

I loved doing gigs with Dinah, Billie, and many of the great musicians around. Duke didn't mind my doing extra gigs on the side, as long as I fulfilled my obligations to him. He knew that we were all doing other things. But whenever his baton went up, we knew that we'd better be *there*, or else.

Duke was also a great poet and he used a lot of unusually creative language. He used to talk about little germs with kissy pink moustaches, and a lot of his titles were sexual innuendos, like "Cottontail" and "Old King Dooji." One tune in particular that I loved to hear him announce was "Passion Flower." He'd say, "A passion flower is one that is more *enjoyed* than discussed."

Duke seemed pleased with me most of the time. But the most difficult task that I had to master was learning what Duke's limits of tolerance were with me. He always made it very clear when one of us band members crossed the "limit line."

31. Duke's Team

You'd have to read Duke's book *Music Is My Mistress* to see what an outstanding roster of professionals he had. Absolutely Grade A musicians. Not one single B. He had a certain thing in mind when he recruited: the signature sound of each individual; how they blended; and how they interpreted his arrangements. It was like a choir of masterful voices, or a palette of colors that he'd use to paint a song.

He wrote something unique for *each* member of the ensemble. He knew exactly what everybody could do and what they couldn't do. He used characteristic sounds, like the one that Rex Stewart got when he played a concert D—which is a trumpet E. Rex had a way of semi-suppressing the third valve and, along with the note, he would get a sort of guttural sound that became known as the half-valve tone. Or like the unique sound that Harry Carney had in the upper register, which was not the register designated for baritone saxophone. Or how Jimmy Blanton could play fast passages on the bass, so Duke used that in compositions like "Pitter Patter Panther" and "Plucked Again." Or how he would write a drum part, then flatter the hell out of the drummer, have the part played—then take the sheet music back and tear it up. Then he'd have the part played without the sheet music, so he could hear the drummer's original interpretation, and he'd say, "Your version is better than mine."

He gave us the freedom to express ourselves in our own ways. And all of us got chances to play solos. That was another one of his knacks of keeping everybody satisfied. He also wrote our names on our parts. It wasn't like in other bands with the traditional "1st Trumpet," "2nd Trumpet" and that kind of thing. He had the copyist put "Rex," "Cat," "Root" (Ray Nance), and "Clark" on our parts.

For solos, Duke had listened to people practice or warm up from time to time and he would write "little ditties." These were passages of what he had heard—someone would play a warm-up riff, and then he'd encourage that person to "stretch it out." Or he would just use a passage like the warm-up riff that Cootie played—which ended up being "Do Nothing Till You Hear from Me." He knew that it was just a warm-up thing for Cootie. But Duke heard so much more and stretched it out into a song, which Cootie might never have done. Or when Bigard used to warm up with a riff that inspired Duke to write "Mood Indigo."

He encouraged individual freedom and compiled ideas. Used things that were seemingly insignificant and made beautiful tunes. He got results that were not just out of his head, but also what was in his musicians' heads.

He asked Jimmy Hamilton and me to write two choruses each on "Perdido," then he orchestrated it. Another time, Duke said to me, "I want you to write me a little ending for this final swift movement. It's gotta be swift, and make it kinda boppish. You don't have to orchestrate it. Just write the line." So what I wrote ended up being the last eight measures of "Newport Up."

And Duke knew how to put the right crescendo or decrescendo sections in the right passages. He had such a variety in his writing. Beautiful ballads and up-tempo things. Gutty-funky-bluesy things. Soul-touching things. Meaningful, serious things. He knew which musicians to feature to get the full impact of his thoughts delivered like no one else.

When the Duke Ellington Orchestra played, the music could shoot you up to the stars with tunes like "Cotton Tail," with Ben Webster's famous solo, because he was known for his big fat, powerful tone. Or float you in the clouds with pieces like "Moon Mist," a ballad that featured Johnny

Hodges, who could go chromatically from the bottom to the top and back to the bottom in one smooth glissando.

Duke had a brass section that could wail up the high register and punctuate the notes precisely. His reed section could play low and smooth and full-bodied with people like Harry Carney, Paul Gonsalves, Ben Webster, Johnny Hodges, Russell Procope, and Jimmy Hamilton.

A few of his all-time-great percussionists were Sonny Greer, George "Butch" Ballard, Louie Bellson, Panama Francis, Ed Shaughnessy, Rufus Jones, Jimmy Johnson, Sam Woodyard, and Dave Black. They used a huge assortment of elaborate equipment—bells, chimes, tympani, tom-toms, snares, bass drums; all kinds of cymbals and temple blocks, to name a few things. The sound effects they created sounded so *real*—thunder, trains, or truck whistles that would transport you to a scene in life. On a tune like "Take the A Train," you could feel the vibrations of the train, then hear the whistle, and you'd think you were at a train station getting ready for a trip. It was more than music. It was an emotional experience.

Duke *mastered* the art of swinging. When he wrote "It Don't Mean a Thing If It Ain't Got That Swing," he knew what it was all about. He wanted to make his music felt. He knew how to make the audience's heads bob and feet tap. All the elements of pure enjoyment were there. Everybody moved when we played, including the band.

Ivie Anderson was the first vocalist in Duke's band, and there were many other extraordinarily talented vocalists who were able to portray exactly the mood that he wanted. Betty Roche was one of them. She could sing or scat anything with precision and feeling. She could sing the hell out of "Take the A Train." When she belted, "Hurry, hurry, hurry," you could feel yourself rushing.

One of my favorite singers was Ozzie Bailey. Not only was he endowed with an incredible voice, but his articulation and intonation were superior. Some of the other top-notch vocalists were Lil Greenwood, Jimmy Carnes, Jimmy Grissom, Ray Nance, Jimmy "Pretty Boy" Britton, Lloyd Oldham, Kay Davis, and Barbara Winfield. Della Reese was also a featured singer, and she was a real show-stopper. Her powerful delivery reminded me of my old days with Big Mamma Hut—hard-hitting, demonstrative, and impacting.

Tom Whaley was Duke's copyist for years. Each time Duke would write a score, he'd give it to Tom to copy the individual parts for the band. Sometimes the ink would be barely dry when we were handed our parts. I struggled sometimes, trying to read notes where the ink was smeared, but I played my best always.

There were times when Duke would do something that was mind boggling, like when he wrote a piece for the queen of England. We played it. Then he collected the sheet music and tore it up. I guess he just wanted to hear it once. Nobody questioned him, so we never found out why he did that.

Duke was very superstitious. One time he was on an elevator coming down to the stage in the Roxy Theater, and when the elevator stopped, a light bulb fell down and cut his hands. He was holding some music that was written on yellow manuscript paper and, coincidentally, he was wearing a yellow suit, yellow tie, and yellow shirt. I guess he needed something to blame for the mishap. So he told Tom to take all the music written on yellow paper out of the book and rewrite it on white paper. He never wanted anything to do with yellow manuscript paper after that.

He didn't like the number thirteen, and he didn't like for anybody to eat peanuts in the dressing room. I never found out why.

I watched him like a hawk. Learned so much from him. Although the personnel changed often, he never had to find a sub for me. I played every gig for eight years. I knew this was the chance of a lifetime, to learn from the world's best.

He always had a seventeen-piece band, a male and a female singer, and two valets—Bobby Boyd and Tommy . . . I can't remember his last name. I got along pretty well with everybody except Cat Anderson. He was a short, robust, pot-bellied, dark-complexioned guy. Eyes like a cat, hazel brown. He had almost no neck, so his head looked like it was sitting right on his shoulders. He was a very dependable musician, a lead trumpet player with great chops—that I will say. He read very well and he played powerfully, with good intonation. Duke was happy with his playing. But Cat was a real cut-up. He would take the music and destroy it, like the time he threw the book over the side of a ship.

Once Cat stole Johnny Hodges' magazines and sat on them to hide them while we were on a stop during a bus tour. Johnny said, "Get up, motherfucker! I know you got my books!" Cat got up and there were Johnny's books. Cat acted like *he'd* been done wrong and stormed off the bus.

He had a habit of staying on the bus at rest stops and pretending he was sleeping. Then when everybody got off the bus, he'd ransack our things. Duke had just gotten a gift of twelve beautiful silk handkerchiefs. Because Duke never locked his bag, Cat went in it and stole all the handkerchiefs and put them into his own bag. We were watching him from the restaurant window. When we came back, he faked like he'd been sleeping and pretended to awaken. He said, "What? You cats made a stop and didn't tell me? I've got to go in there, too."

So when he went into the restaurant, I opened his bag and took Duke's handkerchiefs out and put them back into Duke's bag. When we got to the gig, Cat was pissed off. Somebody asked him, "What's wrong, Cat?"

He said, "Some son-of-a-bitch stole twelve beautiful silk handkerchiefs out of my bag!"

Still and all, he could definitely play. I guess he never crossed the line of no return as far as Duke was concerned, since he never fired Cat.

It could be that Cat's antics were molded from his childhood, since he was raised in the Jenkins Orphan Home in Charleston, South Carolina. Cat pulled all sorts of pranks. But he knew not to mess with *me*.

All the cats from St. Louis carried a shank—in common language, a knife. So did I. When I'd come to work, before I took my music out of the book, I'd push the switchblade button. *Bling!* The sharp metal would flash in the lights. Then I'd throw the knife so that the point of the blade would stick in the fiberglass music stand. *Boing!* I'd shoot a look at Cat, then say, "Good evening, everybody." He'd ignore me, but I knew he got my message.

Harold "Shorty" Baker got his nickname because of his height. Sometimes we'd call him "Shorty Boo," just to mess with him. I loved him because he was a fun cat. Always joking around and pronouncing words in a joking manner, with accents intentionally on the wrong syllables, like "Now, that's a funny coin*CI*dence." On a long bus ride, knowing that we were hungry and thirsty, he'd rattle an empty sack and say, "Well, I guess I'll o*PEN* this bag of fried chicken and this big bottle of lemonade." He had a gorgeous sound on his trumpet and played beautiful and interesting solos. Raymond "Ray" "Root" "Little Dipper" "Sag" Willis Nance played trumpet, too. He had a lot of nicknames, but he and I called each other "Sag," which was short for Sagittarius. He was a short dude, but a real hip cat. A funny little motherfucker, too, who cracked me up when he danced. Sometimes he'd crack me up so much that I couldn't play. He'd flail his arms and do a real dopey step from side to side while rolling his eyes and contorting his face. There's a film with him doing that; in it I'm trying to play, but I can't stop laughing. Every time I see it, I crack up.

We called Ray "Little Dipper" in honor of Louis Armstrong, whose nickname was "Big Dipper." Ray was the sweetest cat in the world. Never harmed anybody. He smiled most of the time, and there was always a pleasant atmosphere around him. He played elegant trumpet solos and was an accomplished violinist, tap dancer, and vocalist as well. He was what was called an all-around man. Fantastic sound.

Willie Cook came over from Dizzy's band. He was playing "à la Birks," a term coined after Dizzy's middle name and bebop style. Willie was a good lead trumpeter with great sound. Very small but a powerful player with interesting solos. Dark-skinned with nice features—almost like a Native American. He wore a conk all the time.

Fats Ford was another trumpet player. His name had previously been Andre Maringuito, which meant "butter fat," according to him, and he was also known as "Lord Plush Bottom." Medium-brown skinned, average height. His wife was Spanish and he developed a Spanish accent, which was humorous. He had a good set of chops and was a good lead player and soloist.

We called Johnny Hodges "Rabbit" because with his long ears and small eyes, that's what his face resembled. He was a marvelous lead alto player with a very mellow sound. Quiet and unassuming, but he could play his ass off.

Russell Procope played alto. He was short and more portly than Rabbit. Kinda intellectually talkative at times. He was from the old John Kirby band. He was a dependable reader and had a beautiful sound.

Jimmy Hamilton was a tenor player who was featured more on the clarinet. His old nickname was "Joe Trump" because he had played trumpet in Philadelphia years before. Everybody loved his playing. He was a little shorter than me, of average complexion and with a little moustache. Sort of slow of speech.

Harry Carney had been with Duke for a long time—ever since he was seventeen. Ended up staying with Duke for forty-five years. An incredible musician. First cat in the band I saw doing circular breathing. I'd learned that technique back in my old days while I was with the Reuben and Cherry Carnival, but there's always something new to learn about anything old. Harry played clarinet, bass clarinet, and baritone sax. He was a big guy with intelligent conversations, and he was Duke's favorite riding buddy. They rode together often in Harry's Chrysler while we rode on the bus.

Juan Tizol played valve trombone beautifully. A Cuban who spoke broken English. Olive complexion, and he wore glasses. He was a hell of a composer, too. Wrote "Caravan," "Perdido," and many more. A great player.

Britt Woodman was a studio man who played slide trombone. Phenomenal chops, beautiful tone. And he could sight-read like nobody's business. Such a delightful person to be around. Kinda short, with a light complexion. He was also sedentary, and would go to sleep on you in a New York minute. He and Jimmy Woode—one of our bass players—and me, we were golf buddies.

Quentin "Butter" Jackson was a master with the slide trombone and the plunger. He filled a great void with his incredible plunger techniques after

Tricky Sam left the band years before. Butter was a true friend of mine—a real compassionate guy.

There were so many master musicians. Even if another band played Duke's charts, they couldn't come close to the sound that Duke got, because he had personnel that could deliver what was in his head. Punches, accents, and color. Duke was a true artist.

He was into many art forms. He did a film in the '70s for Norman Granz in a sculpture garden, showing the direct relationship between music and art. He was not only a master of his instruments—his band and the piano; not only a master arranger and composer, but he was also a master at dealing with anybody, anywhere, at any time. He had a true grip on the art of persuasion. He even persuaded me to do something I thought was impossible.

32. Duke's Management Arts

When we recorded Duke's suite "A Drum Is a Woman," I had no idea what was in store for me. The suite was written with a flavor of the New Orleans Mardi Gras. Lively, celebratory, and colorful. Just before the recording date, Duke said to me, "Clark, you're gonna portray the role of Buddy Bolden."

I said, "Maestro, I don't know anything about Buddy Bolden."

He said, "Sure you do. Buddy Bolden was suave and debonair. Always traveled with a couple of ladies on each arm. Had a great big sound, a powerful tone. He could tune up in New Orleans and break glasses in Algiers!"

He said, "Man, he could bend a note. He could bend a note almost to the point of breaking it, then bring it back again. And moans and groans, he was famous for. He always applied them in his diminishes. He was known for his diminishes. As a matter of fact, you *are* Buddy Bolden. Play me some diminishes and bend a few notes."

So I played some diminishes and bent a few notes.

He said, "See, *you* are Buddy Bolden."

Then I played the passage like I was Buddy Bolden.

Not only could he persuade you jazzwise, but I knew a couple of ladies who told me that Duke could talk to them on the telephone and cause them to have a *climax*. Lester Young told me that Duke could talk the birds out of the trees.

Duke had full command of the English language, and his diction was flawless. He had a compelling tonality in his voice that would make it difficult to doubt whatever he was talking about.

He said, "You are here for a reason. I'm not a disciplinarian. I expect you to do your best at all times. I've surrounded myself with top people, top musicians, and I expect you to do what you're here to do."

That was the gist of Duke's managerial position. He had to deal with the high strung, the low strung, and the strung out. And he did it with finesse.

On top of that, he knew how to make each man feel important and appreciated, which garnered absolute devotion. He knew each musician as well as he knew his own music—what motivated them, what their problems were, how to encourage them.

Paul Gonsalves once told me, "I'm gonna stay here with Duke till I die!" And that's exactly what he did.

If just a few players straggled in and the rest weren't there on time, Duke would start anyhow. Sometimes this would be an element of surprise or just a psychological thing of his. It made you feel bad, like I felt when I was late for a gig at the Blue Note in Chicago. I'd been invited to one of Josie Child's chitterling brunches and stayed for a second helping. As I entered the Blue Note, the band was already playing. I rushed to the bandstand and got my horn out. Duke cut the number that they were playing and went into "Perdido"—my only feature at that time. Instead of playing it in a groovy moderate tempo, he kicked it off in a swift tempo. Then he announced, "We'd like now to present the *late* Clark Terry in Juan Tizol's 'Perdido.'"

I'd had just enough chitterlings and Dry Sack sherry to act the smartass. I went down front and played the whole thing with my horn upside down, using my left hand—something I'd been practicing for a while.

Well, Maestro didn't speak to me for a couple of months. After that, I learned where his "no tolerance line" was drawn. I never did anything stupid like that again!

33. Miles and Bird

While I was with Duke in the early '50s, we were playing at the Bandbox, and Charlie "Yardbird" Parker was on the bill. We all called him "Bird." He liked to play fast tempos, as did Jimmy Hamilton, Paul Gonsalves, and me.

Bird was into the modern harmonies and bebop style, and he did a set with us. I suggested that we play "Scrapple from the Apple," since it was one of his tunes. It was a song about a dish that was made with parts of a pig—the ears, the feet, the nose, everything all ground up and mashed together and formed into a square. Sliced, then fried. Usually eaten for breakfast. They even put the grunt in it.

When we finished playing it, he said, "Aw, fellows. It's so nice for you to like my little ditties."

He was such a beautiful cat, but it was a sorrowful thing to see him going through that drug trip, which he regretted. He was light years ahead of most cats with his approaches. Blew everybody's mind!

I remember one time after he'd played a gig at Birdland, he was standing outside the club among some young admirers, and he was giving them a sermon about not getting hooked like he and Miles had done. They listened with wide eyes because here was their hero literally begging them not to follow in his footsteps.

I hated drugs. Hated what they had done to many of the cats. Talented cats! Good friends of mine. Like Miles.

While I was with Duke, around '53, we were getting ready to pull out of New York and I had a few hours before we had to get on the bus. I was walking to the Ham and Egger, a restaurant on 52nd and Broadway, when I noticed this bulk lying in the gutter on Broadway. I walked closer and looked and discovered that it was a person. I rolled him over with my foot and I couldn't believe my eyes. It was Miles Davis!

After I sat him up and brought him around a little bit, I took him into the Ham and Egger and bought him some breakfast. He knew that I knew he was a junkie. It hurt me so much to see him like that because I loved him and I loved his son, Gregory.

Miles and I ate, and then I walked him back to 47th Street to the Hotel America, where I was staying. We made it up to my room, where I put him to bed. I said, "Don't worry about anything. I'll be back to check on you before we go on the road."

I went and hung out for a couple of hours over at Jim and Andy's, a bar and restaurant on 48th Street, then I went back to my room to get my stuff and my horn. When I got off the elevator, my door at the end of the hall was open. That shocked the hell out of me.

I went to my room. No Miles, no clothes, no horn, no radio. No nothing. I was pissed off. I didn't have time to look for Miles because it was time to get on the bus, so I had to borrow somebody's horn. Luckily, my uniform was on the bus as usual.

When we finished the out-of-town gig, I came back to New York and the first thing I saw was Philly Joe Jones walking down Broadway wearing my brand-new maroon Phil Kronfeld shirt with the "Mr. B." collar and a diagonal zipper across the front. I wanted to walk up and rip it off. Instead, I called the Homer G. Phillips Hospital in St. Louis, where Pauline worked as a switchboard operator.

I said, "Pauline, call Doc Davis and tell him that Miles is fucking up. Doc thinks he's going to Juilliard, but he's going to Yardbird. I rescued him off the street and took him to my room and he stole all my shit!"

When Pauline called me back, she said, "Doc Davis refuses to believe that Miles is on narcotics and he said that if musicians like you would leave him alone, he wouldn't be into that kind of traffic."

Like they say, "No good deed ever goes unpunished." Even though Miles did that to me and his father didn't appreciate how I tried to help him, I felt bad for Miles. He had such a bright future. So I just closed my eyes and said a prayer for him.

It was a long time before I saw Miles again. I walked up to him at Charlie's, a bar where musicians hung out in Manhattan. He said, "Man, I know you're pissed at me. I'm sorry, but I couldn't help myself. I know you're my friend." While he was telling me his story about what had happened, I took his change off the bar and put it into my pocket. He said, "Yeah, I know I owe you." He knew not to start a fracas with me because he knew that I was a boxer, like he was, only I was bigger. He was a lightweight. I was a middleweight.

His son, Gregory, was a bitch of a fighter, too. I'd always wished that he'd let Gregory become a professional fighter. Archie Moore was a heavyweight champion who had dated my sister Lillian. When he saw Gregory, he said, "Man, this cat's got the fastest hands I've ever seen!"

But Miles didn't want him to box, and he didn't want him to play trumpet, either. He said that he didn't want Gregory to be subjected to that kind of life.

I spent a lot of time with Gregory. Giving him trumpet lessons. Trying to make up for what Miles wasn't able to give him. We spent so much time together that a lot of people thought he was my son. In a way he was, because I was giving him the love I'd wanted to give to Hiawatha.

So many of the cats were on dope. It broke my heart, but there was nothing I could do. I tried talking to them about it, but nothing mattered. What bothered me even more was when they kept trying to get me to check it out. They said, "Man, you are missing out on some great shit!"

But I didn't want anything to come between me and my career. I didn't want to become dependent on anything, to blow my money or end up dead. I just wanted to play my music from my heart and soul only.

One night during an engagement at the Apollo Theater, a few of my colleagues enticed me to check out something in one of the dressing rooms way up top. I didn't know what was happening, but they made it sound like it was something really interesting. So I went up there, only to find them shooting up. They said, "Man, you should try some of this new shit! You'll play your ass off!" They saw that I wasn't digging it, so they grabbed me and tried to force me to get involved. I knocked a couple of them down. One of them still had the works in his arm. I fought all of them off.

I never did try any narcotics. Just marijuana—I tried that because the cats were telling me that you couldn't get hooked on it like the hard stuff. But even weed came to a screeching halt one time when I was at a party.

We were all drinking and smoking and having a good time, when somebody starts beating on the door. Bam! Bam! Bam! I thought it was the cops, so I grabbed the bag and went to the bathroom and flushed all the pot down the toilet. I didn't want any headlines about me and some weed.

Well, it wasn't the cops. It was just some cats who said they were beating on the door because when they knocked, no one let them in. I guess the music was too loud and we didn't hear them.

Everybody at the party was mad at me because all the smoke was gone and I was the culprit. Well, after that—it just wasn't worth the hassle. So I exed it out of my life.

Gambling was the only addiction I'd dealt with. And that was enough. It had taken a lot for me to curb it. The thrill of winning was so powerful. But I'd seen small fortunes lost. I knew I'd never be as lucky as Cootie Williams, who went to the racetrack daily just like he was going to *work*. He took his lunch with him and would go home every night with money. But I'd usually lost more than I won. For a long time. With all the hell I'd been through with gambling, I damn sure wasn't going to add another addiction.

34. Billy Strayhorn

Duke's alter ego was Billy Strayhorn. I don't know the origin of the nickname Duke called him, which was "Sweet Pea." I referred to him like a lot of the cats did, as "Strays." He called Duke "Edward." Like Duke, Strays was an elegant dresser. He liked colors. Not overly flamboyant, but different from Duke, who had a more calm taste—like pastel colors.

We all wanted Strays on our recording dates because he was an absolute master. He played beautifully and he had a way of calming Duke, of which Joe Morgan was jealous.

Strays was like a breath of fresh air. He was really friendly. Suave and debonair. Confident of himself and his music. He made sure that things were done in a timely manner, no matter what kind of pressure had built up. He knew how to handle the heaviest of situations without showing worry. No one could back him into a corner. He'd just stand there, firm and flat-footed, and say, "Relax. Let's get this thing done."

He knew how to write music and lyrics that were well respected. He had an almost spiritual touch in his writing. Deep undertones that would draw emotion and dig into the psyche. His positiveness was uplifting and motivating. Yet, he could handle a challenge by shooting a look that cut through the crap like a sword slicing a peach.

Duke had originally hired Strays as a lyricist when he was very young. Strays had come up with things from his tune "Lush Life" like ". . . those come what may places where one relaxes on the axis of the wheel of life to get the feel of life from jazz and cocktails . . ." He was so clever. He had outdistanced most everybody in the field of lyricism.

Then Duke found out that he was a great arranger and composer. Strays was loaded with ideas. So Duke gave him complete freedom to explore his super intelligence and talent.

Strays was a man who lived the most unique life style of anybody. He had no bills: no hotel bills, no apartment bills, no food bills, no clothes or tax bills. No nothing. He didn't have a salary, either. He just signed a tab. Duke paid for everything.

If Strays decided that he wanted to go to Paris and have breakfast, he'd just get on a plane—fly to Paris and have breakfast and come back. Then go wherever else he wanted to go. Just signing and using his credit card. And Duke paid for it all. If he needed some pocket change, he'd write himself a check, cash it, and have some cash in his pocket.

Strays' tunes "Take the A Train" and "Lush Life" later became classics. We all admired the chord changes and moods of his work. He'd always ask, "Did you *enjoy* your part?"

It was as though their partnership was made in heaven. Although they rarely communicated directly on the bandstand or in the studio, they understood each other. Like they could read each other's minds. They complemented each other even when they disagreed.

Strays told me that Duke was doing a movie soundtrack, which we recorded, for *Anatomy of a Murder* with Jimmy Stewart and Lee Remick. Duke was writing in Hollywood in a hotel suite and Strays was in New

York. One day, Duke called Strays up. He said, "Sweet Pea, I'm in the middle of a problem here. Maybe you can help me. I'm at the point where I have a choice of going 1-3-5-7 or 5-3-2-1."

So Strays pondered a moment. Then he replied, "Well, Edward, you're better at this than I am." There was silence. Finally, Strays said, "I'd go 1-3-5."

They hung up, and Duke went the opposite direction.

35. Endurances

When it came time for handling chaos, Duke knew exactly what to do. I remember one time when we were on a bus tour and Oscar Pettiford—God bless him!—was in a rage. Oscar was one of Duke's bass players. Great bassist! So, Oscar was walking down the aisle raising an uproar. When the bus stopped, he moved off into the forest, shouting, "I'm an Indian! I understand the wolves and the animals of the forest. They *talk* to me."

It was fifteen or twenty minutes before we could locate him, capture him, and bring him back. But when he was on the bus again, he was still raging. He wanted to talk to anyone and everyone about anything and everything. So he picked Duke.

It was one of those rare occasions when Duke was riding on the bus, up front, instead of riding in Harry's Chrysler. We were going through some serious mountains and Duke liked to be with a bunch of people when hazardous trips surfaced.

So Oscar walked up to him. He said, "Duke, you so-and-so, I want you to know one thing, blah, blah, blah . . ."

One word led to another, but Duke tried to cool him down. With a calm voice, Duke said, "Yeah, man. Solid. Yeah. Crazy."

Oscar got violent and took up the subject of money.

Duke said, "I don't want to hear all this! Talk to Al Celley. He's hired to take this grief *off* me."

Oscar became even more furious because he couldn't understand why, if he worked for Duke, he couldn't talk to Duke about what he wanted to talk about, which happened at this point to be money.

So Duke closed his eyes and went to sleep. Just like that! He was phenomenal at being able to exclude himself when he wanted.

Then there were times when he had to fire people, like the time when Ben Webster slapped him. I never found out what happened between them.

Or like the time when we were playing in the Apollo Theater.

After every show, Mingus would take his bass upstairs to the dressing room and practice. Charles Mingus was another member of Duke's bass player roster. Hell of a bassist! It so happened that Mingus, Tizol, and I were in the dressing room after the first alert had sounded for the next show. We were the last ones in the dressing room. I called Tizol "Juanito." So, Juanito pulled out a piece of music. Since Mingus had his bass there, he said, "Charles, play this for me."

So Mingus played it. "Bing, bing, bing." And at one spot on the music, he played an A-natural.

Juanito told him, "Charles, that's an A-flat. Not an A-natural."

So Mingus said, "It's an A-natural, man. I'm looking at it. I can read *music*."

Juanito said, "Well, it's Duke's music and I know that it's an A-flat!"

Mingus said, "Don't tell me how to play my music. I know an A-natural when I see one!"

So one word led to another and the anger mounted on both sides. Mingus reached up to grab an emergency fire ax off the wall. Then he drew back to swing the ax at Juanito, and Juan pulled out his Cuban frog sticker, pushed the button, *bling!* A six-inch blade jumped out.

In the midst of this ax in the air and the frog sticker about to be used, I didn't have anything to protect myself. I grabbed Juan's frog sticker hand and Mingus' ax-wielding hand—he had the bass in the other. I said, "All right, both you motherfuckers! Cool it!" It took all my strength to keep them from killing each other.

Just then, from the wings, there came a voice: "All on."

Finally, Tizol walked off toward the stairs. Then Mingus grabbed his bass and he and I headed for the stage, too.

That wasn't the only time Mingus had a scrap, but I was glad that I'd been there to cool things off. The show went on as usual. Afterward, Duke told Celley to pay Mingus off, and he called Oscar Pettiford for the next show that night. When Oscar came, he was laughing as usual, "Ha, ha, ha." Maybe he was laughing about the time he'd cold-cocked Mingus in Birdland. I don't know. But what I do know is that when he took Mingus' place in the show, the show didn't suffer a bit.

Of course, Duke had to deal with racism, like all of us. Like the time when we were at the Flamingo in Las Vegas. The sign said, "No Coloreds, Whites Only." We entered through the kitchen each night, being told, "No fraternizing with patrons. Stay in your dressing rooms between sets." If we wanted to have any fun, we had to go over to the colored section of town, to a gambling joint where there were brown-skinned beauties, crap games, and the only swimming pool in town for us, which we nicknamed the Inkwell. The maître d' was Joe Louis, the ex-champion boxer.

Then there was the time in Texas when the band received an invitation to come to an after-hours joint. Duke accepted and, naturally, his limousine came early. Before the rest of us could get over there, Duke had already been busted for patronizing an illegal after-hours joint. Out of all the people who were there, the police arrested Duke just to embarrass him. To add insult to injury, the next day the local paper had a *big* picture of Duke being put into the Black Moriah—a nickname for a hearse but our nickname for the paddywagon.

When Duke was released, nothing was discussed. He hit his pace without missing a stride.

On that same tour, Tony Scott was with the band. He was a Caucasian clarinetist who had loved to play Ben Webster's book. While he was following his dream, we were suffering all sorts of indignities in the South that he never knew existed. In those days, there were no toilets on the buses, so we had to go into towns and go into the Greyhound or Trailways bus stations for relief stops. Otherwise, we had to stop along the roadside, which was dangerous down South, since the police could have busted us for indecent exposure.

Tony was totally flabbergasted when he discovered that bus stations had a white waiting room and a colored waiting room. All of us were on the colored side, with only Tony on the white side. A little partition divided us. He'd say, "Hey, man! How does the water from the colored fountain taste? This 'white' water tastes like shit!"

On one of the infamous Southern trips, we were playing a one-nighter in Dothan, Alabama—Joe Louis' hometown. We were setting up the bandstand in this huge dancehall. Sometimes at venues like that, white people sat in the balcony while the colored people danced, and then they would switch. But in this particular place, a rope separated the white dance area from the colored area. Bobby Boyd was our band boy. He was setting up the music stands, and the musicians were joking around. A couple of cops walked up to Louie Bellson—we called him "Skoonje"—who was busy putting his drums together.

One of the cops grabbed him and said, "Hey! We don't allow no fraternizing around here!"

Skoonje said, "What do you mean, fraternizing? I'm getting ready to *work*."

The cop said, "You playin' with this band?"

Skoonje said, "Yes."

The cop said, "I told you, we don't allow no fraternizing. No whites playing with niggers!"

Skoonje said, "I'm Haitian." Which was a lie.

So the cops looked at each other and scratched their heads, while Skoonje kept putting his drums together.

Skoonje said that the ten or twelve minutes that it took him to put his drums together seemed like hours, because they kept their eyes on him, watching him like two hawks. He was sweating up a storm. He knew the shit could hit the fan at any moment.

Then Skoonje said, "Bobby! Where's my motherfuckin' goddam drumsticks?"

The cops looked at each other and smiled like they finally believed him.

We all hated racism and being stereotyped. But we had to contain our resentment. There were all sorts of uprisings and killings happening around the country. It was horrible, enough to make you want to do something drastic. Although we were all armed to protect ourselves, we never encountered a bloody incident.

While I was with Duke, I figured the best way for me to support the civil rights movement was to keep praying and participate. So whenever I was invited to be a guest artist, I'd go to the fund-raisers for the movement if Duke's band wasn't gigging and I'd play for free. I wore a dashiki and an afro at those performances. People who were active in the movement wore garments and hairstyles like that to let everyone know that we were involved.

There is a saying that money is the root of all evil. But I believed that the *lack* of money was the root of all evil. I wanted to help the movement have the necessary money to eradicate the evil of racism. So, even if I was dog tired from recording, gigging, and trying to do my best as a husband, I played benefits for them.

Each year the Congress for Racial Equality, or CORE, had a fund-raiser at Jackie Robinson's house in Connecticut, and these were very successful. I was proud to wear the equality pin representing our efforts. Jackie was a famous baseball player who had certainly suffered his share of bigotry. In spite of the racism scene, his career was amazing. He was the first Negro in major league baseball, breaking the color barrier that had existed for fifty years. In his rookie year, he was chosen Most Valuable Player. And those were only *part* of his great accomplishments.

We all loved Jackie. He was a great cat and he had a hell of a house.

Private lake, horses. Huge trophy room of baseball bats, balls, caps, and uniforms. And a lot more. So it was a great place to raise money and hob-nob. Martin Luther King and other great leaders were there sometimes, and I felt proud to be a part of it all.

There were lots of other fund-raisers, celebrations, and special events that I played for free. It wasn't easy to fit these into my hectic schedule, but it was the least I could do.

And believe me, my schedule was *packed*. I could handle it most of the time. But the only thing about constantly traveling on tours with Duke, was missing home and family. I did pretty well. But sometimes it really got to me.

36. Flugelhorn

Being away from Pauline was a drag on both of us. But she knew I had to keep going. By this time, she'd quit her job at the hospital in St. Louis and moved in with me in my hotel room in Manhattan. It was a little cramped, so I got us a small apartment.

She was pretty cool with the situation—especially since she'd met some of the other "jazz wives" and had gotten involved in some of the charities they supported. She wanted to get a job, but I told her I didn't want her to work because I was making enough to take care of us. Plus, I wanted her to be available if situations came up where I could send for her to meet me—gigs with longer stints or places I thought she'd enjoy.

Sometimes she rode with me on the bus, but not too often. She wasn't too comfortable with the way the cats carried on, gambling, cussing, drinking, joking around.

I was rarely gone for more than two or three weeks at a time, maybe four or five, because Duke's band was based primarily out of New York. I was really glad that she understood that I had to go and play. I couldn't sit around and just be a *husband*.

To make up for being gone so much, I showered her with gifts or paid for her to go back to St. Louis for visits. That cooled things out some, but she knew how things would be before she moved to New York. I had to get out and play my music, and if my work took me away for periods of time, then that was the bottom line!

After a while, Strays pulled some strings for me and hooked me up with some influential connections so I could try to get approved by a co-op board for a brand new apartment in Queens. The building was named in honor of a famous black navy hero who had received the Navy Cross back in '42. The Dorie Miller was a real nice building with a board composed of some of the residents. They had to vote "yea or nay" for anybody who wanted to live there. I was praying hard.

When word came down that I was approved, I was thrilled. Thanks to my man, Strays! Now, Pauline and I had a nice roomy apartment in a hip setting—trees, close to a bus stop, less traffic and noise, a slower pace. We fixed it up with some hip furniture, had friends over. Things were looking good.

The best part of the whole scene was that folks from the jazz scene lived in the area, most within walking distance. Man! You had Jimmy Rushing, Ella Fitzgerald, Dizzy Gillespie, and Louis "Pops" Armstrong. A slew of musicians.

And you *know* that I checked Pops out. Most times I'd go alone. But sometimes, whenever Diz and I were in town at the same time, we'd meet up and head over to Pops' house together. Real nice pad. We'd sit up in there with Pops and listen to some of his wild stories and crack up! And man, he could tell some stories! You'd better believe it! All about his episodes of being on the road—the music, the musicians, the women. He *was* the history of jazz—in person! We couldn't get enough. Hated to leave. Now, he never gave us any lessons or anything like that; he just liked to talk and laugh. He was into herbs and health food. And he damn sure loved Swiss Kriss, which was a laxative. He used to say, "Leave it all behind, daddy." Great advice, man.

Our new neighborhood was all the rage. Pauline loved the whole scene, but I knew she missed me a lot when I was on the road. Still, it had to be that way.

Meanwhile, I had some great things going on in addition to the incredible music I was a part of with Duke's orchestra. A long time before, I'd fallen in love with the plush sounds and fat pulsations of the flugelhorns in Lunceford's band. I'd tried for years to get that intimate sound—covering the bell of my trumpet with a felt hat, cutting the plug out of a plunger, using various mutes and mouthpieces. Nothing worked.

We were doing a gig in Chicago at Frank Holzfeind's Blue Note in '57 in the Loop. We'd been gigging there for a while, and I was staying on the south side with my old friend Sykes Smith. Since I was advertising for the Selmer Instrument Company at that time, Sykes and I used to go over on Saturdays to Gary, Indiana, which was his hometown and the home of Selmer.

I had a good buddy there named Keith Ecker. He was the technical advisor for brass with Selmer, and we'd talk about my love for the sounds of the flugelhorn. Although a few guys were fooling around with flugelhorns at that time, like Shorty Rogers and Emmett Berry—and Miles, too, who named his "Fat Girl"—I didn't think they were using the instrument to its fullest potential. They'd use a trumpet mouthpiece so they could play more in the upper register. Instead of doing that, I wanted to go back to that old mellow sound that I used to hear.

Miles and I talked about the horn's potential. But he wasn't digging what I had to say. All he wanted, as far as the flugelhorn was concerned, was for me to fix his valves to be faster. I had a special procedure of twisting the springs and other things. He used to say, "Hey, man. You wanna take my Fat Girl home tonight?" After I did my thing to his horn and brought it back to him, I continued talking about how great the flugelhorn's sound was. How it should be more respected and used more often in our music. Still, he couldn't dig it at that time.

So one day at Keith's house in Gary, he and I sat down and we drank some of his dad's homemade red wine. We were talking, drinking. and fondling a whole bunch of brass fixtures, like lengths of tubing for the lead pipe and receivers. Curvatures, apertures, fittings, pistons, pumps, portholes, matchings. We tried all sorts of combinations, like different mouthpieces and bends of the pipes. Finally, we came up with a sort of rehash of a "good ol'" flugelhorn. It was really close to what I'd been wanting for years. Later, Keith sent it over to Paris where the Selmer factory tested it, gold-plated it, then sent it back to me at Sykes' home.

It was November '57. I was at a recording session for Billy Taylor, unaware that the horn had arrived. Billy was making an album entitled *Taylor Made Jazz*, using the entire Ellington Band with the exception of Duke. We were in downtown Chicago at Universal Studios taking a break when Sykes walked in with the horn. We opened the case and I took out this beautiful golden horn. When I blew that horn, I closed my eyes and thanked God!

I played a couple of warm-up riffs. Some intervals and some fast passages. That smooth, fat sound floated into the air. It got all down in my *soul*. It was more than love at first sight, it was the climax of a dream!

Billy came over and tilted his head toward the bell. He asked me to use it in the session, and I did. While I played, I was thinking about all the things I wanted to learn about it. How I wanted the whole world to hear it.

That night, I took it with me to the club and Duke welcomed it. Later, he wrote a tune for me entitled "Juniflip on the Flugelhorn." He had never written anything especially for me before then. I felt extremely honored. Even though I never found out what "Juniflip" meant, it was still the greatest thrill to know that he liked that mellow sound enough to compose something.

I told Keith all about the tune. Told him that I'd checked out everything on the horn, and it was A-okay. After that, Selmer began producing them. I had the first one off the line. I stayed with the company for a long, long time.

Eventually, I went over to the Olds Company and worked with a crew there for a couple of years. We developed an improved flugelhorn. They called it the "CT Model." We developed a trumpet as well, also with my initials on it. But then things took a dive. I was devastated when I learned that as soon as we'd built up a backlog of several hundred orders, the company went kaput. Then the worst thing of all happened: I was told that the owners had separated and spoiled all the tools and dies so that no one would ever be able to put that same horn together. I felt like somebody had dropped an anvil on my dream! Wham!

At least I had a few CT Models to hold on to, and I guarded them with my life. I'd learned a long time before that even when there's nothing you can do about a situation, you can't let that stop you. You gotta keep on keepin' on! So that's what I did. I kept on playing my blues away, just like I'd done when I was a boy in St. Louis, dreaming about playing all over the world.

I'd still never been overseas, but those dreams were about to come true, too.

37. Europe

Duke was uncomfortable with flying. So when he told us that we were going overseas on the *Île de France* in '58, I thought, My first time to Europe and I'll be riding on peaceful waters in a beautiful cruise ship— now, *that's* the way to travel! I was also ready to play my new flugelhorn, determined to introduce more people to that mellow sound and, hopefully, give them some appreciation and respect for it.

Duke knew that I was a crusader for the flugelhorn. Not only did he write a tune about it for me, but years later, in '73, he wrote about it in his autobiography, on page 230: "When a trumpet player imitates Louis Armstrong, Louis gets the credit. When a trumpet player decides that his style is to be built on Dizzy Gillespie's, Dizzy gets the credit. The same thing with those saxophone players who copied Coleman Hawkins and Charlie Parker. But today, although I hear a whole new world of flugelhorn stylists formed behind Clark Terry, I hear none of the prime authorities on the subject say, 'Clark Terry did this sixteen years ago.' If this is not recognized soon, he could grow up to be the Barzillai Lew of the flugelhorn."

I was speechless when I read that! Although I didn't know who Barzillai was, I was told that Duke had written a composition for him, which his band played on the radio in '42 and '43. He must have really thought a lot of this cat.

Eventually I found out, first of all, how to say his name: BAR-zeal-ya. I also found out that he was born a free black man in 1743. He was a cooper by trade, and he was also a musician who played a fife and drums. He must have been a pretty smart guy, because when he decided that he wanted to marry a woman who was born a slave, he bought her freedom. Paid something like twenty-eight grand for her! That was a lot of money back then *and* today. He was also a soldier who fought in the American Revolution back in 1775. From what I could gather, Barzillai boosted the morale of the soldiers by playing his fife when they were fighting the British at Bunker Hill. This helped the Americans succeed, and he got great reviews from the "higher-ups." Today, his powder horn is a treasure on display at the DuSable Museum of African American History in Chicago.

But I didn't know any of this on that ship back in '58. I just knew that I was on a mission with my flugelhorn.

Before we had gotten too far from port, we found out that Fats Ford had missed the embarkation. So he and his wife rode a tug boat out to the ship, where somebody threw a rope ladder over the side. Then Fats and his wife had to climb up that treacherous thing. We nearly died laughing watching the two of them. The ladder was swinging back and forth and they were holding on for dear life. He was below her, looking up at her butt and looking down at the choppy water, climbing that flimsy contraption. The cats were all leaning over the rail watching them and cracking up! Funny as it was, I knew then that I'd always be early when it came time to getting on a boat because I didn't want to have the cats laughing at *me* like that.

That cruise was so great that I decided to get some cats together and play for the crew down in the belly of the ship. It was more fun than playing for the passengers because the crew dug the shit out of us. It was a special treat for them, since they were usually working and didn't have a chance to hear the musicians playing.

Things were great until we got to England, when I had to deal with the foreign currency scene. I'd heard about the trouble that Sonny Greer had with the English pound. It was equivalent to five dollars, which is why it was nicknamed "American five dollars." Well, Sonny thought one pound was the same as one dollar. All over France, he wondered why the bellmen and waiters jumped over Duke to get to him. He was tipping with pounds like they were dollar bills. He thought he was giving dollar tips but he was dropping five dollars each time.

We went on tour in several countries, and here I was dealing with pounds, marks, kroner, guilders, lire, and a whole slew of other bills. All different sizes, shapes, colors, and denominations. A thousand lire in Italy wasn't much, but a thousand pounds in England was. I didn't want to do a Sonny Greer, so I was dividing, multiplying, adding, and subtracting like crazy. I even bought one of those special calculators for conversions. And each time I needed to change the currency from one country to the next, I had to pay a conversion fee. It was a nightmare.

Today they have the euro. Instead of many different kinds of money, they have the same currency for a bunch of the countries over there. A lot of the citizens fought against giving up their individual currency. They said it took away their identity, their national pride. But the law was passed anyway, and even though I can understand both sides, it is less confusing.

Our accommodations in Europe were far superior to those in the States. It wasn't like staying in mediocre hotels or at the homes of Mrs. Jones, Mrs. Green, or Mrs. Smith down south, even though those women had always been quite cordial. In Europe, we stayed in three-star hotels or better. Great food, great service, nice beds. I understood why a lot of jazz musicians had become expatriates.

On top of that, the European audiences were far more appreciative of jazz than Americans. They respected jazz the way Americans respected classical music. Overseas, they loved to hear jazz played by American musicians who were the composers, recording artists, or performers of jazz. They said that Europe had made a major contribution in the world of art, but jazz was created in America. We were the original musicians, the creators. They made us feel so good that I started thinking about moving there myself.

Back home, audiences were accustomed to too much, for too little, too often. They liked the package deal, like "The Big Show." Merchants who put shows together like that ruined the whole scene, because when Americans went to see Duke Ellington and His Orchestra, they would expect to see other acts, too—like Count Basie, Ella Fitzgerald, Woody Herman.

But in Europe, the audiences felt fortunate to see just one orchestra.

They truly loved jazz. They knew that we'd come from far away to perform for them. Man, they cheered for us and gave us long standing ovations. They clapped their hands and stomped their feet and yelled for encores. "More, more, more, more, more!" they'd yell, until we had to come back on stage and play another number or two.

It was great. And the ladies. Wow! They were beautiful. All over us. There wasn't all that racism like back home. You didn't have to risk getting killed over some blonde. Of course, since I was married, I just looked . . .

We played in nice clubs and concert halls. And the people were real friendly. Lots of smiling faces and cameras flashing. We could really stretch out and play our best.

Everywhere we went, I played my trumpet and my flugelhorn, and I got a lot of compliments on my new horn. Whenever Duke kicked off "Juniflip on the Flugelhorn," you can imagine how good I felt!

38. Norman Granz

While I was with Duke, Norman Granz booked gigs for us whenever the orchestra was off for a while. That kept us busy, kept money in our pockets, and kept us doing our favorite thing—playing jazz.

Norman was one of the most important people in the world of jazz. He did more to escalate the respect level of jazz and raise our salaries than anybody else. He absolutely loved jazz and jazz musicians. He managed Basie, Dizzy, Ella Fitzgerald, Oscar Peterson, Coleman Hawkins, Zoot Sims, Eddie "Lockjaw" Davis, Harry "Sweets" Edison, Roy Eldridge, Charlie Shavers, Louie Bellson, Lester "Prez" Young, Johnny Hodges, Ray Brown, and a slew of others.

Norman was also one of Duke's great jazz associates, and from time to time he traveled with us. He was a real nice cat, Jewish, a few years older than me. A real smooth persuader, and he never cussed.

When we were talking about heading off on another cruise, he encouraged Duke to fly instead. Showed him on paper where the buck falls. Made Duke realize how much money he'd lose if we continued to travel by boat. Norman said, "Flying is faster. The ship takes a week over and a week back. You've lost two weeks just traveling. Or you fly today, do a concert, then fly back home the next day."

So Duke took his advice. And we were on a flight together, when a man walked out of the cockpit to go to the restroom. I was sitting across the aisle two rows behind Duke and Norman.

Duke looked at the gold braids on the shoulders of the man passing by, and he turned to Norman. "Who is that?" he asked.

Norman said, "That's the captain."

"Well, who's flying the plane?"

"It's probably on auto-pilot."

Duke slumped down in his seat and pulled out his prayer beads. Norman was chuckling, but I wasn't. If I'd had some prayer beads, I would have pulled them out, too.

It was Oscar Peterson who gave Norman the affectionate moniker "Smedley," saying that Norman's profile reminded him of a British butler named Smedley. A few select cats like O.P., Ray Brown, and me called him that. But only in private settings.

Norman called Ray Brown "Ice Cream" sometimes, because Ray often wore a white suit that, Norman said, made him look like the Good Humor ice cream man.

Ray, O.P., and I, meanwhile, all referred to each other as "Bogen." This was taken from a syndicated comic strip called *Smoky Stover*, which featured a fire chief named Chief Bogen. After a particularly hot solo we'd say to each other, "Man, you played hotter than Chief Bogen. You should've worn an asbestos suit!"

Norman always called me Clark, and he referred to Oscar as O.P., like I did.

Ray, on bass, and O.P., on piano, man, they were extraordinary musicians. All they needed was to add a good drummer and you'd have the greatest rhythm section in the world. They were both serious musicians and their timing was impeccable.

We all loved each other very much. We were like a family. This meant a lot to me, being on the road most of the time. It helped my loneliness for Pauline and the rest of my family, who by this time had multiplied and scattered to various parts of the world. My sister Lillian—or Lil as we all called her—had passed, and her son, Donald, had moved to Sweden. Margueritte, Juanita, and Ada Mae were in Detroit. Mattie, Marie, Odessa, Ed, and Bus were still in St. Louis, and Hiawatha was there too. I missed them all, but being close to Norman and a lot of the jazz cats kept me going.

Norman and Pablo Picasso were friends. Norman had quite an extensive art collection, and he loaned some of his pieces to the Louvre and other renowned museums. He even named his company after Picasso—Pablo

Records. Because I loved art, I admired the fact that Picasso was one of Norman's associates. To see the two of them hanging out together was a real treat for me. Picasso did a sketch of Norman sitting at a bar, which in later years was worth a lot—close to a million dollars. I fooled around with cartoons and sketches too, sometimes on my band music or on manuscript paper—like one time, when I drew a "masterpiece" of Harry Carney's feet. It wasn't worth a million dollars, but it was fun to me.

Eventually, the lie I'd told Basie came back to haunt me when Norman booked a Jazz at the Philharmonic tour, known as J.A.T.P. It included me and a whole bunch of other cats, and Basie, too. When I saw him again he welcomed me like nothing had happened. Seeing the smile on his face and knowing that I'd lied to him made me feel as small as a cork in the ocean. I said, "Basie, I wasn't honest with you when I left. I told you I was sick, but I really just wanted to join Duke's band."

He laughed and said, "I know. Why do you think I took that raise out of your last check?"

All of a sudden, I felt like a big weight had been lifted off my heart. As we laughed and reminisced, I promised myself again that, no matter what, I'd never tell another lie like that.

When I was around Norman, working or just hanging out, he made me feel proud of being on his team. I loved how he lifted jazz musicians up from the norm to the upper echelon. Referring to us as "First Place," he made sure that we stayed in the finest hotels and ate the best food. He went out of his way to make us happy. Everybody got top-class attention. If things didn't go right, Norman would quickly rise to the occasion. He was on top of everything.

And when it came to serious problems, he stepped right up to the plate and definitely took care of business. As happened in Germany.

39. Norman's Battles

On one of Norman's J.A.T.P. tours in Europe, I can't remember the year, we got off the plane in Germany—two busloads of us—and went immediately to the venue, which was a big tent the size of a baseball park. A common type of setup in Germany. It was close to a few hours before performance, and we just had time to dress.

Norman asked the impresario, "Where's Miss Fitzgerald's dressing room?"

The man laughed and pointed toward the buses. He said, "You got two dressing rooms there."

Norman said, "You don't understand. We have a tour, an entourage of mostly men. Miss Fitzgerald is a lady and she is the headliner of our show, as you can see on your marquee—Ella Fitzgerald, Count Basie, and all the rest up there. So Miss Fitzgerald has to have a dressing room."

The man said, "Well, she doesn't have one. She can dress on the bus like everybody else."

Norman said, "Oh, you don't have a dressing room for Miss Fitzgerald?"

The man said, "No, we don't."

Norman said, "Then you don't have a concert!"

The man laughed and said, "You're kidding. We've got eighty-five thousand people out there."

Norman said, "Well, you're going to have to refund eighty-five thousand tickets."

The man said, "You can't do this! I'll sue you!"

Norman said, "That's exactly what I want you to do. But before you do, I want you to look down in the lower left-hand corner of your contract and you'll see it stipulates that Miss Fitzgerald has to have a dressing room. So sue me. I'll hear from your lawyer and you'll hear from mine."

Norman told us that the gig was off. We got back on the buses and went to a famous Indonesian restaurant a few miles away. We ate and drank all night long, *and* we got paid.

Norman's J.A.T.P. tours were extensive, as I learned over the next four decades doing gigs for him. Some of the places we toured were Norway, Sweden, France, Italy, Switzerland, Spain, Holland. In the United States we played at the Hollywood Bowl in Los Angeles, Carnegie Hall in New York, Keil Auditorium in St. Louis, the Civic Opera House in Chicago, Oakland Auditorium in Oakland, and a whole bunch more. All top shelf.

There were a bunch of cats who wanted to be on Norman's team. On one particular occasion, we were playing the Hollywood Bowl and a well-established musician came up and grabbed Norman's collar and started shaking him. The guy said, "Why do you always hire all of these old motherfuckers like Coleman, Vic Dickenson, Illinois Jacquet, Clark Terry, Zoot Sims, Dizzy Gillespie. and Lockjaw? Why don't you give a young blowing cat like me a chance?"

Norman looked at me and said, "What's wrong with this Tommy Tucker?" That was his way of saying MF. That was as close to cussing as Norman got. I never heard him use one curse word. Ever.

He didn't let the tirade upset him, and eventually the kid walked away. I guessed that cat never learned the lesson "You can catch more flies with sugar than with shit."

Norman had a lot of crap to deal with—attitude from musicians who weren't on his team, perils of travel with lost luggage or missing passports, men who became ill, and racial prejudice, especially since he was a Caucasian and a promoter of black musicians. But no matter what was thrown in his face, he never cussed and he always took affirmative action.

Talking about racism, I remember another incident that happened many years later. Way later—after I'd left Duke's orchestra. It was in 1981 when I had some time between gigs. Norman and I were talking, and he brought up my first recording date with Cleanhead Vinson back in '45, how I had backed Cleanhead up while he sang "Railroad Porter Blues" and "Kidney Stew." So Norman thought it would be a good idea to set up a record date with Cleanhead backing me up, just for fun and to celebrate my first recording date.

Norman got things organized and set up the recording date in Marina Del Rey, California, with Art Hillery on piano, John Heard on bass, Ron McCurdy on drums, George "Harmonica" Smith on harmonica, and Cleanhead on alto sax and vocals—with me featured on trumpet. Norman said that he had chosen the title "Yes, the Blues" for the album.

Before I could get to the gig, racism reared its ugly head. When I arrived at the hotel near the studio where Norman had made a reservation for me, I went to the front desk. The desk clerk said, "We don't have any more rooms."

I said, "Well, Mr. Norman Granz made a reservation for me."

He looked through his book, then said, "Well, we don't have anything like that."

I wanted to deck him, but I knew that wasn't smart.

A Mexican doorman witnessed the whole thing. When I left the desk, he told me, "This kind of thing happens all the time. Why don't you go across the street. It's a better hotel and I'm sure you can get the accommodation you want."

When I arrived at the studio, late, I told Norman what had happened. He said, "I'll take care of that Maryland Farmer." That was another one of Norman's ways of saying "MF" the clean way.

I don't know what he did. He probably sued the hotel—he was famous for lawsuits. He usually won his cases because he had the bread to hire top lawyers, and he didn't take on anything that he couldn't win.

During the recording date, Norman said, "Play one of your original blues, and don't name it. I have a title for it." I did, and he called it, "Marina Bay Rednecks."

Another reason that I loved working with Norman was that he liked to use some of my ideas, and he asked for my help from time to time. I remember one of Norman's recording dates in 1976—*Basie Jam 2*—with Basie, Benny Carter, Al Grey, Eddie "Lockjaw" Davis, Joe Pass, John Heard, and Louis Bellson. They all entered the studio with egotistical attitudes, like "Okay, you called us. So here we are." There was no written music and no one was thinking about what we were going to play. So we wasted almost an hour just lollygagging. Then Norman called me into the control booth. He said, "Hey, why don't you go out there and just start something. Anything that you think might be befitting, and tell them that it's the first number."

I went back out and said to Basie, "Holy, do you remember how we used to make up lyrics to your solos a long time ago?" Then I sang, "Neighbor, keep those bitches quiet. Disturbing my peace . . ." This was a tune we'd clowned around on while Basie was playing one of his famous solos. The whole band used to sing it except for Basie. The audience couldn't really hear us, but Basie could. He remembered it, so I ran it down. Basie laughed; then the cats played it.

Everybody was happy. Basie said, "You got any more like that?"

So I started thinking about some other old Basie band jargons, like "Yo' mammy don't wear no draws." We used to sing that just for laughs, to break the monotony. I remembered the riff that had sparked that line and kicked it off. Everybody joined in, and we stretched it out and made a blues out of it. After we played it, Norman liked it and all the cats liked it, but Norman changed the title to "Mama Don't Wear No Drawers."

The only problem Norman and I ever had was about the fact that he didn't like my flugelhorn. He liked a powerful sound and aggressive playing, and the flugelhorn was just the opposite. It just wasn't blatant enough for him.

So Norman paid a cat to steal my flugelhorn, but I caught on to the situation and I didn't let that horn out of my sight. The thief got mad at me because I'd spoiled his gig to steal my horn. I don't know if Norman still paid him or whatever, but later on Norman and I both laughed about the whole scene because after *that*, I really understood that Norman was just a trumpet lover from his heart. He'd loved trumpet players for a long time—cats like Roy Eldridge, Louis Armstrong. Same legendary cats that we all loved.

On one of Norman's tours in Europe with Diz, Roy, Sweets, and me,

Norman said, "This is called 'The Trumpet Kings,' not 'The Funny Horn Kings,' so leave that funny horn at home." Now, I truly loved my flugelhorn and I still felt a little sad that Norman didn't. But I'd learned a long time before that everything just ain't for everybody. I respected his feelings, and I knew that I'd play my flugelhorn on other gigs. So I didn't bring it. One of the few times in my career.

The tour was successful, and at the end when we were in Zurich, Norman caught me when no one else was around. He said, "I want to office with you." This was his terminology for paying us. He counted off a fistful of money and handed it to me. Twice as much as I would have hoped for. (We never asked Norman what he was paying; we knew he'd pay more than anyone else.) Then he said, "Now, just to prove to you how satisfied I was by your leaving that funny horn at home, here's a token of my appreciation," and he handed me more money.

I counted it after he'd walked away, thinking that it was probably enough to buy some champagne or something. I was shocked when I saw that the bonus money was a *grand* more. A thousand dollars!

Just as I was wondering why so much, he whirled around and came back up to me. He said, "How much bonus did I just give you?"

I said, "Yeah, I know, you made a mistake. You gave me an extra thousand dollars."

He looked at me and said, "Yes, I did make a mistake. I intended to give you two." Then he counted out another thousand and handed it to me. I stood there with my mouth hanging open.

His production at the 1977 Montreux Jazz Festival in Switzerland was a classic. We were doing a set with trumpets. Diz and I happened to have a number with a rhythm section of Oscar Peterson on piano, Niels Pedersen on bass, and Bobby Durham on drums. On the last tune of the set, a *very* up-tempo number, Diz and I gave it our all. We were sweating up a storm. It was one of those rare nights when everything is right and you can play from your soul. It was powerful! We traded fours and some choruses. Diz played some awesome shit, then I played. Meanwhile, Oscar was playing some mean keys, Bobby was swinging his ass off, and Niels was plucking the strings like there was no tomorrow. It was a really hot set. Unforgettable.

When we finished and everybody went to the lounge to relax, Basie was sitting near the video monitor enjoying a drink. As Diz and I passed by, he said, "Ali and Frazier."

When I looked at the videotape later, I understood why he said that. The way Diz and I went back and forth with our horns, it was like we were slugging it out in a boxing ring. I loved it. Everybody did. Norman named the video *Improvisation,* and it's one of my all-time favorites.

Norman was a great guy and a great businessman. He made my years in Duke's band even better. But by the time '59 rolled around, I was thinking more and more about having my own band and doing my own thing. I wondered how much longer I would stay with Duke. And based on how bad I'd felt about lying to Basie, I knew that when the time came for me to move on, I'd look Duke straight in the eyes and tell him the truth.

And that time was coming up fast.

40. Q

When the time comes for change, you can feel it. I knew that I wasn't like Paul Gonsalves, wanting to stay in Duke's band until my dying day. Although Duke never had to get a sub for me during the entire eight years I was with his band, I was ready to move on.

So when Quincy Jones called and offered me a position as straw boss—a kind of assistant music director—for a hot new show he'd gotten involved with, and told me how he had gotten top-notch musicians and that the gig would pay a whopping salary of $350 a week, I was gassed!

He had come a long way from our days together in Seattle when I'd given him early-morning trumpet lessons, to now offering me $140 more per week than my salary with Duke. He was organizing a dream band for an international show based on a Harold Arlen musical that was slated to debut eventually on Broadway. And Q was only twenty-six years old. I'd kept up with his career, and we'd recorded a few albums together over the years—*Birth of a Band* and *Around the World*—but never in my wildest dreams did I ever think that the skinny boy I'd taught a while back would be offering me a reason to leave Duke Ellington.

The opportunity that Q was offering me to be the straw boss was the first like it since my days with George Hudson, when I rehearsed and stylized George's band.

I didn't have to think long about this opportunity, even though I was getting ready to do another European tour with Duke. At first Duke was upset when I gave my notice. He said, "You *have* to go to Europe with us."

I said, "I don't think it's necessary."

He said, "Well, you have to go."

I said, "I can get you a trumpet player for less than half of what you're going to pay me."

He said, "Yes, but it's not you!"

I said, "Well, maestro, if you want me to go, you're going to have to give me four hundred and fifty dollars a week."

He said, "You drive a hard bargain."

Finally, we agreed that I'd stay on and go to Paris, but that would be it.

After the Paris gig I went to him again and told him I was leaving. He said, "So, where are you going?"

I said, "Well, I've gotten a small group together and I'm opening at a little club on the Rive Gauche called Chat Qui Pêche, until Q gets the cats here."

He said, "Okay, I'll come down and see you."

It was a famous club down in an old wine cellar. Just a small little joint, but very popular. Owned by a lady named Madame Ricard. She was beautiful but very cantankerous. The name of the club meant "Fishing Cat." It was in the neighborhood of Notre Dame, and when I walked to work I was scared that I'd see the Hunchback of Notre Dame. Thank God I never did.

On our opening night I had Sahib Shihab on sax, Alice McLeod on piano, Oscar Pettiford on bass, and me on trumpet and flugelhorn; I can't remember who the drummer was. Duke came down into that wine hole with a big party and wished me well. His party almost filled up the little room. It felt good to have Duke's encouragement.

I really loved him and I was going to miss him and the cats, like John Sanders, who was one of the sweetest cats in the world. He went on in later years to become a priest. I'd miss all the cats. Jimmy Woode, Rick Henderson, Wendell Marshall, Sam Woodyard—everyone. I was going to miss being one of the "Fly Boys." That's what Duke called Jimmy Hamilton, Paul Gonsalves, and me because we loved to play fast passages.

And I was going to miss our softball team. Duke could really hit that ball, but he almost had to take a *bus* to get to first base. Jimmy Hamilton was a great pitcher, and Ella Fitzgerald—or "Fitz," as we sometimes called her—swung that bat like you wouldn't believe. And me, I was a pretty good catcher.

I'd had a great time and there were so many memories. Like the time we played Lake Tahoe and had to cook for ourselves, since there were no restaurants where we could go. Wendell Marshall tried to cook a steak. Somebody had told him to sear it in salt, and when he turned it over, the whole side of the steak had salt stuck to it. We cracked up laughing. But we ate it anyway, even though it tasted like brine.

We also ate my disastrous effort to make salmon croquettes with a bunch of special herbs and seasonings. I didn't know that I was supposed to use crackers or bread to hold them together, so they looked like a skillet hash. Jimmy Hamilton tasted it and said, "Well, it doesn't look good, but it tastes all right."

Even though there was a lot I'd miss, Duke made me feel like it wasn't the end of our relationship. He also made it clear that he endorsed what I was doing.

Q had offered Quentin "Butter" Jackson some heavy bread, too, so he left Duke's band along with me. With high hopes and big dreams, Butter and I went to Brussels, Belgium, for the rehearsals and opening of Harold Arlen's blues opera *Free and Easy*. It was a first-class venue at the American Pavilion of the World's Fair, which had been held in Brussels the year before, in 1958.

In the town square in Brussels, there was a brass statue of a person lying down with an arm extended alongside its body. Legend had it that if you rubbed its arm, it had the power to bring you back to Brussels. I rubbed it a few times because I thought the city and the people were beautiful. I rubbed it for a few other reasons, too. My big dream was to buy a nice house and a luxury car for Pauline and me. I figured if the statue had special powers, maybe it could help make that dream come true, too.

The show was fabulous! So was the stage set, which was huge and had a balcony built across the back. We wore dapper costumes that made us look like the old-time riverboat gamblers—fancy hats, spats, vests, and big bouffant-type bow ties; large cuffs on the shirts with cufflinks. We were sharper than a mosquito's peter! Bud Johnson loved his outfit so much that he kept it after the show ended.

Except for the rhythm section and me, the whole band started out in the lobby of the theater, mingling with the people who were coming to see the show. I was on the stage balcony, where I opened the show by announcing, "Della Green is back from Texas! Della Green!" But instead of saying it, I played it. With the help of my plunger, it was almost as intelligible as speaking.

The band got their instruments quickly from some hiding spots and struck up a marching tune from the lobby. This shocked the audience. Then the band marched down the aisles and up the stairs on either side of the stage. It took so long for them to march in that we nicknamed the opening music "The Tapeworm."

The show's theme was taken from the 1946 Harold Arlen musical

St. Louis Woman, about a murder at the horse races. The star of our show was Harold Nicholas of the tap-dancing Nicholas Brothers. He played the role of a top jockey named Little Augie. Sammy Davis, Jr., was slated to replace him when we got to London.

The leading lady was Irene Williams. She was a wonderful vocalist. Many extraordinarily talented people were part of the show, including Robert Guillaume. He did a vignette with a former St. Louis dancer by the name of Othello Dallas. There were all sorts of well-choreographed dances, and the band was absolutely incredible. It was really a hot show, just like Q had said it would be.

Seven-year-old Patti Austin sang in the show. Her parents were actors. She was so cute. When we checked into the hotel, Patti walked into the bathroom and saw the bathtub and the bidet. She said, "Look, Mommy. They've got a big bathtub for you and a little one for me."

Even at such a young age, Patti could really belt out a tune. She was amazing! She did an album in her later years entitled *To Ella* that was awesome. That album is living proof that she had it all together.

What I loved about *Free and Easy* was its uniqueness. All the music was memorized, and some of the musicians had acting and speaking parts along with the actors and actresses. It was beyond the norm of just playing music, more like stepping into another zone. We weren't just part of the show; we *were* the show.

Top-shelf musicians were involved, and the music was beautifully scored. Quincy, like Ellington, surrounded himself with the greatest cats, and I was honored that he had chosen me as his straw boss. I was so proud of Q. He had reached a stage in his career where his voicings were original and signature. Like Duke and Monk. You immediately knew whose voicings they were. And his charts were different. He told me how he had tried many approaches of putting chords together, and with this show he had come up with a winner.

We had a piece called "Blues All Day Blues All Night." It had some fancy plunger manipulations in it, and unless you had been around the Ellington band, or at least part of the Ellington band, it would have been impossible for you to interpret it the way Q wanted. There was a plunger duet that wouldn't have worked unless you knew how to play the plunger with contrapuntal phrases that moved from the first trumpet to the second trumpet. All the experience I'd had with Duke kicked in and we were able to perfect the music.

All the cats were the best in their fields. On saxes we had Jerome Richardson, Phil Woods, Porter Kilbert, Ernie Wilkins, Bud Johnson, and Sahib Shihab; trumpets were Benny Bailey, Lennie Johnson, Floyd

Standifer, and me, with Floyd doubling on tenor sax. Floyd's book was very different from the rest of ours because Quincy could use him in either section. Trombones were Butter, Jimmy Cleveland, Melba Liston, and Åke Persson, the top trombonist in Sweden and a close friend of Q's and mine. Our drummer was Joe Harris, our pianist was Patti Bown, Buddy Catlett was our bassist, and Julius Watkins played French horn. We called Julius "The Phantom" because he did weird things. One night, for instance, he left his mouthpiece at the top of the Eiffel Tower, which caused the show to be delayed until somebody went up there and got it for him. Billy Byers was with the show, too. He was a very good and quick writer, and he assisted Quincy with the arrangements.

One evening, Porter Kilbert, one of our sax players, fell through the black tarp that covered the orchestra pit, which wasn't being used for the show. Everyone was in shock, but Porter was all right. Ironically, the fall cured a problem he'd had for a while. Usually, he couldn't play with his fingertips touching the keys of his sax, for some strange reason; so he'd rigged up a system where he put cork on the top of the keys. But when he made it back up the stairs after his fall, his fingers were working fine, and he never needed the cork on the keys again.

Q conducted majestically and accurately, and he had a suave look. We were all good buddies in the trumpet section. The whole band was friends.

When our show in Brussels ended, off we all went to gay Paree! There were more people traveling with that show than rocks on Pebble Beach. More than just the musicians, dancers, actors, and the crew. There were wives, kids, Chan Parker and her mother—Chan was Phil Woods' wife. Around seventy people. It was *incredible*. And we were having the time of our lives.

Pauline called me from St. Louis, where she was visiting her parents. She told me of some interesting developments. Apparently the Urban League was doing an inquiry into the major television networks as to why there was not more Negro representation. When they went to the National Broadcasting Corporation (NBC), they were told by the powers that be, "There aren't any qualified Negro musicians to play on television." Then the Urban League made up questionnaires and sent them to a bunch of people, asking them to name qualified black musicians. When the surveys came back, my name was on most of them. Recently, Aaron Levine from NBC had called Pauline asking her to contact me to see if I'd be interested in working for the network. I told her to tell them that I was under contract with Harold Arlen's *Free and Easy*. Anyway, I was digging the show and working with Q.

Just before opening night in Paris, I sent for Pauline to come over from the States. She'd learned a teaspoon of French and loved ordering room service, especially *petit déjeuner*. It was great to have her with me. We did some sightseeing and shopping during the day, then went to the show.

That's when the shit hit the fan. Our English-speaking show in a French-speaking country was like trying to sop gravy with a wet biscuit. It didn't work—at all. I gave *Free and Easy* a new name—*Free and Greasy*.

Pauline went back home a couple of days later, and a few weeks later, the show closed. We were all disgusted because it was a great show, with some of the greatest musicians in the world. Nobody wanted to see that band break up, so instead of taking a plane back home like the actors and the crew did, Q lined up some dates and we stayed.

Things started out all right. We gigged from town to town in several countries. But by the time we played at the folk parks in Copenhagen, the money was getting really thin. I knew we were in trouble. It was like trying to play a high note on a trumpet without tightening your ass.

Q was doing his best to hold things together. But the money just wasn't enough for all our people to survive. So I contacted Pauline to see if she could get in touch with Aaron Levine. If that job was still open, I wanted it. She called me back a few days later and told me that the offer still stood.

I told Q that I had a potential job offer back in the States. I hated to leave him, but he wanted me to go and he said he was happy for me. Still, I wished there was something I could have done to save the situation. I felt as bad as I had ten years before when Basie got in trouble from gambling debts and told me and the cats the band had to break up.

As I packed my bags, I said two prayers. One was that Q and everybody would be okay. The other was that I would be able to take the pressure of being the first Negro musician on staff at NBC.

41. NBC

I knew that the Urban League and a whole lot of folks had raised sheer hell for me to be on staff at NBC. Like ABC and CBS, NBC maintained a staff of 175 musicians. Without the civil rights movement, my chances of being there would have been as slim as a toothpick.

I was grateful, but it also meant that I was representing my race.

Pioneering a way for the future. So I minded my p's and q's. I wasn't just on time; I was early. I wasn't just clean; I was dressed sharp, with a spit shine on my shoes. Ready to play and deal with whatever they threw at me.

On my first day, March 21, 1960, I parked my blue Eldorado Cadillac in the 49th Street garage, between 5th and 6th, then walked across the street to Rockefeller Center, home of the NBC studios. They were located in Rockefeller Plaza, bordered on the east by the only street in New York City that wasn't owned by the city. John D. Rockefeller owned it *all*: the skating rink, the Atlas statue, the world's largest Christmas tree each December. And a skyscraper that was surrounded by the jewelry district, airline offices, and international designer stores.

I opened the door and walked on the marble floors of that block-wide building into a busy atmosphere of stores, eateries, offices, and hundreds of people. Long before I walked up to the office of the music contractor for NBC, Aaron Levine, I'd learned never to think you're too hip, because "two hips make an ass." Plus, I'd been warned: "When you go on staff at one of the networks in New York, you're in a house. But a house is not always a home."

I took a deep breath and opened the door. Aaron's secretary, Mrs. Gordon, welcomed me with a soft voice and a firm handshake. She was an older lady. Very friendly.

Initially, Aaron assigned me to *The Arthur Murray Show* and *The Morning Show*. The musicians showed no prejudice at all. They seemed friendly, just like the cats had been in Charlie Barnet's band. We immediately got down to business on the bandstand. They just wanted to play music, like I did.

Eventually I was assigned to the Jack Paar *Tonight* show. It was black and white television at that time, and we wore black suits, white shirts, black ties, and black shoes. Color broadcasts didn't start until that fall. We played a wide variety of music—tailored intros and exits, and charts brought by the guests. The band was nicknamed "The Proof Reading Band" because it was said you didn't know how a piece *could* sound until we'd played it.

We whipped the music out and played it right. Didn't waste a lot of time rehearsing, because everybody was a top professional. The sound was tight. It was all about reading, listening, and paying attention. Believe me, I watched everything and everybody, trying to understand the lay of the land. How things worked. Even though we played a variety of music, I was happy that jazz was usually the type of music played before and after station breaks for commercials.

It was a great band. Usually the trumpets were Doc Severinsen, Jim Maxwell, Mel Davis, Carl Poole, Ricky Trent, Joe Ferrante, Dick Perry, and me. Trombones were Will Bradley, Dick Lieb, Roland Dupont, Bob Alexander, and Paul Faulise. And saxophones were Tommy Newsom, Hymie Shertzer, Paul Ricci, Al Klink, and Walt Levinsky (I can't remember who was on baritone). The rhythm section included Bobby Rosengarden or Franky Garisto on drums, Bobby Haggart on bass, and Bucky Pizzarelli on guitar. José Melis was on piano, and he was the band leader. They had all worked with great band leaders like Benny Goodman, Glenn Miller, Tommy Dorsey, and Gene Krupa. Things were cool.

I was immediately propelled into the world of "first-call musicians." The *top* of the list. We were the musicians most sought after by the contractors for television commercials, radio work, and recording sessions. Those contractors had to be confident about whomever they called because some of the dates were very short. Had to be completed in twenty minutes. You couldn't be doing multiple takes. It was blap, bup, thap, bam! Next . . .

When we were called for dates for cola, beer, candy, cigarette, or soap commercials, we came in expecting almost anything as far as personnel or material was concerned. Anne Phillips was very big with the new Pepsi Cola spots and I was on first call for all of her dates.

Many times we were booked for an hour with a possible twenty minutes of overtime. If it did go into overtime, we'd have to hustle like mad to get to our next date—which might mean covering the distance from 52nd to 59th Street, a five- to ten-minute jump. We had to allow enough time to get a ride or hire a sub to mark the parts before we got there.

When we'd finish, we'd all say good-bye to each other and scurry off to the next jingle, only to discover that many of the same cats were on that date, too. Between jingle dates, maybe we'd do a recording session, as I did for Mark Murphy's first album, *Rah.*

I found myself saying hello and good-bye to the same musicians all day long. Play, sign the W9 form, and hurry to the next date. Or hike it back over to the studio, zip to my locker, change clothes, get on the bandstand, and rehearse the show music from three until four thirty. Then take a dinner break and come back about an hour and a half later and do the show.

If I'd ever thought I was busy before, that was *nothing* compared to what I stepped into at NBC. This was like being a leaf in a tornado.

There was no way I could keep up with my schedule all on my own, so I hired a service called Radio Registry, like the other cats did. The registry would receive calls from the contractors, look at my schedule, and book or turn down dates for me. We all kept personal calendars in case we ran into an opportunity, but we'd always double check with the registry.

I was making a truckload of money, working with a truckload of stellar musicians at these commercial dates. Britt Woodman, Jimmy Cleveland, Earl Warren, Seldon Powell, Wynton Kelly, Freddie Green, Sam Herman, Sam Jones, Jimmy Cobb, Cecil Payne, Duke Jordan, Charlie Persip, Ron Carter, Frank Rehak, Urbie Green, Dick Hixon, Ed Caine, Sol Schlinger, Gene Quill, Jimmy Buffington, John Barrows, Buddy Clark, George Duvivier, Hank Jones, Mundell Lowe, Mel Lewis, Don Lamond, Louis Hayes, Gus Johnson, Joe Newman, Kai Winding, Tony Studd, Phil Woods, Danny Bank, Willie Rodriguez, Ernie Royal, Jimmy Heath, Julius Watkins, George Dorsey, Arthur Clarke, Bobby Timmons, Herb Pomeroy, Willie Dennis, Billy Byers, Ed Wasserman, Al Cohn, Oliver Nelson, Jim Hall, Kenny Burrell, Joe Benjamin, Osie Johnson, and Gary McFarland— to name a *few.*

So far, things were going all right, but I was about to face a big challenge.

42. Jim and Andy's

Jim and Andy's was the place to see and be seen. Nice lighting. I'd been hanging out there for years. Real popular restaurant and bar near NBC. The music contractors hung out a lot there, so the musicians were regulars, too. Cats from the *Tonight Show* and other musicians like Alec Wilder, J. J. Johnson, Bob Brookmeyer, Stan Getz, and Zoot Sims. There were composers, arrangers, all types of musicians. Literally everybody came into the place. It was a real melting pot.

It had the hippest jukebox in town. Huge! Red, white, and blue, with the hottest jazz tunes that you could think of. Bebop things, big band stuff. The number of selections was somewhere between one hundred fifty and maybe two hundred songs. It was playing constantly. Great music.

Jim Koulavaris, the owner, was the nicest person in the world. Most folks didn't know it, but Andy was Jim's cat. Jim tended the bar, kept track of all our tabs, cashed our checks, and even made loans to some of the cats.

We nicknamed the place "The Gym," which was a takeoff on Jim's name. It was a hell of a place. We ate there, drank there, and it even had its own lady of the evening. Just one lady. If one of our friends came to town and needed a little "quick pleasure," we'd just call Jim, even from Europe, and ask him to put it on our tab.

Great place for connections, too. Jim would get phone calls from contractors like, "Hey, Jim, you got any sax players there?" And if you fit the bill, Jim would run the info down to you. Or while socializing, somebody might say, "Such and such is happening at such and such studio. You wanna do it?" And just like that, you got word on what was going on. The musicians who hung out there were capable of doing whatever was asked of them. Top-shelf musicians.

The place also had great service and great food, and the aromas hit your face as soon as you opened the door. Steaks, shrimp, spaghetti, onions and garlic. The kitchen was straight back and Rocky, the cook, always had at least an inch of cigar ash hanging on his smoke, but he never spilled any ashes on anybody's food.

Romeo Penque frequented the place and ate most of his meals there. He was a woodwind musician, and he loved shrimp. So Jim concocted a special dish called "Shrimp Romeo." Jim was cool like that. He also loved to shock the ladies who came there to eat, by placing rolls and breads shaped like male genitalia in the bread basket. We called them "cock and balls." Jim had a special baker to make these things.

Eventually, Rockefeller bought the property where Jim's place was. So Jim bought another place and moved up to 52nd off 8th Avenue. It had a couple of steps down from the street to the door and was set up similarly to his first place. We all went there, too. It had wooden floors, a bar on the right, booths and a few tables.

Jim and Andy's was a "home away from home" for us. Far different from the "house" that NBC represented.

43. Johnny and Ed

Our required time at NBC was between four and eight in the evening. So I had plenty of time to work afterward at my favorite jazz clubs, like the Half Note down on Spring and Hudson. It was owned by the Canterino family, Mike, Sonny, and Judy, and had great Italian food. We loved them all, even their waiter, Al. If somebody pulled out a cigarette, he'd appear out of nowhere with a lighted match, like magic. In response to a "Thank you," he'd say, "It's a pleasure to serve you." After leaving the Note, I'd find a couple of jam sessions, then go to some parties.

Things were cool at NBC until Will Bradley, up in the trombone section, made a whoopee-cushion sound while we were on the air live. Word was that it cost somebody a lot of money because some sponsors were pissed. After that, the show was taped. That meant that we had longer hours, but I still managed to hang out after the show and make it to early recording dates the next morning. I did as many dates as possible each day before time for taping at NBC.

When Jack Paar left the show in '62, they brought Johnny Carson in, and Skitch Henderson replaced José Melis as the band leader. Carson's sidekick was Ed McMahon. The two of them were great!

There was a buzz around the show that they had to hire another Negro. Sure enough, Aaron came to me and asked me to find a black trumpet player. He said, "He has to be married with children, be a highly respected lead player, a great jazz soloist, and an excellent reader." Now, I knew that not everybody in the band was married with children, so I almost lost my temper. But I knew I had to be smart and not disappoint the folks who'd helped to get me the job at NBC. It wasn't just about a gig; it was about opportunities for my race.

A few days later, after I'd cooled off, I decided to call Snooky Young, who had just returned to his old spot in the Basie band. They were doing one-nighters, and at that point they were in Seattle. I talked to his wife, Dottie, who called him, and he called me back. When I told him about the position, he accepted because he wanted to get off the road.

Unbelievably, after Snooky had been at NBC for a while, Aaron came and told me that Snooky wasn't getting along with Skitch. Now, I knew that was a lie because Snooky got along with all the cats! He was responsible. We worked together every day, and without fail we both arrived at work way ahead of time with our trousers pressed, hair cut, faces clean shaven, shoes shined; we'd be tuned up, in our seats, and ready to hit the first note every night at least fifteen minutes early.

Aaron said, "We're going to have to let your boy go."

I said, "He's not my boy, Aaron. He's my *friend*. And I'll tell you what you can do. You fire Snooky, write his notice out—and when you do that, you can write mine, too! And you'll have a lily-white band just like you had before." Then I stormed out of his office and went home.

When I opened my front door, Pauline told me that Aaron had phoned several times. The next day at the studio, I got off the elevator on the sixth floor and Aaron was standing there like he was waiting for me. He grabbed me and said, "Let's go down to the coffee shop." Then he told the conductor, "Clark will be a bit late."

When we sat down in the coffee shop, he reached into his pocket and pulled out a tea bag. Then he ordered a cup of hot water. He said, "I don't have to let Snooky go."

I said, "Aaron, it's quite all right because before I got this job, neither Snooky nor I knew you, and I'm sure we can get along just fine again without you."

They didn't fire Snooky. We both stayed on, and he didn't find out about that whole scene until a few years later.

For the first time in my life, I was making some serious money. Enough to bank big and make plans for a house.

44. Mumbles

On his show, Johnny played a popular game called "Stump the Band," in which someone in the audience asked us to play a particular tune, and if we didn't know it, that person would get a prize. We knew how to play most requests, and if we didn't, we had fun faking it by creating something on the spot. It ended up being fun for everybody.

One night somebody gave us a title that sounded like an old Girl Scout campfire song. Of course, none of us had heard of it. So I started clowning around, and I came up with a tune that went way back to my old days with Gus Perriman, the pianist at the Lincoln Inn in St. Louis. I was thinking about folks getting drunk and slurring the words to their songs so much that no one could understand *what* they were singing. What I did on the show that night was a mix of scat singing and unintelligible words; at the same time, I put on serious and comical facial expressions that made everybody crack up while I was singing the song in what sounded like a funny, weird language. The band cracked up. The audience cracked up. And Johnny loved it! In the long run, folks loved it so much that I started getting requests for it on an ongoing basis. I named it what it sounded like to me—"Mumbles."

I recorded the tune at a Norman Granz session with Oscar Peterson in '64, for an album called *Oscar Peterson Trio + 1*. I was the "+ 1." Now, Norman didn't believe in wasting time, and he liked to catch things naturally. First takes were his thing, his theory being that you lose the spontaneity after that, the "fizz."

After we finished the main tracks, we still had some recording time left. I said, "Oscar, I'd like to hear this thing I have. Just some wordless blues."

So he said, "Okay, sure. Let's try it."

I gave him the tempo and he started playing some blues. Ray Brown and Ed Thigpen were hitting it hard too, real funky blues.

I joined in with my mumbling. When I looked at Oscar, he was cracking *up*. Practically on the floor.

When we finished, he said, "Hey, that's great. Let's do it again and we'll put it on the album."

Then I said, "Well, I've got another one. A slow blues."

He put that one on the record, too. I named it "Incoherent Blues."

Later, I recorded "Mumbles" with Bob Brookmeyer. Aretha Franklin recorded it, too. It was a riot and I loved doing it. Sometimes I'd sing it in different accents that I'd learned while traveling internationally. Everywhere I performed—concerts, festivals, and clubs—people would say, "Sing 'Mumbles'!" I performed it with a different twist each time, and it was never rehearsed. Always spontaneous.

Sometimes I'd do it to cool out some crackpot in the audience who was being disruptive. I'd point at him during the song and involve the audience in squashing his antics. I also did it as a duet, with Red Holloway and Jimmy Heath and a bunch of other cats. We'd have a ball mumbling back and forth like we were having a conversation. We'd crack everybody up—including ourselves. When I did it in Copenhagen with Richard Boone, it was filmed. Every time I look at it now on DVD, I crack up again.

"Mumbles" took on more depth each time I performed it because the musical lines that I sang were actually the way I'd phrase if I were playing a solo on my horn. Meanwhile, it became more and more popular. I got the biggest kick out of going to gigs and watching others do it. Some had gotten it pretty much down. That made me feel like I'd contributed another branch on the "Tree of Jazz"!

Bob Brookmeyer and I had a "mutual admiration society," loved playing together, so much so that we got a little group together in the early '60s. We named it the Clark Terry/Bob Brookmeyer Quintet and got a nice gig going at the Half Note—Eddie Costa on piano, Osie Johnson on drums, and Joe Benjamin on bass. It was one of the best groups ever.

The harmony that Bob and I had was super. I was digging the valve trombone that Bob played because that was the first instrument I was given in high school, but the way its sound married with my flugelhorn sound was something special. We could feel each other's next moves and enjoyed the way we managed to play simultaneously throughout the changes. We called it "noodling." Usually one player wants to outshine the other, but we had a way of blending together that allowed both of us to shine. We really tried to make each other sound beautiful.

We were both from Missouri and we had a special friendship that lasted through the years. In '63, we won the *DownBeat* Jazz Critics Poll award. In '64 we recorded the album *Quintet* for Mainstream, and later we recorded *Tonight, The Power of Positive Swinging,* and *Gingerbread.* We did some things overseas, too, like an episode of the BBC Television show *Jazz 625* in '65, which is on the Internet today (see http://keepswinging.blogspot .com/2008/01/clark-terry-bob-brookmeyer-quintet.html). It was a gas playing with Bob.

Our album that featured "Mumbles" was nominated for a Grammy, but we didn't win. Still, that song became one of the most requested tunes of my career. Its popularity amazed me, since it started out as just a silly game on the *Tonight Show.* Why, out of everything I've done in my career—doing circular breathing, or playing my horn upside down, or switching from my right hand to my left, or holding my trumpet in one hand and my flugelhorn in the other and switching from one to the other, or playing duets with myself—*that* song was such a hit, I'll never understand. But Pops—Louis Armstrong—had told me long before, "People love to hear you sing, Daddy. Plus, it gives your chops a break."

During the time that Bob and I gigged together, I got him involved in playing some benefits with me, including one for C.O.R.E. I loved playing their fund-raisers. But with my hectic schedule, all of the other fund-raisers for different charities got to be too much and I started having stomach pain. Turned out it was an ulcer. So my doctor told me that I had to slow down and learn how to tell people no.

Bob was tired of all the free gigs anyway. He said, "Cee Tee, you've got to practice saying no in all kinds of ways. Hell no! Shit no! Fuck no!" So I had a T-shirt made that featured at least a hundred profane ways of saying no. And I finally learned how to say no to all benefits that weren't associated with the civil rights movement. I'd play benefits for the NAACP and the Urban League and organizations like that, but that was it.

My ulcer healed. But I was about to catch hell from another direction.

45. First House

I was making some really nice bread from the *Tonight Show* and all the gigs on the side, so I decided it was time to buy a house. I wanted to live in a residential area not too far from Manhattan. When I started checking out neighborhoods, I zeroed in on Queens.

There was a nice house in Bayside on a raised lot, with a nice backyard from what I could see as I drove by. I parked my black Cadillac, which I'd bought from George Duvivier. He bought a new one each year, and I liked this black one because it had the first bucket seats ever made for a Cadillac. It had lots of custom details, too, and a trunk big enough for a full-sized bass.

When I rang the doorbell, a white man answered with an unfriendly look on his face. I told him that I'd read about the house in the newspaper. He said, "Well, you're just a bit late because someone put a binder on it last night."

I hadn't seen any Negroes in the neighborhood, and I had a sneaking suspicion that he was lying, because he looked like he'd just gotten off the train from Racism, U.S.A. He never looked me in my eyes. He might as well have said, "You ain't welcome here!"

So I went to one of my Caucasian friends, Jim Maxwell. He was my buddy and section mate on the *Tonight Show*. I said, "Jim, I tried to buy a house in Bayside. The owner said somebody else had already put a binder on it, but I think he was lying."

Jim said, "Let's go back there tomorrow. I'll check it out."

The next day we met in Bayside. I parked a block away from the house where Jim could see me from the front porch.

He told me later how things went down. He said that the guy invited him inside to check things out. Jim asked him, "Is the house available?" The guy said, "Yes." So Jim looked it over again. He said, "This is a nice house. You don't have a binder or anything on it?"

The owner said, "No. Fortunately, we don't have one."

So Jim stepped out on the porch and signaled for me. I walked up looking at the owner's shocked face. Jim said, "Since you don't have anybody in line for this house, I want you to sell it to my friend here."

Jim was a big man, over six feet tall, and he weighed at least two hundred pounds. He meant business, and the owner knew that there would be trouble if he didn't cooperate. Jim was standing there with a piercing look on his face staring at the owner.

That's how I bought 218-14 36th Avenue in Bayside, New York, in 1963.

My first house! It was a raised ranch style, brown brick, with nice curb appeal. I loved the location because it was near my old apartment at Dorie Miller, so I could easily visit my neighbors there.

I couldn't wait to show it to Pauline. When she saw it, she loved it right away. We checked out the three bedrooms, two bathrooms, and the roomy basement with a nice bar. It was a great party room, and we talked about adding a bathroom down there. The backyard was very private, and it had a big concrete barbeque pit. After we moved in, we had frequent parties and backyard barbeques with steak, chicken, hot dogs, hamburgers, turkey, ribs, fish, and even armadillo—all cooked by R. T. Holley, who was a friendly cat, not a musician, just a nice guy. He and his wife lived up on 110th Street. We'd have between fifty and a hundred people at our parties—inside the house, in the backyard, and in the side yard, which had a nice little patio.

The neighbors didn't like us living there at first. Some of their kids threw trash on our front yard. But I didn't let that break my spirit. I built that front yard slope up almost five feet high with loads of dirt. Then I put a brick wall up to support all that dirt. The kids would have to reach way up high to throw anything on *my* grass.

One day, I decided to take those neighborhood kids up to the Carvel ice cream store on Bell, where I bought them loads of their favorite flavors. After that, the neighbors and their children got more friendly. They even waved at me when I drove down the street.

One of my first home improvement projects was to hire a carpenter to enlarge and enclose the back porch and make it into what I called "a drive-in closet" and an office. It was fantastic.

Pauline was busy furnishing the house and I felt like I was on top of the world. The only problem was that I was so busy making money that I couldn't always come home. So I stayed in the city a lot, which meant more shoes, clothes, diamonds, and minks for Pauline.

I managed to keep my gig playing with Bob Brookmeyer at the Half Note after the *Tonight Show*. Kept hitting a few jam sessions around town here and there. When I didn't have time to get a hotel room and get some decent sleep, I went to the TransLux, which was a newsreel theater. Since I only had a few hours before I'd have to be ready for an early studio commercial call, I'd pick a seat in the back row to cop some quick z's. I'd sit down, set the alarm on my watch, and use my wrist as a pillow next to my head so I could easily hear the alarm. Then I went to sleep. When the beeps started, I got up and went to the Horn and Hardart on the east side of 42nd Street. They had a nickel vending machine where you could get beans, macaroni, meat, and snacks like cakes, pies, coffee, and ice cream. Or I went to the Ham and Egger or Nedick's, which was a little restaurant that served hamburgers, hot dogs, and stuff like that.

Eventually, I realized that burning the candle at both ends was catching up with me. I decided to take a few days off and send for Hiawatha.

On the day that he arrived, we were all smiles, but soon the winds of happiness turned chilly. Too much time apart and not enough roots to our relationship. For almost thirty years, I'd been holding on to that happy father and son dream, and I'd worked hard to make it come true. I thought he'd understand why I'd been gone. But he thought I should understand why he was angry about all those years of his life *without* me.

I'd done the best I could. So had he. But our relationship just wasn't the dream that either of us had in mind. We argued a lot, and things escalated to the point where we realized that it just wasn't going to work. So I sent him back to St. Louis. My last words to him were, "When you decide to be a man, let me know!"

That was a hard time for me. But when times got hard, I turned to my music. No matter how hard the times were, I never gave up my music!

That was when I forgave my father for the way he'd treated me. I realized that he had done the best that he could, just like I'd tried to do for Hiawatha. I imagined that maybe my father pushed me harder than anyone else because I bore his first name—even though I was his third son. I felt that maybe he really *had* wanted me to make it. Maybe the only way he knew how to encourage me was to dare me, to threaten me.

Hearing Hiawatha yell at me, expressing all his anger about what I had done wrong when I'd only had good intentions, made me realize how long I'd been angry at my own father. It occurred to me that maybe *his* intentions were good, too. In letting go of all that anger, it was like I finally unhooked a rusty weight that I'd been dragging around all of my life.

The pictures I had of Pop in my mind changed. I could see him looking down on me, and for the first time, I could see him smiling. I imagined him saying, "See. I had good intentions, too. You thought I didn't love you, but I did. I worked hard to take care of you ten crumb snatchers. I did my best."

With Hiawatha gone, I felt like I had just lived through a horrible nightmare. I wished I could take back those harsh words I'd said to him, but it was too late. He was too angry at me. At that moment, nothing I could have said would have made any difference. Only time could help. So I picked up my horn and kept going, hoping that one day we'd be friends.

46. Big Bad Band

In '67 when Skitch Henderson left, it was rumored that I was up to lead the *Tonight Show* band. But the word came down that if they had a black person in front of the band, it would ruin the ratings in the southern market. So Doc Severinsen got the job. I loved Doc and I was happy for him, but I was also pissed!

When I opened at the Club Barron in Harlem later that same week, I was introduced as "the *real Tonight Show* band leader." That was cool. But it still didn't make up for the racist crap. The only thing that cooled me down was the picture in my mind of me standing in front of my own band. I knew that it would take time and some serious bread to get a big band together, so I accepted more dates and started a buzz, scouting for players. And I kept on smiling.

Another thing that eased my mind was my new grandbaby boy, who was nicknamed "Butch." My stepson, Rudy, and his wife, Betty, were the proud parents, and Pauline was a doting grandmother. Her smile was bigger than ever, and I was glad that she had more family to keep her company, since I was gone so much. Later, Rudy and Betty had two more children, Michelle and Terrence. Pauline brought Terrence straight home from the hospital. We took all three of them on trips from time to time.

Each time I saw Pauline holding Butch and I saw how happy she was, that gave me more strength to face the bigotry I had to deal with each day. It also made me more determined to have my own band. So I laced up my bootstraps and kept making contacts.

There was a buzz at the Gym about organizing some softball teams with some of the cats who hung out there. We had enough guys for four teams. So we bought uniforms and got the okay to use the ballpark that was across the street from Milt Hinton's house. Milt was an extraordinary bassist and a close friend.

I always liked to be the backstop—the catcher. There was one cat who was a little older and he preferred managing instead of playing. He was a good manager, so we nicknamed him Casey Stengel after the legendary manager of the Mets, Yankees, Braves, and Dodgers.

At one of our games, with an opponent on third base, our pitcher threw fast and hard and the batter hit a ground ball to the pitcher. Our pitcher wanted to throw the runner out at home, and the guy on third looked like he was going to try to score.

I was holding the ball between third and home, waiting to tag him. Then he put his head down and barreled into me with his cleats. Something in my back went, *Crack!*

That was the beginning of one of my worst nightmares. Pain became a way of life. I went to doctors, took lots of aspirin. But nothing did any good.

One day my friend Dougal House out in California suggested that I try one of those back stretchers, where I'd realign my spine by being suspended upside down. He ordered one and had it sent to me. I tried it several times, but it didn't help either. Nothing helped to get rid of that pain. Not special contraptions, not chiropractors, not acupuncturists, not orthopedic specialists.

But I'm not a quitter, so I kept trying suggestions that came across the table. I took more aspirin, ate healthier, drank herb teas, took vitamins and minerals, and drank elixirs of over-the-counter remedies. I slept with pillows between my knees. Tried various standing and sitting positions. The one thing I didn't try was heavy pain-killing drugs. I wanted to keep my mind as sharp as possible for playing. No nodding or glazed eyes or half-assed performances for me. I hated what drugs had done to my friends anyway.

At one point I read *The Power of Positive Thinking* by Norman Vincent Peale. After I thought about some of the suggestions in that book, I decided that it was "mind over matter" for me. My pain could have been a lot worse—I knew that. My chops were okay. So I made up my mind that if back pain was what I had to deal with, then so be it. I could handle it.

I scurried from one gig to the other, in town and out of town. I kept recruiting for my own big band, talking to the cats at the different gigs. They were really digging the idea. So I took more dates to make more money. I got busier that a one-armed paper hanger with crabs! Dates were coming almost faster than I could handle. But I was determined. So I did it all—records, jingles, the *Tonight Show*, tours, concerts, the Half Note gigs, and more.

Eventually, I got enough cats organized for my band. I was above cloud nine!

One of the cats I chose was Ernie Wilkins. Our friendship went way back to my high school days in St. Louis, and then when we were in the navy together. We'd always kept in touch, and I was proud of how he had grown over the years since he'd written that megahit for Joe Williams, "Everyday I Have the Blues." That was a long time ago when I'd helped him and his brother, Jimmy, get in Basie's band.

By now, Ernie was a highly respected musician, composer, and arranger. I was gassed when he joined my new big band! When I told him about some of the other cats who were in the band, he said, "Why don't you name it 'Clark Terry's Big Bad Band'? Man, those cats are *bad* enough to play everything I've written. I want to write some new things for you, too." He was so proud of my band, *and* he wanted to write things for us!

I loved that name—"Clark Terry's Big Bad Band." In those days when something was spoken of as "bad," that meant it was the absolute best!

I'd recruited cats who loved to play, who knew how to swing. Super talented cats who loved my original music and who themselves had written music that I loved. Cats who didn't look like they were working at a factory when they were on the bandstand. But instead were enjoying the music and the audience. I had gotten cats with signature sounds, sounds that I wanted to hear. Cats who could blend together to give the band a hot, unique style. I knew we would enjoy working together because we'd all played together in the past and had a blast.

It was also very important to me to acquire musicians who understood the fact that we were "public servants" and that if our audience was happy, then we'd done our job. I didn't need anybody on my bandstand who had an attitude like they were some kind of god or goddess. Sending a message like "Pay attention to *me* and don't move while I'm playing."

Since I hated prejudice of any sort, I wanted a multiracial mix, and I wanted chicks, too. I also wanted a small band within my big band in case we needed to do some more intimate settings or smaller venues. Most of all, I wanted to have a hell of a roster so that I wouldn't run into any problems finding people to play, whether it was in the States or overseas.

After booking A & R Studios on 48th, we started rehearsals. My rhythm section was Ron Carter on bass, Patti Bown on piano, and Grady Tate on drums. Trumpets were Ray Copeland, Lloyd Michaels, Lew Soloff, and Woody Shaw. On trombones, I had John Gordon, Sonny Costanzo, Jack Jeffers, and Melba Liston. The saxes were Phil Woods, Arnie Lawrence, Frank Wess, Ernie Wilkins, Jimmy Heath, and Danny Bank.

We had an incredible repertoire of original and classic arrangements that Ernie, Phil, Melba, and Frank had written. Eventually I got other arrangers, like Allan Faust, and an old Ellington colleague of mine, Rick Henderson, got involved, too. That music has stood the test of time because those arrangements are still part of my big band book today.

Everybody was digging the hell out of our arrangements. We did some of my tunes, like "Sheba," "Etoile" by Ernie Wilkins, "Take the A Train" by Strays, Duke's "Come Sunday," and a slew of others. Since rock and roll was popular, we even did one tune from that scene called "Dirty Old Man."

My big band was tight. We had a hell of a sound! Soon we tested the waters in the Club Baron up in Harlem. I checked out the fingers popping, heads bobbing, and shoulders moving. When we got cheers and requests for encores, I knew we were in the pocket.

There were lots of positive vibes around town about my big band, with great reviews in the media. So we kept going strong. I was incorporating all those lessons I'd learned from Duke and Basie and others. How to connect with my audience. How to keep the band happy with fresh and interesting music and personalized arrangements. Keeping on top of the idiosyncrasies of each member. Helping them with their problems so they remained happy. Of course, I had to keep hustling to make sure everybody got paid. Even if it was out of my own pocket.

I didn't have deep pockets like Duke or the royalty checks that he received from his music being used in movies and from his hit tunes on radio and television. And I didn't have Picasso paintings like Norman had. But even though I didn't have that kind of bread, everybody in my band got paid. I worked hard to make sure of that!

We were great. Duke even sat in with us later at one of our concerts in New York. That was one of the greatest thrills of my life, and luckily, somebody snapped a photo.

On most weekends, I booked dates as a featured soloist or I put together a quartet or quintet and we'd gig in other U.S. cities or in Europe—Scandinavia and other countries. I especially enjoyed those gigs because I only had to perform one or two times a night, and that meant I could get some sleep. On Mondays, I was back for the New York City whirlwind of studio gigs, the *Tonight Show*, and club dates. And my big band, man! Took me a few years to organize a hip roster.

I had some of the baddest cats around. Trumpet players like Mike Vax, Willie Singleton, Bob Montgomery, Virgil Jones, Lew Soloff, Lloyd Michaels, Ray Copeland, Greg Bobulinski, Dale Carley, Paul Cohen, Richard Williams, Jimmy Nottingham, Ernie Royal, Marvin Stamm, Jimmy Owens, Randy Brecker, and Oscar Gamby. Our reed roster included cats like Jimmy Heath, Ernie Wilkins, Phil Woods, Arnie Lawrence, Charles Davis, Chris Woods, Bobby Donovan, Zoot Sims, Ron Odrich, George Coleman, and Joe Temperley. And we had trombonists like Sonny Costanza, Jack Jeffers, Dave Bargeron, James Cleveland, John Gordon,

Eddie Bert, Wayne Andre, Jimmy Wilkins, Janice Robinson, Tony Studd, and Chuck Conners.

Our rhythm section was always right on the money, with players like Ed Soph, Grady Tate, and Mousey Alexander on drums; bassists like Victor Sproles, Ron Carter, or Wilbur Little; and on piano we had Duke Jordan, Ronnie Matthews, or Don Friedman.

All those cats knew what to do and how to do it. We were getting rave reviews. More than anything, we all loved playing together. But rock and roll was coming on strong, which made me more determined to find ways for jazz to survive.

We hit the road and did some jazz festivals and parties in the United States, and then we played in Europe. The audiences loved us. Before long we were making plans to perform in Carnegie Hall!

I had a real scare in '68 while I was working in Chicago at my cousin's club with Lurlene Hunter. She was a show-stopping vocalist. She did the Campbell's Soup commercial, "Mmm, mmmm, good. Mmmm, mmmm, good. That's what Campbell's Soups are—Mmm, mmmm, good!" Lurlene could sing! Man, she would blow you away! But she wouldn't leave Chicago and go on the road. I begged her, but she refused. It was such a shame.

Anyway, I was trying to change my tire while I was there, and I had to take the hubcap off. I didn't know that the inside of the rim was razor sharp. Before I knew it, that sharp metal had cut the skin off three fingertips of my left hand. Talk about panic!

First thing I thought about was playing my horns. I prayed harder than I'd ever done in my life. Thank God, I had a good doctor and he fixed me up. But an overseas correspondent for *Melody Maker* magazine reported that I had *severed* three fingers on my left hand in a car accident, that I'd probably lose use of them permanently. Well, that caused quite a ruckus. And just like that, I started getting a bunch of calls like the ones from British fans who were offering personal skin grafts for me. I couldn't believe it! It brought tears to my eyes.

I didn't know what to do to let them know that I was all right, but the Old Man Upstairs fixed it because *Jazz Journal* magazine reported the truth: that my fingers would be okay.

With that incident, the power of the media was more obvious than ever for me. I couldn't believe how lies were so easily spread. Eventually the chaos over the whole thing died down. I kept on gigging and planning for my big band's debut in Carnegie Hall, which was coming up on February 15, 1970.

1. My mother, Mary Scott Terry. "My mother's name was Mary. She died when I was around six or seven. I don't remember too much about her because she was always gone. Working, they said."

2. My father. "His name was Clark Virgil Terry, and we called him Pop, but everybody else called him Mr. Son, because his nickname was Son Terry. All my friends were scared of him, and I was, too."

3. That's me in the mid '20s, when I was around four or five. I'm dressed in a sailor suit and there's a toy trumpet in my hand. Looking back, I guess it was more than a coincidence that I enlisted in the navy and became a professional trumpet player.

4. My son, Hiawatha, and me in the mid '40s. "Bought him the latest clothes like mine, had some pictures taken of us dressed in sailor suits."

5. One of the Great Lakes navy bands in 1945. As Len Bowden said, "Recruits in this particular branch of the navy, for the first time, will be signed up as musicians! We'll have a handsome new rating, an insignia of a G clef instead of a 'C' on the cuffs." This went down in history as "the Great Lakes Experience," helping thousands of colored musicians. I'm in the trumpet section on the far left, third row from the bottom.

6. The George Hudson Band in 1946. "When the patrons came to dance at the Club Plantation after hearing some new pop tune earlier that *day*, George's band was known for being able to play it that *night*." Personnel changed from time to time. Top row, from left: Singleton "Cocky" Palmer, John Orange, Earl Martin, Ed Batchman, George Hudson, Fernando, Blott (I can remember only one name for these last two), William Rollins, Kimball Dial. Bottom row, from left: Jimmy Grissom, Robert Parker, me, Paul Campbell, Cyrus Stoner, Willie "Weasel" Parker, Cliff Batchman, Edgar Hayes.

GEORGE HUDSON
AND HIS ORCHESTRA

GADE AGENCY, INC.
48 WEST 48th STREET
NEW YORK CITY

7. My first publicity photo, circa 1946.

› 8. Top: Publicity shot of Charlie Barnet, circa 1947; his band was very popular nationwide, with hit tunes. "That was the first time that one of my compositions ["Phalanges"] was recorded!" Bottom: That's me on the left and Jimmy Nottingham on the right, while we were in Charlie's band in 1947. "Nott was an awesome player. So much so that Charlie decided to feature our hot trumpet routines."

CHARLIE BARNET
And His Orchestra

9. I married Pauline in '48 in Detroit at Carl and Rachel Davis' house. "As I slid that band of gold on her finger, I thought, 'Now, I have the right woman.'" Top row, from left: Johnny "Pops" Davis, Willie "Weasel" Parker from George Hudson's band—my best man—and his lady (unidentified), Pauline and me in the middle hugged up, Carl Davis (Johnny Pops' brother), and Henry Smith, a friend of Carl's. Bottom row, from left: Murlene (Margueritte's daughter), Count Basie, my sister Margueritte, and Rachel Davis (Carl's wife).

❯ 10. "Crooning" my heart out to the ladies, circa late '40s.

11. Count Basie's band (the small group), circa early '50s. "His feel of time and the way he articulated was totally original and very effective." From left: Basie at piano, Freddie Green on guitar, Jimmy Lewis on bass, Buddy DeFranco on clarinet, Wardell Gray our sax player behind Buddy, me on trumpet, and Gus Johnson on drums.

12. Circa mid '50s: Being in Duke's band was amazing. "My favorite quote of his was, 'I'm easy to please. Just give me the *best*.'" From left: actress Betty Grable, actor Harry James, me, and Duke Ellington.

13. I'm trying to get a more mellifluous sound by putting felt over the bell of my trumpet at the Newport Jazz Festival in 1956.

14. In '59, I was in the awesome band that Quincy Jones put together for the *Free and Easy* musical in Europe. I'm on the stairs playing my trumpet. "I was so proud of Q. He had reached a stage in his career where his voicings were original and signature."

15. Playing softball in the mid to late '50s. My favorite position was backstop. I don't know who's on the left, but that's me on the right. "I was going to miss our [Duke Ellington] softball team. Duke could really hit that ball, but he almost had to take a *bus* to get to first base."

16. My first honorary doctorate, from the University of New Hampshire in 1978. From left: Paul Verrette, Mark DeVoto, Cleveland "Buddy" Howard, me, and Dave Seiler.

17. The Clark Terry Youth Band in '79. "Most of them went on to become professional musicians." On bass, Peter Dowdall. Bottom row, saxes, from left: Randy Russell (obscured by music stand), Branford Marsalis, Danny House, Ned Otter, Diane DeRosa. Middle row, trombones, from left: Conrad Herwig, Kenny Crane, Ron Wilkins, and Matt Finders. Top row, trumpets, from left: Tony Lujan, Byron Stripling, Steve Rentschler, and Gary Blackman. Our drummer, Mike Baker, is out of range in the photo, but he was there. That's me out front playing flugelhorn.

18. Clark's Terry's Big Bad Band, circa late '70s. A longtime dream come true: "I had gotten cats with signature sounds, sounds that I wanted to hear. Cats who could blend together to give the band a hot, unique style." From left: Richard Williams, I think that's Greg Bobulinski above him with the headband, can't tell who the guy next to him is, below them is Charles Davis, below him is Janice Robinson, next to her is Jimmy Wilkins (you can only see his head), then Reggie Workman; above him looking to the left is Jack Jeffers, below him is Ernie Wilkins, above him is Oscar Gamby with the cigarette, seated below is Duke Jordan wearing glasses, standing next to him is Sonny Costanzo in the middle of the photo, seated below him is Jimmy Heath, then Arnie Lawrence with the big cap on; standing behind him is Jimmy Nottingham, on the far right is Ed Soph, and I'm reclining on the sidewalk.

19. That's me playing two horns, circa mid '80s. I loved playing duets with myself.

20. Me on the left and Diz (Dizzy Gillespie) on the right, circa mid '80s. We always supported each other. Loved hanging out at Pops' (Louis Armstrong's) house. "We would say, 'Let's go bug Pops and get our batteries charged!' That was our way of saying that we wanted to learn from him."

› 21. Clark Terry's Great Plains Jazz Camp, June of '80. "For the first time, I had my own jazz camp. I was totally gassed! It was at Emporia State University in Kansas." Used with permission of Bob Montgomery.

› 22. Gwen and me on our first date in New York, at the "Hearts for Ella" tribute in February of '90. "She caused a lot of rubbernecking with her short sexy black dress." Photo by Rosalie Soladar.

21

22

23

Lionel Hampton   AL GREY

24

‹ 23. The three wise men in Anne Phillips' Christmas musical production *Bending Towards the Light* (www.jazznativity.com), December of '91. Bob Kindred was the musical director. "I'd been involved every year since the first one in '85. Incredible, stellar cast. I'd just gotten out of the hospital after back surgery. The pain just about killed me, but I was so glad to be there that the pain was second-ary." From left: Hamp (Lionel Hampton), Al (Grey), and me. Used by permission of Judy Kirtley, Photographer.

‹ 24. Hanging out in Manhattan in '91 after that hospital scene. "Big Prez [God] made another impossibility become possible, and I got there." Lots of friends helped, too, and I'll always remember that. From left: me, Al (Grey), Wynton Marsalis, and Gwen. Don't know who is in the background.

25. "On Valentine's Day in '92, I kept my second promise to Big Prez. I married Gwen. Pastor John Gensel flew down from New York to do the ceremony. It was down in Rockwall, Texas, at a yacht club." You can barely see her because she's only around four feet tall, but that's my sister Margueritte standing to Pastor Gensel's right.

26. This was around '93: playing my trumpet with my plunger—a necessary ingredient for certain sounds, like when I played some mean, low-down, chitlin-eatin' blues.

27. President Bill Clinton was pointing at Gwen when she took this photo in '93. We were hanging with him in D.C. at one of his inaugural galas in connection with the Monk Institute. Behind us, from left: Jimmy Heath, Joe Henderson, and Jon Faddis. © Pasgtel Music Marketing.

28. Circa '94: Here I am enjoying my new hobby—painting with acrylics. I was in a supply room in a gallery in Albuquerque, putting the finishing touches on a painting that I named *Cosby's Creek* for Bill Cosby. My teacher in the photo is Arlene Wackerbarth, the close friend of one of my old buddies, a trumpet player named Bob Farley; he passed in 2004.

29. That's Dianne Reeves giving me a kiss in the mid '90s. "I've always helped her in any way possible. And she's gone straight to the top!"

› 30. That's my man, Q (in black suit), in New York conducting a suite entitled "Sonic Convergence" with an international orchestra at the Ross School in 2001. An *awesome* experience. Extremely talented students. I'm on the left, sitting in as a guest artist.

› 31. Late '90s: We're all shooting the breeze, relaxing and reminiscing. That's my buddy from way back, Gerald Wilson, on the right, and I'm in the middle. I can't tell you who the gentleman is on the left. Wish my eyes were better.

32

33

‹ 32. Bill (Cosby) and I have been friends for many years. Here he's doing his "Screech Jones" routine on one of my sets at the Village Vanguard club in Manhattan in the late '90s. "He played up the suspense, making the audience hold their breath each time he'd put the horn up to his mouth. But instead of playing, he'd take it down again and keep talking." Everybody was cracking up. Genius!

‹ 33. I'm on the left, and O. P. (Oscar Peterson) is on the right, circa early 2000s. His daughter Celine is standing behind him. He was a great, great pianist. I always said that it sounded like he had four hands when he played. Celine is my goddaughter.

34. Circa late '80s: "It's always been fun to play my flugelhorn upside down. My trumpet, too, except the time with Duke's [Ellington] band when I was being a smartass. I never did anything stupid like that again!"

35. My 2010 Grammy Lifetime Achievement Award. It was such an honor! "The thing that touched me the most was that some of my students came to celebrate with me." On the left is my son Gary Paris; my student Quincy Cavers is behind me; my wife, Gwen, is to my right; and Neil Portnow is on the far right. GRAMMY ® and the gramophone statuette and logos are registered trademarks of The Recording Academy and are used under license. Photo © 2010 Rick Diamond / WireImage.

47. Carnegie Hall

Everybody was dressed to the nines in black tuxedos. I wore my blue tux with tails and matching 'gators on my feet. When I stepped out on that stage, heard the applause, and saw my name on the placards in front of the music stands, I declare it was almost better than sex!

"A one. A two. A little dab will do." That was how I counted off one of the most emotional concerts of my career. I looked at the faces of my friends. A stellar bunch of cats, seated there in my band, and they seemed as thrilled as I was.

We had Virgil Jones, Lew Soloff, Lloyd "Karate Chops" Michaels, and Ray Copeland on trumpets; Frank Wess, Chris Woods, Ernie Wilkins, George Coleman, and Joe Temperley on reeds; Sonny Costanza, Jack Jeffers, Dave Bargeron, and John Gordon on trombones; and our rhythm section was Don Friedman on piano, Victor Sproles on bass, and Mousey Alexander on drums. Our arrangements were done by Phil Woods, Frank Wess, and Ernie Wilkins.

Thank God our performance was recorded that night because I can't remember much after I counted off the first number. I was frazzled! Just like the first time I joined Ellington at that big show gig on Armistice Day back in '51.

To sum up my state of mind on the night my big band debuted at Carnegie Hall, after all the intense rehearsals, no sleep, shoveling out huge wads of bread, hectic scheduling, and "acute butterflies," I'll use one of my favorite phrases: "I was overwhelmed with whelment!" I guess the audience enjoyed it, because they gave us a standing ovation.

All I can say is that you'll have to listen to the recording from that night to get an idea of what happened. My hat goes off to Helen Keane and Bob Swartz, our producer and engineer, and to Martin Koeniges, who did the cover photo for the album. I couldn't have done it without them. *That,* I do remember.

The reason the whole thing cost me so much bread was that I had to pay the Carnegie Hall crew *and* the crew that I'd hired. Their rule was that you had to pay their people whether you used them or not. Dollars were jumping out of my pockets like grasshoppers! I prayed that I could get good distribution for the record, and recoup my investments that way.

Trying to get a record company to pick up the album was like trying to sell bikinis in Alaska. Since Helen had been successful getting Polydor to release a record we'd done in Montreux the year before, I went to her for help. She tried her best, but she couldn't make a connection.

At first, I felt really down about the whole scene. It wasn't at all like the dream I'd had when I was a kid in St. Louis, wanting a band like Duke's. There was a hell of a lot more involved than I had imagined. More bread than I had thought, by far! Things I didn't know about the record business. And not enough time to learn, since I was traipsing all over the globe doing gigs, trying to foot the bill for everything. Too tired to think straight. In constant back pain.

I got mad at the record companies. Then I got mad at myself. After a while, I cooled down. I'd always been a fighter, so I decided just to keep on fighting. I thought, At least we debuted in Carnegie Hall, one of the most renowned concert halls in the world. The band was happy, and they'd gotten paid. That standing ovation showed that the audience was happy. So I kept stepping. But more hard lessons were lurking around the corner.

48. Etoile

Eventually, I got two distribution deals for some of our records—one with a British company and the other with a company from Japan. Things looked promising. But all of that was taking up a hell of a lot of my time, which was already *packed* with gigs. So I decided to get some help and the proper setup.

First thing I did was to get a nice office at 756 7th Avenue, right in the heart of Manhattan. It was a two-room suite on the sixth floor. I copped some nice office furniture for the reception area. Made my office a home away from home with a beautiful desk and a comfortable sleeping chair where I could rest my bones between dates. It had a nice closet for my wardrobe. I said good-bye to hotel rooms and the Trans Lux.

I hired a secretary and a couple of cats to do booking and marketing. Milt Hinton, Seldon Powell, Frank Wess, Ernie Wilkins, and Jack Jeffers also used my office for short breaks between their dates or to conduct business.

For years, I'd been happy just playing my music, but the time had come for me to stop losing so much money. I decided to start my own publishing company. Before now, I'd never thought twice about suggesting little riffs here and there, creating tunes on the spot at recording gigs for the record companies. But I wasn't getting one wooden nickel for what I'd contributed, and it pissed me off when I heard my original material on the radio and jukeboxes.

I realized that the record companies were taking my creativity all the way to the bank. Something had to be done—and I wasn't the only one who felt like that. No more playing just for the love of it. It was time to get paid in as many ways as possible—publishing, copyrights, whatever!

It was also curtains for cameras rolling at my gigs when I hadn't signed a release. I cut off my performances many times. "I won't play another note unless the camera stops!"

Even in our jam sessions, I'd catch snakes with a camera or a tape recorder, bootlegging our gigs, cheating us out of our bread. Our jam sessions were our most sacred times, when we could all congregate after a hard day's work and feel free to play from our souls. There was no pressure of being hired; we could just play whatever we felt with whomever we wanted. And then somebody would sneak in a tape recorder, while we were blowing our hearts out for *free.* So I had to stop and threaten them. It was enough to make you want to mash somebody's nose through their face. Luckily, I never had to do that, but I knew I had to do *something.* I felt just like the member of the 197 union when he made a demand at a meeting in St. Louis years back: "The time have came when something is got to be did!"

So I invited Melba Liston and Phil Woods to my office, and we started Etoile Music Productions. *Étoile* means "star" in French. We also started a record label under the same name. And to seal the plan, I started a publishing company, which I named Pastel Music in honor of Duke, because he liked pastel colors.

We had big dreams. We wanted to do it all. Jingles, recordings, and performances. One of our initial objectives was that Phil and Melba would write arrangements and I would hawk them—sell them, you know. So when an opportunity came for me to do a concert with the Buffalo Philharmonic Orchestra, Melba said, "I'd like to write the arrangements. I'd love the challenge." So she wrote the arrangements for the symphony orchestra and jazz band combined.

Our first venture hit a roadblock when we went up to Buffalo to rehearse with the orchestra. We were told, "Oh, no. We can't read this. If you have more than four measures on a line, it's not acceptable." We never knew about that rule for orchestral music.

So we did a U-turn and went back to our office, where Melba rewrote the whole thing. We also had to spend more money to make new copies. We were only getting two grand, and it cost more than half that to copy and recopy everything. A tiny profit was left for Melba and me by the time we deducted the expenses for the two trips to Buffalo for a rehearsal and the concert. The bottom line was just enough for me to get a dinner.

That Buffalo concert was a big success, though. The guest conductor was a young cat named DeFalo. He loved the arrangements and used them with several other symphonies, including Denver, St. Louis, Kansas City, Cleveland, and Pittsburgh. So in the end, it all worked out.

We had to laugh about the lessons we learned in those early days with Etoile. The best thing was that we stayed friends through it all, even though "our outgo usually exceeded our income."

I remembered something Shorty Mac had said a long time before, when I was heading out on my first road gig with the Reuben and Cherry Carnival. He told me to lighten up and laugh more about life. I tried to keep things light, because I wanted it all to work out. I didn't want to be a drag. But the money was coming out of *my* pockets.

I had already suffered a heavy fine that the IRS slapped me with, to the tune of seventy-six thousand dollars! They said that I was responsible for deducting taxes from my big band payroll. Hell, I didn't have time to do all that paperwork. I had hired my musicians as independent contractors and I thought they were responsible for their own paperwork. But I got stuck holding the bag.

On top of those taxes, Uncle Sam got me again! At one point I took my band over to Europe for a one-week gig that paid ten thousand dollars. They all went back to the States, but I stayed on for a few weeks to do some gigs that I'd lined up for myself. The IRS got it all wrong and charged me taxes on ten thousand dollars per week that *I* was there, even though the big band only performed for one week.

Between Uncle Sam and my back pain, which was getting worse, I was close to losing control. But I was also determined not to give in to the left hooks that life had thrown at me. So I had some ballpoint pens made with the initials K.M.B.B.G.A, and I distributed them. Those letters stood for the words "Kiss my big black greasy ass!" My friends cracked up when they saw them. I still have some of those pens today. Funny how something like that can ease the tension. And I kept steppin'. Nothing was going to stop me from playing jazz.

In those early '70s, Ken Demme got me hooked up with some endorsements for a bus line and a beer company. I also took Louis Armstrong's advice and did some cigar endorsements—even though I had stopped smoking. I remembered back to when Pops did some beer endorsements, even though he told me, "I don't drink that shit, Daddy." And I did a few things for Chevrolet, with Eydie Gormé doing the vocals. She hit a high note and I hit a high note on my horn, while the car was sitting up high on a rock.

My schedule was getting busier with more endorsements, television interviews, cover stories for newspapers and magazines. But jazz dates were the most important things on my calendar, and my big band was the love of my life.

There were some rumors that I had "sold out" on jazz because I was doing all kinds of other music in the jingle market and on the show. I did interviews to try and set the record straight, but finally I just passed out some more of my K.M.B.B.G.A. pens, deciding that folks are going to believe what they want to believe. Meanwhile, I kept zigzagging across the world, playing my music all over the place and then jumping back into New York dates. I needed the bread to stay ahead. If they couldn't dig it, then it was their problem, not mine.

I played with lots of other musicians, and I took my big band on as many gigs as we could get. I loved every minute of it—in all corners of the Earth. And I really enjoyed going to local schools and talking to the kids about jazz. Little did I know that I was being introduced to a whole new world of jazz perpetuation.

49. Jazz Education Arena

In the early '70s, local schools invited musicians from the *Tonight Show* to come and talk about what we were doing in our careers. So Doc Severinsen, Jimmy Maxwell, Bernie Glow, and I spent time at some schools, playing, talking, and answering questions.

The students dug it, and I realized what an impact we were having. I saw this as a great way to perpetuate jazz. With rock and roll all over the place, I felt that the big band scene was slowly fading away, and unless we all did something it was going to vanish completely. So I became committed to exposing as many kids as possible to jazz. The schools provided us with a captive audience, and I saw that the students enjoyed it as much as we did.

Generally speaking, things hadn't changed from when I was a young kid in school and we were learning all that classical music. Only now it was jazz that needed to be taught on a grand scale. Instead of being pissed about it, I just made time to go to as many schools as I could. I wanted the students to know about all the jazz greats—Duke Ellington, Basie, Roy Eldridge. The pioneers. I wanted to teach them, wanted them to hear us play. I saw that when we made it interesting and fun enough, they wanted to learn more.

While I was gigging in Harlem in the early '70s, I met some young cats who wanted to play jazz. James "Short Stop" Scott was around fourteen years old. He reminded me of Q (Quincy Jones)—eager and persistent. Short Stop wanted to play trumpet, and he had some friends who wanted lessons, too. So before I knew it, I was involved with a bunch of young "tough guys" who needed my help. I decided to spend my own money and help them start a jazz youth band.

One Saturday afternoon I called an open rehearsal at the Club Baron, where Miles or Dizzy (I can't remember which one) had been gigging that week. The kids were excited. A few dozen young musicians from all over showed up, and I gave everybody a chance to play. I could see that they needed some serious direction. When we'd finished, the man who was cleaning up the club complained about all the bottles and trash we'd left behind, so I told Short Stop to get a studio booked for the following week, and I'd pay for everything.

We rented Penn Studio on 125th, which was a five-flight walk-up on the same street as the Apollo Theater. In the heart of Harlem. I remembered all of that electric energy that I felt when I came to New York for the first time back in '45, on leave from the navy. Although it was a hell of a hike up those stairs, the place was perfect. We could make all the noise we wanted—get down to the business of jazz. The studio proprietor, George Penn, was an ex-trumpet player, and he welcomed us with open arms.

I called a friend of mine named Fred Wayne, who was a serious writer. He put together a book for the band that had at least fifty tunes in it. I pulled some of the tunes out of my big band book, too. So we had plenty of music for the young cats. They were so excited. It was great knowing that I was doing something to help keep them off the streets and out of trouble. *And* to teach them about jazz.

In our trumpet section, we had Jerry Gonzales, Sinclair Acey, Short Stop, Chip Coles, Carl Jennings, and later, Cyril Green, Billy Skinner, Joe Gardner, and a kid named Kamal Abdul Alim. The saxophones were Bill Saxton, Rene McLean (Jackie McLean's son), Gene Ghee, and Quentin Lynch, and later on, Kenny Rogers and Lawrence Ramsey. Our trombones were Bernard Pettiway, Milton O'Neal, Marvin Neal, and Ray Murray. On bass we had James Benjamin and Andy Gonzales, who was Jerry's brother. Dennis Tate was our guitar player. The drummer was Dennis Davis. On piano we had Lewellen Matthews and, later, Billy Gault. Miles Matthews played congas.

Those kids stole my heart! I bought Bernard a trombone, Quentin a baritone sax, and Gene a tenor sax. Even though my other obligations kept me almost too busy to fart, I kept working with them.

Right away, I saw that they were a bunch of knuckleheads. Coming in late, missing sessions, making lame excuses, and showing *attitude*. So I told them, "I'm not here to babysit anybody. I'm paying for everything, and I don't have time to waste. I don't need any shit from any of you little motherfuckers! We're here to play some jazz." After that, I didn't have any trouble.

I taught them how to read music and all about phrasing. How to solo and how long to solo. The particulars of music theory. Notations, quotations, chords, and progressions. They learned how to play a big band book, and I looked over their arrangements. Encouraged them, just like I'd done with Q.

It was one of the best feelings in the world to see the joy in their faces. They had a lot of potential, made a lot of progress.

I had musicians from my big band come and teach them at my office. Had section rehearsals there, too. Frank Wess oversaw the reeds, Lloyd Michaels oversaw the trumpets; Arnie Lawrence, Kenny Dorham, and Ernie Wilkins taught the whole band when I was on the road. Their little Harlem band was really good, and they became popular.

I let the Penn Studio go because the stairs were a drag with my back condition. So we had rehearsals in a studio on 42nd Street, then at Wilbur De Paris Studio on 23rd Street. Finally, I arranged for them to rehearse at the Manhattan School of Music. I knew a cat there and he got us a classroom. I was so excited that they were in an accredited university!

At one point I had to go out of town for some gigs, so I got a trumpet player friend of mine named Don Stratton to teach the kids for me. When I got back, Don said, "The attendance is falling off. Sometimes, no more than two or three kids show up."

I asked one of the cats what was going on. He said, "We don't need no *whitie* teaching us about our music."

That pissed me off! I said, "You just don't get it! What difference does it make if my sub is black or white? You were learning!" I was so mad, I started to say, "Fuck it!"

I decided to take a break from them, thinking I'd wasted my time and money. But then I found out that some of the cats had enrolled in college on scholarships based on the experience they'd gotten with me. And shortly after that, I learned that the government had funded a program that encompassed the same concept as my youth band. The program was named Jazz Mobile, and it was headed by Billy Taylor. Later, one of my former drummers, Dave Bailey, headed it. After Dave, one of the baritone sax players in my youth band, Kenny Rogers, was an executive with Jazz Mobile, and stayed with the program until the day he died.

I'm glad I didn't get too upset with those young cats because many of them went on to become quite successful. The Gonzales brothers had an act known as Fort Apache Band. Gene Ghee became head of the music program of Boy's High in Brooklyn. Sinclair Acey taught theory, arranging, and composition at old Westbury College and at a school in the Bronx, eventually becoming assistant principal. Bill Saxton became a regular in my Big Bad Band, as well as a successful independent musician and the owner of his own club in Harlem. James Benjamin became Harry Belafonte's ace player and a first-call musician. Dennis Davis became a successful drummer in Hollywood and worked with George Benson and Sting. Miles Matthews became a politician. Carl Jennings became a teacher at the University of Maryland. Billy Gault ended up teaching at Hart College in Connecticut, and Rene McLlean became a first-call musician. Short Stop became a trumpet teacher and traveled with me internationally. A lot of people thought he was my own son. In a way, he was.

Jazz had taken up most of my time, but I loved every minute of it. It was the only thing that had never let me down, and I knew I'd never let it go. Watching the young cats in that Harlem youth band grow in their careers made me feel proud. They were all like family to me. I had to make sure I did my part to continue perpetuating jazz.

One day Billy Taylor asked me, "Man, why don't you come to Cleveland with me to teach a clinic?"

It was one thing to go to the local schools, talk with the students, play for them, and answer questions. I'd had fun working with the young cats from Harlem putting together the youth jazz band. But when Billy told me that the clinic was at a college and that I'd be actually teaching like a real professor, that was ridiculous! I'd been kicked out of high school, after all. So I didn't want to put myself in an embarrassing situation where somebody could say, "How in the hell is this man going to jump into the education scene when he doesn't even have a high school diploma?"

I said, "Man, I don't know anything about teaching a clinic."

He said, "You're a natural. Just come on and do your thing."

When we got to Cleveland, I felt like a young mouse on a cat farm. But once I got going, I was hooked. The students were so interested in what I had to say. They kept asking me questions, and all of us wished we'd had more time.

I realized that what they were being taught wasn't coming from a real-life experience, like I'd had in all those big bands. What it was like to be on the road. The difference between classical music performance and the guttural sounds and swinging rhythms that jazz encompassed. The phrasing was different. The tonguing was different. There was so much I wanted them to learn.

They were hungry to learn how to interpret the language of jazz. How to play phrases like Louis Armstrong, like Basie and Duke. Those students made me feel like I was offering them something unique—so much so that I knew this was something I wanted to do for the rest of my life! I decided that my crazy schedule had to go. I *had* to make room to teach.

Just like that, I told all the contractors to take me off their lists. I'd been hiring too many subs for the television shows anyway. Running from studio to studio had gotten old. I realized that I wanted something more. It wasn't that I didn't enjoy making all that bread. It was simply that I loved working with those students more. So I squeezed clinics in between performance dates, and the more clinics I did, the more enjoyment I got. I started judging schools' ensemble competitions, performing and recording with the students, too. At one school, I even played with their marching band on a football field in the pouring rain. Stood out there when we finished our performance while they presented me with an award. We were all as wet as biscuits in the river, but I loved it!

They wrote me letters and I answered them. It got to the point where I was traveling with a suitcase of mail in addition to my other luggage. Then their parents started calling, telling me how much the kids had improved on their instruments. Sometimes they asked for my help with more than music. I talked one kid out of committing suicide, for example. That was a heavy trip. But it made me realize the responsibility I'd taken on. It meant a lot to me to know that I was making a positive difference in these young people's lives.

All this meant that my jazz family was growing. And it gave the perpetuation of jazz a boost because all of a sudden there were all of these young folks practicing and learning. They wanted to know all sorts of things, like how to do circular breathing, what kind of person Miles was, what I'd learned from playing in bands like Basie's or Duke's. They wanted to know whether to play a flatted fifth here, a raised ninth or a minor third there. They wanted to learn the difference between playing classical and jazz.

They wanted to learn *all* about the language of jazz—how to bend a note, slur it, ghost it. How to improvise. I loved teaching them how to buzz to get a different sound. How to play by huffing air from the lower diaphragm like Ben Webster did. How to play soft and sweet "lull" sounds like Prez did. How to play through their teeth for the "th" sound.

Somebody asked me about the plunger, how to play it. I told them, "Listen!" Like Duke used to say. "Listen to the masters like Ray Nance, Rex Stewart, Tricky Sam, and Tyree Glenn. Cats like that." Then I told them to say, "How. Now. Brown. Cow." Slowly. Told them to look in the mirror at their lips as they said it, watch how their mouth moved, because that's the way the plunger has to move to say those words. I told them that their plunger has to be soft, so they can manipulate it. Just like lips. I told them to cut the plug out and leave the hole open so they could play the plunger in tune. And I said, "You've got to practice, practice, practice. It doesn't happen overnight." That made sense to them.

I loved finding ways of teaching them with things they could relate to. Things that would hit home. When I showed them how Mexican mariachi players learned how to play ascending and descending glissandos on their mouthpiece only, without even picking up their horn, from the looks on their faces I knew I was on the right track. I went on to explain how having chops like that helped Sweets Edison play his old Reynolds trumpet in tune, even when it got jammed. They were like sponges, soaking it all up.

They wanted me to tell them what it had been like to perform at the White House, for the 1969 salute to Duke on his seventieth birthday. They enjoyed stories about my travels. Like the time that a taxi driver in France was taking me in the wrong direction so that he could make more money. He'd pretended that he couldn't understand English. His eyes got real big when I pushed the button on my switchblade. *Bling!* Then all of a sudden he understood everything I was saying. English and all!

I told them the truth, and their laughter was sincere. They were so happy to tell me all about the compliments they'd gotten after incorporating what I'd taught them. At my concerts, they'd bring their parents backstage to meet me. Those were some beautiful times.

In jazz education, Billy Taylor had introduced me to a whole new world, and I was sincerely grateful. I followed his lead and got others involved—Snooky Young, Ed Shaughnessy, Louis Bellson, Red Holloway, Marshal Royal, James Moody, Frank Wess, and a slew of others. By '71, I was working with so many high schools, colleges, and universities that an article about me in the National Association of Jazz Educators magazine bore the title "The World's Busiest Jazz Clinician."

I wanted as many ways as possible to teach jazz. So in 1973, with a cat

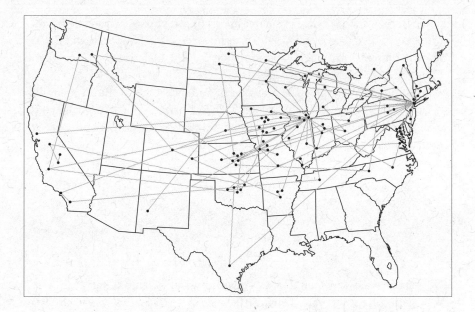

HIGH SCHOOLS	Lawrence, IN	Kent State U.—Kent, OH
Flint, MI	York, PA	DeAnza College Festival—Cupertino, CA
Butler, MO	Wayzata, MN	U. of Pittsburgh—PA
Raytown, MO	Long Island, NY	Morningside College—Sioux City, IA
McPherson, KS	Endicott, NY	Washington St. College—Cheney, WA
Derby, KS		St. U. of N.Y.—Albany, NY
Davenport, IA		Fresno St. College—Fresno, CA
Indianapolis, IN	COLLEGES	
Burlington, IA	State College—Glassboro, NJ	
Houston, TX	Doane College—Crete, NE	FOREIGN
Little Rock, AR	Memphis St. U.—TN	7 weeks Europe
Weatherford, OK	Grinnell College—IA	2 weeks Japan
Kirksville, MO	Quinnipiac Festival—Hamden, CT	Toronto, Canada
Appleton, WI	Southern Ill. U—Carbondale, IL	
Russell, KS	Park Valley College—Rockford, IL	MISCELLANEOUS
Riley, KS	U. of North Dakota—Grand Forks, ND	Youth Workshops—Oklahoma City
Union, MO	U. of the Pacific—Stockton, CA	Jazz Workshop—Tulsa, OK
Troy, MO	Eastern Washington College—Cheney, WA	Community Youth Workshop—York, PA
Jefferson, IA	Oklahoma City College Festival—OK	IAJ—Youth Concert—Long Island, NY
Los Alamos, NM	American College Festival—U..of Ill.	CMP Seminar—Binghamton, NY
Topeka, KA	Mich. St. U.—East Lansing, MI	Dick Gibson Jazz Party—Denver
Buffalo Center, IA	Lenoir Rhyne College—Hickory, NC	Blues Alley—Washington, D.C.
Greenville, OH	U. of New York—Binghamton, NY	Left Banks Society—Baltimore
Terre Haute, IN	U. of Md. summer workshop—College Park	Donte's—Los Angeles
Edwardsville, IL	New York U.—NY	London House—Chicago
Sioux City, IA	Monterey Jazz Festival—CA	
	Morgan St. College—MD	

"World's Busiest Jazz Clinician": Some of the places across the country and overseas where I led classes, clinics, workshops and performed concerts within a few years. Adaptation of a map in the National Association of Jazz Educators magazine, from an article written by Allen Scott.

named Phil Rizzo, I tried my hand at writing a book; it was called *The Interpretation of the Jazz Language*. A few years later, in '77, we did *Let's Talk Trumpet: From Legit to Jazz*. Then I did a little brochure entitled "The Art of Circular Breathing."

Writing these books was a lot of work and it cost a wad. But if it could get the message across to the students, then I had to do it. Plus, it helped take my mind off my back because the pain was on the rise. It still wasn't more than I could bear, but it sure was talking louder.

50. Those NBC Years

No matter what aches and pains I had, physical or emotional, I always kept going. Kept steppin'. During the twelve years that I was with the *Tonight Show*, from 1960 to 1972, I must have recorded more than a hundred albums. Each one was unique and challenging. Like the time I was at a rehearsal in '60 with Charles Mingus for a record date.

This was the first time that Charles was bringing his original music to New York. Britt Woodman was from California like Charles was, and they had known each other from childhood. Since Britt was a well-respected trombonist and had established himself in New York, he helped Charles out by putting a band together for the date, which included me. A bunch of cats were there. I can't even begin to start naming them. Serious musicians.

Charles passed out the charts for his tune "Mingus Fingers," which he had written for Lionel Hampton's band and Hamp had recorded on Decca Records in '47. I looked at the chart, which was torn, fondled, and watermarked. Very difficult to read.

After trying to figure it out for a while, I finally gave up. Put my horn in the case, picked it up, and walked to the front. I said, "Charles, I'm very sorry, but I'm a pretty busy cat at this period and I really don't have time to sit here and try to decipher this music. I really can't tell whether a note is on a line or in a space. So I'm going to have to cut out instead of wasting your time."

Now, he had a reputation for getting into fisticuffs, like one time when he knocked out Jimmy Knepper's and Jackie McLean's teeth. I could tell that he was pissed because his nose was flared out more than usual. His nostrils looked like tuba bells!

I laid my horn down. I wasn't wearing glasses at that time, and I was ready in case he made a move. Especially since I'd had that training with Kid Carter and I'd won some boxing matches in his gym back in St. Louis when I was a boy. Some things you never forget, and boxing was *still* in my blood.

I'd learned to never lower my gaze when facing an opponent because their first move is usually telegraphed from their eyes. So I stood there and looked him straight in the eyes, ready to throw a counterpunch if he tried to punch me.

He checked me out. My stance. And the fact that my horn was laid down. After a few seconds, his rapid breathing subsided and his nostrils went back down to their regular size. He said, "Okay, man. Okay."

That was the end of it and I walked on out. I'm happy to say, though, that we recorded that album later, in May of '60, and we became good friends. The name of the album was *Pre-Bird*, and later on it was reissued with a new title, *Mingus Revisited: Charles Mingus and His Orchestra*.

I also worked with him at a Town Hall concert in '62. He'd requested that we wear tuxedos. But then out he walked on stage in a pair of dungarees, a tank shirt, and tennis shoes. He looked at the audience, grabbed the mike, and said, "I don't know what you people think this is, but for us, it's a record date." He wasn't really prepared for the concert—we hadn't rehearsed the music properly before the gig. But the house was packed. So he opened, to the surprise of everyone in the band, with a jam tune, asking me to come down front and improvise. He named that tune "Clark in the Dark." Later on that night, he did the same thing with Eric Dolphy.

Most cats might not have pulled the whole thing off as smoothly as Charles did, but he was endowed with the capability, like Ellington, to maneuver out of what would normally have been a serious problem. All in all, I had a great time playing with my friends at that "record date," as Charles put it; a great time in spite of the challenges, because I'd always had a lot of respect for Charles.

He and I remained friends, and I'm sure that since I'd confronted him face to face at that rehearsal in front of his whole band, he knew I meant business. My involvement with boxing played a key role in my life many times because it gave me confidence to deal with obstacles without fear. I also had friends who were professional boxers. Like Archie Moore. He had one hundred twenty-seven knockouts, and nobody has ever matched his record. Archie and I had a mutual admiration for each other because I thought he was a hell of a champion, and he loved my trumpet skills—so much so that he asked me to come and play at his training camp while he worked out.

Once when Archie was a guest on the *Tonight Show*, I played a tune for him named "Undecided" while I was wearing boxing gloves! On that same show, I played a little tune that I had written for him called "Lil' Ole Mongoose"—that was his nickname, the "Old Mongoose"—while he kept rhythm by bombarding a speed bag. It was a gas.

I'm glad that I never had to use my boxing skills at any of my recording sessions. I enjoyed playing with the cats. Enjoyed my record dates. Like the one on December 10, 1960—"Gerry Mulligan and the Concert Jazz Band at the Village Vanguard." That date was a lot of fun.

A few weeks earlier, after I'd gotten off from work at the *Tonight Show,* I had gone to the Vanguard and listened to Gerry and his band. I'd known him for a while, and I liked the cats in his band. I'd played with some of them on dates for commercials around town for months—sometimes twice in one day, before I went to work at NBC each afternoon.

Gerry had Nick Travis on trumpet, playing some awesome solos—a great lead trumpet player; another excellent cat on trumpet was Don Ferrara. Then there was Bob Brookmeyer, who was one of the all-time great valve trombonists; Mel Lewis, a great drummer we used to call "Tailor" because he played so well until everything would *fit* just right; and Bill Crow—he was a very good bass player. Then there was Gene Quill, one of the top alto players around town. Matter of fact, he was often referred to in the local saying "Phil (Woods) and Quill"—both great sax players. But Phil wasn't in Gerry's band, just Quill. A whole lot of really talented cats were in Gerry's band. Very good musicians.

And Gerry's band was very different because they didn't play the ordinary run of arrangements. They played his original things—tunes that I liked. And I liked Gerry. Suave cat. Hollywood actress wives. Fun to be around.

He had some great arrangers, and he wrote his own arrangements, very good arrangements. Al Cohn, Johnny Mandel, and Bob Brookmeyer were doing arrangements, to name a few. I dug Gerry's band scene, so I made time in my hectic schedule for a few rehearsals, starting around the end of November.

On that December 10th record date, Gerry had Don Ferrara, Nick Travis, and me on trumpets; Bob Brookmeyer, Willie Dennis, and Alan Raph on 'bones; Bob Donovan on alto sax, Jim Reider on tenor, Gene Allen on baritone, and Gerry Mulligan played baritone and piano; Bill Crow was on bass, and Mel Lewis on drums.

There was a tune on that album that I really liked named "Blueport." I can still remember the melody. Fast blues tune, nice chart—it became a hit tune.

It was cool playing with Gerry and his band, and I played with them for around four years whenever I could. Did a few dates here and there, two or three other albums, and some concerts on the college scene where I loved watching the excitement on the faces of the students. They really dug us.

Fun cat, Gerry was. Used to announce one of the tunes that we played, "You Took Advantage *on* Me," just for fun, instead of saying "*of* Me." We all got a big kick out of that.

There were so many bands that I played in and recorded with—Herbie Mann's Orchestra, Lalo Schifrin, Woody Herman's Orchestra, man, so many bands. Woody was one of the all-time great band leaders. He kept the band going for forty years. He wrote great music and he always had great musicians because he was such a nice guy and the cats really liked working with him. I liked his style a lot.

Some of the other albums I did during those *Tonight Show* years were *Big Band Bossa Nova* with Q, *Really Big* with Jimmy Heath, and *Genius + Soul = Ray Charles*. On that one, Q hired me to contract the date, which meant choosing the musicians.

So much was happening so fast, but it was a lot of fun. I did a few albums with Skitch and the *Tonight Show* orchestra, and I did some records with Strays, Lionel, Babs Gonzales, Joe Williams, Earl Hines, and Shirley Scott, to name a few.

It had been a while since my first album as a leader back in 1955, when I recorded *Clark Terry* for Mercury Am/Arcy. So during the *Tonight Show* years I made a few more, sometimes paying for them myself. Worked with record companies and used my own quartets or quintets. Put things on wax like *Trumpet Giants: Sarah Vaughan and the Clark Terry Quartet, Clark Terry: Color Changes, Everything's Mellow, All American*, and *Tread Ye Lightly*.

I already knew I didn't like being signed to any one label. Didn't want anybody controlling my life. I wanted to call my own shots. So I worked with all of them—Columbia, Epic, Riverside, Mercury, Mainstream, RCA, Old Town, Verve, and dozens more. They called, they paid, and I played.

George Wein was still heading up the Newport Jazz Festival while I was with the *Tonight Show*. We did some recordings together. George liked to sing a little and play piano. A nice guy to work with, and a great businessman. I'd worked with him back in the '50s up in Boston at his club, Storyville, and then later at the Newport Jazz Festival, some tours overseas, and, eventually, the Nice Jazz Festival and the Playboy Jazz Festival.

George had connections worldwide. He also had a beautiful wife, Joyce, who was responsible for all of the great food at the festivals. I remember once I was visiting their home in Vence, France. Beautiful place up in the hills with views of mountains. A fishing pond. Nice trees and flowers. We were having dinner, and I wanted to make a toast to George and Joyce. So I made my little speech, got a quick laugh, then when I clinked glasses with Joyce, the crystal goblet I was holding broke.

I was so embarrassed. But she was a great hostess, and she tried to make me feel okay about it. She just smiled and said, "Don't worry, Clark. I'll get you another glass." So she goes and gets another glass, and we do another toast. Well, I broke the second glass, too! She got everybody to laugh about it. But I felt like I had three left hands, five thumbs on each one. Long story short, I ended up giving her a set of crystal goblets, even though she said that wasn't necessary.

There was so much recording going on while I was with NBC. So many gigs, dinners, parties. When I look at the calendars that I've saved from that time in my career, I sit back and smile. I say, "I'm glad that I don't have to do that today!" Pages and pages of dates. Three or four dates on a page. Here's an excerpt from my 1963 diary: "Ed Beach, WRVR Radio; Minor Sound—Hotel America, Marty Wilson; Variety Sounds on 46th; Rehearsal at the Waldorf with Lena Horne; Dinah Washington's party; Webster Hall with Milt Hinton; Carnegie Hall benefit with Mercer Ellington; Jazz Clinic with Art Miles; RCA Victor with George Avakian; Gig with Olatunji; Billy Taylor's party at Minton's; Snooky's for dinner; Capitol Records with Freddie Hubbard." And that was just a *few* pages from a few days. All while I was doing the *Tonight Show*! Not to even mention the flying across the waters and back for the gigs overseas.

My schedule was so packed, I hardly had time to take a crap! It was a whirlwind. But I *loved* what I was doing. That's what made it work.

51. Storms

Outside my professional life, the *Tonight Show* years had their share of tragedies. While I was busy running from gig to gig, churches were blown up, children were murdered, there were sit-ins and demonstrations. Racial equality seemed damn near impossible.

I was devastated when John F. Kennedy, Robert Kennedy, and Martin Luther King, Jr., were assassinated. Those events stopped the world cold.

They were such great leaders. And each time something like that happened, there was more violence.

I did the only thing I could, which was to keep playing fund-raisers for the movement, putting my money where my mouth was. And I prayed.

I wished that things could be like they were on the bandstands and in the studios. Jazz was the common denominator at the gigs. We all loved the music. Even when I went overseas and played with cats who didn't speak the same language, we communicated through the music. There was no problem. Just jazz and the freedom of expression.

In spite of the police brutality, high-powered water hoses turned on marchers, the bombs and the blood, schools were integrated. Students spoke up for human rights. More people listened and got involved.

I knew that no matter what the opposition did, they would not be able to stop the movement. Their actions actually made martyrs of the people they murdered. Strengthened the purposes of our efforts. Made us more determined.

Still, we endured a hell of a lot. That was always the lay of the land.

Miles told me about a few encounters he'd had with racism. He owned the building where he lived, on 77th in Manhattan. He lived on three of the four floors and rented out the top floor. One time, he had a vacancy and posted an ad in the *New York Times*. A white guy read the ad, never suspecting that the property was owned by a black man. Miles came to the door when the guy rang the bell and said, "Can I help you?"

The guy said, "I read about an available apartment at this address." He kept looking over Miles' shoulders and past him, like he thought Miles was just the help, answering the door for the real owner. He couldn't comprehend the situation.

Miles said he stood there, checking the dude out. Getting hotter by the minute.

Finally the man said, "I want to speak to the owner." At that point, Miles told me, he teed off on the guy. Decked him with a beautiful right cross and left the man lying unconscious in front of the door. Miles said he closed his door and went on about his business.

He'd always remind me of that story and a few others, like the time when he came up out of Birdland one night, and a policeman tried to chase him away from standing in front of the club. The cop's partner was drunk, and he beat Miles with his nightstick. Then there was the time when Miles was stopped by cops who didn't believe that he owned the red Ferrari he was driving. They beat him up for owning a nice car!

No matter what, racism was on the scene. Blatant or subtle. But we all kept steppin'. And I made sure that I recruited more cats to join me in playing fund-raisers for civil rights. We played as many of those gigs as possible. We were committed to keeping hope alive. Nothing could stop us.

Miles and I always kept in touch with each other, by phone if we couldn't get together in person. We talked about the things we were going through. He'd show up at my gigs whenever he could.

One time he'd played at the Civic Opera House in Chicago and I was at a club nearby, so he came by after his concert. Came in and caught the whole set. Brookmeyer and I had the group together, and we had Herbie Hancock on piano.

Miles and I talked later that night after our gigs, and he told me that he was going to Pittsburgh the next morning. When he got there he called me and said, "Hey, man, that piano player you've got is a bitch!"

I said, "Yeah, he can play."

He said, "You think he might want to work with me?"

I said, "I'm sure he would."

When I told Herbie, he jumped up and down. He couldn't believe it. I told him that it was cool with me, so he went with Miles.

On another occasion, Miles came through Chicago while I was there and I had Miroslav Vitous on bass. Miles came to the set and had to leave to get ready to catch a plane early the next day. He called me the next morning and said, "Hey, man, that bass player you got is a motherfucker!"

I said, "Yeah, he can play his ass off."

He said, "Will you ask him if he wants to play with me?"

When I told Slav, he screamed and moaned and jumped up and down so much, I thought he was going to pass out.

Miles was the hottest thing going in those days and I was glad for the cats. I felt like I was there to *help* the jazz scene. I'd always been fortunate to stay associated with top-notch players, and I always looked forward to helping the next cat. Whenever there was an opportunity for someone in my band to further their career, I was the first one to say, "Go!"

Whenever people said to me that "Miles sold out," I shut them up right away. I told them, "Miles plays what he wants to play!" I always loved and respected Miles, and he felt the same about me. I was happy for him. Happy that he was banking some serious bread. In spite of the bigotry.

At least the cats in the *Tonight Show* band had been beautiful. No bigotry there, from any of them. But in the spring of '72, the show was getting ready to move to the West Coast. Burbank, California. Doc Severinsen asked me to join him, Snooky, and a couple of the sax players in making the move, but I knew that wouldn't work for me. I wanted to stay in New York. I turned his lucrative offer down.

Doc called me from California. He said, "Come on, we'll help you get a beautiful home out here. You know we need you."

My contacts in New York were too heavy to just uproot everything I'd worked for. I wanted the freedom to do my own thing. Freedom to work with my big band and in the jazz education scene. Doc was cool with that. From then on, whenever I was in California, I'd do a guest spot on the show or I'd sit in with Doc and the band.

That April, I was honored at the fifth annual Quinnipiac Intercollegiate Jazz Festival in Connecticut, and who was the toastmaster but Ed McMahon! It was an emotional thing for me to see Ed and to hear tribute speeches from Stanley Dance, Ernie Wilkins, Reverend John Gensel, and other friends of mine. That meant a lot to me.

I knew I'd made the right decision to stay in New York because I was enjoying my big band dates and other performances, and my passion for jazz education was growing at a fast pace. My newest dream was to organize a youth band and take them overseas so they could experience jazz on the other side of the world.

52. Black Clouds

In the spring of '74 I was gigging in Europe, and one day I called home to see how things were going. When Pauline told me that an early Christmas card had arrived from Duke, with a postmark of April 17, 1974, my stomach did a dive. I said, "A Christmas card in *April*?" I knew something was wrong. I knew he had been in the hospital and I'd wanted to go and see him while I was back in the States, but word came back that he didn't want any visitors. I was hurt, but I imagined that he didn't want us to see him in bad condition.

Well, the news about the card put a big damper on things. I still have the card. Kept it all these years. It's an original card in a white envelope. On the front, it has the words "Love God" printed in blue ink and shaped like a cross. "Love" is written vertically and "God" is written horizontally. Inside, the message says, "Merry Christmas is Merrie, Happy New Year is Happie. You are beautiful. Compounded with Luv and Blessings. And may your total future be the greatest."

After Pauline told me about the card, I kept asking around. Nobody had any good news about Duke's health. On May 24th somebody told me that Duke was gone. That was definitely a heavy day. I knew I'd miss him and love him for the rest of my life. I knew that his music would live forever, and I would always do my part to make sure it did.

As I thought about that early Christmas card, I wondered if he knew that he was close to the end. But the thing that touched me the most was that he thought of me before he left.

Since I was still in Europe during his funeral, I thanked him for what he had done for me by playing tributes to him. Performing, recording, and teaching his music. A few years later I did an album in Hollywood for Norman Granz entitled *Memories of Duke*, with Jack Wilson on piano, Joe Pass on guitar, Ray Brown on bass, and Frank Severino on drums. The first song was the one that I used to love to hear him announce, "Passion Flower." The last one was "Come Sunday," which is one of the most emotional ballads I've ever played. He was such a genius.

In '76, I bought a summer house in Pleasantville, New Jersey, with a wrap-around porch for Pauline and our grandchildren. It was close to Atlantic City, where I hoped to open a little jazz club. And I wanted my family to enjoy a different setting and have some things that I didn't have in my childhood.

The only downside was that things between Hiawatha and me hadn't improved, so I didn't ask him to join us. But each time I looked in the faces of the growing numbers of my students at the schools where I was teaching jazz, I thought, Well, at least I've got wonderful relationships with *them*. They couldn't replace Hiawatha, but they gave me something to hold on to, and so did my grandkids, Butch, Michelle, and Terrence.

Pauline enjoyed the summer home, and she did a fantastic job of making it comfortable for all of us. We went there whenever I could squeeze time out of my schedule.

In '78, I noticed that she wasn't looking as healthy as usual. Something was wrong. She was coughing a lot and losing weight. I took her to our family physician, Dr. Hoffman, for a checkup and x-rays. His office was a few blocks from our house in Queens, so after dropping Pauline off back home, I drove straight back to see him instead of waiting for a phone call about the report.

I sat in the consultation room with him, surrounded by stacks of papers. He slid the films under the clip of the white board on the wall. When he turned on the backlight, he jerked. He said, "Oh, shit!"

I said, "What is it?"

"It's cancer."

I felt like somebody had just rammed a sword in my heart. The gray clouds came back, just like that day in the navy when I'd gotten the letter from Margueritte telling me that Pop was delirious. I couldn't think, couldn't speak.

I don't know how I made it back home. When I opened the front door and looked to my right, Pauline was sitting in her favorite chair in the living room, staring out the front window. I started crying and she got up to hold me.

She said, "It is, isn't it?"

I could barely talk. I said, "Yep."

We hugged each other and cried.

Later, I called Dr. Hoffman and he recommended some specialists. He said that she'd probably have to have a tracheotomy.

As I walked down the hallway from my office in the back, I tried to think of what I could say. Pauline was still lounging in the gold brocade chair like she was in a trance. I said, "I don't care what it costs, baby! We're gonna get you the best care that money can buy."

She just smiled a thin smile. I sat down next to her and we talked about whether I should come off the road and stay with her. But knowing that our insurance didn't cover all the things she needed for her recovery, we both agreed that I should continue to work.

While I traveled, I thought about some of the things that Pauline and I had done, how happy we'd been together for thirty-one years. How she had always been in my corner. She was with me in '76 when Charles Swartz got me the gig at the Whitney Museum, featuring jazz with classical music on a recording entitled *Professor Jive,* using part of the Boston Pops Orchestra. I thought about how she'd loved going to Boston with me to visit Jimmy Hayes and Cannonball and Nat Adderley. The fun-filled trips with the whole family to the little house in Cape Cod with the rambling roses all around the fence. The house in the Bahamas that we'd enjoyed. I'd ended up buying a lot there with a fifty-foot dock in hopes of one day building a dream home for us with a flugelhorn-shaped swimming pool. I remembered how we'd enjoyed visiting with Count and Catherine Basie in their home there. How Pauline loved taking Terrence with us overseas— Spain and other countries. He could barely talk. He said, "I went to 'Pain on Granddaddy's big plane." She'd been so proud of me when I received my first honorary doctorate from the University of New Hampshire that May of '78.

Whenever I was back home, I had to watch her go through all kinds of barbaric procedures. She was steadily losing weight, and the sparkle in her eyes was getting dimmer. I felt totally helpless.

During her recovery from the tracheotomy, I wanted so much to be there with her, but I knew I had to make some bread. I worried about her so much until I started having battles with my blood pressure and struggled to keep my sugar levels under control. Almost every night when I finished my gig, I wrote to her from my hotel room. Sometimes I mailed the letters and sometimes not.

Friday, July 27th, 1978
Geneva, Switzerland

Dear Pauline,

I just wanted to write you a note to let you know that we are All with you Every Minute of your Ordeal!!! You're in Good Hands and we all Love you and pray Daily for you and I'm Sure that the 'Old Man Upstairs' will answer our prayers.

I'm sure that you know that we're seeing to it that you're going to get the BEST medical attention that there is available. And I don't care what the costs will be.

After I finished that two-page letter, I wrote another one that same night.

Dear Pauline,

I would like for you to call Liz [Pauline's cousin] and ask her if she can get a leave of absence and come and stay with you for a couple of weeks when you first go home. Tell her I'll pay all her expenses and the salary that she makes at Barones for the two weeks—just to take care of you.

I told Betty to tell Rudy [Pauline's daughter-in-law and son] to get you some Vitamin E, A, B, and C and B12 and Brewer's Yeast, and you must start taking them religiously. 3000 units of E; 3000 units of C; one A, B, and C and two B12's and Six Brewer's Yeast (2 after each meal) DAILY!!! I have spoken to several vitamin experts about you and your case since I've been here.

As soon as you get well, we'll take a beautiful VACATION somewhere! Ok, Sugar?!!! I'll be home in just a couple of weeks after you get home."

When I got back home, Pauline was still going through the maze of treatments. New medicines. New doctors. I was grasping for straws, so I said, "A change of scenery might help." And I took her with me to my next gig near Disney World and set us up in an apartment. I was working at the Village Lounge with a house trio—Louise Davis on bass, Harvey Lang on drums, and Bubba Cobb on piano.

I tried to cheer Pauline up before going to work one night by cooking one of the few dishes I knew. "Slumgullion," I called it. A mixture of scrambled eggs, hot dogs, onions, and herbs that I'd learned to fix while in the Boy Scouts.

She was reclining on the sofa, smiling and watching me as I sliced, stirred, and cooked the concoction. When my gig was over that night, I couldn't wait to get back to our apartment to see how she'd liked it. But when I walked into our living room, she was still lying in the same position on the couch. The food stood untouched.

I had brought a box with me from home—photos, resumes, and cassette tapes of students who wanted to be in my youth band. I'd put the word out to public and private high schools, colleges and universities, that I was putting this band together. So each day, while Pauline rested, I read the resumes and listened to the tapes to keep my mind busy and stop worrying.

Eventually, I chose Steve Rentschler, Byron Stripling, Tony Lujan, and Gary Blackman for my trumpets; Kenny Crane, Conrad Herwig, Matt Fenders, and Ron Wilkins for my trombones; for saxes, Danny House, Branford Marsalis, Ned Otter, Randy Russell, and Dianne DeRosa; for the rhythm section I picked John Campbell on piano, Peter Dowdall on bass, and Mike Baker on drums. They were from colleges and universities across the United States—New Mexico, Texas, Georgia, New Jersey, Oklahoma, California, Louisiana; Danny was in high school; and Peter was all the way from Australia.

The Florida trip didn't do a lot to lift Pauline's spirits. When we got back home in New York, we sat together in our kitchen. She wouldn't eat much. I watched her struggle for breath to talk by covering the hole in her throat. Her voice was raspy. I felt like we were fighting a losing battle with the Grim Reaper. But I refused to give up.

I stayed busy getting the youth band off the ground. The kids came to New York and I put them all up at the Edison Hotel on 47th Street, just off Broadway, where I'd rented a rehearsal hall. We practiced for a week from sunup until sundown, stopping only for food and bathroom breaks.

It was a phenomenal band. An incredible female vocalist, too—Michelle Beckham—and very talented writers and arrangers—Jimmy Heath, Frank Wess, Ernie Wilkins, Harold "Crooksville" Crook, David Slonaker, and David Leach. Smokin' hip charts!

The kids were really satisfied with the music. That was one of my goals: to get positive answers when I asked them, "Did you enjoy your part?" as Strays used to ask back in my days with Duke. And talk about working hard—these kids were serious. No problems with any of them. They worked on their styles, explored new accents, learned the art of swinging and different phrasings, and everything necessary to get that "in the pocket" sound. When I tell you they *got* it, man, you'd better believe it!

Eventually, I took them all to Europe—first time overseas for all of them except Branford. And they were fantastic. The audiences *loved* them. I was so proud. Real promising futures, all of them. Most of them went on to become successful musicians, and some joined the education scene. It was a life-changing thing for them. When they got home, all of a sudden they were being called for lucrative gigs. They were gassed! It was good for them, and for me. Gave them a boost and gave me the courage to keep on going while Pauline was so sick.

I stayed on the merry-go-round, as I call my hectic lifestyle, constantly gigging all over the place. After I did a Dick Gibson Jazz Party, I did an African Safari of Jazz. "Clark Terry and his Jolly Giants." I had wanted to go to Africa for a long, long time. Sierra Leone, Ghana, Nigeria, Kenya, Mauritius, Madagascar, Ivory Coast, Mali, Guinea, and Liberia. The U.S. State Department had set the African tour up for me, with Chris Woods on sax, Dave Adams on drums, Charles "Sluggo" Fox on piano, Victor Sproles on bass, and vocalist Joe Williams. It was a hell of a group, really tight. And you know Joe was fantastic!

On the six-week tour, we played for some of the most beautiful people anywhere on earth. The scenery was breathtaking: white beaches, aqua waters, mammoth mountains, beautiful sunsets. We spent time hobnobbing with dignitaries, African, European, and American, and promoting good will. (The wife of the governor of Sikasso, I remember, wore enough gold to make a solid-gold flugelhorn.) Politics mixed with jazz mixed with dinners. I ate lots of "different" foods, but there was one thing I couldn't eat, even though it was a "special treat." Fish eyes. I just couldn't eat the fish eyes.

The tour had its challenges, too. We had to wait hours for flights that were delayed until the planes were full. I received a blow to my head from falling luggage jammed in an overhead rack. On the road to Kaduna, we had to navigate potholes as big as trucks. And Victor's seven-thousand-dollar bass violin ended up with a twelve-inch crack.

During the six weeks, I closed my eyes many times and said prayers for Pauline, wishing she could have been with me, enjoying our music and some of the African musicians we were hearing. Incredible musicians like Madagascar Fats, a Fats Waller–styled pianist; Joseph Kobeem on xylophone; Koo Nimo's Ashanti drum group, with two young dancers. Those Malagasy musicians surprised us! They had an incredible sense of jazz swing-time. They could really *wail*. Seriously. They were as good as any of the best jazz musicians I'd ever heard. We did a collaboration with their musicians on saxophone, harmonica, guitar, and bass, three vocalists on stage with us in an Afro-American musicfest. It was all about cohesive spontaneity from two different cultures on the same bandstand. Talk about *soul*. Man!

I wished Pauline could have heard the authentic African drummers. Just unbelievable. And Dave's talking drum. Even though Dave was Caucasian, they loved him. Gave him roaring applause.

While we were in Nigeria, there was a huge Independence Day celebration, accompanied by the transfer of power from a federal military government to elected civilian government. That was really something—historic. I wished she could have seen that.

Healthwise for me, everything was okay. For a few days I had a case of the "African quickstep," meaning diarrhea, but Paregoric cooled that out. And every Friday was Aralen day, when I took the Aralen drug to protect me from malaria, since there were millions of mosquitoes.

All during this time I kept up a façade of things being all right, even though I was so afraid for Pauline. Part of my assignment from the State Department was to write about our experiences, so I kept an extensive journal, which I couldn't wait to read to her.

When the tour ended and I finally got back to Bayside, I was horrified to see how Pauline's health was failing. I had spent a river of money, but nothing seemed to be doing any good. She smiled a little while I read my tour journal, but mostly she was too weak to respond to much of anything.

I kept gigging, then flying back home to check on her. The last time I saw her, she was in intensive care. My next performance was scheduled for a club in Chicago. I tried to tell her that I wasn't going to go, but she wouldn't listen.

I said, "Do you *really* want me to go?"

"Yes."

"I *can't* go. I don't want to leave you."

She whispered, "Rudy is here. He'll take care of everything."

I kissed her; then, as I walked out the door, I turned around and waved good-bye. She gave me a tiny smile and waved back. I prayed for a miracle as I left for Chicago.

A few nights later—it was November 22, 1979—Rudy called. The gray clouds had turned black.

I can't remember much about the next few days, except that Dougal House came all the way from California just to give me a hug. Then he went back home. Now, *that's* a friend. He was the father of Danny House, the kid in the youth band that I took to Europe. But man, my heart was heavy like lead.

Pauline's funeral was like one big black cloud. I remember crying a lot. There'd been a lot of death around me. Usually, I was on the road; never went to funerals. But with Pauline gone, I started thinking about all the people who weren't in my life anymore. Mom and Pop had been gone a long time. My brothers, Bus and Ed, were both gone. My sisters Ada Mae, Lillian, and Marie were gone; only Margueritte, Juanita, Mattie, and Odessa were left. Duke was gone. A lot of my friends were gone. And now, it was Pauline who'd died. Sitting at Pauline's funeral was one of the hardest things I'd ever done.

53. Keep on Keepin' On

The only way I knew how to keep going was to keep going. I recorded more albums, played more concerts, did more interviews, and then a wonderful thing happened in June of '80: the Clark Terry Great Plains Jazz Camp.

For the first time, I had my own jazz camp, and I was totally gassed! It was at Emporia State University in Kansas, a beautiful, hip campus. Dozens of eager young students came there for a week. It was organized by Bob Montgomery, who'd played trumpet in my Big Bad Band. We'd done a few festivals and gigs together in the States. Traveled around Europe on one of my bus tours.

When he told me he was getting a jazz camp together, that was one thing. But when he told me that it was ready to go, I was thrilled! We'd worked to get some of the other cats from my band to be special guests— Chris Woods, Frank Wess. and Carl Fontana. Bob also got some members of the Emporia State faculty as special guests—Pat Coil on piano, Bob Bowman on bass, Jay Sollenberger on trumpet, Jack Petersen on guitar, and Jack Mouse on drums. And finally, we had our camp faculty members: Bryce Luty, C. L. Snodgrass, Roger Kugler, and Don Meredith on trumpets; Chuck Schneider, Charlie Molina, Chuck Berg, and Jerry Noonan on saxes; Steve Slater, Gary Blauer, Jon Burlingham, and Ray James on trombones; our percussionist was Howard Pitler, and Dick Wright taught jazz styles.

For one week, our students learned how to improvise and play in big bands and combos. They had a ball, and so did we. It was a lot of work, but it was very successful. So much so, that we did it for eleven years. Then we went over to Central State University in Oklahoma for four years.

During all those years, we had professionals like James Moody and Rich Matteson come to the camps and work with our students. The greatest thing of all was to see and hear the students' progress. They had the brightest smiles when they'd catch on and listen to their own accomplishments.

I tried to give them as much as I could. I wanted them to know that way back when I first got started, I didn't know how to read music, so I had to listen. And I was determined to memorize the tunes I heard. Commitment was the key for me. These kids needed to learn to use their ears, too. I told them it was by listening intensely that I developed a good memory. Memorization was both visual and oral. I told them about a saying back in my old days, "You have to learn the lyrics to the tune in order to play it."

I gave them examples. If I'm playing a beautiful ballad about a lovely lady, I play it like I'm telling her, "I love you." I'm talking to the lady in a mellow voice. I'm playing passionately and seriously. I made them laugh when I made a funny face of exaggerated anger and I told them that I wouldn't play it roughly. Make it sound like, "I LOVE YOU!" I got a kick out of using comedy to get a serious point across.

I tried to think of creative ways of helping them understand the *language* of jazz. Like when I told them that making up lyrics to a song was one way that helped me to imagine more effectively how to *phrase* the song. How to create different rhythmic patterns. Instead of playing notes, I wanted them to learn how to play lyrical passages.

When they'd listen to me actually *talk* through my horn while playing a passage, they laughed because I made it funny. But some of them caught on that I was showing them how many things they could learn if they just let go and tried.

I told them about the time Prez visited a jazz club one night to hear a new disciple on the scene. The player was impressed that Prez had come by to hear him. After the set he eagerly rushed up to Prez and greeted him. He asked Prez, "How did you like my playing, Mr. Young?" Prez replied, "You sound nice. But what is your *story*?"

I wanted my students to understand that if they didn't find the proper interpretation, then their playing—like that young disciple's—would sound like mundane speech. Absolutely no transfer of feeling to the listeners.

Sometimes I got disgusted with students who obviously weren't practicing enough. It was a waste of my time if they weren't serious about their instrument and about jazz. I told them, "You've got to do it over and over and over until you perfect it! In France, rehearsal is called *répétition:*

repetition. I played 'A String of Pearls' many, many times before I learned all the highs and lows. Before I really understood the *language* of that tune. Even Bobby Hackett's solo. And *that* tune got me in the door with George Hudson's band."

For the drummers, I taught them that their rhythms should have accents like a tap dancer makes. I'd demonstrate a boring tap dancer with no accents: "Doop be doop be doop." Then show them how to put in some accents: "Um Bop doo POW shoo shoo WHOP!"

At one of my camp rehearsals, the drummer was playing a mundane pattern, "Bingity bing, bing." So I walked up to him, took his music, and tore it up. I said, "Now, play the piece and *swing* it." With no music, he played from his soul. He felt it and made us feel it. He swung it.

A lot of my students had been taught by people who were involved in the theory of music, harmony, and composition, which was good in its own way. But I wanted them to know how to play from their hearts. How to play it *right*.

I wanted them to find *ten thousand ways* to do things with their instruments. Determination. That's what I wanted them to have. How to make it out there on the road, no matter what. How to "get that *hump* in their backs." Bottom line—how to pay dues by sticking to a dream no matter what obstacles come around. How to learn *from* obstacles and realize that they make things better.

To give them an example, I told them about the time when the drummer didn't show up for a record date. And we did the date *anyway*.

It happened back in July of '78. Philippe Gaviglio was a producer and he had booked a bunch of dates for me over in France. We were scheduled to make an album down in the south of France, in the middle of a vineyard that was owned by one of his friends. We booked Red Mitchell on bass, Ed Thigpen on drums, and Horace Parlan on piano. All incredible musicians.

And Horace, man, talking about overcoming obstacles—he'd had some kind of childhood illness that left his hands slightly handicapped. Said he'd studied piano like there was no tomorrow. And to compensate for the trouble with his hands, he learned to play arpeggios with his *left* hand and chords with his *right*. Sometimes he'd cross his hands when he played. You could never tell which hand was in the treble keys and which was in the bass keys. Absolutely amazing.

So, Philippe, Red, Horace, and I, we all went to a little studio hidden up in the nooks and crevices of the grape orchards. The wine orchards. It was a nice place to hide out and get in the mood for recording. There were all sorts of beautiful wines there, and we enjoyed ourselves while we waited for Ed to show up.

Time passed and Philippe got itchy. He said, "Let's just make a track, for fun. Without the drums."

We were all astonished that it came off well, rhythmically. So Philippe said, "Hey, let's do the rest of it."

So we made the rest of the album, just the three of us—piano, bass, and trumpet. As a matter of fact, we made enough material for two albums. Philippe was thrilled with the outcome, including the fact that you had to listen very closely to detect that there were no drums. In some instances, it was impossible to tell.

After it was all over, Philippe said, "I have a great title for the album. I think I'll call it, '*Fuck* the Drummer.'"

I said, "Aw, man. You can't do that."

He said, "Why can't I do that? Hell, it's *my* money."

I said, "Yeah, but it's *my* name."

So Philippe ended up naming it *Intimate Stories* and releasing it much later, in '98.

I can't remember why Ed didn't show up for that gig, but, like I told my students, "We didn't sit around and complain. We used what we had—and it worked." When Ed and I came across each other later, we were cool. Didn't let that incident put a drag on our friendship. Played many other gigs together. And our friendship extended to the point where I grew to love his family and they loved me, too.

Same thing for Philippe. He was like a son to me, and all about business. I made a *ton* of money working on the gigs that he got for me. Months and months of work.

As a matter of fact, it was at one of the festival dates that he booked for me—the Cliousclat Festival in France back in '75—that I first heard Michel Petrucciani. This cat was born with a disease that caused him to be extremely short in stature, maybe less than four feet tall. Needed help getting up on the piano bench. But a hell of a pianist. Only *thirteen* years old when I heard his debut at that festival. Man! I was blown away with his talent.

I told some of the cats that I knew over there, "We gotta help Michel, man! Get him on some more gigs." Then I told Philippe to set things up so Michel could play with me on some of our tour dates—and he did. Michel went on to become very successful. Highly respected. Shows what can be done when you're determined.

That's just one of the reasons that I dug working with Philippe. He was compassionate. I told my students that when they climb up a little on the ladder, don't just stand there and say, "Hey, look at me." I told them to turn around and help somebody else. That's the real deal. That's what family is for.

Cats like Philippe and Ed and other jazz musicians around the world felt pretty much the way I did—that we were one huge *family*. And we usually worked out our differences.

At my jazz camp in June of '80, my students loved hearing stories like these. Everybody said the camp was successful—the students, the faculty, and my friends. I thought so, too. Teaching was what I loved the most. Absolutely. Whenever I could give jazz lessons to students, I did. The rest of the time, I was traveling and gigging.

My students wrote to me, and I wrote postcards and letters back to them. I did a lot of letter writing while I was on the road. Kept in touch with my friends and my family. That cut down on feeling homesick, lonely, disconnected.

Between gigs in the States, Norman Granz hired me for a tour in Japan, and I did a lot of work around Europe. Sometimes my nephew Odell McGowan traveled with me, and at other times one of my other nephews, Don Gilliam, went with me, too. We had a lot of fun together. They made some bread and I had some help.

As for my son, Hiawatha, we were still estranged. He rarely came to the family reunions in St. Louis—but I did, whenever I had the chance, and I was glad to see Margueritte, Mattie, Odessa, and Juanita. My sweet sisters. There were some new additions to the family who thought that I was a "money well waiting for their bucket," and that put a damper on my visits. But I still went because my sisters were so proud of me.

They were very understanding about my career. It takes a special support system to be out on the road constantly, and my siblings had *always* encouraged me to keep going. They knew that I hadn't been able to go to the funerals of my father, my brothers, or my other sisters because I had to work. They *knew* that I had to do what I had to do. I'd always shared my successes with them. Taking care of expenses or wiring money, buying gifts. Visiting whenever I could.

A few times, I arranged for my sisters to come to my concerts. It made me feel good to listen to them bragging on me. I took them to nice dinners afterwards. I remember one of my nieces coming along one time, and for an extra special little touch, I ordered pheasant under glass for her. When I asked how she enjoyed it, she said, "It tastes just like neck bones, Uncle John!" We all cracked up.

As usual, Margueritte kept in touch regularly to lift me up when I felt low about Pauline being gone or any other problems I had. She wrote letters. Came for visits. Or she called me to read a scripture and pray. We all kept in touch. I don't know how I would have made it without my sisters in those hard times during the '80s. Especially Margueritte.

The letters I got from my students helped, too, when I felt downhearted. There was one in particular from a little elementary schooler. At one of the clinics I did in the schools, my group performed "The Flintstones," among other selections, and one of the letters I received afterwards said, "Dear Mr. Terry, Thank you for doing the show at Cactus Wren. I liked win you sed yapudu. Yours truly, Jesse." That was his way of writing, "When you said, Yabba, dabba, do!" One of the lines from the lyrics. I loved it!

My students meant *everything* to me. I was so grateful that I was able to teach them about jazz. Even if, on occasion, I got carried away. One time at the Kennedy Center in Washington, D.C., I was supposed to be in the wings, getting ready to go on stage for a concert. But nobody could find me. They looked all over the place. Then somebody heard my horn down in the basement. I was teaching a student and had gotten so involved with the lesson I was giving I had forgotten about my concert!

I remember once when I was in London, I met a young trumpeter named Guy Barker. After the show, we talked for a while. He came backstage to meet me and he told me that his mother was an actress and his father was a stunt man. When he played his horn for me, I could see that he was a promising player, but I noticed a problem. I said, "You've got a pretty little girlfriend standing here, but somebody's going to take her away from you."

He looked at me with a shocked face and said, "Why?"

I said, "When you play, you look ugly because you're playing all on the side of your mouth and twisting your face because you have the wrong embouchure." I showed him how to tuck his lips properly, find his natural embouchure in the middle of his lips. That way, not only would he look better, but he wouldn't damage his chops. Then I said, "Do you have any time off?"

He said, "Well, I've got a light schedule coming up. Why?"

I said, "I want you to practice what I've shown you. And even when you don't have your trumpet with you, just do it on your mouthpiece."

He kept in touch with me and let me know that I had helped him to play better. He was even able to make higher notes. Later, he ended up playing in a group with the British pop star Sting. Even though Sting's band wasn't into the jazz scene, I knew that Guy had our music in his blood, and so in some way he would be a part of keeping jazz alive. I was really proud of him.

It was the greatest feeling in the world to think that I had something to do with the careers of my students. The *greatest* feeling. I loved the awards that came from here and there, but the thing I loved most was to see those young people grow. Watch their dreams come true.

I had worked with some students at the University of Pittsburgh a few times, and in the late '80s I got a phone call from Nathan Davis, who was the jazz seminar director there. He asked me to donate some of my personal things to the university for a display that they were putting together. At first, I was shocked. It was a total surprise to realize that people would want my memorabilia for an exhibit. Nathan ran it down to me, told me about some sample things they'd like to have. After I hung up, I started feeling real good about the whole scene. Honored, in a sense. So, I got some things together for them—some of my Clark Terry valve oil, an old passport, a golf ball, some valve springs, a few payroll deduction receipts from the Duke Ellington Orchestra, and a slew of other stuff.

They were so happy when they received everything, and it gave me a deeper sense of connection to my students. Another means of joy in the midst of dealing with the challenges of road life—delayed flights, close connections, crowds, no sleep, pain in my back.

Among the many gigs I was doing, I did some sets with Jon Faddis, like the Madarao Festival in Japan. Did a Japanese commercial for Suntory whiskey together. Record dates, too. He was a very talented young trumpeter, eager to learn, and he was just starting to come into his own as a soloist. He'd done a lot of work with Dizzy, and although there were traces of Diz in his playing, I was glad to hear Jon playing in the middle register and developing his own ideas.

I remember one particular album that we cut together for a Japanese label, Nippon Phonogram. It was recorded in Switzerland and New York. Had some power hitters on the gig. Cats like George Mraz and Jimmy Woode on bass, Mino Cinelu on percussion, Terri Lyne Carrington and Ed Thigpen on drums, Harold Danko and Dado Moroni on piano. Jon played trumpet—hitting those notes dead on. Strong chops. Most of the time on that album, I played flugelhorn. Beautiful album. *Take Double.*

I was so proud of Jon, loved working with him. And I liked the hip cover for that record, with us dressed in sharp white suits and photographed to look like we were standing on the wings of a private jet.

By this time in my life, I'd received quite a few awards and other forms of recognition, but I never let it go to my head, because I always whispered,

"There but for the grace of God, go I." And before I'd go to sleep each night—no matter where I was in the world—I rubbed the front of the Bible just to make a personal connection with God.

In 1987 a jazz landmark happened! On September 23, the House of Representatives declared that jazz was a "rare and valuable national American treasure." Finally, all the thousands of musicians who had spent their lives playing and teaching jazz, like I'd done, could say, "Thank you!" to the American government.

As I read the official wording, I zoomed in on a few of the phrases used, like "Jazz has achieved preeminence throughout the world as an indigenous American music and art form," or "outstanding artistic model of individual expression," or "bridging cultural, religious, ethnic and age differences," or "has become a true international language." I shouted, "Yes! Yes! Yes!" That resolution said *exactly* what I'd been teaching for years. I couldn't have been happier if I'd found a sack full of hundred-dollar bills!

Before that resolution, jazz parties had been just a whole lot of fun—fantastic jazz played by top musicians in private resorts or other beautiful venues, tons of tasty food, and hobnobbing leisurely for a few days with lots of friends and fans. Annual gatherings, you know.

Now, as I played at the different jazz parties like the ones given by Dick and Mattie Gibson or Don and Sue Miller in Arizona, or the Minneapolis Jazz parties, or the even the ones in Holland by Hans and Annette Loonstijn or wherever I went, when I thought about that September 23rd resolution, I felt like jazz was well on its way to being perpetuated. *That* was my lifelong mission.

When I played overseas—like when I did Norman Granz's Jazz at the Philharmonic tours around France, Scandinavia, and England or Gerd Meyer's tours with the "Basie Eight" around Germany, or when I did record dates in Belgrade and Yugoslavia with Boško Petrović—I had a little more pep in my step. The only drag was that my back was really bothering me.

So I went over to Switzerland and had some microsurgery done. Dr. Sooter arranged the operation, with Dr. Rohner doing the surgery for a herniated disc. Wish I could remember their first names. Afterwards, Dr. Sooter told me that he was a sax player and he asked me if I'd ever taught at the Swiss Jazz School in Bern. I told him that I had and we talked a lot about jazz. It was great to have doctors who loved jazz, and they did a pretty good job on my back because, after a short recuperation, *most* of that horrible pain was gone.

But another problem was bugging me. My vision was getting blurry and I was having trouble reading charts. I hadn't taken the time to go to an eye specialist because I was making it okay. I'd just ask for extra lighting when I needed it. And besides, my calendar was filled to the brim, as usual. Still, I could tell that my eyes were getting close to being a drag.

54. New Love

It was January of 1990 and I'd been gigging hard, as usual. I'd met a woman who told me that she knew someone who would be a nice lady for me. Since I'd heard useless predictions like this hundreds of times, I fluffed her off—just like I'd done to Miles years ago in Carbondale, Illinois, when he was asking me about playing the trumpet while I was checking out all the pretty young girls dancing around the Maypole.

But something kept nagging at me to check out this "nice lady." So I made a few calls to some friends and asked them to do a little Sherlocking. Eventually I received a box in the mail that was filled with news clippings, photos, and other info about Gwen Paris. All positive stuff. She was forty-two, single, attractive. Co-founder of a charity to help high school students get into college—Students Targeting Adult Responsibility, or STAR.

Reports came back that Gwen had gotten some info about me, too, and that it was all green lights to call. So around the middle of January I phoned her office in Dallas, Texas. I was looking at a picture of her. I said, "Hello, Ms. Paris."

She said, "Hello, Mr. Terry."

While going through the initial formalities, I was digging her voice— honey sweet. Her grammar and her diction were impeccable. Definitely a plus.

I said, "Is that your real hair?"

She laughed and said, "Yes. Is that your real beard?" She described the photograph that she had of me. I knew it was the one with my Van Dyke look.

She told me that she'd listened to some of my music for the first time. She said, "So, you're a jazz musician. How long have you been playing trumpet?"

I said, "Almost fifty years and I'm gonna keep on doin' it till I get it right."

She was honest enough to tell me that she didn't know much about jazz. For a moment I got quiet. Jazz was my entire life, and I wondered if I could find enough common ground with someone who knew nothing about it. But I stayed cool and changed the subject. I said, "And you—you help kids go to college?"

She told me about how students were unaware of the millions of dollars that were out there in scholarships, didn't know how to get those funds. How STAR helped with all of that. I listened, hoping that she'd keep it short. She did.

As I listened to her talk about her concerns for the "future leaders of our world," I was thinking about how I'd devoted most of my life to helping young people learn how to play jazz. I said, "I *love* to teach. If we don't help our youth, they'll end up like blind mules in a meadow." She chuckled.

Even though I had a photo of her, I said, "How would you describe yourself?"

"Well, let's see. I'm around five-four, maybe a hundred and twenty-five pounds, brown-skinned, and that's about it. What about you?"

"I'm a big, fat, bald-headed greasy dude." She laughed. Then I said, "How long are your eyelashes and how long is the hair on your arms?"

She was giggling. "I don't know, I never measured it."

I asked a ton of questions and she did, too. I explained that I'd been single since Pauline passed in '79, and that I didn't have a special lady now.

She told me that she was a real estate broker, divorced, no boyfriend, no ex-husband "escapades." She had two sons, Gary and Tony, twenty-two and sixteen. Man, the more we talked, the more I was interested. Seemed like she felt the same, but you *know* I maintained my cool.

I told her about Sissy and Hiawatha, and some of my experiences with my students—how they were like family to me.

I found out that she was also raising another sixteen-year-old kid from Rome named Peter because his father, David, had fallen on hard times. She went on to explain that David's girlfriend, Victoria, wasn't able to take care of Peter. They'd all been neighbors and she loved Peter like a son. Said she'd never been involved with David.

As far as the music scene, she said that she'd studied classical piano for seven or eight years. Played some flute in high school and sung R&B in college. Said she'd written a few tunes as a hobby—R&B and country. No jazz anywhere.

"Can you cook?"

She said, "Is fat meat greasy?"

Now, I'm sitting there thinking, She has a great sense of humor; she's raising *sons*, so she knows about the male species; she can cook; loves to help young people, and I can see from her photo that she's a real knockout. If she was as great in person, I *knew* that I would marry her.

For the next thirty days, we talked almost every day, and I'd send funny postcards and letters from places where I gigged. When I got back home to unpack, check on personal business, and repack, there would be letters, cards, and poems from her.

She told me that she was born in Pine Bluff, Arkansas. Had only been to a few places in the United States. I couldn't wait to show her my world!

There was a strong sense of integrity about her. I loved hearing her talk about how much she loved God. Made me think about the way I always rubbed the Bible on the road. How I held it in my arms while drifting off to sleep.

We covered a lot of ground by telephone in those thirty days. She said when she was growing up in Pine Bluff, she had to starch and iron everything, from her father's handkerchiefs to sheets and pillow cases. She made it clear that she wasn't going to iron *anything* of mine. She said, "The only reason I own an iron is for my sons and guests to use."

I said, "That's okay. I don't like to iron either. I have a lady who takes care of that for me." But meanwhile, I was wondering if she was too undomestic for me. I knew I didn't want a woman who put all of her energy into her job and not enough into her home. After all, I needed plenty of help.

I found out that her sister was in the education scene and that her mother had retired from it. Her father and grandfather, both deceased, had been lawyers. Her brother was a corporate executive. We also covered a few things about my health and hers. When we talked about my back pain, diabetes, trouble with my vision, and high blood pressure, she said, "Don't worry. I'll do some research." Now, that was music to my ears.

Finally, she accepted my offer to fly her to Chicago, where I was scheduled to perform. I couldn't wait!

The way the tickets worked out, she arrived at the airport before I did. When I walked toward the gate where she was waiting, she stood up, and I was bowled over. Wow! She was everything I'd hoped she'd be, and more. Svelte, classy, graceful, with long pretty hair, and just the right height.

I tried my *damnedest* to be laid back. I was decked out in my black leather trench coat and black leather fisherman's cap cocked "acey-deucy." She looked sexy in her knickers, which showed off her shapely legs. And her sweater dipped just enough to accent her nice bosom. I wanted to dive right in!

When we got within reach, we hugged tighter than Dick's hat band. Then I kissed her. That was *it* for me, and she was all smiles, too. But I knew I couldn't look like an easy target, so I dragged things out with small talk. "How was your trip? Are you hungry?"

My friend Ed Crilly drove us straight from the airport to the gig and he was talking to us, but I was too busy kissing Gwen to pay him any mind.

He said, "Are you gonna come up for air?"

I said, "Are you kidding?" All I could think about was Gwen's sweet kisses and her intoxicating perfume. I just couldn't get enough. Finally she looked at me and laughed.

I said, "What's so funny?"

"Your moustache has turned pink from my lipstick." Then she handed me a Kleenex.

I said, "That's why I don't like lipstick on my ladies. Plus, it messes with my chops."

When her smile died, I mustered up a grin and said, "That's okay. I'm not playing *now*. I'll just wipe it off later."

After the gig that night, she was so excited about the concert. She went on and on about how her students should know about me and jazz. She also told me what a kick she'd gotten out of "Mumbles."

I said, "Some folks call me, 'Mr. Mumbles.' I don't care what they call me. Just don't call me late for dinner."

She was just beautiful. When we went to my hotel room, she said, "My mother told me to never give up the booty on the first date."

I said, "That's okay. My mother told me the same thing."

We talked for a long time about my career. Where I'd been, where I was going, who I'd recorded with, and why I didn't have an autobiography. I told her that I had a writer working on it. Then we finally went to bed. To *sleep*.

The next morning, we flew together to New York, where I was scheduled to do the "Hearts for Ella" tribute to Ella Fitzgerald. When we got to my home in Bayside, I tossed the house keys on the dinette table in my dark kitchen. I'd wanted to improve the lighting in the room, but I hadn't had time. And the last time I'd been home, it was just for a couple of days. I didn't have time to set things up for my friend Lady K. to come and freshen things up. I wondered what Gwen thought about my house. And I declare, I don't know what got into me, but I said, "This place is really dusty! No food in the fridge. And I've got a pile of dirty laundry. You've got *lots* of work to do!"

She shot me a piercing look. Then she started walking from room to room and yelling with a fake French accent, "Lil*lee!* Lil*lee!* Where *are* you? You need to clean up like you're getting *paid* to do! Clark is not *pleased!* You *need* to do your *job!*" When she walked back into the kitchen, I was standing dumbfounded. She raised her arms like she was totally disgusted and said, "I was looking for zee maid but I can not *find* 'er." Then she smiled at me.

I'm thinking, Okay, I've met my match! So I grabbed her and kissed her.

Later that evening, I asked her to model the dresses that she'd told me she'd brought to wear to the next day's concert. When she was modeling the last dress, I ran my hand down the back of my head. I hadn't said a word, so she knew I didn't like any of them. Then I said, "May I make a suggestion without hurting your feelings?"

She said, "Sure." She was smoothing her dress, which looked like a blue sack of potatoes.

I said, "Ditch those dresses and take my credit card up to InCognito on Bell Boulevard tomorrow while I'm at the rehearsal. Buy something sexy. Okay?"

She said, "You don't like any of my dresses?"

I said, "No. They don't accent your figure. Like Duke Ellington said, 'I'm easy to please—just give me the best.' And *you* deserve the *best*."

I knew I'd have to stay at the concert venue for rehearsal all day the next day. Since it was her first time in New York, I hoped she could make it to the gig in Manhattan on her own. Before I left that morning, I laid some bread on her and said, "No offense, but please check out one of the manicure shops." As I headed out the door, I prayed that she could handle me and my world.

55. Whirlwinds

Not only did Gwen make it to the gig just fine, but she caused a lot of rubbernecking with her short sexy black dress. Rosalie Soladar, Al Grey's lady, took a picture of us that night that is still one of my favorite photos.

Things were great except for the fact that my eyes were starting to give me more hell. Everywhere I looked, it looked like somebody had turned all the lights way down low. Even though the dressing room had bright bulbs all around the mirror, everything seemed *dark*. To add to my misery, my back pain was getting worse. I tried to fix it with more aspirin, but that did as much good as trying to paddle a canoe with a baseball bat.

The concert was a tribute to Ella, and it was incredible. Ella completely stole the show! After spending the evening in the audience listening to us play and receiving all those emotional tributes, she decided that she wanted to sing. She stepped up on stage and took a mike; then she called for Joe Williams and me to come back on stage. We did a "Mumbles" threesome. The standing ovation seemed like it would go on forever!

When Gwen found me among the fans and musicians backstage, she said, "Clark, I cried so much during the show, and especially at the end. I wished I'd known about all of these great musicians. I feel horrible that I've never seen Ella or Joe or Lena or those other legends perform in person until tonight. You all were fantastic! I'm going to do all I can to educate people about jazz."

I thought, Bingo!

When Gwen got back to Texas, she arranged for her friend Maxine Ragsdale to take charge of her office, and then she got an executive-on-loan grant from IBM. I wanted her to move in with me, but she wasn't ready for that yet. At least she was able to travel. First, I took her to Don and Sue Miller's Paradise Jazz Party in Scottsdale, Arizona. Then I arranged for her to meet me in Nice, France, for George Wein's Parade du Jazz, better known as the Nice Jazz Festival.

She had to fly to Paris and make it to Nice on her own, but she aced it.

Miles was at the festival. I took her over to where he was performing; it was in one of the three venues there. We stood in the wings backstage. When he got wind that I was there, he walked over to where we were. We talked for a few minutes and he invited me to sit in. But I had to get back to my own gig. Gwen was totally digging all the jazz legends.

She said, "It's a shame that all we're taught about in American schools is classical music. Not a drop about jazz. It just isn't fair!"

She kept bugging me about the progress on my autobiography, said she wanted to see it. I said, "I've got that all under control. Allen Scott is working on it. It's coming along." I told her that Allen was a freelance writer that I'd met while I was with the *Tonight Show*. We'd hung out together and talked about my life and career. He'd written an article about me for one of the jazz magazines. Real intellectual cat. Wrote for *Navy Times* newspaper.

She wanted to know more, and the only thing that cooled her questions out was when I agreed that she could do some research, ask me a few questions about my career, "to help Allen."

After we left Nice, we toured a few more French towns where I did mostly one-nighters. Then we headed back home.

A few weeks later, we went to see Dr. Cheryl Kaufman about my vision. Dr. Kaufman said, "If you hadn't come in today, Clark, you might have completely lost the vision in your left eye." That scared the shit out of me! All the times I'd been too busy to see someone about my eyes were coming back to haunt me. Now I was sitting in an office getting ready for emergency laser surgery to stop the bleeding behind my retina so it wouldn't be "curtains" for my eye!

Thank God that Gwen had put her foot down and demanded that I go to the ophthalmologist. After that, I promised her that my schedule would include more time for my health. Another one of the hundreds of reasons that I had to keep her in my life.

She was a great help to me, taking over responsibilities. Flight arrangements, negotiations and confirmations for gigs, phone calls, fan mail, wardrobe maintenance, and a bunch of other stuff. I felt like a big load had been lifted off my shoulders. And I loved her cooking!

The updates she made to the house were hip—new kitchen cabinets, new refrigerator, and something I'd never had, a dishwasher. She even had me helping her to clean out the freezer in my basement. Then she changed one of my guest rooms into her office, with filing cabinets, a computer, and a printer. Next thing I knew, she replaced my two rotary dial telephones with the latest two-line, pushbutton model. Had a phone put in her office, too. Man!

Before I could catch my breath, the master bedroom got an overhaul. Then she opened up the storage bins in my office and dusted off all of my awards. She nailed them up on the living room, dining room, and kitchen walls. All down the hallway. She was so proud of my career. That made me feel like I'd hit the jackpot in Atlantic City!

Her sons joined us in November for a New York recording session with Chesky Records at the Village Gate. The band was hot, and it was a real tight set. We had Jimmy Heath on tenor, Don Friedman on piano, Marcus McLaurine on bass, and Kenny Washington on drums. Paquito D'Rivera sat in with us on sax. We all had a fabulous time.

The audience had been really patient while we were taping and doing retakes, so at the end of the set I created a new tune that they could participate in. I named it, "Hey, Mr. Mumbles." They'd sing, "Hey, Mr. Mumbles, what did you say?" Then I'd answer them in the "Mumbles" language. They cracked up each time I answered them. Everybody loved it!

In early December I did a live session for TCB Records at the jazz club

Q4 in Rheinfelden, Switzerland, with the George Robert Quartet. It was an incredible session, with George on alto, Dado Moroni on piano, Isla Eckinger on bass, and Peter Schmidlin on drums. Those cats were unbelievable! It was a gas! Man! They even had a surprise pre-birthday celebration for me.

Milt Hinton happened to be on the same plane with us coming back from Switzerland. Milt and I would run into each other from time to time—either coming from or going to gigs, and sometimes we were booked on the same gig. We weren't seatmates on that flight, but when we landed in New York we spent a few minutes catching up on things. Reminiscing about those days when I got the Harlem youth band together and bought instruments for some of them; how Milt taught them in my Manhattan office; how well most of them were doing and how that whole scene planted the seed for Jazz Mobile.

Eventually, we hugged each other and I said, "See you down the road a piece, Judge," which was the nickname I called him. "And give my love to Mona." She was his wife—great lady. Used to travel a lot with him. Everybody loved her. He always smiled when I called him Judge, and then he'd say, "Thirty days!" which was his "sentence time" for me as if we were in court and he was a real judge.

On December 14th, the University of New Hampshire was throwing a big seventieth-birthday bash for me. My relationship with UNH went back to the mid-'70s, when I'd taught there. I'd taken their jazz band with me to the Montreux Jazz Festival in '76. My first honorary doctorate was from UNH back in '78. And we'd hosted the Clark Terry Jazz Festival and other events there annually.

Dave Seiler was the head of the jazz department there. He had placed a rocking chair on stage for me because he knew about my back. So I rocked in that chair, thinking that I was part of the show that Dave and I had planned. Hip local musicians and students in the Clark Terry 70th Birthday Celebration Big Band. But then, as I sat there rocking, out walks Milt Hinton! I was shocked. We had seen each other only a few days before, and he never said a *word* to me about coming to UNH. I was truly bowled over. We did a tune together, and he pulled the strings on that bass as only he could do. I loved it!

Now, Milt's surprise appearance would have been enough for me. But that wasn't all that Dave, Paul Verrette, and Gwen had concocted. Paul was a professor at UNH and he was very involved with the jazz scene there. A great friend. One by one, more friends came out and played. James Williams, Louie Bellson, Hal Crook, and Gray Sargent. I couldn't believe what was happening. The cherry on the cake was when one of my students, Ryan Kisor, walked out on stage, followed by Herb Pomeroy and Doc Cheatham! Doc was eighty-five years old at the time, and he played "Just Friends" so beautifully. They were all fantastic!

After the show, they brought out a huge cake and I blew out the candles. Then they handed me the mike. I could barely talk because it had been so overwhelming to see so many friends, both on stage and in the audience. They had come from near and far to wish me a happy birthday.

A few days after that, Norman Granz gave me an unforgettable gift: a luxurious trip to California, where Oscar Peterson was getting married to a lady named Kelly. That was the first time I'd ever flown on an all-first-class plane, complete with a chef carving filet mignon in the aisle. It was wild!

When we got to Beverly Hills, Norman and his wife, Greta, put us up at L'Hermitage. Talk about posh! Complimentary caviar and limousines. Everything, including the wedding, was unforgettable. It was beautiful to see how happy O.P. was with his new wife.

All in all, my seventieth birthday was probably one of my best birthdays ever! The only drag was that my back pain was talking louder and louder, making it more of a hassle for me to fly and gig. Plus, the other eye was giving me problems.

I decided that maybe it was time to slow down a little. Maybe buy a nice home in Dallas, since Gwen was still living there sometimes. Nice international airport, nice weather. Do my business from there.

The next year, Gwen and I bought a waterfront home on Lake Ray Hubbard in Heath, Texas. It was a dream home for both of us. Lake views from the master bedroom, living room, kitchen, and den. I'd always loved the water, and I was eager to buy a boat and do some fishing. We got the keys to 626 North Sorita Circle on May 6th of '91. As we walked through the house—*our* house—for the first time, I kept looking at Gwen's smiles. I was thinking of all the fun we were going to have.

Duty called, though, so I left her there on the 9th to fly to New York to do a guest appearance on the Joe Franklin television show in Manhattan. A talk show with guests, similar to the *Tonight Show*.

I'm glad I still have my personal calendar pages from those days, to help me remember all the things that went down at that time. Life sure was hectic!

On the 10th, I taught a master class at Princeton University in the afternoon, then played at Struggles nightclub in New Jersey that night. Then next day, I performed at Rutgers University in the evening and later on played again at Struggles.

On the 13th, Gwen flew to New York to join me when I received the Beacons of Jazz Award along with Billy Eckstine at the New School in Manhattan. Two days later we flew to Vienna for a tour put together by Boško Petrović; I played a concert there on the 16th; another in Graz, Austria, on the 17th; and flew to Zurich on the 19th to make a connecting flight back home.

On the 22nd I returned to Bayside for more laser surgery on my eye. The next day, I got my tooth recapped, then we went to St. Peter's Church for a gig that Pastor John Gensel organized, which was a tribute to Gary McFarland. We'd all been shocked to learn that Gary had been poisoned in a bar. Real nice cat, Gary. Hell of a musician. Died in '71.

On the 24th we flew to Columbia, South Carolina, for the annual jazz festival there, which was coordinated by Johnny Helms. Three days later it was back to Bayside for more laser surgery and more dental work. A Queensboro Community College gig was next, on the 31st, with Jimmy Heath, Frank Wess, Marcus McLaurine, Sylvia Cuenca, and John Campbell, with vocalists Carrie Smith and Irene Reid. After that, we took a break to answer mail, pay bills, and do personal errands. On June 6th, we jetted to Dallas for a couple of days of down time.

On the 9th, it was back to work, with a concert in Mt. Vernon, New York, followed by more dental work on the 10th and a rehearsal at the Blue Note with Lionel Hampton on the 11th, for a gig on the 12th. That gig was recorded, and it was fantastic! There were two albums made from our performances there, with Lionel on vibes, Sweets Edison and me on trumpets, James Moody and Buddy Tate on tenor sax, and Al Grey on trombone. The rhythm section was Hank Jones on piano, Milt Hinton on bass, and Grady Tate on drums. The afternoon of the 13th, I did a performance at Charlie D's in New York with a doctor who was a good drummer. Bob Litwak was his name. He played in an annual gig with some of his friends who were also doctors, and I was their guest artist. They had a nice sound and we all had a lot of fun.

I left Gwen in New York and flew to Birmingham, Alabama, for a concert there and then continued on to Iowa to another one of my wonderful student encounters—"C.T.'s Band Camp," which was run by Cliff "Wheels" McMurray—for a few days.

On the 20th I was back in New York, where Gwen went with me to an afternoon rehearsal at the Manhattan School of Music for a gig coming up on July 1st and 2nd; then later that evening we went to a sound check at Carnegie Hall for a concert that night with Mel Tormé—a great concert.

Gwen and I flew to Oklahoma for a fantastic five days at "Clark Terry's

1991 All-American Jazz Festival" at the University of Central Oklahoma, until the 28th. This was one of Bob Montgomery's productions and, as usual, we all had a ball. An absolute gas!

When we got back to New York and I went to see Dr. Hoffman on the 29th about that pain in my back, he suggested that I should have a CAT scan and an MRI. Since I was booked so heavily, I postponed the tests. I wasn't too interested in doing them anyway, since I'd heard that the MRI procedure was "Claustrophobia City." Just the thought of being confined inside of a metal contraption scared the hell out of me!

After the two-day gig at the Manhattan School of Music, Gwen and I flew to Amsterdam for another George Wein tour. I gigged in Holland for Hans Loonstijn's Jazz Party on the 5th of July, then started on the first part of George's tour, playing in The Hague on the 6th; Strasbourg, France, on the 7th; and Cossiac and Bordeaux on the 8th. After a few days off in a hotel on the Riviera, I did the Nice Jazz Festival on the 14th and 15th, and then we continued with the rest of George's tour, heading to Romatheul on the 16th; Montreux, Switzerland, on the 17th; Pori, Finland, on the 18th and 19th; Gordes, France, on the 20th; and back to Nice on the 21st. After a brief stop at the house in Bayside, we flew to Los Angeles where I had a gig at the Catalina Club on the 23rd and 24th.

Gwen said she loved traveling with me. I had wondered if she'd have the stamina for it, but she was hanging right in there. My friends around the world loved her. They thought we made a nice couple. This was all a routine schedule for me, and normally it wouldn't have been a problem because I was doing what I loved. But I was catching hell because it felt like a fire was slowly spreading in my back.

56. Through the Storm

Everything I wore had aspirin in the pockets in '91. Pants, vests, shirts— even my horn bags. I slept in my bed with my legs over an ottoman, a chair, a box, anything I could find to position my back where it didn't hurt so badly. Nothing helped. The pain was excruciating. Something had to be done because I couldn't make it much longer.

Between concert gigs, I had some record dates in New York. *Jazz* with Cleo Laine and Johnny Dankworth, Gerry Mulligan, Toots Thielemans, and a bunch of other cats. In January, I did *Memories of Louis: Teresa Brewer and Friends* with Nicholas Payton, Freddie Hubbard, John Hicks, Cecil McBee, and Grady Tate. I flew over to Graz, Austria, in April and recorded *St. Louis Blues* with Boško Petrović, Damir Dičić, Mario Mavrin, and Vito Lesczak. Then I went to Boston to do *Almost Blue* with Fred Haas, Jeff Auger, Marty Ballou, Les Harris, Daryl Bosteels, Melissa Hamilton, Val Hawk, and Christopher Humphrey.

By June, I was really struggling. But I kept going. I did a recorded concert called "Live at the Blue Note: Lionel Hampton and the Golden Men of Jazz." Sweets Edison, James Moody, Buddy Tate, Al Grey, Hank Jones, Milt Hinton, Grady Tate, and Hamp. I nicknamed us "The *Olden* Men of Jazz." We loved working together.

When summer of '91 came, I just couldn't take it anymore. So Gwen set things up for me to go to Booth Memorial Hospital in Flushing, New York, for the MRI that Dr. Hoffman had suggested a while back.

John Simon ended up driving me there. He was a great tenor player, and I'd nicknamed him "Faithful" because he had always stuck with me through changes in my health. He had just played with me on a gig a few days before, like we had done many times. Years later, I recorded some tunes on his album *John David Simon and Friends*, featuring Etta Jones and me.

While I was at the hospital with John, Gwen was at home waiting on Triple-A to jump-start the battery in my car, which was dead from sitting up while I'd been gigging. Wynton Marsalis and I had talked the night before about the whole scene with my back, and he had told me that he would help out with the battery situation.

I'd always loved Wynton. He is such a fantastic musician, and we enjoyed shooting the breeze from time to time. I'd been so proud of his career, and I'd always done whatever I could to help him. He'd done the same for me, too. Can't remember recording together, but we played together at a gig that was set up by the Thelonious Monk Institute. It was at a gala for President Clinton later in '93—Wynton, Herbie Hancock, Thelonious Monk III, Al Grey, Ron Carter, and me. Bill Cosby introduced our band.

Wynton's family was very talented, starting with his father, Ellis. All of them were incredible musicians—Wynton, his brothers, Branford and Delfeayo. Branford was in my youth band back in '78, and ended up being the music director on the *Tonight Show* later. I helped Delfeayo out many years later—around 2009—when he called me about a recording project that he was doing with some of Duke's music.

Well, when Gwen and Wynton walked into that hospital room where John and I were, I felt better seeing them, but still, I was scared shitless. I told Wynton that I just couldn't make the MRI because I was too terrified of that big iron tube. Just thinking about it made me crazy. So we're all there together in my room. I'm dressed in the hospital garb, and my back feels like it's breaking in *half*.

Wynton said that he'd called one of his personal doctors, who could come and give his opinion. I felt like the dregs in the bottom of a wine bottle. Hopeless. I really didn't want to deal with more doctors, but Wynton insisted. I cussed for a while and then I gave in. Well, his doctor made it there in no time, and after we had our intros, he did a quick analysis and put his bid in for me to see a neurologist.

I said, "I've got a good doctor and I don't need anybody else!"

Wynton took my hand and said, "Well, Cee Tee, what do you have to lose? We need you out here. Nothing else has worked. So will you please try what my doctor is saying?"

I thought about it, knowing that I damn sure couldn't go on like I was. So I said, "Okay, Wynton. I'll try anything."

A few days later, after I got the okay from my doctor, an ambulance took me to the Long Island Jewish Hospital. Reverend Taylor and his wife drove behind the ambulance with Gwen. He was the pastor of Galilee Baptist Church, which was down the street from my house. That was our church. I'd played there, and Al Grey had joined me a few times with his trombone. We played things like "When the Saints Go Marching In." Beautiful things.

Al and I hung out pretty regularly, and we enjoyed playing together. He had a real nice sound on his horn. Our friendship went way back to the old navy days in '42. A lifetime friendship and great jazz memories. We'd been on a lot of George Wein's tours together, and I loved the way he worked the plunger. His girlfriend, Rosalie, and Gwen were close.

When we got to the Long Island hospital, John Simon was there to meet us. Al and Rosalie showed up, too. I felt like I had no control of my life anymore. I was pissed and scared, praying that things would work out.

After several days of tests, I ended up in spinal stenosis surgery, which was done by Dr. Lowenthal. I'd been told that he was one of the best neurosurgeons on the scene. When I woke up in the recovery room, John and Gwen were there. I tried to move, but I couldn't. I was scared. Scared that I'd never play again. When I was moved into my own room, I wanted to hear some jazz, so somebody brought me a tape player and a radio.

Days passed. People came. Flowers were delivered. The phone rang so much that the hospital complained. But they cut me some slack and allowed the calls. I couldn't even hold the phone! Someone did it for me.

At the end of the day, I couldn't remember who all I'd talked to. So I kept just listening to my radio and praying.

There were two nurses. Both were hefty, like football linebackers. They came each day and flipped me like a pancake with the sheets, since I couldn't move. It reminded me of sleeping in the hammock when I was in the navy. Only this time, I *couldn't* flip myself. At least I could push the red nurse's button. And believe me, I did!

My world was falling apart. I thought, What if I have to spend the rest of my life without being able to play my horns? Or teach my students?

After three weeks, the doctors came to my room and talked with Gwen. I faked like I was sleeping. I heard them say that patients with the same kind of surgery normally had more response than I was having. They were concerned that I might not be able to walk or play again.

Gwen said, "He'll play again *and* walk again. He'll run again, too! I've got faith!"

I was glad she had faith, because I didn't. All I could think about were the concerts I wasn't going to make. All the preparations for my gigs that people had made, all the money they'd spent on advertising, and I couldn't play. My quintet had turned down other gigs to work with me. Now my gigs were canceled. I wouldn't get to see all my friends who'd planned to come to my concerts. I was devastated.

Most of all, I thought about my students. The clinics I'd planned to do. The school bands. I thought about the students from UNH who'd been looking forward to playing with me on a cruise in a few weeks—one of the cruises that Hank O'Neal and Shelly Shire produced each year. All the months those UNH students had spent rehearsing. It was going to be their first time playing in the Floating Jazz Festival. I pictured their hurt faces. Those faces haunted me.

I wanted to get up out of that bed and stay involved with my students. Stay involved with projects like the Thelonious Monk Institute of Jazz. We had worked hard to set the thing into action. "T" and his wife, Gale, and his mother, Nellie; the institute's president, Tom Carter, and his wife, Cheri; Maria Fisher—real hip lady, used to be a successful opera singer. Jazz musicians like Jimmy Heath and Wayne Shorter. Famous actors Clint Eastwood and Billy Dee Williams helped, too. So many folks, I can't remember everybody. We'd planned to organize an international competition. Give students around the world a chance to be heard, help them with their jazz careers. Maria had given a million-dollar grant, and we had made plans for our first fund-raising concert. We wanted Bill Cosby to be our headliner. He and I had been friends for a long time.

I smiled when I thought about how Bill loved coming by my gigs and doing impromptu comedy bits. He'd come on stage and say that his name was Screech Jones. Make a big build-up about playing a bent-up horn that I'd given him. He played up the suspense, making the audience hold their breath each time he'd put the horn up to his mouth. But instead of playing, he'd take it down and keep talking.

I remembered the night Bill came to my set at the Vanguard and played the piano. I declare, a few passages of his rendition actually resembled something Monk would play. It was a gas!

Well, since we wanted Bill to get involved with the Monk Institute, I had arranged to have one of his favorite cigars sent backstage to him after one of his concerts. I'd sent a note with the cigar, asking for his help. He accepted.

The institute was only a few years old, and we were all looking forward to watching it grow.

For a moment, I thought about Monk. I remembered the time in '56 when I was working at Birdland with Duke. Monk came by to check things out, which he usually did. After the date he cornered me and said, "Hey, man, I want to have you on my recording date which I'm doing tomorrow. When you get off work tonight, we'll go uptown and talk about it."

Later, we took a taxi and went uptown to Central Park West to the home of a lady called "The Baroness." It was wintertime, really cold. We went up to her apartment—real nice apartment, big fire burning in the fireplace—and the first thing that Monk did was to open a bag and throw something in the fireplace. The flames turned orange. A few minutes later, he threw some more stuff in there, and the flames turned blue. He kept doing this, with the flames turning many colors. We just sat and watched. After an hour and a half, there'd still been no discussion of the record date. Now, we'd gotten to the Baroness' around three in the morning. Three hours later, I glanced through the blinds at the daylight and I said, "T, you know I have to get home to Queens before I come back for the date."

He said, "Yeah, man. Okay. I'll see you at the studio." And he gave me the address and the time.

When I got to the studio later that day, Monk had Max Roach on drums, Paul Chambers on bass, and Sonny Rollins on tenor; Monk was on piano, and I was there with my horn. The tune that we recorded was "Bemsha Swing," named for a Bahamian town that was Adam Clayton Powell's favorite hangout.

As I walked into the studio, I was surprised to see several timpani drums.

Max had an intricate setup with the drum set and the timpani, and he managed to play both during the tune, which was something very different for that day and time. I *loved* it.

He kept this idea in mind for many years, because forty-six years later—in 2002—he and I made a recording entitled *Friendship* where he used tunable drums to give the same effect as the timpani. Pure genius.

When we got down to work, we didn't rehearse (the standard saying was, "Rehearsing is like polishing a turd"), and we didn't have any written music . Monk just ran it down on the piano, and we listened; then he said, "Okay, let's make it." That album was named *Brilliant Corners*.

Monk was such a talented musician. And I wanted the institute named for him to be a success. Now, lying in that hospital, I worried that I wouldn't get a chance to do my part.

Days slipped by, and the next thing I heard was Gwen talking to the doctors about transferring me to another hospital. A therapy hospital, Helen Hayes, in Jersey. I didn't want to go there. I just wanted to go *home*.

The doctors suggested that maybe I could have a home therapist instead. But Gwen kept pushing for Helen Hayes. She was standing before a team of doctors demanding that they transfer me. She said, "You can't send him home like this. He can't even sit up!"

I wanted to tell her to shut up. But there was no fight left in me. I thought it was curtains. I knew she meant well, but it all felt like a waste of time.

Al and Rosalie came or called daily, and they also tried to encourage me to go to Helen Hayes. I didn't listen to them, or to Reverend Taylor and his wife, or to Wynton or John, or anybody.

I felt like the thing I loved was being taken away from me. My jazz. And the thing that I loved the most, encouraging my students, was over.

Usually, I could rally from any situation. I used to say, "It's a poor mouse that doesn't have but one hole. If you can't go one way, find another. That's what improvisation is all about." Those words didn't help this time. All that talk I'd done about "Keep on keepin' on" didn't matter a damn.

I couldn't even hold a glass of water. All I could do was lie in that bed. Doctors and nurses kept coming and going from my room. No hope in their eyes. They'd just kind of glance at me and then look down, like they didn't know what to say.

I'd heard them tell Gwen that it had been thirty days and things weren't looking positive. She tried to inspire me. Quoting the Bible about faith and all of that. But I didn't want to hear anything she had to say. She kept trying to convince me to give my permission for the transfer. But I closed my ears to everything but my music. If I was going to die, I damn sure didn't want to die in a hospital.

The walls of my room were lined with get well cards. The phone kept ringing, but I didn't feel like talking. I just shut my eyes and listened to my jazz. Tried to ignore the sounds of the leg pumps, which were going all the time to help the circulation in my legs.

A few days later, Gwen brought my sister Margueritte to see me. I was *so* happy to see her. All four feet of her. She stood on one side of my bed and Gwen was on the other side. They each took one of my hands. Margueritte said, "Clark, I want you to give it a try. You're not a quitter. I believe you'll make it if you want to. You can play your music again—I know this. I'll stay with you all the way while you're in that therapy hospital. I *know* you'll come out okay."

Gwen was crying, and I was, too. I looked at Margueritte. She was pleading with me. She said, "Now, I know you're scared. But God is with you. He won't let you down. Gwen is right. You shouldn't go home like this, and you know it. So come on and let's go."

They transported me by ambulance to the rehab hospital. On the way there, I promised God three things if he'd let me make it out of there alive. One—I would work harder to make amends with my son. Two—I'd marry Gwen. Three—I'd spend more time with my family, my friends, and my students. Especially my students.

When they rolled me into the foyer of Helen Hayes Therapy Hospital, I felt even more depressed to see so many people in wheelchairs and strapped to rolling beds. One man was lying on his stomach in an inclined bed with his feet higher than his head. He turned his face toward me and smiled. I managed to smile back at him.

When the nurses came to my room the next morning, they said, "All right, Mr. Terry, we're gonna take you to the shower." They used my sheet to transfer me onto a rolling bed and they pushed me to a huge room with a big square basin in the center of the room. On top of the basin was a metal top riddled with holes. They put me on the metal top and stripped me naked. Then they pulled a shower head down from the ceiling. I had to admit, that water felt great.

Some doctors came to see me back in my room. They told me that for the next few days there would be rigorous exercises. They said that the staff was experienced and knew exactly how much to push me. I was thinking, Well, here we go.

That afternoon, Margueritte and Gwen stood beside me while some nurses strapped a brace around my chest to support my back. The nurses slowly raised me up to a sitting position. Excruciating pain shot up and down my spine. I thought I was going to pass out. I cussed everything and everybody! But they ignored me. Told me things would get better.

The next day they propped me up in the wheelchair. I screamed from the pain. Cussed and screamed. But they kept on hooking up all the straps and gadgets and got me secured in that chair. When they rolled me out into the hall, I gritted my teeth. Tried to focus on what Margueritte had said: God won't let me down.

A few minutes later, the nurses rolled me into a room filled with exercise equipment and strange-looking contraptions. They said, "We're going to do some rotation exercises. We know you'll feel some pain. If it gets too tough, we'll stop for a while."

The pain was horrible! I kept my eyes closed and balled up my fists as they raised and lowered my legs, rotated my arms, turned my head from side to side. I kept thinking about my students. The Monk Institute. Kept telling myself, I'm not a quitter. Whatever I have to do to play again, teach again, I'll do it.

Each day, Margueritte and Gwen waited for me while I went back to that workout room. After a few days, the rotation exercises hurt a bit less. Just a bit. The easiest thing was the squeeze ball to help strengthen the muscles in my hands and arms. The weights weren't too bad either.

Around the fourth day when I was rolled into the exercise room, the nurses said, "Now we're going to stand you up." I'd never felt so much pain in my entire life! I hollered loud enough for God to hear me up in heaven! Eventually, they got me on my feet. I pleaded, "Don't let me go! Don't let me go!"

They said, "We've got you, Mr. Terry. We've got you." And they did. They were really nice. I felt safe with them.

A few days later they said, "Now you've got to try walking." They rolled me over to a pair of horizontal bars about hip height, then struggled to get me standing. They said, "Just hold on to these bars and try to take a step." They made me feel like they'd rescue me quickly, so I tried. But I just couldn't. They were very patient with me, and I kept trying. Eventually, I took a step.

About a week later, I was able to take a few steps while holding on to the bars. Then the nurses said, "Now you're ready to do the stairs.

Stairs—there were three of them—never looked so *tall*. They seemed custom made for Kareem Abdul Jabbar. In about a week, though, I made one stair. I was gripping the hell out of the side bars. A while later, I could do all three stairs. Man, talk about feeling thankful! I felt like the Old Man Upstairs was smiling on me again. And finally, I began to really believe that I might be okay. Play and teach again. That made me more determined than ever.

After I'd done pretty well on the stairs, they rolled me over to another room where there was a center portion of a car. Just the part where the doors and seats were. They said, "You've got to master getting in and out of a car now, Mr. Terry."

All the things I had taken for granted were haunting me. Simple things like being able to walk to a car. Get in and close the door. Turn the ignition and drive.

Now, I was sitting in my wheelchair and looking at that car contraption. All I could think about was how much pain it was going to cause to get inside. But a week later, I was sitting behind the steering wheel. All smiles.

I heard that Miles was in a hospital, too. I called him and he sounded real low sick. I said, "Inky, you can make it." Silence. He wasn't talking, but I knew he was there. I said, "Man, if you die, I'll kill you." I tried to make him laugh. Nothing. I prayed for him when Margueritte hung up the phone for me.

Dizzy and his manager, Charlie Fishman, came to see me during my fifth week at Helen Hayes. I had just finished participating in a wheelchair race. Diz said, "Man, you'll be back out there in no time."

Visitors, cards, and phone calls increased. Funny how when folks thought I was going to die, communication lessened. There was even a rumor that I had died.

Margueritte and I said a prayer together every day that she'd gotten from one of her books: "Breathe in God and breathe out frustration. Breathe in God and breathe out limitation. Breathe in God and breathe out hesitation. Now you are renewed, refreshed, and revitalized, and ready to begin again."

I was so glad she was there. It worried me that Gwen had to drive her to the hospital every day, sixty-five miles each way, but I needed Margueritte. Needed her encouragement. She had always been in my corner. When she told me how dark it was going back each night through the mountains near the hospital, I just asked, "What time are you coming tomorrow?"

When I found out that Miles had died, something inside me *fell*. W-a-y down! He had always beaten the odds. But now he was gone, too. So many of my friends had died. My family. Life seemed so unfair. And then I got a phone call from Anne Phillips.

57. Second Chance

Six weeks of commitment finally paid off, and I was released from my physical therapists in the hospital where they'd worked me like a rock-bustin' prisoner! But things were definitely better. I was so glad to get out of there *alive*. I could walk short distances with crutches and use a wheelchair for everything else. I also had to wear a thick back brace, but I didn't give a hoot. God had given me a second chance!

Another great thing was that those students at the University of New Hampshire made that cruise while I was in the hospital. I heard from my friends on the boat that they did a fantastic job. Those young lions made me really happy. They even sent me a huge card with everybody's signature, including Dave Seiler's. I couldn't wait to see them again. Keep the ball rolling.

I was so grateful, I even gave God a nickname: "Big Prez." I appreciated *everything*. From the biggest things like still having my ass above the grass, to the smallest things like holding the phone. If I could have flown up to heaven and thanked him in person, I would have.

Luckily, I got a chance to thank him in Manhattan instead, when Anne Phillips called me about being in the Christmas story that she and Bob Kindred produced every year. I said, "Yes!" I didn't know how I was going to do it, but I'd made up my mind. And that was *it*.

Since 1985, I had always been invited to play a part in their production, which she had written—the birth of Jesus with jazz music. "Bending Toward the Light—A Jazz Nativity." I was one of the original cast members, playing one of the three wise men.

That December of '91, I sat in my wheelchair in the foyer of a beautiful church in Manhattan—St. Bartholomew—near the Waldorf Astoria Hotel. I was dressed in a really hip robe and an ornate head wrap with a lot of feathers. Jon Faddis had told me that he would push me down the aisle. But I said, "No, I want to you to hold me up. Help me to *walk*."

A lot of my friends and fans had called and said they were coming to see me in the show. And I was eager to see *them*, talk with them, laugh with them. Especially after those horrible rumors that I had died while I was in the hospital.

When the big wooden doors opened into the sanctuary, Jon and a man I didn't know held me up on each side and helped me to walk down the long aisle while I played my horn. The place was completely packed. Sold out show. Slowly, we made it all the way to where they had built a manger on stage. The pain just about killed me. But I was so glad to be there that the pain was secondary.

They told me later that people stood and watched me with tears in their eyes as I made my way down that aisle. I didn't see *anybody*. I was totally focused on holding my horn and blowing those notes. Making it to that manger straight ahead. And I got there. Man!

I think the other wise men were Al Grey and Tito Puente, but I'm not sure. Gail Wynters sang her heart out as Mary. She was one of the finest vocalists in New York. It was an incredible production. I felt so much love!

The next day, I thought about the list that I had promised Big Prez if I made it out of that hospital alive. Those three promises: reconcile with Hiawatha; marry Gwen; and spend more time with the folks I love. Folks who love me. Family, friends, and especially my students. I felt more dedicated to my students than ever before. I wanted to keep encouraging them. Other musicians, too. Everybody!

I realized that things that I used to think were the most important in my life, that I thought I couldn't live without, like playing as many gigs as possible, making a lot of records, making a whole lot of money—I realized that it was more important to be blessed with *time*. That time was a *gift*, and what I did with that time was what mattered. Like helping others, you know.

I thought about the first time that Jon had come to my office on Seventh Avenue in Manhattan. I had invited him to come by and play. He was just getting started then, and I'd watched him climb straight to the top! His career had really taken off.

After that surgery in '91, more than ever, I understood why it was imperative that I should encourage my students. When I was teaching them what I knew as far as playing the music was concerned, it was really about establishing relationships. Of course, it was extremely important to me that they would perpetuate jazz far and wide, but it was mostly about spending time together and listening to what their dreams were. To me, jazz was love. And like the old saying goes, "It's better to give than to receive." It worked out well for them and it felt great to me, thinking that I could contribute something to make their dreams come true.

Like when Branford Marsalis called me for some advice. He had been offered the gig as music director for the *Tonight Show* at NBC. Having been a member of the show's band for twelve years, I had a few private suggestions that he should hang on to. I was so proud of him. Still am.

Being able to play again after that hospital scene was great. But the way that Hiawatha and I got along—or *didn't* get along—still bothered me. I wanted a better relationship with my son, like I had promised. I didn't want us to stay at odds with each other. So I called him and told him I'd like to spend some time with him down in St. Louis that next summer. We talked about his health—he'd been having some stomach problems, but he was better now—and we discussed my recent hospital scene. I wanted to keep more in touch, and he was cool with that. After the phone conversation, I wrote him a nice long letter and I included a money order in it.

As far as my career was concerned, I was glad to get back into action. Glad to get back to working with the Monk Institute, be an active part of it again. Glad to work with the students.

I got a new manager, too. Tom Cassidy had been my agent, and we had always seen "eye-to-eye." But Gwen's son Gary had started helping out a lot—setting up publicity for gigs, arranging photo sessions, helping me pack, traveling with me—and as I watched Gary grow in his management skills, I decided to give him a chance. Help him out like that.

He did a great job of taking care of things for me. Turned out to be one of the best managers I've ever had. Real particular with fine details. He even created a newsletter that he sent to my friends and fans. Named it "Mumbles." For the first time, folks could keep up with my itinerary, read things about how I was doing and what was going on. It got to be such a success that I was getting letters forwarded from *DownBeat* magazine from folks asking for subscriptions to "Mumbles."

I was enjoying my life so much more. And I was glad to be *able* to. Enjoying more personal involvement with people around me.

That January of '92 I did an album called *Friends Old and New* with Greg Gisbert, Al Grey, Joshua Redman, John Hicks, Ron Carter, and Grady Tate. I'd been to hundreds of sessions before, but this time I was *especially* glad to mix with my old buddies. And those young lions, Greg and Joshua—it felt good to see them; to *play* with them; to help them in any way I could. Believe me!

Early that February, Bill Cosby initiated a bachelor party for me. It was just four of us: Bill, Jimmy Heath, Max Roach, and me. We were sitting in the dining room of the new apartment that Bill and Camille had just moved into in Manhattan, all at one end of his very *long* dining room table. It must have been fifteen feet long.

A chef was in the kitchen cooking. Man, those aromas had my mouth watering! We were shooting the breeze, laughing, telling jokes. As it was getting close to time for us to eat, Max fell asleep momentarily, Jimmy took out a nitroglycerin pill and popped it in his mouth, and I pulled out my insulin syringe and gave myself a shot. Bill was staring at us. He said, "Should I call an ambulance?"

On Valentine's Day in '92, I kept my second promise. I married Gwen. Pastor John Gensel flew from New York to do the ceremony. It was down in Rockwall, Texas, at a yacht club. Two hundred friends came from different parts of the world. Hans Friedland, a journalist, and Bengt-Arne Wallin, a hell of a trumpeter, came all the way from Sweden; Alan Matheson, another great trumpeter, came from Canada; and Randi Hultin, a writer, came from Norway—to name just a few. Surprised the hell out of me! I didn't think anybody would come way down to that remote little town.

Gwen's family and friends, and my family and friends—we *all* got joined together that day. We turned it out! Had a ball. Great jazz, fantastic musicians and their wives. Jimmy and Cynthia Wilkins, George and Joan Robert, Al Grey and Rosalie Soladar, Plas Johnson, my old buddy Willie "Weasel" Parker and his wife, Milt and Mona Hinton—and my friend Sweetie Mitchell sang some awesome blues. Keith Loftis and other STAR students who played jazz were there, too.

Lots of friends came—Tom and Cheri Carter from the Monk Institute, Ann Sneed from the International Art of Jazz, Jackie Harris from the New Orleans Jazz Festival, and a slew of other people. Man, everybody was gassed!

The only song at our wedding that wasn't jazz was one of Gwen's picks. She wanted to hear "Wind Beneath My Wings" because she said that was what she wanted to be for me. So her friend Benita Arterberry sang it. *Great* voice.

When we left the yacht club, everybody headed to our house that we'd bought the year before, and we partied some more. Had a jam session until three o'clock the next morning. So many folks in that house. Ames Growe and his friend Gwen came from New Orleans and brought gumbo, shrimp, beans and rice, all kinds of stuff. Talk about chowing down!

And our dining room was the jam session room. No furniture in there, just drums and a piano, and a whole bunch of musicians taking turns and keeping the music hot.

Folks were up dancing, and eating, and talking, and that jazz was echoing off the waters of Lake Ray Hubbard, just like the jazz in my neighborhood back in St. Louis had echoed off the waters of the Mississippi River.

A few days later, I took Gwen to Disney World for our honeymoon. Now, I didn't know that when I had talked with Bill and Camille Cosby a few days earlier, they had gotten wind of our accommodation plans and had made some "Cosby" changes. They surprised us with a limo, a penthouse suite, cigars and hot sauce. We were completely gassed! Then, one of the "Veeps" at Disney World gave us a private tour. Man! Gwen and I enjoyed all the rides, and we rode one of them three times—the one with the song "It's a Small World."

After a few months of traveling and gigging, and between record dates in Oslo, Norway, and Los Angeles, I kept my first promise to Big Prez. In August, I went to visit Hiawatha at the apartment complex where he lived in St. Louis. Gwen and Margueritte went with me, and some other family members did, too. We all had a good time together, sitting at one of the picnic tables in the courtyard under some shady trees, sipping on sodas and munching on snacks. Hiawatha looked good, and he seemed to be doing pretty well.

We stayed for a good while, telling jokes and shooting the breeze, then he walked us to the front. I told him that there was something I wanted him to have. Then I handed him a copy of the custody papers that I'd gotten back in the '40s. I'd never thought about showing him those papers before.

He read them. Then he looked up at me with tears in his eyes. He said, "I never knew you wanted me."

We hugged each other real tight and I said, "Of course I wanted you, but I did what I had to do. *Somebody* had to pick the cotton." That made him laugh. I told him how I had thought about him while I was on the road; how we couldn't go back and change the past but that we could make things better now.

Of course, we had a long way to go to mend our fences. But maybe we were finally on the right track.

I got back on the "international merry-go-round." And I was lovin' it! Schedule packed like sardines in a tin can. Back-to-back gigs.

On March 1st of '94, I did something really different. I performed at the Grammys with a trio of young rappers. Called their group "Digable Planets." Really knowledgeable about jazz, and I dug them a lot. Cat named "Butterfly" was the leader. Real nice cat. And the best part was that they won a Grammy that night! It was wild, man.

I didn't let any grass grow under my feet, because I was too glad to be back out there. Stayed busier than a one-armed paper hanger with crabs! Here's an excerpt from my date book in '94: April 2–8, "Ultimate Caribbean Jazz Spectacular," one of Hank O'Neal's jazz cruises with a bunch of incredible musicians, including my septet featuring Nicholas

Payton, Jesse Davis, Joshua Redman, Don Friedman, Marcus McLaurine, and Sylvia Cuenca—a shipload of great jazz.

Then on April 9th in Winter Park, Florida, at Robbins College, I did a clinic, and I played a concert there on the 10th. I had a chance to work with more students two days later on April 12th in Manhattan at New York University. After that, on April 16th in Jersey City at the New Jersey Public Library, Marcus McLaurine, Don Friedman, Sylvia Cuenca, and I played an intimate concert for some beautiful people.

About a week later, on April 22nd and 23rd, I went up to Boston where I had a chance to play with the Alan Dawson trio at Sculler's Club—great concert, man.

Then a few days later, on April 26th and 28th, I did an elementary school clinic and concert with my cousin Lesa Terry, Mark Elf, Bill Crow, and Al Grey. It was at Fort Totten for the Bayside Historical Society in Queens. One of my dear friends, Della Stametz, organized the whole scene, and it seemed like she had a hundred kids there. They really enjoyed our music, and they asked some interesting questions like, "Why did you pick jazz?" Man, that was a lot of fun.

Those kids didn't want to leave when it was over so I lined them all up and they did the *bunny-hop* around the room while we played the theme from the *Flintstones*. Finally, they hopped on outside where their buses were waiting.

The Charlin Jazz Society booked a gig on April 29th in Washington, D.C., and I had a chance to play with Paquito D'Rivera, Stanley Cowell, Keter Betts, Harold Sumney, Nnenna Freelon, and Fred Irby with the Howard University Jazz Ensemble. Beautiful concert.

On May 3rd I played at the Manhattan School of Music in New York City with Phil Woods, Jimmy Heath, Doc Cheatham, and Dick Lowenthal with the MSM Jazz Orchestra. It was a gas, man, up there playing with those cats. Then on May 5th there was a salute to me at Pace University. It was one of Jack Kleinsinger's productions, and he had some fantastic musicians there: Al Grey, David "Fathead" Newman, Lew Soloff, Lewis "One" Nash, Marcus McLaurine, Don Friedman, and a bunch of other musicians. Playing with all of them was a real treat!

At the Clef Club in Philadelphia on May 8th, I had a chance to play with some dear friends, Trudy Pitts and Mr. C. We had a ball! Trudy played piano and sang some low-down funky blues, and her husband, Mr. C, played some mean drums.

Then on May 20th I went to Stockholm, Sweden, to do a gig for the Duke Ellington Society Convention. Played with my dear friend Bengt-

Arne Wallin and an All-Star Swedish Big Band, and on May 21st I did a concert there with Louie Bellson, Britt Woodman, Jimmy Woode, and a bunch of other cats. Such great times, man.

After that, on May 24th and 25th I played in Vienna, Austria, with Louie Bellson, Jimmy Woode, Britt Woodman, Norris Turney, and Heinz Czadek with the Vienna Conservatory Band. Bill Dobbins played on that gig, too. It was good to see him. He was one of the students in a clinic that I'd done a while back at Kent State University in the U.S.

From May 27th until June 5th I did the "8th Annual Jazz Festival at Sea" on a ship in the Mediterranean, where a bunch of cats did a tribute to me. It was very emotional for me, and I enjoyed playing with Red Holloway, Willie "The Picker" Pickens, Eddie Jones, Buster Cooper, Butch Miles, and Gray Sargent. Lots of other musicians. Great music and some beautiful ports, too—Venice, Kalamata, Bodrum, Volos, and Athens.

And it went on and on and on: Le Mars, Iowa, from June 27th to July 2nd; July 4th, Copenhagen, Denmark; July 5th, Lyon, France; July 6th, Paris, France; July 7th, Fano, Italy; July 10th, The Hague, Holland; July 12th, Timisaora, Romania; July 14th, Dournenez, France; July 17th, Bayonne, France.

I took off for a few days so Gwen and I could catch our breath. We went to Texas to spend a little time at our home there. Just relax a while. Even bought a fishing pole, but all I caught was a stick.

Still, I enjoyed watching the sunsets across the water, sipping my sherry, and thanking Big Prez for another day. And I enjoyed my new hobby— painting with acrylics. Years later, Hank O'Neal used one of my pieces, "Ode to Picasso," on the CD cover for *The Clark Terry Spacemen*.

In the summer of '94, since I never really had time to enjoy our Texas home, we sold it and the one in Bayside, and we bought another beautiful waterfront home in New York. It was on Long Island, in a little town named Glen Cove. Another dream home—24 Westland Drive. Nice layout, swimming pool, and beautiful sunsets over the Long Island Sound. Loved watching that big orange sun go down over that water. Did some painting out on the patio whenever I could. Made time to spend with my friends and family. And definitely with my students.

From August 1st through the 5th, I went to the University of New Hampshire for my annual summer residency. Really enjoyed hanging out at the Acorn restaurant with Dave Seiler, Paul Verrette, Alan Chase, and Buddy Howard. And the young musicians there, man, they were just beautiful. I loved teaching them, performing with them, answering their questions, and they loved my stories.

I always made sure that my calendar included opportunities to work with students. And I did a variety of annual festivals, cruises, club dates, tours, and concerts for people who booked gigs with me. They were like family—Norman Granz, George and Joyce Wein, Hank O'Neal and Shelly Shire, Philippe Gaviglio, Boško Petrović, and some I haven't mentioned before, George Robert, John Lee, Jordi Sunol, Jenny Wilkins, Anita Berry, and many more. They were all great people, and their friendships have stood the test of time. The friendships of my students, too.

I kept a pretty hectic pace going for years and totally enjoyed all of my gigs, but I started slowing down in 2001. Just didn't feel that good healthwise. Needed to let that dream home go and scale down on expenses. I knew that I was no "spring chicken."

We were right in the middle of planning a move to New Jersey when I found out that I had "the big C"—cancer. Colon cancer.

Q helped me get through that whole scene. He organized a "dream team" of doctors for me at Sloan-Kettering Hospital in Manhattan. Dr. Larry Norton was the "captain" of that team. All top-shelf doctors. I'd gotten a new personal doctor since Dr. Hoffman's office was so far from Jersey. My new doctor, Steve Fochios, had an office in Manhattan. He was right there with me, too.

Don't know what I would have done without Q's help, checking on me and talking with the doctors and Gwen, sending flowers, lifting my spirit. Steve Tyrell came to give his support when I had my surgery. Real nice cat, Steve. Sings his ass off! My friends from Chicago, Mickarl and Carol Thomas, came, too. And, as usual, John "Faithful" Simon was there, doing whatever he could for me.

Lots of people helped me through that crisis. Bill Cosby called often, telling jokes and encouraging me. Hundreds of people helped, man. Made me feel like I could make it.

Right in the middle of my chemo, radiation, and surgeries, Gwen took care of business and moved us to Haworth, New Jersey—420 Ivy Avenue. Nice house—corner lot, trees everywhere. Just a short ride over the George Washington Bridge to Manhattan.

Took me about a year to recover, and when I was well again, I jumped right back on that merry-go-round. Not quite as busy, but still all over the place. And my first priority, between gigs, was to organize another youth band—part of my third promise. At eighty-two years old, I wanted to find a special school nearby where I could teach jazz on a regular basis. One that wasn't too far from the LaGuardia airport or the one in Newark. Convenient to Manhattan, you know.

So I asked around, and one afternoon I ended up talking to Bob Kindred in the den of my new home. He told me about William Paterson University in Wayne, New Jersey. Bob said, "William Paterson has a serious jazz studies program that Thad Jones started around twenty years ago. Rufus Reid headed it up later. They've got some *really* talented students." He ran it all down to me. Sounded interesting.

He told me that Marcus McLaurine was teaching there. Well, Marcus had been the bassist in my quintet for around twenty-five years. That was a big plus. James Williams was teaching there, too. He was a great pianist and also a good friend. So I decided to check it out. Found out that Richard DeRosa and Harold Mabern were teaching there, too. More good buddies of mine.

Before long, I was hired as an adjunct professor at William Paterson University, and the students were making themselves at home in my kitchen. Hanging out for long hours. Alan Hicks, Cameron MacManus, Stantawn Kendrick, Justin Kauflin, Crystal Torres, Andy Shantz, and other students. Even students from UNH like Chris Klaxton, Steve Guerra, and Chris Burbank would come down. I was an adjunct professor there, too.

Musicians would come by. So many musicians—Arturo Sandoval; Jon Faddis and his wife, Laurelyn; Tony Lujan and his wife, Lilliana; Roy Hargrove; Nicholas Payton; Russell Malone; Marcus McLaurine and his wife, Miyuki, and their children; Sylvia Cuenca; Jeff Lindberg; Lee Hogans and his girlfriend, Anja Nielson; John Simon. Older musicians like Jimmy Heath with his wife, Mona, and Red Holloway.

Stopping by was a regular thing when I was in town. "Hey, Clark, what are you doing tonight?" That was it. Friends always visiting. Lots of friends—Tad Hershorn telling jazz history stories; Donya "Mama D" Kato cooking something tasty; Milt Jackson's widow, Sandy, and Ray Brown's widow, Cecelia, and Milt Hinton's widow, Mona, laughing and talking and dancing; Alyce Claerbaut talking about her uncle, Billy Strayhorn, and singing karaoke with Gwen and Russell Malone; Kariyma Nelson helping with my book, taking trumpet lessons, and sharing time with her daughter, Asha.

I can't remember everybody. Over the years, damn near thousands of people have visited me wherever I've lived. Spent time with me in my hotel rooms, dressing rooms and backstage, too. Man, I'd have to damn near write another book to name all the folks who were just beautiful.

That house in New Jersey *stayed* jumping, and the relationship that I had at William Paterson was incredible. I really dug teaching those students at school *and* at home, and my other students, too. We'd eat something and then jam with anybody who came by. They'd ask a thousand questions, and then everybody would listen to my stories until I'd fall asleep in my chair with my horn in my lap.

It reminded me of the '50s when Dizzy and I used to go over to Pops' house. Louis Armstrong, you know. We would say, "Let's go bug Pops and get our batteries charged!" That was our way of saying that we wanted to learn from him. He was usually typing something on his old typewriter. Peck, peck, peck. We'd hang around listening to him telling stories about his career. A lot of dirty stories, but all of them great stories.

David Demsey was the head of the jazz studies scene at William Paterson. He was a cool cat. Played some mean tenor in my big band a few years later at the Blue Note. Arnie Speert was the university's president. To show you how hip he was, he sang my tune, "Mumbles," at the ceremony when they gave me an honorary doctorate—my fourteenth!—in 2004.

David—I nicknamed him "Dr. D.D."—called me one day and said, "Now, Clark, we don't mind our students hanging out with you at home. But you've got to make sure they stop going to sleep in class." Well, I didn't want to get the kids in trouble, so we cooled it with the late nights.

Finally, I got it together with my newest big band, Clark Terry and the Young Titans of Jazz. On trumpets we had Frank Greene, Stjepko Gut, Tony Lujan, and Crystal Torres. Our trombones were Barry Cooper, Conrad Herwig, Stafford Hunter, and Dion Tucker. Lakecia Benjamin and Brad Leali were on alto, with Steve Guerra and Whitney Slaten on tenor. Adam Schroeder handled baritone. Our rhythm section was Helen Sung on piano, Derrick Hodge on bass, and Marcus Gilmore on drums. Helen had won one of the Monk Institute's piano competitions.

Lots of incredible students, man. They came from William Paterson, UNH, and other schools all over the United States. Stjepko was from Austria. Some of them were still in school, some were already playing professionally. Marcus Gilmore was just sixteen, a high school student. Of course, I had to get permission from his mother to be in my band.

They sounded great! They had worked *hard* to get that swing, that cohesiveness. I was proud of *all* of them. In 2004, I wanted to take them to Hans Zurbrugg's annual jazz festival in Bern, Switzerland. I'd played it for many years and was excited to give the Titans the experience of being up on that stage.

Unfortunately, my age and health challenges had been putting a damper on travel. My back was starting to hurt again, and all that cancer therapy had taken its toll. Still, I really wanted to get to Bern.

Since I wasn't doing as many gigs, I couldn't lay the usual bread on Gary, and since he'd gotten married back in '94 and been blessed with a pretty little baby girl named Legacy in '98, he needed a steady income. So his wife, LaJuana, took over managing me. She'd been helping Gary for most of the ten years he'd worked with me, so she was familiar with how things went down.

Her very first assignment was to work out the details for the Titans' trip to Switzerland. Now, that was an acid test, but she came through with flying colors. Been managing things for me ever since.

The trip to Bern was beautiful. Hans was glad to see us. He had a hip jazz club, Marian's, named after his wife. He also owned the Hotel Innere Enge. Some of the rooms there had names on the doors instead of numbers—the Milt Hinton Suite, the Louie Bellson Suite, the Lionel Hampton Suite, the Clark Terry Suite. Memorabilia on the walls. Milt's bass was suspended from the ceiling in his suite. Oscar Peterson stayed in my suite at one point, and afterward Hans decorated an Oscar Peterson Suite. They're all really something to see.

Everybody loved the Titans! They were just outstanding. We made an album over there, too. Before long, they played at William Paterson University in Jersey at the kickoff ceremony for a new Clark Terry Archive, headed by Dr. D.D. It was part of their "Living Jazz Archives." Bill Cosby was the conductor that night. For that event, we called my Titans the Bill Cosby Dream Band. That was in 2005. It was an unforgettable concert. Great music and lots of laughs. Bill was hilarious. The audience loved it.

My Titans played at the Blue Note in New York in 2006. There was *no* standing room! Jon Faddis sat in; Sylvia Cuenca and Marcus McLaurine, too. A few of Dr. D.D.'s students joined us—Alan Hicks on drums, Roxy Coss on tenor, and Stantawn Kendrick handled tenor and alto. Justin Kauflin played up some piano. Cinnamon was on trombone. His real name was Cameron MacManus, but I nicknamed him Cinnamon 'cause I could never think of his first name. Dr. D.D. joined in with his tenor. And "Mr. Low Blow" played bass trombone. His real name was Jack Jeffers, and he was in my big band years ago.

Things were going great. But then our neighborhood started changing. Huge multimillion-dollar homes were going up, older homes were being torn down. Taxes were on the rise. By that time, I was having more trouble getting around. You know, Father Time was doing his thing. So I started looking for a retirement locale.

58. The Biggest Surprise

Searching for a place to retire ain't easy in the "Golden Years," better known to me as the "*Olden* Years." I checked out Chicago, Florida, St. Louis. Then the possibility of an adjunct professorship came up at a university in Virginia, where the cost of living wasn't as high as in Jersey. I figured Virginia wasn't too much of a drive to William Paterson, maybe five hours.

The daughter of Jim Maxwell, my section mate on the *Tonight Show,* lived near the school in Virginia. Her name was Annie Megabow, and she helped out in the search for a new home. My family team Patsy and Larry Clark looked, too. They had moved there from Long Island. Patsy still called me Uncle John, a name from long ago when I lived in St. Louis.

Then one day I got a call from a cat named John Graham. He wanted me to be the Grand Marshal in the 2006 homecoming parade for the University of Arkansas at Pine Bluff (UAPB). We talked for a while about this and that. Then I told him about the Virginia school. He said, "You know, Clark, it would be great if you could teach some of our students down here in the Delta. They don't get as many opportunities as the students on the East Coast. They need to know about you and other jazz masters."

A few days later, he came to Jersey for a visit. Went with me to an ASCAP ceremony where my name was placed on the wall at the headquarters in Manhattan. Next thing I knew, he got the UAPB Chancellor, L.A. Davis, involved. When they made a better offer, I accepted. Anyway, I thought it would be a gas for us to live near Gwen's family in her hometown.

She cried and begged me not to consider moving there. "Virginia is closer to William Paterson University. There's not as much to do in Pine Bluff as there is in Virginia. You might be bored down there."

I knew she was a little sensitive about her small hometown. Didn't think I'd be happy there. But hey, I grew up near the river bottom of St. Louis. So I kept making plans to move to Pine Bluff. I figured that she'd be happier there in the long run. But more than anything, I wanted to keep my third promise—more time with family.

I loved her family and they loved me. Her son Gary spent lots of time reminiscing with me about our travels together, and I could always count on him for whatever I needed. His wife, LaJuana, loved trying new recipes, and she was still doing a beautiful job with the details for my gigs. Gwen's other son, Tony, and I enjoyed swapping jokes and hanging out in the kitchen. He also had some serious "chef abilities," and he kept me informed about the latest medical developments regarding my health challenges. The grandchildren, Legacy, Nikki, Li'l Tony, and Max, called me "Grandpop." Gwen's brother, Harry, could definitely handle the barbeque grill and tell some mean jokes. We were a great family. I'd nicknamed Gwen's sister "Baby Sis," and I nicknamed their mother "Pretty Girl."

My brothers and sisters were all gone. Even Margueritte. Her death in 2005 had been especially hard on me—my sweet sister. Don't remember what got her, just knew that she was gone. Man, real *dark* clouds then.

So I thought Pine Bluff would be a good place to settle down. It wasn't too far from Dallas, where Gary, LaJuana, and Legacy lived. Harry and his youngest children, DeAndra and Theo, were living there, too. The thing that cemented my decision was that I believed what John Graham had said. "The students *need* you down in the Delta. Give them a chance."

Since we moved to Pine Bluff in '06, I was honored to ride in that UAPB homecoming parade as Grand Marshal, and UAPB has had two Clark Terry Jazz Festivals. My other daughter-in-law, Olivia, filled in when LaJuana got sick. Arranged all the flights and hotel rooms for both festivals. It was her first time working with musicians. She did great!

A whole lot of folks worked on those festivals. The first one featured my quintet, with Don Friedman on piano, Sylvia Cuenca on drums, and Marcus McLaurine on bass. Stantawn Kendrick, my alto man, had previous commitments for that date, so my old buddies Red Holloway and Jimmy Heath bailed me out on saxes. Now, you *know* what Red and Jimmy can do. Both masters!

The second festival featured Clark Terry's Big Bad Band. Frank Greene, Stjepko Gut, and Richard Bailey on trumpets. Richard was a UAPB trumpet professor, and he was sitting in for Tony Lujan, who had a flight delay that caused connection problems. Crystal Torres was busy gigging with Beyoncé, and even though she couldn't make it, I was really proud of her. And I was glad when I learned that Roy Hargrove had agreed to sit in as our special guest on trumpet. They were definitely doing it right. On saxes, we had Adam Schroeder, Dr. D.D., Lakecia Benjamin, Stantawn Kendrick, and Whitney Slaten. Tearing it up! In the bone section we had Jack Jeffers, Barry Cooper, Stafford Hunter, and Cinnamon. That whole section was smokin'! In our rhythm section, Helen Sung was on piano, Marcus McLaurine on bass, and Sylvia Cuenca on drums. In the pocket!

That band was so together. Definitely taking care of business. Choice charts that I'd been cherry-picking for sixty years. They played their asses off! It was the *best* time for all of us. Made me so proud of all the work we had done. The audience loved us. Loud cheers and standing ovations! All of those ingredients made it worthwhile.

I kept in touch with my students around the world. One of my William Paterson students, Lee Hogans, was called to tour with Prince! Now, you *know* that made me happy. Students were flying to Pine Bluff to study with me, and they were bringing friends with them. One time Cinnamon, Justin Kauflin, Alan Hicks, and a friend of Alan's named "Steps" came down and set up in my living room—"Steps" on his trumpet, Cinnamon on trombone, Justin on the piano, and Alan kicking those drums. Those young lions had my house *jumping*. Glad we live in a secluded neighborhood, or somebody would've complained about all that loud music!

Listening to those students grow reminded me of when Dianne Reeves was just getting started. I was blown away by her talent! She was debuting at the Wichita Jazz Festival back in the '70s, I think, and some creep didn't want to let her sing. Well, after I got through cussing a few people out, things cooled off and they let her sing. I've always helped her in any way possible. And she has gone straight to the top! You know, when she calls me and talks about how I've helped her, it just makes me so happy.

The members of my quintet have told me that I've helped them over the years. Former members, too, like Jesse Davis and Dave Glasser—both extraordinary sax players. They will always have a special place in my heart. All the members of my quintet mean a lot to me. Marcus McLaurine has been in my quintet since the early '80s. I'd needed a bass player for a gig in New York at the Blue Note and another gig in Canada, so I called Melba Liston, and she recommended Marcus. He's been with me ever since. He's a *masterful* bassist.

Don Friedman and I have been playing together for more than fifty years. We met back in the '60s when we played some dates in Jersey. He's a skillful and incredible pianist.

Sylvia Cuenca came to a jam session back in the early '90s at the Village Vanguard. She walked up on stage looking svelte and beautiful. I wondered if she could really play jazz. But when she sat in and got down to it, there was *no* doubt. She definitely filled the bill. So I hired her and she's grown into a Class-A percussionist.

Stantawn Kendrick was one of my students at William Paterson University. His remarkable talent on the sax was totally natural. He used to come to my home in Jersey, not far from the school. I spent a lot of time with him and the other students who came and hung out with me. Jamming until dawn, sounding phenomenal.

Sometimes Helen Sung would play in my quintet. She was one of the winners of the Monk Institute's piano competitions. When I first heard her play, I thought, One day she's going to be among the best! That day has come. She is a tiny little lady with a strong grip on jazz. When she sits down, she has total command of those keys. And she can spellbind an audience.

Some of my friends added to the festivals, too. Teaching, judging, performing. Frank Foster, Kevin Mahogany, Denise Thimes, Ernie Andrews, Shawnn Monteiro, Deborah Brown, and others. Folks in Pine Bluff said they couldn't believe their ears and eyes! Everybody's feet were tapping. And Ernie had folks crying, singing some "down-home" blues. They were all top-caliber musicians. Roy's jam session was *smokin'*.

UAPB has had two huge exhibits of my memorabilia. Henri Linton, who's in charge of the art scene, headed them up. He put together some really hip displays in the gallery. It really moved me to see all my work so beautifully arranged. They did a fabulous job.

Then I looked up, and there were fifteen or twenty jazz groups coming to the music department to show off their jazz skills. Jimmy Heath, Roy Hargrove, and Frank Foster did some of the evaluations. High school and college students from as far as Memphis and Oklahoma. Unbelievable! First time UAPB had something like that.

Ron Carter came down from Northern Illinois University to do some clinics. I'm not talking about Ron Carter the bassist. I'm talking about Ron Carter the woodwind player. As far as I'm concerned, he's one of the best jazz teachers I've ever met. He worked with those students until they surprised themselves. Shawnn did some great clinics, too.

UNH and Southeast Missouri State University have annual Clark Terry Jazz Festivals, too. I'd like to think that Big Prez is cool with the way that I've tried to keep my promise to him about helping the young jazz musicians.

Looking back over my life, I feel really blessed. Oh, I've had other health storms. A heart attack in 2007, but Dr. Ferrell took care of that. And my new pacemaker has given me a better rhythm. More swing. Thanks, Dr. Berenbom. Almost had to have my finger amputated from a bone infection the next year, but Dr. Armstrong came to my rescue.

I smile when I think about all of the students I've had a chance to help. The awards from some of their schools. Honorary doctorates. Once I got two in one day in *two* different cities: in the morning at the Manhattan School of Music in New York; that afternoon at the New England Conservatory in Boston, along with Ted Kennedy and Aretha Franklin.

I even got an honorary high school diploma from Vashon High in St. Louis back in '95. Finally graduated from high school at seventy-five years old. And they included the fact that I was Salutatorian of my class. Man! What a gas.

Talking about St. Louis, I was honored with a star on the Walk of Fame on Blueberry Hill in '96, and then about three years later the Griot Museum unveiled a life-size wax statue of me with a hip display of my memorabilia. I really appreciated that hometown support.

Sometimes I'm amazed at how much I've been blessed. I think of all the music that I've been fortunate enough to record. Like the great privilege of making *Porgy and Bess* in August of 2004 with Jeff Lindberg and the Chicago Jazz Orchestra. Outstanding musicians like Danny Barber and Arthur Hoyle, friends like Alyce Claerbaut. That album got several five-star reviews.

I couldn't see very well at the time. My eyes were giving me trouble. So Jeff made me some charts that were three feet tall. Problem *solved*. Talk about beautiful.

I think of all the special people I've met who love jazz. People like Peter Jennings, Bill Clinton; Kris Colley and his wife, Janet—volunteers at the Monk events, always there to help me out and keep the ball rolling for jazz; J. D. and Michelle Day, too—part of the production staff with the Monk events; Bill Cosby's wife, Camille, and her National Visionary Leadership Project that documents the contributions of some of our jazz musicians and some really legendary folks. I think about Wendy Oxenhorn and her great Jazz Foundation of America, helping musicians in need. I close my eyes and see thousands and thousands of faces of others who love jazz like I do. And it makes me feel so good.

I've lived to watch the inauguration of the first black president, Barack Obama. Never thought I'd live to see *that*.

Still, there are two things that have bugged me for a long time.

One is that one of my most favorite recordings, *Clark After Dark*, never got proper distribution. It was such a beautiful album.

When I got to the record date back in '77 in London, I walked inside the large building looking for the recording studio. I opened a door and saw a huge orchestra with strings. A lot of folks. Looked like a hundred people. I thought I'd opened the wrong door. So I said, "I'm sorry. My name is Clark Terry. I was looking for the room where I'm supposed to record."

Somebody said, "This *is* the right room. Come on in."

That session was more than I ever expected. Those arrangements were some of the best I've heard. Most of them were done by a real good buddy of mine named Peter Herbolzheimer. I told all of my friends about that record, and they wanted to hear it. But only a few copies were released. For thirty years, that has boggled my mind.

The second is that I never heard from Shitty since that Christmas Day a long time ago back when I was a young boy in St. Louis. I can still remember those good times we had with my first little street corner band, and how Shitty played that junkyard bass that we made. I can still see him tapping up a storm with those PET Milk cans smashed underneath his shoes, which substituted for real taps. He was such a friend. Even went with me to that old funky junkyard to help find some old things that I could use to make my first trumpet.

That was almost eighty years ago, and yet it still seems like yesterday. Like I've said before, people come and people go, but Shitty was the only one to just disappear.

Life isn't always fair, but at least there are some beautiful things that happen, too. Like in November of 2009, I got a call from Neil Portnow that knocked my socks off. He told me that I had been selected to receive a Grammy Lifetime Achievement Award! I couldn't believe it. At first, I thought it was a joke. After I hung the phone up, I just sat on the side of the bed wondering if it was for real. But I knew I wasn't dreaming.

Two months later, on January 30th, 2010, I was sitting in the front row in the Wilshire Ebell Theater in Los Angeles. It was all true! It was the all-time biggest surprise of my *life*. My whole life! I wondered why they chose me, all those people who'd voted for me. Gwen later read me the names of everybody who had gotten the Lifetime Achievement Award before, and I was *shocked*. Whatever the reasons were for choosing me, I was glad to be there.

The thing that touched me most about the whole scene was that some of my students came to celebrate with me. I was told that it was going to be a small, private ceremony, that I could only invite a few guests. Well, I didn't know who to invite. So I just said yes to the first people who said they wanted to come. Didn't know they would be mostly students.

My youngest student is a sixteen-year-old kid from California named Josh Shpak. Real promising on his trumpet and flugelhorn. His godfather brought him to the ceremony. What's ironic is that I taught his godfather, a cat named Michael Miller, when Michael was sixteen years old. That was at a clinic in California back in the '70s with a high school jazz band. Michael also brought Josh's brother, Noah. A fourteen-year-old kid who's just learning to play guitar.

Alan Hicks came all the way from Australia. A few seats down from me was Quincy Cavers, one of my UABP students. His main instrument is the sax. Bright future ahead of him. My cousin Teri Terry and a few close friends were there, too. Alan Matheson and Kris and Janet Colley.

Some of my other students were working in the bands of stars who had been nominated for R&B Grammys. They wanted to be there with me, but they were busy with rehearsals for the televised awards show that would be broadcast the next night. Which I saw as a good thing! Crystal Torres was busy with Beyoncé's band, and Derrick Hodge was working with Maxwell's band. Roy Hargrove didn't get in to L.A. till the next night for the television show. He was up for another Grammy. He's one of the young lions that I've encouraged from the beginning of his career, way back when he was in Gwen's STAR program.

I was really nervous sitting there at the ceremony. I asked Gwen how many people she thought were there. She guessed around two hundred. I couldn't see a thing; it just looked dark in there. But I could see the stage in front of me a little bit. Lots of lights up there.

Six other people received awards that evening. Some I'd heard of before, some I hadn't. The inventor Thomas Edison I was familiar with. Michael Jackson and André Previn. But I didn't know much about the others. It was all really interesting, though. Watching the other winners and their families, as much as I could see. Listening to the acceptance speeches and all made me a little nervous about what I was going to say when it was my turn, you know. The films that were shown for each recipient looked nice. I just wish I could have seen things better.

When Gwen told me that Quincy Jones had just walked in, I was speech-less. I was so glad that he came! Especially with his hectic schedule. Gwen gave him her seat next to me. He hugged me real tight, and tears rolled down my face. What an awesome thing for him to come. My *first* student from sixty years ago!

Lots of cameras flashed as folks took pictures of us. I wiped my eyes, and then he whispered in my ear. "Sack, I love you. I can't stay long. I left a recording session to come here. I've got fifty people waiting on me. We're doing a remake of 'We Are the World' to raise money for Haiti."

I thought about Haiti. That terrible earthquake. Generations of people killed. The news reported more than two hundred thousand. It was kinda hard to feel happy when there was so much sadness around the world for Haiti.

Quincy had to go before I received my award. He had stayed for a good little while, but my turn hadn't come yet and I knew he had to leave. We hugged each other again, and then he left. Gwen moved back to the seat next to me.

A little while later, Neil introduced me. Gwen took the oxygen tube off my face—I'd already told her that I could do without it while I was up on stage. I could go up to around an hour without it, but not much longer than that.

The stage lights went down, and then they showed a film about my career. I could see some of it. They had things in it like Zoot Sims and me playing together. Bob Brookmeyer. My Big Bad Band. Dianne Reeves giving me a kiss. They even had a segment of the *Little Bill* television show, one of Cosby's shows, when I was a cartoon character. I was singing a song called "Never." A version of "Mumbles."

When the film ended, Neil called me up to the stage. Alan Hicks, my son Gary, and Quincy Cavers helped me to walk up the stairs that led to the middle of the stage. I'll remember that climb for the rest of my life. It took a few minutes because I was using a cane, and they were holding me up on both sides and behind. I was told later that there was a standing ovation from the time I got up from my chair until I made it on stage. All I remember is trying to raise one foot above the other to get up there as fast as possible. I'm glad I had a lot of help doing it!

When I made it, Neil walked up beside me. That's when I saw the Grammy up close. My Lifetime Achievement Grammy. Man, there it was! He held it for me while their photographer took some pictures. I guess Neil knew it was too heavy for me to hold, since it was an effort for me just to stand up there.

Quincy and Gary helped me over to the podium. There was a tall chair there for me. I was half sitting in it and half standing with Gary supporting me. All I remember saying is, "I just want to thank God!" I can't remember much else of what I said. It was so exciting. My first Grammy Award! It meant a whole lot to me. I'd been nominated for a Grammy a few times. Gotten a couple of Grammy Certificates. Even a Grammy President's Merit Award. But I never dreamed of getting a Grammy Lifetime Achievement Award. It was *very* encouraging.

It gave me the idea of giving my *students* an award. Like my nephews Jason McGowan and Charles "Chuck" Hopkins, who've both come a long way on their horns. Or like my cousins the Terry sisters: Zela plays first cello with the Nice Symphony Orchestra in France; Teri sings like an angel; Mona plays beautifully on her harp; and Lesa is one of the finest jazz violinists on the scene, teaching and performing worldwide. Lesa called me the other day and told me that she had just received her first honorary doctorate. And she thanked me for the lessons I'd given her. I'm grateful that I was able to help her to get started.

My goddaughter, Shawnn Monteiro, calls me from time to time and tells me how happy she is that I encouraged her career and inspired her to get into the jazz education scene. She's a very talented lady. A singer and a teacher. The daughter of one of my good buddies, Jimmy Woode. He was a great bassist. I'm really proud of Shawnn.

I've taught others my formula for success: emulate, assimilate, and innovate. I want to give awards to those who have used this process to encourage and help others.

Like Annie Megabow. When she was just a little girl, I told her that she was "my little dancer." I said, "You're going to be a great dancer one day." Well, she grew up and actually became a professional dancer *and* dance teacher. In one recital, she danced to one of my recordings. Man!

Then there are friends of mine who have told me that I've encouraged them. Like Jimmy Heath. He wrote about me in his book that just came out, *I Walked with Giants*. He said that I helped his career. Funny thing—when Jimmy was sick a long time ago, I went to the hospital to visit him and I gave him some money. You know, just to help him over that rough spot. Well, don't you know he gave it back to me when I was sick last year! Even gave me *more* than I'd given him.

I've thought of a name for my award: the Clark Terry Award. That's what I'm calling it. And I want to give the first one to my first student—Q. Maybe I'll even have some kind of ceremony to present my awards.

I had my ninetieth birthday on December 14, 2010, and my prayer is that I can keep on inspiring folks. Especially jazz students. I want to encourage as many people as possible. And I want all of them to do the same thing as they continue in their careers. So I want my award to have a special message on it: "Keep on keepin' on to encourage!" There are thousands of folks who say I've helped them, and I feel good about that. I'm looking forward to being real busy giving out awards.

And I'd sure like to know what happened to my old friend, Shitty.

Acknowledgments

There are so many people to thank, I don't know where to start.

Okay, well just start with the most important first, and then go from there.

Above all, I want to thank Big Prez—my special name for God—for making it possible for me to go back so many years and remember all of these super-important things for my book, and for letting me live to see it become a reality.

Keep going.

Well, I feel like I was extremely blessed—at a young age—to have been a member of Corinthian Baptist Church. I thank the folks in that church, especially Reverend Sommerville, who helped me to keep in touch with God throughout my life.

Some of the people aren't here anymore, but I want to acknowledge them, too. I know they're up there with Big Prez, looking down from Heaven, and they're happy for me.

Well, we can put an asterisk beside their names. Is that okay?

Okay. I'll start with my family. All of them. My father* and mother*, my older sisters* Ada Mae and "Skeety Reet" (Margueritte) who always believed in me, and "Lil" (Lillian); all of my younger sisters* "Sugar Lump" (Mable Myrtle), "Neet" (Juanita Alberta), the twins Marie Louise and Mattie Lucille, and my sweet baby sister "Dessie" (Odessa). And my brothers*, "Bus" (Virgil Otto) and "Shorts" (Charles Edward).

My son, Hiawatha*, who just passed away as I was finishing my book—I wish I could have been around for you more often, and I'll always love you.

To my favorite niece, Murlene Davis; my nephews, Charles "Chuck" Hopkins and Donald Gilliam; and my special niece "Patsy" (Pat Clark)—I appreciate your support and understanding while I was on the road. Patsy, extra thanks for helping with the family history, and love to Larry (Pat's husband). To my grand-nephew "Lonzo" (Alonzo Davis) thanks for helping me out with the photo names.

To all of my other nieces, nephews, cousins, and my specially chosen nephew, Odell McGowan—your mother* "Red" (Edna McGowan) was one of my favorite people—I thank you for always being there. My four "California cousins"—Mona Terry, Lesa Terry, Zela Terry, and Teri Terry-Renty—your help was always so appreciated. And to my other cousins, Billy Scott* and Clyde Scott*—thank you. (I've still never met anybody who could fart the B-flat scale like you, Clyde.)

I'm grateful for all of my family and friends from our old hometown neighborhood in St. Louis—Carondelet. Especially grateful for my brother-in-law Sy McField* (Ada Mae's husband) for being such a guiding force in my life; for Aunt Gert*, who was like a mother to me; and for my friend Shitty (Robbie Pyles), who will always be in my heart. And I'm grateful for all the musicians at home who welcomed me and who remained friends during my career.

What about your family? They helped, too.

That's nice. Keep talking and I'll keep taking notes.

Okay, to our son Gary Paris—thanks for motivating me, filming the editing sessions with Gwen, giving such great suggestions, and helping to spark my memory. LaJuana (Gary's wife)—your critiques were cool; I enjoyed your "serious vittles" and your encouragement. To our son Tony Paris—thanks for prompting my memory with those great jokes, helping with my health issues, and for always being there for me; and to Olivia (Tony's wife)—thanks for the hip suggestions, for encouraging me, and for always lending a helping hand for whatever I needed. To "Pretty Girl" (mother-in-law, Versie Spearman) and "Bo" (her husband, Charles Spearman*)—thanks for always lending an ear and sharing your ideas. "Baby Sis" (sister-in-law, Georgette Wiley)—your editing skills were awesome, and thanks for cheering me on. To Harry Golden (brother-in-law), thanks for keepin' the faith, and for your prayers. And thanks to the "grands" (Legacy, Nikki, Little Tony, and Max) for the giggles and the hugs, which always helped me keep a smile on my face.

Did I leave anybody out?

Well, you've heard me talk about my father (Theodore Jones), and although you didn't have a chance to meet him, I'd like to thank him and my mother for their love and words of wisdom. And I want to thank my childhood pastor, Reverend Davis* at St. Paul Baptist Church here in Pine*

Bluff, for my spiritual roots. And you never met my sister Janice Jones*, but you've heard me talk about her, too. I'd like to thank her for her love.

All right, and I feel like Pauline* and her mother* (Fannie Mae Reddon) and father* (Henry Reddon) are glad for me. And I want to thank Rudy and Betty White (Pauline's son and daughter-in-law), for hangin' with me through the years. And to my grandchildren Butch (Rudy III), Terrence, and Michelle—I'll always love you.

Now I'm at the really hard part. I know if I start naming friends, I won't remember everybody. Somebody's gonna say, "That jive turkey, he didn't mention me!"

It's impossible to remember and thank everybody, Clark, considering all of the people who have been involved in your life or helped you with your book. Just do the best you can.

FRIENDS ON THE BOOK COVER

Q (Quincy Jones), you'll always have a special place way down deep in my heart. You were my first student and I'm so proud of your accomplishments. You've been with me through the good times and the serious storms. I love you, man, and love to your family. "B" (Bill Cosby), I still can't stop thanking you. Your friendship has been beautiful and rare. Thanks for always coming through for me for so many years; I love you and Camille (Bill's wife) and your wonderful family. "Dr. D.D." (David Demsey)—I'm grateful for your beautiful friendship, the Clark Terry Archive at William Paterson University, and for all the hours you put into my book. Love to Karen (David's wife) and your beautiful daughter. "Hee-hoo!" (my special greeting for Jimmy Heath): you have never let me down, always lifted me up. Thanks, man. You and Mona (Jimmy's wife) are the greatest. I've always loved you and I always will. And love to your family. Nancy Wilson— you've always been a beautiful lady with an elegant flair, and you've definitely got a special place in my heart. Thanks for your beautiful words. Keep on keepin' on. Wynton Marsalis, in spite of your hectic schedule, you've always been right there when I needed you, and I've tried to do the same for you. Keep making beautiful music. Love you and your family always.

TOM LORD'S DISCOGRAPHY

The remarkable job that you did on my discography is unparalleled. I appreciate the selected discography that you put together for my book, and that huge discography for my website and my publisher's website. I'm very grateful.

OUR ADVISOR

Our great friend and attorney, Jeremy Nussbaum (of Cowan, Liebowitz, and Latman—New York City)—without you, I don't know where we'd be. Man, in my court, you'll always be in first place.

OUR PUBLISHING TEAM AT UNIVERSITY OF CALIFORNIA PRESS

Mary Francis, it's hard to believe that you did all of that work, but you did it, and I appreciate you. Thanks for believing in my manuscript and for the expert guidance you've given. Jacqueline Volin, thanks for all that extra work that you did to help make my book become a reality. Anne Canright, I'm very proud of your super editing scrutiny. Kim Hogeland, thanks for all of your fine details that kept things in order. Eric Schmidt, thanks for laying it all out and giving us great direction. Steve Isoardi, your critical review was fantastic, very informative. Thanks, man. I hope you like the final product. Kenny Chumbley, thanks for taking care of the photo business. And I appreciate the Editorial Committee at UC Press who voted to publish my autobiography.

FRIENDS WHO GAVE ME GUIDANCE

"Judge" (Milt Hinton*), thirty days! I hope you're ruling in favor of my book. I'll love you and Mona* (Milt's wife) forever. "Magic" (Frank Wess), man, you know I'll always love you. You've never steered me wrong. "Flankson" (Frank Foster), you've been beautiful since the beginning. You and Cecelia (Frank's wife) are two great people. George and Joyce* Wein, much love to both of you. You've always lent a helping hand for years. "Hankles" (Hank O'Neal), I'll always be grateful for the good times that we've shared. You and "Muscles" (Shelly Shire, Hank's wife) are the best. Gary Giddins, thanks for all the beautiful articles you've written about me, and for your love. Marie Brown, thanks for sharing your wisdom, for believing in my book from the very start, and for keeping the faith for so many years. Tad Hershorn, your friendship has been beautiful, and I love the music collection. You've done so much, man. Thanks for your help and the incredible research documents, and good luck with your new book about Smedley (Norman Granz*). Phoebe Jacobs—whatever we needed, you always got it, and fast. I'm grateful to be endowed with your friendship. Laura Ann Parker-Castoro—I really appreciate your encouragement and expertise, even though you were neck-deep in your own writing. You and Chris (Laura's husband) have been beautiful. Lois Gilbert, the job you've done on my website is extraordinary, and I'm grateful for your faith and involvement in my book. Love to our friend, Duke Lee, too. Bill Saxton, you were in my first youth band. Thanks for your great suggestions and for helping to spark my memory. You and "St. Louis" (Theda, Bill's wife) are very special to me. Save my group a date at the club. "Brownie" (Chaunston Brown), you've been with us all the way; please stay with us. Jenny Wilkins, thanks for all the help that you and Charlotte Armstrong (Jenny's daughter) gave me. I'll always miss Ernie* (Wilkins, Jenny's husband). David Berger, thanks to you and Holly (David's wife) for sharing your expertise whenever we needed your help.

FRIENDS WHO PRAYED CONSISTENTLY

Mickarl Thomas and "Cat" (Carol Ann, his wife)—man, I always felt like I could count on you two, and you always came through. Love you. John Graham—your friendship has meant the world to me. I'm grateful for you and Laura (John's wife). Dianne Reeves, I'm so happy with how you've grown in your career. Thanks for always giving me encouragement and for being there whenever I've needed your help. Monte and Yvette Coleman and Ford and Cindy Trotter—thanks for being great neighbors, and for always wishing the best for me and my book. Monte, love your great sermons. And Ford, your dad has been great, too. Randy and Sherry Witt—I'm grateful for how you always rolled up your sleeves to help. You two are absolutely beautiful. "Wheels" (Cliff McMurray) and Tina (his wife), I'll never forget all of the support and encouragement that you two have given to me. I'll always love you and your family very much. Maxine Ragsdale—you've helped from the jump, and that will always be remembered. Much love. Emily Cowan*—thanks for your "ears," from the beginning, and for keeping the faith. Wendy Oxenhorn—you and the Jazz Foundation of America have been absolutely unbelievable. Thanks for your help. Couldn't have made it without you. Denise Thimes—thanks for hangin' in there with me. I'm digging how your career has grown. Keep the melodies flowin'! "Momma D" (Donya Kato)—thanks for that encouraging attitude. Love you. Gaye Wilson—thanks for keeping hope alive, and for helping in so many ways with my book. Love to Al (Gaye's husband), too. Pastor Taylor* and Sister Taylor (Don and Mable Taylor)—man, I'll never forget those great sermons, and Sister Taylor, I'll always remember your words of consolation. I love both of you. And the beautiful Bellon Family in Haworth, New Jersey—you guys were so inspiring and supportive; as well as Alan and Norma Mihlstin in Long Island, New

York—I really appreciate you. To Odell McGowan's family, you all were always in my corner—Ruth Ann (Odell's wife) and Jason (his son); and we can't forget "Bates" (Sheila Bates, their friend). You guys always helped me out whenever I needed a lift.

FRIENDS WHO SPARKED MY MEMORY

"Shortstop" (James Scott*)—you were always like a son to me. I appreciate the time you spent traveling with me and taking trumpet lessons—for years—and thanks for helping me to remember so many things. I hope you like my book. Alan Hicks—you've been like a son, too. The travels, the lessons, the love and friendship. Keep the beat going! Much love. "Co" (Bob Brookmeyer)—you're the greatest! Thanks for helping me through the good times and the rough waters. Keep making that beautiful music. "Brother Red" (Holloway)—you've been my inspiration for years. Thanks for helping me with my book, for your friendship, and for believing in me. "Fab" (Al Grey*) and Rosalie Soladar*—thanks, "Bro and Sis," for your beautiful love. I'll never forget you. Bob Montgomery—thanks for all the Clark Terry Jazz Camps, for helping me to fill in the gaps, and for your never-failing friendship. Jon Faddis—thanks for letting me always count on you and Larelyn (Jon's wife). I love you both. I really appreciate the beautiful musicians who played in my quintet and were always in my corner, and I'd like to give special thanks to "Cuencs" (Sylvia Cuenca), Don Friedman, Helen Sung, Stantawn Kendrick, and Marcus McLaurine. And Marcus—your family has always been special—Miyuki (Marcus' wife), Mizuki and Malik (his children). Tony Lujan—thanks for letting me be your "Jazz Father" and for helping with so many details for my book. Keep up the good work, and love to Lilliana (Tony's wife) and your beautiful family. Mike Vax—you've been with me for a long time; please stay with me. I love you. And love to Pat (Mike's wife). Stjepko Gut—thanks for your help, for sharing so many years together, and for your friendship. Keep blowin', man, and love to your beautiful daughters. "Faithful" (John Simon)—man, you've been in the mix a long time. Thanks for straightening out the rough edges. I love you. John Eddinger—thanks for helping out with my health scene, and for staying with your ax (trumpet).

FRIENDS WHO HELPED WITH EDITING MY DRAFTS

Alan Matheson—what you did, man, I'll never forget. You've always made things better for me. I'm digging all the beautiful music you've sent to me. Love to you and Riina (Alan's wife). "Cinnamon" (Cameron MacManus)—

thanks for all that time you spent with editing, your suggestions, and our friendship. You've been great as a student, traveling with me, and being in my corner. Much love. Robert and Sophia Phillipson—thanks for the critiques, the flowers, the cheese, and your love. You two are very special. Kariyma (Jo Ann Nelson)—thanks for all that editing, your critiques, and your friendship. Hope you like the changes.

FRIENDS WHO MOTIVATED ME

Billy Taylor*—thanks for being with me for decades, and for all of your encouragement. You'll always be in my heart. Johnny Dankworth* and Cleo Laine (Johnny's wife)—thanks for all that royal treatment! I've loved the times that I spent with you guys. Benny Powell*—thanks for all the years of encouragement and your incredible friendship. "T" (Thelonious Monk III), Gale Monk, Tom and Cheri Carter, and all the folks at the Monk Institute—thanks for having me at all the events, for your kind words of encouragement, and for years of love and support. You're all very dear to me. Milt* and Sandy Jackson—thanks for keeping the fires burning when my spirit got chilled, and for pushing me when I got tired. Heinz and Helga Czadek—thanks, for all of those beautiful things in Austria, and for your support and love for so many years. You two are unforgettable. To my dear friend, and a great classical trumpeter, Maurice Andre, thanks for motivating me for years, man. Keep on keepin' on. "Ar" (Eilene Soladar, Rosalie's* daughter)—welcome to "Mommy's Place." I love you, and thanks for your faith. "Shithouse Shorty from Local #40" (Irv Williams)—keep bein' on *it*, and thanks for your help over the decades. Matt Domber—thanks for your help, your kindness, your friendship, and your support. "Migueligans" (Michael Miller)—thanks-a-million is not enough, but please keep on keepin' on, and keep bringing Josh and Noah (Shpak) for lessons. Love you all. Jimmy and Stephanie Owens—you two have always been above the norm. Thanks for the years of help and the tasty steaks. Henri Linton—thanks for doing those fantastic exhibits at UAPB; I had forgotten a lot of those things. Your help has been priceless and your friendship is very much appreciated. Alyce Claerbaut and Rochelle (her daughter)—your love has meant a lot. Thanks for that extra push when I needed it. Kris and Janet Colley—thanks for talking me into believing that I could get it done, for all of your support throughout the years, and for always helping me with my health challenges. I love you both. "M.P." (Mason Prince)—thanks for that delicious Omaha beef, the motivational cards, and for your incredible friendship and encouragement over the decades. Marvin and Angela Floyd—thanks for helping out, driving me around, and for your love. A big hug to Camille, too. Dennis and Bunny* Reynolds, you two never stopped supporting me. Love you both. Dennis, I want you to keep blowin' that trumpet and hangin' on in there. To "Pablo" (Paul Verrette*), Dave and Linda Seiler and their beautiful daughters, Buddy Howard*, Alan Chase and the other fantastic folks at UNH, I'll always remember the decades that we spent together with warmth and a lot of love. I appreciate you all! George and Dana Pettigrew—you guys never gave up on believing that I'd get my book done. Thanks for your wonderful friendship. Ian Carr*—thanks for believing in my writing style from the beginning. Wish you could celebrate with me. To all of my friends at William Paterson University, I'll never forget the beautiful times we've shared, and I'm looking forward to more times together—Arnie Speert, Mulgrew Miller, Harold Mabern, Dave Rogers, Cecil Bridgewater, Gene Bertoncini, and all of the other fantastic people. Thanks so much for encouraging and supporting me, and for that beautiful Clark Terry Archive. Quincy Cavers—thanks for helping to log the facts and find albums and awards, for traveling with me, and for being a good student. Keep blowin' those horns. Carl and Trudy Redus—thanks for your help with the Clark Terry Jazz Festivals that were presented by the University of Arkansas at Pine Bluff. And congrats, man, for being the first black mayor here! You and Trudy have been beautiful. Chancellor L.A. and Ethel Davis, Vice Chancellor Mary Benjamin, Margaret Hall, Michael Bates, James Horton, Darryl Evans, and all of the beautiful people at UAPB, especially "Baby Sis," thanks for your support, for your encouragement and your love. Let's keep the jazz going! To Tommy May, John Garrison, James Horton, Al and Ann White, Stella Thornton, Kenny and Sandra Fisher, Archie Sanders and all of the wonderful folks here in Pine Bluff—you all have made me feel welcome. Much love to each of you.

MY HEALTH TEAM

To my doctors who weren't mentioned in my book: David Nixon (your mom and dad have been super, too) and Pete Menger—thanks for helping out with my sight. Guindan Bai—thanks for that great acupuncture and for getting rid of my back pain. Alexander Navarro, thanks for taking such good care of me. Tommy Ray—I appreciate that "back and neck" help, and for limbering up my hands so I can play better. Jeffrey Glick—thanks for all that you did when my health was a drag.

To my home health aides: "Bunny" (Brenetta King)—thanks for all that good food and for your patience; "My Buddy" Marilyn Turner—thanks for lifting my spirits when I felt disgusted; "CT" (Camille Walker)—I love your great jokes and encouragement; J'Mille Walker—thanks for your special care and those outside strolls; Antoinette Broady—thanks for your prayers and motivation. John "Pee Wee" Jones—thanks for traveling with me and for always lending a helping hand. Your assistance means a lot.

AND . . .

That was great, Clark. Is that it?

No, and I thank all the musicians I've ever played with, composers and arrangers, the people who voted for me to receive awards and the ones who presented them, all the journalists who wrote nice things about me, the photographers, my drivers, promoters who booked my gigs, secretaries who kept things straight, jazz instructors who helped to perpetuate jazz, my friends and fans, and all of the wonderful folks who let me stay in their homes while I was on the road. And I especially thank all of my beautiful students everywhere.

Everybody whose name I didn't think of, I hope you will forgive me. And I want to thank all the U.S. presidents that I had a chance to perform for at the White House—I only mentioned President Clinton in the book. I feel bad that I didn't mention the others, but I also had a chance to perform at the White House for other former presidents—Kennedy, Johnson, Nixon, Carter, Reagan, Bush, Sr., and Bush, Jr.

So, now we're down to a very special lady I want to thank—you. I couldn't have done this without your love, patience, perseverance, traveling with me, taking care of me, entertaining my friends and students, writing and rewriting all those pages, reading them to me for years, and sticking with me until we completed my book.

Some of my friends have asked me how and why you ended up helping me with my book. I told them that, sadly, the first three writers passed before we could get anything done. Allen Scott*, Floyd "Fluji" Williams*, and Marc Crawford*, who was a dear friend of mine and a fantastic professor of Jazz Studies at New York University in Manhattan. Dempsey Travis and I had different approaches to the ways and means that my story could be told, and Quincy Troupe, my longtime hometown friend, was busy working on a screenplay for Miles Davis. I appreciate each of them for wanting to help me, and for their words of encouragement. During all of those years when I was trying to find a writer, you kept the faith, kept gathering information and putting everything together. I thank you for all of that.

You're welcome, Clark. It's been such an honor. Thanks for your love and for letting me help you. I thank God so much for answering my prayers for your book, and for all of the people at our church here—First Assembly—who prayed for us to complete your book.

I'll always be grateful for the beautiful song that you wrote for me— the one you recorded with the Metropole Orchestra—named "Gwen." That was really encouraging while I worked with you.

I also appreciate the Writer's Colony in Eureka Springs, Arkansas; the Frederick Douglass Creative Writing Workshops in Manhattan; and the Greater Dallas Writers' Association.

So, Clark, are you ready to wrap it up now?

No. I want to thank a few more people. Can't forget my personal barber, Devlon Chandler. Thanks for doing your thing to keep me "neat and trimmed." Love to your beautiful wife, Arinitra, and your sweet children. Talking about artists, I've got to mention Kyle Lane. Your work is *incredible*. That piece you gave me, "Trumpet's Preeminent Perspective," man, I'll be thanking you forever. Much love to you and your lovely wife, Sherry, and your beautiful family. To Robbie Todd, thanks for traveling with me and helping me out with my health challenges, especially that heart attack. I'll never forget your support and compassion. There are many photographers who have helped me tremendously during my career, and although I can't name them all, there are two I must thank. *Herman Leonard, you definitely had an "eye" with that camera. Your photos have stood the test of time, and so has our friendship. I miss you. To my man, Herb Snitzer, can't forget your awesome photos. Our association has been a gas! Hope your new book, *Glorious Days and Nights*, is a huge success. And to my friends in Kansas City—Leon Brady, Gary and Angela Hagenbach (keep singing, Angela), Becky Lenge, Brian McTavish, Greg Carroll, and all the others—thanks for hanging with me during that heart attack. Couldn't have made it without you. Greg, please stay on top of that American Jazz Museum there. You guys are doing a great job. To my newest grandson, Liam (Tony's son), welcome to the family. To my sweet goddaughter, Celine Peterson (*Oscar Peterson's daughter), I love you and your mom, Kelly. Please keep O.P.'s memory alive. He was such an *excellent* musician. I'll miss him till the day I die! Okay, Gwen. That's it. If I don't stop now, I'll keep on keepin' on forever.

All right, that was super! I hope you're happy with your book. And for all the stories and names and facts that you didn't include, maybe they can be in the next one.

The next one! It took me twenty years to do this one!

Honors and Awards

GRAMMY AWARDS

National Academy of Recording Arts and Sciences

2004   NARAS President's Merit Award
2010   Grammy Lifetime Achievement Award

GRAMMY NOMINATIONS

National Academy of Recording Arts and Sciences

1964   Best Instrumental Jazz Performance, Small Group or Soloist, with Small Group, "Mumbles," Oscar Peterson and Clark Terry
1965   Best Instrumental Jazz Performance, Small Group or Soloist, with Small Group, *The Power of Positive Swinging*, Clark Terry and Bob Brookmeyer
1976   Best Jazz Performance by a Soloist, album *Clark Terry and His Jolly Giants*

GRAMMY CERTIFICATES

National Academy of Recording Arts and Sciences

2001   Contributor to *Q*, Grammy award–winning recording
2001   Performance on Dianne Reeves' *The Calling*, Grammy award–winning recording

LIFETIME ACHIEVEMENT AWARDS

1991   National Endowment for the Arts
1997   International Association of Jazz Educators

1997	Borough of Queens, New York
2001	WBEE Jazz Radio AM 1570, Chicago, IL
2002	Jazz Foundation of America
2002	Jazz Journalists Association
2003	University of Pittsburgh Academy of Jazz, Pittsburgh, PA
2004	Melton Mustafa Band Festival, Florida Memorial College, Opa-locka, FL
2005	The Blues Bank Collective, Portsmouth, NH
2008	The Jazz Cruise, Mexican Riviera. Headquarters for the Jazz Cruise: St. Louis, MO
2010	American Jazz Museum, Kansas City, MO
2010	University of Arkansas at Pine Bluff, Pine Bluff, AR
2010	Historically Black Colleges and Universities' National Band Directors Consortium, Atlanta, GA

JAZZ HALL, WALL, AND WALK OF FAME AWARDS

1975	Hall of Fame Award, State of Oklahoma
1980	Hall of Fame Award, Rutgers University, Newark, NJ
1985	William J. (Count) Basie Memorial Award, International Jazz Hall of Fame, Kansas City, MO
1989	Hall of Fame Award, Tri-C Jazz Festival, Davenport, IA, Rock Island and Moline, IL
1996	Hall of Fame Award, Vashon High School, St. Louis, MO
1996	Walk of Fame Award and Star, Installed on Blueberry Hill, St. Louis, MO
1999	Hall of Fame Award, Lionel Hampton/Chevron Jazz Festival, University of Idaho, Moscow, ID
2006	Wall of Fame Award, ASCAP—American Society of Composers, Authors and Publishers, New York
2008	Bugler Extraordinaire Medal, Buglers Hall of Fame

JAZZ MASTER AWARDS

1991	NEA Jazz Master Award, National Endowment for the Arts
1997	Jazz Master Award, Music Conservatory of Westchester, White Plains, NY
1999	Benny Golson Jazz Master Award, Howard University, Washington, DC
2003	UCLA Duke Ellington Master of Jazz Award, Friends of the University of California, Los Angeles

2003   Duke Ellington Jazz Master Award, County of Los Angeles, CA

2003   Jazz Master Award, New Jersey Arts in the Park "Giants of Jazz VI"

AWARDS FROM EDUCATIONAL INSTITUTIONS

Honorary Doctorates

1978   University of New Hampshire, Durham, NH

1988   Berklee College of Music, Boston, MA

1993   Teikyo Westmar University, Le Mars, IA

1995   Elmhurst College, Elmhurst, IL

1995   Hamilton College, Clinton, NY

1995   Rowan College of New Jersey, Glassboro, NJ

1997   Manhattan School of Music, New York, NY

1997   New England Conservatory, Boston, MA

1997   University of South Carolina, Columbia, SC

2000   Southeast Missouri State University, Cape Girardeau, MO

2000   Webster University, St. Louis, MO

2002   College of Wooster, Wooster, OH

2004   Purchase College, State University of New York, Purchase, NY

2004   William Paterson University, Wayne, NJ

2007   University of Arkansas at Pine Bluff, Pine Bluff, AR

Honorary Degrees

1981   U.S. Navy School of Music Honorary Degree, Naval Amphibious Base, Norfolk, VA

1995   Diploma from Vashon High School, St. Louis Board of Education, St. Louis, MO

Other Awards from Colleges, Universities, Academies, and Institutes

1968   Guest Soloist Award, University of Northern Iowa, Cedar Falls, IA

1972   Appreciation Medal, Murray State University, Murray, KY

1972   Ellington Fellow Medal, Yale University, New Haven, CT

1978   One O'Clock Award, North Texas University Lab Band, Denton, TX

1979   Appreciation Award, Académie du Disque Français, France

1980   Outstanding Service in Jazz Award, Institute of Afro-American Affairs, Black Student Service Center, New York University, New York, NY

1980   50th Anniversary Appreciation Award, Jersey City State College, Jersey City, NJ

1990   Honorary Director Award, Southwest Missouri State University,
        Springfield, MO

1990   Recognition Award, Instituto Professional Projazz, Portugal

1991   Beacons in Jazz Award, New School for Social Research,
        New York, NY

1993   Appreciation Award, University of Minnesota Morris,
        Morris, MN

1993   Recognition Award, Harvard University, Cambridge, MA

1994   Prix Award, Académie du Jazz, Paris, France

1994   Innovator, Master Musician, Inspiration Award, Highlights in
        Jazz, Pace University, New York, NY

1994   Certificate of Appreciation, Jazz Seminar Committee,
        University of Pittsburgh, PA

1995   SCE Jazz Fellow Award, New York University, New York, NY

2002   Charles Holmes Pette Medal, University of New Hampshire,
        Durham, NH

2009   President's Medallion, Harris Stowe State University,
        St. Louis, MO

Awards from High Schools, Middle Schools, Elementary Schools, and Community Schools

1964   Honorary Lifetime Membership, Berriman Junior High School,
        Brooklyn, NY

1968   Honorary Bandsman Award, Clarence Central Senior High School
        Bands, Clarence, NY

1968   Honorary Conductor Award, Lebanon High School Band,
        Lebanon, MO

1970   Appreciation Award, Jefferson City Bands, Jefferson City, MO

1971   Mayor's Appreciation Award, Lovejoy Schools, Brooklyn, NY

1973   Beautiful Person Award, Southwestern Community High School,
        Flint, MI

1974   Honorary Visiting Ministers of Jazz, Blackshear Junior High School

1975   Appreciation Award, Walterboro High School, Walterboro, SC

1987   Distinguished Alumnus Award, St. Louis Public School District,
        St. Louis, MO

1989   Salute Award, Cardinal Ritter College Prep High School,
        St. Louis, MO

2003   Mentor Award, Manhattan Country School, New York, NY

2005   Appreciation Award, Thurnauer School of Music, Tenafly, NJ

AWARDS FROM JAZZ FESTIVALS AND CONFERENCES

1974   Homer Osborne Award, Outstanding Achievement in Jazz Education, Wichita Jazz Festival, Wichita, KS

1976   Contributions to American Music Award, Americana Festival, University of Minnesota, St. Paul, MN

1991   Medal of Honor, The Midwest Clinic, International Band and Orchestra Conference, Chicago, IL

1991   Musician, Educator, and Ambassador of Jazz Music Award, Clark Terry All-American Jazz Camp Festival, University of Central Oklahoma, Edmond, OK

1992   25th Anniversary Award, Elmhurst College Jazz Festival, Elmhurst, IL

1992   Duke Ellington Memorial Award, 52nd Street Americana Festival, New York, NY

1993   Diplôme de Dégustation, Jazz in Marciac Festival, Côtes de Saint-Mont, Marciac, France

1993   Medal of Honor, Umbria Jazz Festival, Perugia, Italy

1995   Friendship Award, Louie Bellson Jazz Festival, Rock Island and Moline, IL

1995   Three Key Award, Bern International Jazz Festival, Bern, Switzerland

1996   Fish Middleton Jazz Scholarship Fund Salute, East Coast Jazz Festival, Rockville, MD

1996   Guinness Jazz Legend Award, Cork Jazz Festival, Cork City, Ireland

1997   Bird Award, North Sea Jazz Festival, The Hague, Netherlands

1997   Charlie Parker Memorial Award, 52nd Street Americana Festival, New York, NY

1999   The Great C.T. Award, Atina Jazz Festival, Atina, Italy

1999   Great Contribution to Jazz, San Sebastián Jazz Festival, San Sebastián, Spain

1999   Appreciation Award, Northwest Jazz Festival, Northwest College, Powell, WY

2000   Milt Jackson Award, Charlie Parker Festival, New York, NY

2000   Honor for Clark Terry Jazz Festival, Phi Mu Alpha Sinfonia, Southeast Missouri State Chapter, Cape Girardeau, MO

MEDIA AWARDS

1963   Clark Terry/Bob Brookmeyer Combo Award, *DownBeat* Jazz Critics Poll, Talent Deserving Wider Recognition

1992   Gift of Song Award, Voice of America

2001   BBC International Jazz Artist of the Year, British Broadcasting
Corporation

2005   Trumpeter of the Year, Jazz Journalists Association, New York, NY

2011   Honorary Membership, Kappa Kappa Psi Iota Phi Chapter,
University of New Hampshire, Durham, NH

FRATERNITY AWARDS

1968   Honorary Membership, Phi Mu Alpha Beta Zeta Chapter

1981   Dedication to Young Musicians Award, Phi Mu Alpha, Tennessee
State University, Nashville, TN

1981   Honorary Membership, Kappa Kappa Psi Gamma Alpha Chapter,
Honorary Band Fraternity

1985   American Man of Music, Phi Mu Alpha Sinfonia, Southeast
Missouri State Chapter, Cape Girardeau, MO

2006   Humanitarian Service Award, Kappa Alpha Psi Fraternity, Inc.,
Pine Bluff Alumni Chapter, AR

AWARDS FROM ORGANIZATIONS AND CORPORATIONS

1962   Certificate of Accomplishment, Playboy All-Star Jazz Poll

1963   Certificate of Accomplishment, Playboy All-Star Jazz Poll

1966   Achievement Award, North Shore Club—National Association of
Negro Business and Professional Women's Clubs, NY

1968   All Star Band, Established Artist Certificate, Record World All
Star Band

1971   Founding Artist Award, Kennedy Center for the Arts,
Washington, DC

1982   Thelonious Monk Memorial Award, Search For Truth, Inc.,
Chicago, IL

1983   Appreciation Award, Thelonious Sphere Monk Statue Unveiling
Ceremony, New York, NY

1984   Trophy Award, 11th National Convention, National Association of
Jazz Educators

1984   Honorary Member Award, Jazz Disciples, Inc., Atlanta, GA

1985   Honorary Member Award, Central Florida Community Jazz Center

1986   Honor Award for 43 Years of Jazz Purity, Count Basie Jazz Society

1989   Professor Emeritus Award, Pan African Kupigana Ngumi Martial
Arts Federation, Chicago, IL

1990   Louis Armstrong Award, American Jazz Association, Gary, IN

1990	BMI Jazz All-Stars 50th Anniversary Medal, Broadcast Music Inc., Gary, IN
1991	Satchmo Award (Louis Armstrong), Charlin Jazz Society, Washington, DC
1991	Award of Merit, City Stages Jazz Camp, Birmingham, AL
1993	Award of Honor, Bohuslän Big Band, Bohuslän, Sweden
1994	Living Legacy Award, Mid-Atlantic Arts Foundation, Baltimore, MD
1996	Living Legends Award, Harlem Jazz Foundation, Harlem, NY
1997	Wittnauer Award, The Jazz Edge, Inc., St. Louis, MO
1998	Recognition Award, Dorie Miller Houses Concert, Louis Armstrong House and Archives, Queens, NY
1998	Knighted as Sir Clark Terry, Musica et Patria—Musica et Mundus, Ritter der Ronneburg, at Castle Ronneburg, Hesse, Germany
1999	American Eagle Award, National Music Council
1999	Eagle Award, Celebrating the Music of Clark Terry, Anheuser-Busch, St. Louis, MO
2000	Honorary Member, Duke Ellington Society
2000	Honorary Membership, Duke Ellington Society UK, Great Barton, Bury St. Edmunds, United Kingdom
2000	Dedicated Service Award, International Association of Jazz Educators
2001	Lucie Rudd, M.D., Founders Award, Veritas, Friends of Charlie Parker, New York, NY
2001	Benny Carter Award, American Federation of Jazz Societies
2002	Recognition Award, Jazz Rhythms, New Visions, the Riverside Youth Scholarship Project, New York, NY
2004	Best Performance Award, Arts for Life
2004	Don Redman Heritage Award, Don Redman Society, Jefferson County, WV, NAACP and Harpers Ferry Historical Association, Piedmont, WV
2005	Award of Honor, Extraordinary Career, International Trumpet Guild
2007	Sheldon Music Award, Sheldon Concert Hall, St. Louis, MO

CITY, STATE, NATIONAL, AND INTERNATIONAL GOVERNMENT AWARDS

1967	Key to Quinnipiac College and the City of Hamden, Hamden, CT
1970	Talent Search Judge Appreciation Award, New York Housing Authority

1971	Honorary Citizen Proclamation, City of Davenport, IA
1972	Honorary Citizen Certificate, City of Odessa, TX
1975	Commendation Citation, State of Oklahoma
1976	"Aide-de-Camp" Appointment on the Staff of the Governor Proclamation, State of Louisiana
1979	Honorary Citizen Certificate, City of Tucson, AZ
1979	Clark Terry Day Proclamation, City of Hempstead, NY
1980	Outstanding Contributions to Jazz and Jazz Education Proclamation, City of Cherry Hill West, NJ
1983	Honorary Citizen Proclamation, State of Arizona
1986	Key to City of Copenhagen, Copenhagen, Denmark
1988	Medal of Honor, Commune St. Josse-ten-Noode, Belgium
1989	Clark Terry Appreciation Day Proclamation, City of North Chicago, IL
1990	Clark Terry Day, Borough of Queens, NY
1991	Certificate of Appreciation, City of New York, NY
1992	Key to City of Edmund, Edmund, OK
1994	Paris City Hall Medal, Paris, France
1994	Appreciation Certificate, City of Le Mars, IA
1994	Honorary Commissioner Certificate, Shelby County, TN
1995	Outstanding Contributions to Jazz Award, Jamaica Development Corporation, Jamaica, NY
1995	Honorary Citizen, State of South Carolina
1997	Key to City of Scranton, Scranton, PA
1998	Clark Terry Days Proclamation, Chicago, IL
1999	Key to City of Glen Cove, Glen Cove, NY
1999	Black History Month Honor Certificate, City Council, New York, NY
2000	Officier de L'Ordre des Arts et des Lettres, French Government
2000	Proclamation of Honor, Detroit, MI
2001	African American Night Jazz Legends Award, Nassau County, NY
2001	Dr. Martin Luther King, Jr. Award, Dr. Martin Luther King, Jr. Birthday Celebration Committee of Nassau County, Inc., NY
2003	Commendation Certificate, City of Los Angeles, CA
2004	Austrian Cross of Honour—Litteris et Artibus, Austrian Government
2004	Clark Terry Day Proclamation, Cincinnati, OH
2005	Clark Terry Day Proclamation, Fulton County, GA
2007	Proclamation of Honor, "Jazz in the City Week," Pine Bluff, AR

2008 Frank Smith Spirit of Kansas City Jazz Award, Elder Statesmen of Kansas City Jazz, Kansas City, KS

2008 Clark Terry Weekend, Wyandotte County, Kansas City, KS

U.S. MILITARY AWARDS

1967 Commodore Appointment of Navy Intercollegiate Music Festival, IMF Flagship *Sero*, U.S. Navy

1994 Pershing's Own Certificate of Appreciation for Loyalty and Professional Dedication, U.S. Army

1999 "Clark Terry Jazz Heritage Series" Award, U.S. Air Force Band

2001 Certificate of Authenticity, National Ensign Honor Flight, Naval Training Center, Great Lakes, IL

Original Compositions

COMPOSITIONS OF MY OWN

Argentia
Bayside Cookout
Blues for Daddy O
Blues for Daddy O's Jazz Patio
Blues for Etta
Blues for Gypsy
Blues for K.K.
Blues for the Champ of Champs
Boardwalk
Boomerang
Brushes and Brass
Buck's Business
Buddy's Tête-à-Tate
Celita Linda
Champaign and Chitterlin' Twist
Chat Qui Pêche
Chuckles
Clark Bars
Clark's Ditty
Clark's Expedition
Co-op
Côte d'Azur
The Countess
Cruisin'
Daddyo
Daylite Express
Dex-Terry-Ty
Digits

Egdirdle
Electric Mumbles
Evad
Evad Smurd
Finger Filibuster
Flugel N the Blues
Flutin' and Flugelin'
Freedom March Blues
Frog Eyes
Globetrotter
Grand Dad Blues
Groovy Dues
Ground Hog
Gwen
Hawg Jawz
Hey, Mr. Mumbles
Hildegarde
Holy Mackle Sapphire
Hot Sauce (lyrics by Gary Paris)
Impeccable
Incoherent Blues
In Orbit
In the Alley
Jazz Patio Blues
Jones
Joonji
Keep, Keep, Keep on Keepin' On
Kitten

K-9
Latin Blue
Levee Camp Blues
Lil' Ole Mongoose
Love Love Love
Mamblues
Mardi Gras Waltz
Marina Bay Rednecks
Michelle
Miguel's Party
Mine Too
Mr. Mumbles Strikes Again
Mumbles
Mumbles Returns
Mumbling in the Alps
My Gal
Nahstye
Natural Thing
Never
No Flugel Blues
Ocean Motion
Ode to a Flugelhorn
Ode to Pres
One Foot in the Gutter
One More for Diz
On Top of Ole Sugarbush
Opus Ocean
Organism
Owen
Pauline
Payin' Them Berlin Dues Blues
Peaches Are Better Down
    the Road
Pea-Eye
Perdido Line
Peterson Chops
Phalanges

Phat Bach
Th' Phunkie Waltz
Pint of Bitter
Please Blues Go on Away
Putte's Patter
Quicksand
Republic
Return to Swahili
Rive Gauche
River Boat
The Salt Mines
Samba de Gumz
Sapphire Blue
Serenade to a Bus Seat
Sheba
Sid's Mark
Silly Samba
Simple Waltz
Slopp Jah
Slow Boat
Snapper
Snatchin' It Back
Spacemen
Stayin' Over
St. Lucia Blues
Strange Creatures Crawl Out from
    Under the Rocks When It Rains
The Stroller
Swingin' on the Cusp
Take Me Back to Elkhart
Tee Pee Time
Tête-à-Tête
Top and Bottom
Tread Ye Lightly
Trumpet Mouthpiece Blues
Why
Zipcode

COMPOSITIONS WITH OTHER MUSICIANS

Coolin'	Duke Ellington and Clark Terry
Clusterphobia	Duke Ellington and Clark Terry
Dual Fuel	Duke Ellington and Clark Terry
Launching Pad	Duke Ellington and Clark Terry
Sakena	Sykes Smith and Clark Terry
Stop Breaking My Heart	Freddie Green and Clark Terry
That's Why They Called Her Queen	Babs Gonzales and Clark Terry

SOME OF THE FILM SCORES ON WHICH I PLAYED

Calendar Girl (SPE Corporate Service/Columbia)
The Fabulous Baker Boys (20th Century Fox)
The Hot Rock (20th Century Fox)
Mickey One (SPE Corporate Service/Columbia)
The Wiz (Universal Studios)

Selected Discography

Compiled by Tom Lord, editor of the Jazz Discography Online (TJD Online)

The following selected list of 371 releases by Clark Terry includes sessions where he was a sideman and a leader. This list is arranged chronologically in ascending order from Terry's earliest recordings to his most recent. Each entry is arranged by date, leader name, album title, and record company with release number. Long-playing releases are shown with (LP) following the release number. Compact disc releases are shown with [CD] following the release number. Wherever possible, CD releases have been listed, as they are usually more widely available than LP releases.

All releases that do not show one of the following country codes are American:

(And)	Andorra	(It)	Italy
(Can)	Canada	(Jap)	Japan
(Dan)	Denmark	(Pol)	Poland
(Du)	Holland	(Rus)	Russia
(E)	United Kingdom	(Sp)	Spain
(F)	France	(Swd)	Sweden
(Fin)	Finland	(Swi)	Switzerland
(G)	Germany	(Yugo)	Yugoslavia

For a complete discography of Clark Terry, compiled by Tom Lord, see www.ucpress.edu/go/clarkterry or www.clarkterry.com. For complete information on *The Jazz Discography*, by Tom Lord, see www.lordisco.com.

The Clark Terry discography as presented online is based on recording session and is listed in ascending chronological order. It includes leader name, album name, musicians (including instruments played), tune names, and record company and release numbers. Original issues are listed along with large numbers of LP and CD reissues. The discography has been extracted from the popular Jazz Discography Online. Full details can by viewed at www.lordisco.com.

1. April 1947—Various Artists—*Blues Boogie and BOP—The 1940's Mercury Sessions*—Verve 314-525609-2 [CD]

2. September 1947—Charlie Barnet—*For Dancing Lovers*—Verve MGV2031 (LP)

3. December 1947—Charlie Barnet—*Town Hall Concert*—Columbia CL639 (LP)

4. September 1948—Count Basie—*Anita O'Day Meets the Big Bands*—Moon (It) MCD047-2 [CD]

5. April 1949—Count Basie—*Count Basie, 1947–1949*—Classics (F) 1107 [CD]

6. June 1949—Count Basie—*Shoutin' Blues*—RCA Bluebird 66158-2 [CD]

7. May 1950—Count Basie—*Blues by Basie, 1939–1951*—Columbia CL901 (LP)

8. Summer 1950—Billie Holiday—*Lady Day Box, vol. 5*—JUTB (It) 3039 [CD]

9. August 1950—Sonny Criss/Wardell Gray—*Wardell Gray, 1950–1955*—Classics (F) 1463 [CD]

10. November 1950—Count Basie—*One O'clock Jump/Count Basie, 1942–1951*—Columbia CL997 (LP)

11. April 1951—Count Basie—*Count Basie and his Orchestra, 1950–1951*—Classics (F) 1228 [CD]

12. December 1951—Duke Ellington—*Ellington Uptown*—Columbia ML4639 (LP)

13. February 1952—Louie Bellson—*Just Jazz All Stars*—Capitol 15904 (LP)

14. March 1952—Duke Ellington—*The 1952 Seattle Concert*—Bluebird 66531-2 [CD]

15. June 1952—Dinah Washington—*The Complete Dinah Washington on Mercury, vol. 3*—Mercury 834675-2 [CD]

16. July 1952—Duke Ellington—*Live at the Blue Note*—Aircheck 4 (LP)

17. November 1952—Duke Ellington—*Duke Ellington at Birdland, 1952*—Jazz Unlimited (Dan) JUCD2036 [CD]

18. March 1953—Duke Ellington—*The 1953 Pasadena Concert*—Jazz Legacy (F) 500201 (LP)

19. June 1953—Duke Ellington—*One Night Stand with Duke Ellington at the Blue Note*—Century (Jap) 20EL-5503 (LP)

20. December 1953—Duke Ellington—*Duke Ellington and His Orchestra, 1953, vol. 2*—Classics (F) 1432 [CD]

21. February 1954—Clark Terry—*Clark Terry*—EmArcy (Jap) EJD-3091 [CD]

22. April 1954—Duke Ellington—*The 1954 Los Angeles Concert*—GNP Crescendo GNPD9049 [CD]

23. June 1954—Cats versus Chicks—*Cats versus Chicks*—MGM E255 (LP)

24. June 1954—Duke Ellington—*The Complete Capitol Duke Ellington*—Mosaic MD5-160 [CD]

25. August 1954—Jam Session (Mercury Jazz Concert)—*Dinah Washington with Clifford Brown—Complete Recordings*—Lonehill Jazz (Sp) LHJ10165 [CD]

26. Late 1954—Jimmy Hamilton—*Jimmy Hamilton and the New York Jazz Quintet*—Fresh Sound (Sp) FSR2002 [CD]

27. January 1955—Clark Terry—*Swahili*—Lonehill Jazz (Sp) LHJ10244 [CD]

28. March 1955—Duke Ellington—*Les Suites Sinfoniche*—Musica Jazz (It) 2MJP-1021 (LP)

29. September 1955—Johnny Hodges—*Creamy*—Verve MGV8136 (LP)

30. 1956—George Gershwin—*The Complete "Porgy and Bess"*—Definitive (And) DRCD11271 [CD]

31. January 1956—Duke Ellington—*Blue Rose*—Columbia CL872 (LP)

32. February 1956—Duke Ellington—*The Complete Gus Wildi Recordings*—Lonehill Jazz (Sp) LHJ10173 [CD]

33. July 1956—Duke Ellington—*Ellington at Newport 1956 (Complete)*—Columbia/Legacy C2K64932 [CD]

34. August 1956—Duke Ellington—*Such Sweet Thunder*—Columbia/Legacy CK65568 [CD]

35. September 1956—Johnny Hodges—*Duke's in Bed*—Verve MGV8203 (LP)

36. October 1956—Duke Ellington—*A Drum Is a Woman*—Columbia CL951 (LP)

37. October 1956—Thelonious Monk—*Brilliant Corners*—Riverside RCD-30501 [CD]

38. December 1956—Tony Scott—*The Complete Tony Scott*—RCA 7432-142132-2 [CD]

39. March 1957—Jackie and Roy—*Jackie and Roy with the Roy Kral and Bill Holman Orchestras*—Fresh Sound (Sp) FSRCD510 [CD]

40. April, 1957—Clark Terry—*Serenade to a Bus Seat*—Riverside RCD-30189 [CD]

41. April 1957—Duke Ellington—*Such Sweet Thunder*—Columbia/Legacy CK65568 [CD]

42. June 1957—Johnny Hodges—*The Big Sound*—Verve MGV8271 (LP)

43. July 1957—Clark Terry—*Out on a Limb*—Chess GRD819 [CD]

44. July 1957—Clark Terry—*Duke with a Difference*—Riverside OJCCD-229-2 [CD]

45. August 1957—Paul Gonsalves—*Cookin'*—Chess 0007 [CD]

46. September 1957—Jimmy Woode—*The Colorful Strings of Jimmy Woode*—Argo LP630 (LP)

47. September 1957—Duke Ellington—*Indigos*—Columbia CK44444 [CD]

48. November 1957—Billy Taylor—*Taylor Made Jazz*—Argo LP650 (LP)

49. December 1957—Dinah Washington—*Dinah Washington Sings Bessie Smith*—Verve 314-538635-2 [CD]

50. 1958—Billy Strayhorn—*Echoes of an Era*—Roulette RE121 (LP)

51. February 1958—Duke Ellington—*Black, Brown, and Beige*—Columbia/Legacy CK65566 [CD]

52. March 1958—Duke Ellington—*At the Bal Masque*—Columbia (F) 469136-2 [CD]

53. April 1958—Duke Ellington—*The Cosmic Scene*—Mosaic MCD-1001 [CD]

54. May 1958—Clark Terry—*Clark Terry in Orbit*—*Clark Terry Quartet with Thelonious Monk*—Riverside OJCCD-302-2 [CD]

55. July 1958—Duke Ellington—*Live at Newport 1958*—Columbia/Legacy C2K53584 [CD]

56. July 1958—Sonny Rollins—*Tenor Titan*—Metrojazz E(S)1002 (LP)

57. July 1958—Mercer Ellington—*Steppin' into Swing Society*—Coral CRL57225 (LP)

58. August 1958—Charlie Barnet—*Cherokee*—Evidence ECD22065-2 [CD]

59. August 1958—Cat Anderson—*Cat on a Hot Tin Roof*—EmArcy MG36142 (LP)

60. August 1958—Duke Ellington—*Jazz at the Plaza, vol. 2*—Columbia C32471 (LP)

61. October 1958—Duke Ellington—*Live in Paris, at the Alhambra*—Pablo PACD-5313-2 [CD]

62. October 1958—Donald Byrd—*Au Chat Qui Pêche*—Fresh Sound (Sp) FSRCD1028 [CD]

63. November 1958—Duke Ellington—*European Tour*—Bandstand (It) BDCD1509 [CD]

64. November 1958—Duke Ellington—*Duke in Munich*—Storyville (Dan) STCD8324 [CD]

65. November 1958—Duke Ellington—*In Concert at the Pleyel, Paris, 1958*—Magic (E) DAWE39/40 [CD]

66. February 1959—Duke Ellington—*Duke Ellington Jazz Party*—Columbia CK40712 [CD]

67. February 1959—Clark Terry—*Top and Bottom Brass*—Riverside OJCCD-764-2 [CD]

68. March 1959—Mercer Ellington—*Colors in Rhythm*—Coral CRL57293 (LP)

69. May 1959—Quincy Jones—*The Quincy Jones ABC/Mercury Big Band Jazz Sessions*—Mosaic MD5-237 [CD]

70. May 1959—Duke Ellington—*Anatomy of a Murder*—Columbia/Legacy CK65569 [CD]

71. June 1959—Ray Charles—*Genius*—Atlantic LP1312 (LP)

72. July 1959—Duke Ellington—*Live! At the Newport Jazz Festival, '59*—EmArcy 842071-2 [CD]

73. August 1959—Duke Ellington—*Live at the Blue Note*—Roulette CDP7243-8-28637-2 [CD]

74. September 1959—Duke Ellington—*Festival Session*—Columbia CK87044 [CD]

75. September 1959—Duke Ellington—*Duke Ellington 2*—Sarpe Top Jazz (It) SJ1013 [CD]

76. October 1959—Clark Terry—*Masters of Jazz, vol. 5—Clark Terry*—Storyville (Dan) 101-8505 [CD]

77. January 1960—Clark Terry—*Paris, 1960*—Swing (F) SW8406 (LP)

78. February 1960—Quincy Jones—*Live at the Alhambra, '60*—JMY (It) 1004-2 [CD]

79. February 1960—Quincy Jones—*Free and Easy*—Ancha (Swd) ANC9500-2 [CD]

80. March 1960—Ernestine Anderson—*My Kinda Swing*—Verve 842409 [CD]

81. April 1960—Ernie Wilkins—*The Big New Band of the 60's*—Everest LPBR5104 (LP)

82. May 1960—Johnny Griffin—*The Big Soul-Band*—Riverside OJCD-485-2 [CD]

83. May 1960—Charles Mingus—*Pre Bird*—EmArcy 826496-2 [CD]

84. June 1960—Mundell Lowe—*Themes from "Mr. Lucky"*—Camden CAL627 (LP)

85. June 1960—Jimmy Heath—*Really Big!*—Riverside OJCCD-1799-2 [CD]

86. July 1960—Dave Bailey—*The Complete 1 and 2 Feet in the Gutter Sessions*—Lonehill Jazz (Sp) LHJ10220 [CD]

87. July 1960—Bob Wilber—*Evolution of the Blues*—Music Minus One MMO-1008 (LP)

88. August 1960—Budd Johnson—*Budd Johnson and the Four Brass Giants*—Riverside RLP(S)343 (LP)

89. August 1960—Al Cohn—*Son of Drum Suite*—BMG 74321-36409-2 [CD]

90. September 1960—Eddie Lockjaw Davis—*Trane Whistle*—Prestige OJCCD-429-2 [CD]

91. October 1960—Yusef Lateef—*The Centaur and the Phoenix*—Riverside OJCCD-721-2 [CD]

92. October 1960—Buddy Tate—*Tate-a-Tate*—Prestige PRCD-24231-2 [CD]

93. November 1960—Dizzy Gillespie—*Gillespiana and Carnegie Hall Concert*—Verve 314-519809-2 [CD]

94. November 1960—Randy Weston—*Uhuru Afrika*—Roulette CDP7-94510-2 [CD]

95. November 1960—Clark Terry—*Color Changes*—Candid CCD9009 [CD]

96. December 1960—Gerry Mulligan—*Gerry Mulligan and the Concert Jazz Band at the Village Vanguard*—Verve MGV8396 (LP)

97. December 1960—Count Basie—*Easin' It*—Roulette (S) R52117 (LP)

98. December 1960—Teri Thornton—*Devil May Care*—Riverside OJCCD-1017-2 [CD]

99. December 1960—Ray Charles—*Genius + Soul = Jazz*—Impulse A(S)2 (LP)

100. December 1960—Blue Mitchell—*Smooth as the Wind*—Riverside OJCCD-871-2 [CD]

101. January 1961—Count Basie/Sarah Vaughan—*Count Basie/Sarah Vaughan*—Capitol Roulette CDP7243-8-37241-2-3 [CD]

102. January 1961—Cecil Taylor—*Cell Walk for Celeste*—Candid (G) CCD79034 [CD]

103. February 1961—George Romanis—*Double Exposure!*—Decca DL4170 (LP)

104. February 1961—Cannonball Adderley—*African Waltz*—Riverside OJCCD-258-2 [CD]

105. March 1961—Cecil Payne—*Stop and Listen to . . . Cecil Payne*—Fresh Sound (Sp) FSRD193 [CD]

106. March 1961—Dizzy Gillespie—*Carnegie Hall Concert*—Verve 314-519809-2 [CD]

107. March 1961—Jimmy Hamilton—*It's About Time*—Swingville SVLP2022 (LP)

108. March 1961—Nat Pierce—*The Ballad of Jazz Street*—Hep (E) CD2009 [CD].

109. April 1961—Buddy Greco—*I Like It Swinging*—Epic LN3793 (LP)

110. May 1961—Duke Ellington—*Paris Blues*—Ryko RCD10713 [CD]

111. May 1961—Eddie Lockjaw Davis—*Afro-Jaws*—Riverside OJCCD-403-2 [CD]

112. June 1961—Manny Albam—*More Double Exposure*—RCA-Victor LSA2432 (LP)

113. June 1961—Gene Ammons—*Soul Summit*—Prestige PRCD-24118-2 [CD]

114. June 1961—Clea Bradford—*These Dues*—Tru-Sound TRU15005 (LP)

115. July 1961—Johnny Griffin—*White Gardenia*—Riverside OJCCD-1877-2 [CD]

116. July 1961—Clark Terry—*Everything's Mellow*—Moodsville MVLP20 (LP)

117. August 1961—Dinah Washington—*The Complete Dinah Washington on Mercury, vol. 7*—Mercury 838960-2 [CD]

118. August 1961—Kai Winding—*Kai Ole*—Verve V(V6)-8427 (LP)

119. September 1961—Billy Taylor with Jimmie Jones Orchestra—*Kwamina*—Mercury SR60654 (LP)

120. September 1961—Mark Murphy—*Rah*—Riverside OJCCD-141-2 [CD]

121. October 1961—Junior Mance—*The Jazz Soul of Hollywood*—Jazzland JLP63 (LP)

122. October 1961—Tubby Hayes/Clark Terry—*The New York Sessions*—Columbia CK45446 [CD]

123. November 1961—Riverside Jazz Stars—*A Jazz Version of "Kean"*—Riverside RS9397 (LP)

124. November 1961—Bob Brookmeyer—*Gloomy Sunday and Other Bright Moments*—Verve MGV8455 (LP)

125. November 1961—Gary McFarland—*The Jazz Version of "How to Succeed in Business Without Really Trying"*—Verve 314-527658-2 [CD]

126. November 1961—Quincy Jones—*The Quintessence*—Impulse B0009782-02 [CD]

127. December 1961—Billy Byers—*Impressions of Duke Ellington*—Mercury PPS2028 (LP)

128. December 1961—Gerry Mulligan—*Mulligan '63*—Verve (Sp) 840832-2 [CD]

129. 1962—Babs Gonzales—*Live at Small's Paradise*—Dauntless LP4311 (LP)

130. 1962—Clark Terry/Bob Brookmeyer—*Previously Unreleased Recordings*—Verve V6-8836 (LP)

131. January 1962—Ray Brown—*Ray Brown with the All Star Big Band*—Verve V6-8444 (LP)

132. February 1962—Tadd Dameron—*The Magic Touch*—Riverside OJCCD-143-2 [CD]

133. March 1962—Blue Mitchell—*A Sure Thing*—Riverside OJCCD-837-2 [CD]

134. March 1962—Cecil Payne—*The Connection*—Charlie Parker PLP806 (LP)

135. May 1962—Clark Terry—*All American*—Prestige 24136 [CD]

136. June 1962—Oscar Peterson—*Bursting Out*—Verve 314-529699-2 [CD]

137. June 1962—Milt Jackson—*Big Bags*—Riverside OJCCD-366-2 [CD]

138. August 1962—Art Farmer—*Listen to Art Farmer*—Mercury MG20766 (LP)

139. August 1962—Quincy Jones—*Big Band Bossa Nova*—Verve 0602498840399 [CD]

140. August 1962—Stan Getz/Gary McFarland—*Big Band Bossa Nova*—Verve 823611-2 [CD]

141. September 1962—Dave Pike—*Bossa Nova Carnival*—Prestige (Jap) VICJ-23148 [CD]

142. September 1962—Gary Burton—*Who Is Gary Burton?*—RCA-Victor 74321-36403-2 [CD]

143. October 1962—Mark Murphy—*That's How I Love the Blues!*—Riverside OJCCD-367-2 [CD]

144. October 1962—Charles Mingus—*The Complete Town Hall Concert*—Blue Note 8-28353-2 [CD]

145. November 1962—Oliver Nelson—*Full Nelson*—Verve V-8508 (LP)

146. December 1962—Michel Legrand—*Michel Legrand Plays Richard Rodgers*—Philips PHS600-074 (LP)

147. December 1962—Coleman Hawkins/Clark Terry—*Back in Bean's Bag*—Columbia CL1992 (LP)

148. 1963—Al Caiola—*Cleopatra and All That Jazz*—United Artists UAS6299 (LP)

149. 1963—Bill Potts—*Bye Bye Birdie*—Colpix CP451 (LP)

150. February 1963—Joe Williams—*Jump For Joy*—Bluebird 52713-2 [CD]

151. February 1963—Kenny Burrell—*Lotsa Bossa Nova*—Kapp L1326 (LP)

152. March 1963—Clark Terry—*Three in Jazz*—BMG 74321-21825-2 [CD]

153. March 1963—Jimmy Smith and Oliver Nelson—*Hobo Flats*—Verve V6-8544 (LP)

154. March 1963—Milt Jackson—*For Someone I Love*—Riverside OJCCD-404-2 [CD]

155. March 1963—Tito Rodriguez—*Live at Birdland*—Palladium PCD102 [CD]

156. April 1963—Quincy Jones—*Plays Hip Hits*—Mercury MG20799 (LP)

157. April 1963—Kenyon Hopkins—*The Yellow Canary*—Verve V6-8548 [CD]

158. April 1963—Cal Tjader—*Several Shades of Jade/Breeze from the East*—Verve 314-537083-2 [CD]

159. May 1963—Gene Roland—*Swingin Friends*—Brunswick BL7-54114 (LP)

160. June 1963—Clark Terry—*More (Theme from "Mondo Cane")*—Cameo C-1064 (LP)

161. July 1963—Lambert, Hendricks, and Bavan—*At Newport '63*—RCA Victor LSP2747 (LP)

162. July 1963—McCoy Tyner—*Live at Newport*—Impulse AS-48 (LP)

163. July 1963—Joe Williams—*At Newport '63*—RCA Victor 74321-21831-2 [CD]

164. September 1963—Clark Terry—*Tread Ye Lightly*—Cameo C-1071 (LP)

165. October 1963—Herbie Mann—*Latin Fever*—Atlantic SD1422 (LP)

166. November 1963—Billy Taylor/Oliver Nelson—*Right Here, Right Now!*—Capitol T(S)203 (LP)

167. November 1963—Joe Williams—*Me and the Blues*—RCA Victor 74321-21823-2 [CD]

168. 1964—Morgana King—*With a Taste of Honey*—Mainstream S6015 (LP)

169. February 1964—Oscar Peterson/Clark Terry—*Oscar Peterson Trio + One—Clark Terry*—Verve B0009652-02 [CD]

170. March 1964—Clark Terry—*The Happy Horns of Clark Terry*—Impulse GRD-148 [CD]

171. May 1964—Clark Terry—*Live 1964*—Emerald EMR-1002 (LP)

172. June 1964—Lalo Schifrin—*New Fantasy*—Verve V6-8601 (LP)

173. October 1964—Johnny Dankworth—*The Zodiac Variations*—Fontana (E) TFL5229 (LP)

174. October 1964—Lionel Hampton—*You Better Know It*—Impulse A(S)78 (LP)

175. November 1964—Wes Montgomery—*Movin' Wes*—Verve 810045-2 [CD]

176. November 1964—Clark Terry/Bob Brookmeyer—*Tonight*—Mainstream MDCD728 [CD]

177. December 1964—Ruth Brown—*Ruth Brown '65*—Mainstream M56034 (LP)

178. December 1964—J. J. Johnson—*The Dynamic Sound of J. J. with Big Band*—Bluebird 6277-2-RB [CD]

179. December 1964—Donald Byrd—*I'm Trying to Get Home*—Blue Note BLP4188 (LP)

180. January 1965—Ray Brown—*Ray Brown and Milt Jackson*—Verve 533259-2 [CD]

181. March 1965—Clark Terry/Bob Brookmeyer—*The Power of Positive Swinging*—Mainstream MDCD723 [CD]

182. March 1965—Grassella Oliphant—*The Grass Is Greener*—Atlantic LP1494 (LP)

183. April 1965—Stan Getz—*Stan Getz Plays Music from the Soundtrack of "Mickey One"*—MGM E4312 (LP)

184. April 1965—Wes Montgomery/Clark Terry—*Radio 1965*—Vara Jazz (Du) 8219 [CD]

185. April 1965—Stanley Turrentine—*Joyride*—Blue Note CDP7-46100-2 [CD]

186. April 1965—Lionel Hampton—*Jazz All Stars, vol. 1*—Who's Who in Jazz WWLP21010 (LP)

187. April 1965—Cannonball Adderley/Oliver Nelson—*Domination*— Capitol Jazz 77560 [CD]

188. May 1965—Lalo Schifrin—*Once a Thief and Other Themes*—Verve V6-8624 (LP)

189. May 1965—Modern Jazz Quartet and All Star Band—*Jazz Dialogue*— Atlantic SD1449 (LP)

190. June 1965—Billy Strayhorn—*Lush Life*—Red Baron AK52760 [CD]

191. July 1965—J. J. Johnson—*Goodies*—RCA Victor LPM3458 (LP)

192. July 1965—Jean DuShon—*Feeling Good*—Cadet LP4048 (LP)

193. October 1965—Dave Pike—*Jazz for the Jet Set*—Atlantic SD1457 (LP)

194. December 1965—Gary McFarland—*Tijuana Jazz*—Impulse A(S)9104 (LP)

195. 1966—Clark Terry—*Mumbles*—Mainstream S/6066 (LP)

196. 1966—Clark Terry/Bob Brookmeyer—*Gingerbread Men*—Mainstream MDCD711 [CD]

197. February 1966—Gary McFarland—*Profiles*—Impulse A(S)9112 (LP)

198. February 1966—Ray Bryant—*Gotta Travel On*—Cadet (Jap) MVCJ-19019 [CD]

199. March 1966—Sonny Stitt—*The Matadors Meet the Bull: Stitt*— Roulette R25339 (LP)

200. April 1966—Oliver Nelson—*Oliver Nelson Plays Michelle*—Impulse A(S)9113 (LP)

201. April 1966—Ed Thigpen—*Out of the Storm*—Verve 314-557100-2 [CD]

202. July 1966—Clark Terry/Chico O'Farrill—*Spanish Rice*—Impulse AS9127 (LP)

203. July 1966—Sonny Stitt—*I Keep Comin' Back!*—Roulette RS-25346 (LP)

204. August 1966—Shirley Scott/Clark Terry—*Soul-Duo*—Impulse AS9133 (LP)

205. September 1966—Ray Bryant—*Lonesome Traveller*—Cadet (Jap) MVCJ-19009 [CD]

206. September 1966—Jimmy Smith/Wes Montgomery—*The Dynamic Duo*—Verve V6-8678 (LP)

207. October 1966—Hank Jones/Oliver Nelson—*Happenings*—Impulse AS9132 (LP)

208. November 1966—Leonard Feather—*Leonard Feather's Encyclopedia of Jazz All Stars*—Verve V6-8743 (LP)

209. November 1966—Chico O'Farrill—*Nine Flags*—Impulse AS9135 (LP)

210. November 1966—Jazz at the Philharmonic All Stars—*JATP in London 1969*—Pablo 2620-119-2 [CD]

211. December 1966—Charlie Barnet—*Live at Basin St. East '66*—Hep (E) CD2005 [CD]

212. 1967—Doc Severinsen—*The Great Arrival*—Command RS927 (LP)

213. January 1967—Sarah Vaughan—*It's a Man's World*—Mercury 830714-2 [CD]

214. January 1967—Sarah Vaughan—*Sassy Swings Again*—Mercury 814587-2 [CD]

215. February 1967—Jimmy Rushing—*Every Day I Have the Blues*—Impulse 547967-2 [CD]

216. February 1967—Pee Wee Russell—*The Spirit of '67*—Impulse AS9147 (LP)

217. June 1967—Various—*The Greatest Jazz Concert in the World*—Pablo PACD2625-704-2 [CD]

218. July 1967—Clark Terry—*It's What's Happenin'*—Impulse (Jap) MVCJ-19095 [CD]

219. August 1967—Louis Armstrong—*What a Wonderful World*—Decca GRD656 [CD]

220. August 1967—Duke Ellington—*And His Mother Called Him Bill*—RCA Victor 09026-63386-2 [CD]

221. November 1967—Thelonious Monk—*Thelonious Monk Nonet (Paris '67)*—France's Concert (F) FCD113 [CD]

222. 1968—Hank Johnson—*Harlem/The Jazz Heritage Ensemble*—Action Theater XTV144314-1A (LP)

223. July 1968—Clark Terry—*Music in the Garden*—Jazz Heritage 913024F (LP)

224. November 1968—George Benson—*Goodies*—Verve V6-8711 (LP)

225. April 1969—Tribute to Duke Ellington—*1969 All-Star White House Tribute to Duke Ellington*—Blue Note 7243-5-35249-2-0 [CD]

226. June 1969—Sarah Vaughan—*Jazzfest Masters*—Scotti Bros. (Pol) 72392-75244-2 [CD]

227. June 1969—Count Basie—*Jazzfest Masters*—Scotti Bros. (Pol) 72392-75245-2 [CD]

228. June 1969—Clark Terry—*At the Montreux Jazz Festival*—Polydor (G) 24-5002 (LP)

229. February 1970—Clark Terry—*Big Bad Band*—Big Bear (E) 13 (LP)

230. April 1970—Clark Terry/Northeastern State College Stage Band—*Clark Terry Tonight*—Dimension70 Stereo 38155 (LP)

231. July 1970—Louis Armstrong—*Hello Louis!*—GHB BCD-421/422/423 [CD]

232. August 1970—Bengt-Arne Wallin—*Varmluft*—Sonet (Swd) SLP2528 (LP)

233. September 1971—Colorado Jazz Party—*Colorado Jazz Party*—MPS (G) 49.21699-1 (LP)

234. December 1971—Quincy Jones—*The Hot Rock (Soundtrack)*—Prophesy SD6055 (LP)

235. 1972—Clark Terry—*1972 Phi Mu Alpha Jazz Festival*—Audio House AHSPLA1472 (LP)

236. July 1972—Gap Mangione—*Sing Along Junk*—Mercury SRM1-647 (LP)

237. July 1972—Jimmy Smith—*Newport in New York 1972: The Jimmy Smith Jam, vol. 5*—Cobblestone CST9027 (LP)

238. September 1972—Art Blakey and the Giants of Jazz—*Live at the Monterey Jazz Festival 1972*—Monterey Jazz Festival MJFR-30882 [CD]

239. 1973—Clark Terry—*Swing in '73*—Mark Custom MC5803 (LP)

240. January 1974—Ella Fitzgerald—*Fine and Mellow*—Pablo 2310-829-2 [CD]

241. April 1974—Clark Terry—*Live at the Wichita Jazz Festival 1974*—Vanguard 662087 [CD]

242. September 1974—Big Joe Turner—*Stormy Monday*—Pablo PACD2310-943-2 [CD]

243. September 1974—Dizzy Gillespie—*The Trumpet Kings Meet Joe Turner*—Pablo OJCCD-497-2 [CD]

244. 1975—Clark Terry—*Clark Terry and His Jolly Giants*—Vanguard 662131 [CD]

245. May 1975—Oscar Peterson—*Oscar Peterson and Clark Terry*—Pablo OJCCD-806-2 [CD]

246. June 1975—Clark Terry—*Live at Montmarte 1975*—Storyville (Dan) 101-8358 [CD]

247. June 1975—Boško Petrovič—Blue Sunset—Jugoton (Yugo) LSY63041 (LP)

248. July 1975—The Trumpet Kings—*At the Montreux Jazz Festival 1975*—Pablo OJCCD-445-2 [CD]

249. 1976—James Moody—*Sun Journey*—Vanguard VSD79381 (LP)

250. 1976—Clark Terry—*Wham! Live at the Jazzhouse*—MPS/BASF (G) 20.22676 (LP)

251. 1976—Clark Terry—*Professor Jive*—DRG CDSL-2-5220 [CD]

252. January 1976—Cleo Laine—*Return to Carnegie*—RCA APL1-2407 (LP)

253. May 1976—Count Basie—*Basie Jam No. 2*—Pablo OJCCD-631-2 [CD]

254. November 1976—Bunky Green—*Transformations*—Vanguard VSD79387 (LP)

255. November 1976—Elvin Jones—*Summit Meeting*—Vanguard VSD79390 (LP)

256. December 1976—Clark Terry—*Live at Mokuba*—Break Time (Jap) BRJ-4019 [CD]

257. 1977—Clark Terry—*The Globetrotter*—Vanguard VMD79393 [CD]

258. January 1977—Peter Herbolzheimer—*Jazz Gala '77 All Star Big Band*—Telefunken (G) 6.28438 (LP)

259. July 1977—Milt Jackson/Ray Brown—*Montreux '77*—Pablo OJCCD-375-2 [CD]

260. September 1977—Clark Terry—*Clark After Dark*—MPS (G) 529088-2 [CD]

261. April 1978—Clark Terry—*Clark Terry Big Band*—Poljazz (Pol) Z-SX-0682 (LP)

262. July 1978—Clark Terry—*Out of Nowhere*—EPM (F) FDC5500 [CD]

263. August 1978—Clark Terry—*Funk Dumplin's*—Matrix (Dan) MTX1002 (LP)

264. September 1978—Arne Domnerus—*Two Swedes in New York*—Phontastic (Swd) PHONTCD7518 [CD]

265. December 1978—Clark Terry—*Lucerne 1978*—TCB (Swi) 02082 [CD]

266. 1979—UMO Jazz Orchestra—*Umophilos*—RCA (Fin) PL40127 (LP)

267. February 1979—Clark Terry/Charles Schwartz—*Mother, Mother! A Jazz Symphony*—Pablo 2312-115 (LP)

268. March 1979—Oscar Peterson—*The Silent Partner*—Pablo 2312-103 (LP)

269. March 1979—Clark Terry—*Ain't Misbehavin'*—Pablo OJCCD-1002-2 [CD]

270. September 1979—Count Basie—*Get Together*—Pablo PACD-2310-924-2 [CD]

271. January 1980—Oscar Peterson—*The Personal Touch*—Pablo PACD-2312-135-2 [CD]

272. February 1980—Bob Brookmeyer—*Bob Brookmeyer/Mel Lewis and the Jazz Orchestra*—DCC Jazz DJZ-616 [CD]

273. March 1980—Stanley Turrentine—*Use the Stairs*—Fantasy F-9604 (LP)

274. March 1980—Clark Terry—*Memories of Duke*—Pablo OJCCD-604-2 [CD]

275. September 1980—J. J. Johnson—*Concepts in Blue*—Pablo OJCCD-735-2 [CD]

276. December 1980—Jesper Thilo—*Tribute to Frog*—Storyville (Dan) SLP4072 (LP)

277. January 1981—Clark Terry—*Yes, the Blues*—Pablo OJCCD-856-2 [CD]

278. December 1981—Clark Terry—*Ow—Live at E. J.'s.* JLR103.601 [CD]

279. June 1982—Frank Mantooth—*Sophisticated Lady*—Sea Breeze SB2074 [CD]

280. June 1982—Clark Terry—*Live in Belgrade*—RTB (Yugo) 2120984 (LP)

281. September 1982—Aurex Jazz Festival—*Aurex Jazz Festival '82*—East World (Jap) EWJ-80238 (LP)

282. July 1983—Teresa Brewer—*Live at Carnegie Hall and Montreux, Switzerland*—Doctor Jazz W2X39521 (LP)

283. October 1983—JATP All Stars—*Return to Happiness—JATP at Yoyogi National Stadium, Tokyo*—Pablo PACD2620-117-2 [CD]

284. 1984—Jim Cullum, Jr.—*Deep River: The Spirit of Gospel Music in Jazz*—Riverwalk Jazz RWCD8 [CD]

285. 1986—Mercer Ellington/Duke Ellington Orchestra—*Digital Duke*—GRP GRD9548 [CD]

286. January 1986—Clark Terry—*To Duke and Basie*—Enja (G) 5011-2 [CD]

287. February 1986—Clark Terry/Jon Faddis—*Take Double*—EmArcy 830242-2 [CD]

288. October 1986—Flip Phillips—*The Claw—Live at the 1986 Floating Jazz Festival*—Chiaroscuro CR(D)314 [CD]

289. December 1987—Bob Kindred—*Bending towards the Light—A Jazz Nativity*—Conawago 1004 [CD]

290. December 1987—Louie Bellson—*Hot*—Musicmasters CIJD60106X [CD]

291. March 1988—Horace Silver—*Music to Ease Your Disease*—Silveto SPR105 (LP)

292. May 1988—Clark Terry—*Clark Terry–Metropole Orchestra*—Mons (G) MR874815 [CD]

293. July 1988—Clark Terry/Red Mitchell—*Jive at Five*—Enja (G) 6042-2 [CD]

294. December 1988—Clark Terry—*Portraits*—Chesky JD2 [CD]

295. January 1989—Oliver Jones/Clark Terry—*Just Friends*—Justin Time (Can) JUST31-2 [CD]

296. February 1989—Clark Terry—*Squeeze Me*—Chiaroscuro CR(D)309 [CD]

297. May 1989—Clark Terry—*At the University of New Hampshire*—Disc Makers QT011121 [CD]

298. June 1989—Red Holloway/Clark Terry—*Locksmith Blues*—Concord Jazz CCD-4390-2 [CD]

299. June 1989—Jay McShann—*Paris All-Star Blues*—Heritage Jazz 522804 [CD]

300. February 1990—Al Grey—*Fab*—Capri 74038-2 [CD]

301. February 1990—John Pizzarelli—*My Blue Heaven*—Chesky JD38 [CD]

302. February 1990—Abbey Lincoln—*The World Is Falling Down*—Verve 843476-2 [CD]

303. April 1990—Clark Terry—*Having Fun*—Delos DE4021 [CD]

304. June 1990—Joe Sudler—*The Joe Sudler Swing Machine and Clark Terry*—TJA (Can) TJL9457 [CD]

305. November 1990—Benny Carter—*All That Jazz—Live at Princeton*—MusicMasters 5059-2-C [CD]

306. November 1990—Clark Terry—*Live at The Village Gate*—Chesky JD49 [CD]

307. November 1990—Nancy Harrow—*Secrets*—Soul Note (It) 121233-2 [CD]

308. December 1990—George Robert—*Live at the Q-4 Rheinfelden*—TCB (Swi) 9080 [CD]

309. 1991—Cleo Laine—*Jazz*—RCA 60548-2-RC [CD]

310. January 1991—Teresa Brewer—*Memories of Louis*—Red Baron AK48629 [CD]

311. April 1991—Clark Terry—*St. Louis Blues*—Jazzette (Yugo) BPCD-010 [CD]

312. May 1991—The Ritz/Clark Terry—*Almost Blue*—Denon (Jap) COCY-7999 [CD]

313. June 1991—Lionel Hampton—*Live at the Blue Note*—Telarc CD-83308 [CD]

314. January 1992—John Hicks—*Friends Old And New*—Novus 63141-2 [CD]

315. June 1992—The Basie Alumni—*Swinging for the Count*—Candid (E) CCD79724 [CD]

316. August 1992—Newport Jazz Festival All Stars—*Swing That Music*—Columbia CK53317 [CD]

317. October 1992—Louie Bellson—*Duke Ellington: Black, Brown, and Beige*—MusicMasters 65096-2 [CD]

318. October 1992—Dorothy Donegan—*The Dorothy Donegan Trio with Clark Terry*—Chiaroscuro CR(D)323 [CD]

319. February 1993—John Pizzarelli—*Naturally*—Novus 63151-2 [CD]

320. February 1993—Clark Terry—*What a Wonderful World*—Red Baron JK53750 [CD]

321. March 1993—James Williams—*Talkin' Trash*—DIW/Columbia CK66874 [CD]

322. September 1993—Marian McPartland/Clark Terry—*Piano Jazz*—The Jazz Alliance TJA-12009 [CD]

323. December, 1993—Clark Terry/George Robert—*The Good Things in Life*—Mons (G) 2003 [CD]

324. December 1993—Louie Bellson/Clark Terry—*Live from New York*—Telarc CD-83334 [CD]

325. February 1994—David Friesen/Clark Terry/Bud Shank—*Three to Get Ready*—ITM (G) 970084 [CD]

326. April 1994—University of New Hampshire Jazz Band/Clark Terry—*Monk and Then Some*—QT 10273 [CD]

327. May 1994—Clark Terry—*Shades of Blues*—Challenge (Du) CHR70007 [CD]

328. August 1994—Clark Terry—*Remember the Time*—Mons (G) MR874762 [CD]

329. December 1994—Clark Terry/Frank Wess/DePaul University Jazz Ensemble—*Big Band Basie*—Reference RR-63 [CD]

330. December 1994—The Statesmen of Jazz—*The Statesmen of Jazz*—American Federation of Jazz Society AFJSCD201 [CD]

331. January 1995—Clark Terry/Pee Wee Claybrook/Swing Fever—*Reunion*—d'Note Jazz DND2001 [CD]

332. January 1995—Swing Fever/Clark Terry—*A Chicken Ain't Nothin' but a Bird*—d'Note Jazz DND2006 [CD]

333. January 1995—Oscar Peterson—*The More I See You*—Telarc CD-83370 [CD]

334. March 1995—Jim Cullum, Jr.—*Hot Jazz for a Cool Yule*—Riverwalk RWCD5 [CD]

335. August 1995—Claude Tissendier/Saxomania/Clark Terry—*A Tale of Two Cities*—IDA (F) 040 [CD]

336. October 1995—Clark Terry/Red Holloway—*Top and Bottom*—Chiaroscuro CR(D)347 [CD]

337. December 1995—Clark Terry—*Clark Terry Express/DePaul University Big Band/Bob Lark*—Reference Recordings RR73 [CD]

338. January 1996—The IMTS Jubilee All Stars—*When Legends Get Together*—LynRo Music (G) LC3284 [CD]

339. April 1996—Dianne Reeves—*The Grand Encounter*—Blue Note CDP8-38268-2 [CD]

340. October 1996—Clark Terry/Dario Cellamaro—*Manipulite*—Old Magic Music (It) CD97DC01 [CD]

341. April 1997—Harry Sweets Edison—*Live at the Iridium*—Telarc CD-83425 [CD]

342. May 1997—Carol Sloane—*The Songs Ella and Louis Sang*—Concord Jazz CCD-4787-2 [CD]

343. 1999—Rias Big Band—*The Music of Duke Ellington*—Mons (G) MR874-306 [CD]

344. 1999—Steve Tyrell—*A New Standard*—Muze UPC075678-32092-7 [CD]

345. June 1999—Dave Glasser/Clark Terry/Barry Harris—*Uh! Oh!*—Nagel-Heyer (G) 2003 [CD]

346. September 1999—Mike Vax/Clark Terry—*Creepin' with Clark*—Summit DCD273 [CD]

347. November 1999—Clark Terry—*Live on QE2*—Chiaroscuro CR(D)365 [CD]

348. November 1999—Simon Rattle—*Classic Ellington*—Blue Note/EMI Classics 5-57014-2 [CD]

349. December 1999—Clark Terry—*One on One*—Chesky JD198 [CD]

350. January 2000—Ray Brown—*Some of My Best Friends Are . . . the Trumpet Players*—Telarc CD-83495 [CD]

351. February 2000—John David Simon—*John David Simon and Friends*—Warm Groove WGCD1001 [CD]

352. April 2000—Summit Jazz Orchestra—*The Summit Jazz Orchestra and Clark Terry*—Edition Collage (G) EC530-2 [CD]

353. May 2000—Summit Jazz Orchestra/Clark Terry—*The Knight's Golden Trumpet*—Ermatell (Rus) JCD050 [CD]

354. May 2000—Wolverines Jazz Band—*40th Anniversary*—Arbors Jazz ARCD19263 [CD]

355. May 2000—Clark Terry—*Herr Ober*—Nagel-Heyer (G) 068 [CD]

356. June 2000—Hugh Ragin—*Fanfare and Fiesta*—Justin Time (Can) JUST152-2 [CD]

357. September 2000—Dianne Reeves—*The Calling*—Blue Note 41978 [CD]

358. 2001—Steve Tyrell—*Standard Time*—Columbia CK86006 [CD]

359. 2002—Steve Tyrell—*This Time of the Year*—Columbia CK86638 [CD]

360. March 2002—Clark Terry/Max Roach—*Friendship*—Columbia CK87171 [CD]

361. June 2002—Shawn Monteiro with Clark Terry—*One Special Night*—Whaling City Sound WCS022 [CD]

362. 2003—Angela Hagenbach—*Poetry of Love*—Amazon ARCD-2822 [CD]

363. 2003—Steve Tyrell—*This Guy's in Love*—Columbia CK89238 [CD]

364. February 2003—Gerald Wilson—*New York, New Sound*—Mack Avenue MAC1009 [CD]

365. November 2003—Clark Terry/Jeff Lindberg/Chicago Jazz Orchestra—*Porgy and Bess*—Americana Music 9002 [CD]

366. December 2003—The Statesmen of Jazz—*A Multitude of Stars*—Statesmen of Jazz SOJCD202 [CD]

367. May 2004—Clark Terry and the Young Titans of Jazz—*Live at Marian's*—Chiaroscuro CR(D)212 [CD]

368. September 2005—Jon Faddis—*Teranga*—Koch KOC-CD-9969 [CD]

369. 2007—Whitney Marchelle—*Me, Marsalis, and Monk*—Etoile [no #] [CD]

370. May 2007—Louie Bellson/Clark Terry—*Louie and Clark Expedition 2*—Percussion Power PERC2 [CD]

371. April 2008—Scotty Barnhart—*Say It Plain*—Dig 137 [CD]

Index

A & R Studios, 84

Acey, Sinclair, 192, 194

Ada Mae (CT's sister). *See* Terry, Ada Mae McField

Adams, Dave, 210, 211

Adderley, Cannonball, 207, 289, 293

Adderley, Nat, 207

advertisements: CT's endorsements in, 153, 190–91; CT's music for, 172, 191, 200, 218

Africa, CT's trip to, 210–11

albums, CT as performer on: *All American* (CT as leader), 201; *Almost Blue* with the Ritz, 231; *Around the World* with Quincy Jones, 165; *Basie Jam 2*, 163; *Big Band Bossa Nova* with Quincy Jones, 201; *Birth of a Band* with Quincy Jones, 165; *Brilliant Corners* with Thelonious Monk, 235; *Clark After Dark* (CT as leader), 254; *Clark Terry* (CT as leader), 201; *The Clark Terry Spacemen* (CT as leader), 245; *Color Changes* (CT as leader), 201; *Deep Purple/ Jubilee Jump* with Charlie Barnet, 110; *Dinah Jams* with Dinah Washington, 134; *Everything's Mellow* (CT as leader), 201; *Friendship* with Max Roach, 235; *Friends Old and New* with John Hicks, 241; *Genius + Soul = Ray Charles*, 201; *Gingerbread* with Bob Brookmeyer, 178; *Jazz* with Cleo Laine, 230; *John David Simon and Friends*, 231; *Memories of Duke* (CT as leader), 206; *Memories of Louis* with Teresa Brewer, 231; *One Night Stand* with Charlie Barnet, 110; *Oscar Peterson Trio + 1*, 177; *Porgy and Bess* (CT as leader), 254; *The Power of Positive Swinging* with Bob Brookmeyer, 178; *Pre-Bird (Mingus Revisited)* with Charles Mingus, 199; *Professor Jive* (CT as leader), 207; *Quintet* with Bob Brookmeyer, 178; *Rah* with Mark Murphy, 172; *Really Big* with Jimmy Heath, 201; *St. Louis Blues* (CT as leader), 231; *Take Double* (CT as leader), 218; *Taylor Made Jazz* with Billy Taylor, 154; *Tonight* with Bob Brookmeyer, 178; *Town Hall Concert* with Charlie Barnet, 110; *Tread Ye Lightly* (CT as leader), 201; *Trumpet Giants* (CT as leader), 201. *See also* recording sessions, CT's

Alexander, Bob, 172

Alexander, Mousey, 186, 187

Alexander, Willard, 115, 118

Ali, Muhammad, 164

Alim, Kamal Abdul, 192
Allen, Charles ("Chuck"), 70, 118
Allen, Gene, 200
All-Star Swedish Big Band, 245
American Federation of Musicians, 128
American Revolution, 156
Amsterdam, CT's activity in, 230
Anatomy of a Murder soundtrack,
    147–48, 287
Anderson, Cat, 129, 130, 137, 139–40,
    286
Anderson, Ivie, 138
Andre, Wayne, 186
Andrews, Ernie, 253
Apollo Theater (New York), 92, 96,
    133, 145, 149, 192
archive. *See* Clark Terry Archive at
    William Paterson University
Arlen, Harold, 165, 167, 169
Armstrong, Louis, 140, 153, 155, 163,
    178, 190, 195, 248, 294, 295
art, visual, CT's, 160, 245
Arterberry, Benita, 242
Arthur Murray Show, The, 171
ASCAP music publishers, 135, 250
Auger, Jeff, 231
Aunt Gert (CT's maternal aunt). *See*
    Scott, Gertrude
Austin, Patti, 168
Austin, Willie ("Turk"), and CT as a
    member of Turk's band, 23–24, 26,
    29, 33–36, 38–41, 43, 67, 76
Austria, CT's activity in, 229, 231, 245
Avakian, George, 202

"Baby Sis." *See* Wiley, Georgette
back problems, CT's, 183, 188, 190,
    193, 198, 218–19, 222, 225, 228, 230,
    231–32, 237, 239, 249
Bailey, Benny, 168, 288
Bailey, Dave, 194, 288
Bailey, Ozzie, 138
Bailey, Richard, 251
Baker, Harold ("Shorty"), 129, 130, 140
Baker, Mike, 209
Ballard, George ("Butch"), 138
Ballou, Marty, 231

"Banjo Pete," 46
Bank, Danny, 173, 184
Barbara Jean (CT's niece). *See*
    Williams, Barbara Jean
Barber, Danny, 254
Bargeron, Dave, 185, 187
Barker, Guy, 217–18
Barnet, Charlie, 103–10, 114, 129, 171;
    acid test audition for, 2, 102
"Baroness, The," 234
Barr, James, 20, 21
Barrows, John, 173
Basie (bass player in Beaver Palmer's
    gig), 58
Basie, Catherine, 207
Basie, Count, xi, xv, 2, 78, 104, 129,
    132, 157–58, 160, 161, 164, 165, 170,
    175, 183, 185, 192, 207; breakup and
    musicians' talent in band of, 115–16;
    CT accepts Duke Ellington's offer to
    leave band of, 123–24; CT's acid test
    audition for, 108–9; CT joins band
    of, 111; CT records with, 163; CT
    recruits Wilkins brothers for, 125;
    CT returns to St. Louis after leav-
    ing band of, 126; CT teaches about,
    195; JATP tours with Basie Eight
    band, 219; selected discography,
    284, 288, 294, 296, 297, 299; small
    group reunited and traveling with
    band of, 117–22; swinging artistry
    of, 112–14
Bastine, Volley, 87, 88
Batchman, Cliff, 81
Bates, Peg Leg, 37, 80, 128, 131
Bayside, New York, CT's residence in,
    179–80
Bayside Historical Society, 244
BBC television, CT's appearance on,
    178
Beach, Ed, 202
Beacons of Jazz Award, 229
"Beanie Roach," 7, 19, 108
bebop, 107, 110, 140, 143, 173
Bechet, Sidney, 107–8
Beckham, Michelle, 209
Belafonte, Harry, 194

Belger, Blue, 58–61
Belgium, CT's activity in: with "Free and Easy" show, xv, 167–69
Bellson, Louie, 158, 163, 196; concerts with, 245; at CT's seventiety birthday celebration, 227; Hotel Innere Enge Suite of, 249; as member of Duke's band, 138; racial challenges of, 150–51; selected discography, 284, 297, 299, 301
Benjamin, James, 192, 194
Benjamin, Joe, 173, 177
Benjamin, Lakecia, 248, 251
Benson, George, 194, 294
Benson, Red, 106
Berenbom, Dr. Loren, 253
Berg, Chuck, 212
Berry, Anita, 246
Berry, Emmett, 113, 154
Berry, Otis (CT's cousin), 3, 10
Bert, Eddie, 186
Betts, Keter, 134, 244
Betty (Rudy Jr.'s wife). *See* White, Betty
Beyoncé, 251, 256
Bigard, Barney, 137
Big Bad Band, CT's, 182–91, 194, 212, 251, 257, 295
"Big Jim," 43, 45–46, 78–79
"Big Mamma." *See* Hut, Ethel
Bill Cosby Dream Band, 249. *See also* Cosby, Bill
Billy (CT's cousin). *See* Scott, Billy
birth of CT, 3
Black, Dave, 138
Blackman, Gary, 209
Blakey, Rubel, 92
Blanton, Jimmy, 21, 137
Blauer, Gary, 212
Bloom, Curt, 106–7
Blott, 81
Blue Note (club), 133
Blue Note (club in Chicago), 143, 153, 284, 285, 287
Blue Note (club in New York), 229, 231, 248–49, 252, 299
BMI music publishers, 135

Board, Johnny, 91
Bobulinski, Greg, 185
Boggs, Jean Louise, 107
Bolden, Buddy, 142
books written by CT, 198
Boone, Richard, 177
Boone, Russell, 14, 16–17, 66
Borders, George. *See* George Borders' Club
Bosteels, Daryl, 231
Boston, CT's activity in, 119, 231, 244
Boston Pops Orchestra, 207
Bowden, Len, 62–65, 67–68, 72, 73, 78
Bowles, Russell, 89
Bowman, Bob, 212
Bown, Patti, 169, 184
boxing, CT's practice of and comments on, 9, 41, 57, 109, 145, 165, 199, 200
Boyd, Bobby, 139, 150
Bradley, Will, 172, 175
Bradshaw, Tiny, 78, 91
Brecker, Randy, 185
Brewer, Teresa, 231, 297, 298
Bridgewater, Cecil, 55
Bridgewater, Pete, 55
Briggs, Bunny, 104–5, 107, 109
Britton, Jimmy, 81, 138
Brookmeyer, Bob, ("Co"), 173, 177–78, 180, 200, 204, 257, 290, 292, 293, 297
Brooks, Emmanuel St. Claire ("Duke"), 116–17
Brooks, John ("Five-By-Five") 66
Brown, Cecelia (Ray's wife), 247
Brown, Clifford, 134, 285
Brown, Deborah, 253
Brown, Ray, 158, 159, 177, 206, 247, 290, 292, 296, 300
Buchanan, Elwood ("Buke"), 50–51, 86
Buckner, Milt, 54, 91, 92
Buffalo Philharmonic Orchestra, 189–90
Buffington, Jimmy, 173
Burbank, Chris, 247
Burlingham, Jon, 212
Burrell, Kenny, 173, 291
"Bus" (CT's brother). *See* Terry, Virgil Otto

"Butch" (Rudy Jr.'s son). See White, Rudy III
"Butter." See Jackson, Quentin
"Butterfly." See Digable Planet
Byers, Billy, 169, 173, 290

Caine, Ed, 173
Calendar, Mary, 81
Calloway, Cab, 111
Cameron, John, 53, 58
Campbell, Gydner Paul, 66, 81
Campbell, Jimmy, 106, 108
Campbell, John, 209, 229
Campbell, Paul, 70
Camp Robert Smalls. See Great Lakes Naval Training Center
Canterino Family, (Mike, Sonny and Judy), 174
Carley, Dale, 185
Carnegie Hall, CT's performances at, 161, 186–88, 202, 229, 288, 289, 297
Carnes, Jimmy, 138
Carney, Bill ("Mr. C."), 244
Carney, Harry, 136, 138, 141, 148, 160
carnival bands, CT as member of, 23–32, 40, 141
Carondelet neighborhood, St. Louis, 4, 5, 9, 11, 13, 20, 26, 29, 30, 43, 46, 54, 74, 84, 94, 102, 113, 127, 133
Carrington, Terri Lyne, 218
Carroll, Jr., 15
Carson, Johnny, 174–76
Carter, Benny, 91, 163, 298
Carter, Cheri, 233, 242
Carter, Kid, 9, 31, 65, 92, 109, 199
Carter, Ron (bassist), 173, 184, 186, 231, 241, 253
Carter, Ron (woodwind player), 253
Carter, Tom, 233, 242
Cassidy, Tom, 241
Catlett, Buddy, 169
Cavers, Quincy, 255, 257
Cedric, Eugene, 21
"Cee Tee" (nickname for Clark Terry), 178, 232, 258
Celley, Al, 122, 148, 149
Celley, John, 122

Central State University, Oklahoma, 212
Chambers, Jordan, 50, 86, 100
Chambers, Paul, 234
Champaign, Illinois, CT's activity in, 51–52, 55
Chapel, Mattie, 72
Charles, Ezzard, 124
Charles, Ray, 201, 287, 288
Charlin Jazz Society, 244
Chase, Alan, 245
Cheatham, Doc, 228, 244
Chesky Records, 226, 298, 300
Chess Brothers, 71
Chicago, CT's activity in: with Big Bad Band, 186; with Billy Taylor's band, 154; with the Chicago Jazz Orchestra, 254, 301; with Count Basie's band, 113, 117–18; with Duke Ellington's band, 143, 285, 287; with J.A.T.P., 160, 161; as leader with small groups, 204; with Lionel Hampton's band, 92; during WWII, 70–72
Chicago Jazz Orchestra. See Chicago, CT's activity in
Child, Josie, 143
childhood, CT's, 1–21, 33, 43–45, 46–47, 133; musical activity in, 1, 3, 4–8, 10, 12–21
Chippie, 85–87
Christmas production at St. Bartholomew, New York, 239–40
Churchill, Savannah, 80
Church of God and Christ (St. Louis), 4, 16
Cinelu, Mino, 218
"Cinnamon." See MacManus, Cameron
circular breathing, 30, 141, 178, 195, 198
civil rights movement, 151, 170, 178, 203–4
Claerbaut, Alyce (Billy Strayhorn's niece), 247, 254
Clark, Buddy, 173
Clark, Patsy (CT's niece), 250
Clarke, Arthur, 173

Clark Terry All-American Jazz Festival (Univ. of Central OK), 230
"Clark Terry and His Jolly Giants," 210, 295
Clark Terry Archive at William Paterson University, xv, xvi, 249
Clark Terry Jazz Festivals, 227, 251, 253
Cleveland, CT's activity in, 194–95
Cleveland, James, 185
Cleveland, Jimmy, 169, 173, 185
Clinton, Bill (President), 231, 254
Clinton, Larry, 6
Cliousclat Festival (France), 215
Cloud, Doug, 15–17
Clyde (CT's cousin). *See* Scott, Clyde
Cobb, Bubba, 208
Cobb, Jimmy, 173
Cohen, Paul, 185
Cohen, Porký, 106
Cohn, Al, 173, 200, 288
Coil, Pat, 212
Cole, Nat King, 80, 128, 132
Coleman, George, 185, 187
Coleman, Yvette, 163
Coles, Chip, 192
Colley, Janet, 254, 255
Colley, Kris, 254, 255
Collins, Bris, 55
Comegys, Leon, 88
commercials, music for, 172, 186, 191, 200, 218
compositions, CT's, 107, 137; "Gwen," 268; "Hawg Jawz," 110; "Hey, Mr. Mumbles," 226; "Incoherent Blues," 177; "Joonji," 110; "Lil' Ole Mongoose," 200; "Mumbles," 176–77, 178, 223, 248, 257; "One Foot in the Gutter," 110; "Out on a Limb," 71; "Phalanges," 110; "Sheba," 185; "Slop Jar," 110; "The Snapper," 110
Congress, U.S., resolution on jazz by, 219
Congress for Racial Equality (CORE), 151, 178
Conners, Chuck, 186
Cook, Willie, 129, 140–41

Coon-Sanders Original Nighthawks Orchestra, 6, 13
Cooper, Barry, 248, 251
Cooper, Buster, 245
Copeland, Ray, 184, 185, 187
Corinthian Baptist Church, St. Louis, 4, 31, 105, 127
Cosby, Bill, xiii–xiv, 233–34, 246, 254; band with CT at Clinton Inauguration Gala introduced by, 231; the Bill Cosby Dream Band, 249; CT's bachelor party and honeymoon surprises by, 241–43; CT as cartoon character on *Little Bill* television show of, 257
Cosby, Camille (Bill's wife), 241, 242–43, 254
Coss, Roxy, 249
Costa, Eddie, 177
Costanza, Sonny, 184, 185, 187
Cowell, Stanley, 244
Cox, Ida, 33–35, 39, 43
Cox, Katherine ("Lady K"), 223
Crane, Kenny, 209
Creath, Charlie, 46
Crilly, Ed, 223
Crook, Harold ("Crooksville" or "Hal"), 209, 227
Crow, Bill, 200, 244
Cuenca, Sylvia ("Cuencs"), 229, 244, 247, 249, 251, 252
Czadek, Heinz, 245

Daddy-O and Daddy-O's Patio. *See* Daylie, Daddy-O
Dagg, Leon, 127
Dance, Stanley, 205
Daniels, Jerry, 131
Danko, Harold, 218
Dankworth, Johnny, 230, 292
Danville, Illinois, CT's activity in, 52–54, 91
Davis, Charles, 185
Davis, Dennis, 193, 194
Davis, Dewey. *See* Davis, Miles
Davis, Eddie ("Lockjaw"), 158, 161, 163, 288, 289

Davis, Gregory, 144, 145
Davis, Jesse, 244, 252
Davis, Johnny Pops (CT's brother-in-law), 3, 10–11, 23, 95, 111
Davis, Kay, 138
Davis, L.A., Dr. (Chancellor), 250
Davis, Leonard ("Ham"), 46
Davis, Louise, 208
Davis, Mel, 172
Davis, Miles Dewey ("Inky"), xvi, 50, 51, 86–87, 131, 144–46, 154, 192, 195, 203–4, 220, 225, 238
Davis, Miles Henry ("Doc Davis," father of Miles), 145
Davis, Murlene (CT's niece), 94, 102, 111
Davis, Nathan, 218
Davis, Sammy, Jr., 168
Dawes, Bob, 106
Dawson, Alan, 244
Day, J.D., 254
Day, Michelle, 254
Daylie, Daddy-O, 70–71
Dean, William Wallick, 21
DeAndra (CT's niece), 251
death: of CT's father, 72–73, 212; of CT's siblings, 212, 251; of CT's wife Pauline, 211–12; of Duke Ellington, 206; of Miles Davis, 238
DeFalo, 190
DeFranco, Buddy, 118
Delaney Elementary School, St. Louis, 9, 17–18
Demme, Ken, 190
Demsey, David ("Dr. D.D."), xv–xvii; ceremony for Clark Terry Archive headed by, 249; as member in CT's Big Bad Band, 251; musicianship of, 248
Dennis, Willie, 173, 200
DeRosa, Dianne, 209
DeRosa, Richard, 247
Detroit, CT's activity in: with Count Basie's band, 111–13; with Lionel Hampton's band, 93–94
Dewey Jackson and His Musical Ambassadors, 8, 19, 42–44, 48, 51

Dial, Kimball, 81, 83
Dičić, Damir, 231
Dickenson, Vic, 161
Didley, 6, 9, 11, 13–14, 19, 46, 108
Digable Planet (rap group), 243
Disney World, 208, 242–43
divorce, CT's, from Sissy, 73, 74, 98
Dobbins, Bill, 245
"Doc Davis." See Davis, Miles Henry
Dollar Bill and His Small Change band, CT as member of, 25–26
Dolphy, Eric, 199
Don (CT's nephew). See Gilliam, Donald
Donaldson, Lou, 73, 79
Donegan, Dorothy, 71, 299
Donnelly, Ted ("Muttonleg"), 113, 115–16
Donovan, Bob ("Bobby"), 185, 200
Dorham, Kenny, 193
Dorie Miller apartment building, 153, 180
Dorsey, George, 173
Dorsey, Tommy, 78, 172
Dowdall, Peter, 209
DownBeat Jazz Critics Poll, 178
DownBeat magazine, 241
"Dr. D.D." See Demsey, David
D'Rivera, Paquito, 226, 244
drug abuse, 144–46, 183
Duke Ellington Society Convention, 244
Dupont, Roland, 172
Durham, Bobby, 164
DuSable Museum of African American History, Chicago, 156
Duvivier, George, 173, 179
Dyer, Toby ("Hooks"), 53, 54
Dyerettes, the, 80

Eastwood, Clint, 233
Ecker, Keith, 154, 155
Eckinger, Isla, 227
Eckstine, Billy ("Mr. B"), 77, 145, 229
Ed (CT's brother). See Terry, Charles Edward

Edison, Harry ("Sweets"), 113, 115, 158, 163, 196, 229, 231, 300
Edison, Thomas, 256
education, jazz, CT's involvement in, xv–xvii, 2, 191–98, 205, 206, 217–18, 227, 233, 240, 242, 245, 247–48, 250–52, 257–58; and jazz camp, 212–14, 216, 229. *See also* youth bands, organized by CT
Eiffel Tower, 169
Eight Annual Jazz Fest at Sea (Mediterranean), 245
Eisenhall, Aaron, 88
Eldridge, Roy, 95, 158, 163, 192
Elf, Mark, 244
Ellington, Duke, xi, xv, 21, 52, 70, 104, 111, 162, 167, 168, 184–85, 187–89, 192, 209, 218, 224, 231, 234, 244; acid test for joining band of, 2; Billy Strayhorn's collaboration with, 146–48; challenges with Cat Anderson, and superstitions of, 139; CT accepts offer from, 124; CT considers leaving band of, 165–66; CT's experiences with Norman Granz while in band of, 158–60; CT's first experience hearing, 1–2, 3, 6; CT's first gigs as a sub with, 117; CT joins band of, 128–34; CT learns more tunes of, 50; CT leaves Basie for, 126–27; CT scouted for, 122, 123; CT teaches students about, 195–96, 199; death of, 205–6, 212; first composition for CT's flugelhorn written by, 152–54; knowledge, skills and writing techniques of, 136–37; mentioned in autobiography of, 155–57; musicianship of, 138; musicianship of band, 139–41; persuasive abilities of, 142–43; racism and equality movements while in band of, 149–51; selected discography of, 284, 285, 286, 287, 289, 290, 294, 297, 299, 300
Ellington, Evie, 122
Ellington, Mercer, 202, 286, 287, 297
Elnora, 5, 33
Emmett, 22

Emporia State University, Kansas, 212
English language skills, CT's practice of, 30–31, 96
Etoile Music Productions, 188–91
Europe, CT's activity in: with Basie Eight Band, 219; with Big Bad Band, 186; and *Clark After Dark* recording session, 219; with Duke Ellington's band, 156–58; and Duke Ellington's death, 205–6; at Ellington Society Convention in Stockholm, 244–45; with *Free and Easy* blues opera, 167–70; with George Wein's shows, 201, 225, 230; at Nice Jazz Festival, 201, 225, 230; with Norman Granz's shows, 160–61, 163–64, 219; with small groups, 166–67, 214–15, 216, 227, 231; with Vienna Conservatory Band, 245; with Young Titans, 248–49
Evans, Skeeter, 91

Faddis, Jon, 218, 239, 240, 247, 249, 297, 301
family of CT. *See individual family members*
Fannie Mae (CT's mother-in-law). *See* Reddon, Fannie Mae
father of CT. *See* Terry, Clark Virgil
Faulise, Paul, 172
Faust, Allan, 184
Feather, 55–59, 72, 85
Fenders, Matt, 209
Ferguson, Maynard, 134
Ferrante, Joe, 172
Ferrara, Don, 200
Ferrell, Ryan, Dr., 253
Fields, Herbie, 91, 93
Fields, W.C., 53
Fisher, Maria, 233
Fishman, Charlie, 238
Fitzgerald, Ella, 80, 87, 100, 153, 157–58, 161, 166, 168, 223, 225, 295, 300
Flint, Michigan, CT's activity in, 58–62, 197
Floating Jazz Festival, 233, 239, 243, 297

flugelhorns played by CT, 153–56, 158, 163–64, 178, 218

flying, CT's fear of, 94, 102, 106, 119, 120, 159

Fochios, Steve, Dr., 246

Fontana, Carl, 212

Ford, Fats, 129, 141, 156

Forrest, Jimmy, 87, 117

Fort Apache Band, 194

Foster, Frank ("Flankson"), 253

Fowlkes, Charlie, 91

Fox, Charlie ("Sluggo"), 14, 87, 210

Fox, John, 14

France, CT's activity in: with *Free and Easy* blues opera, 169–70; with George Wein's shows, 201, 225–26, 230; with small group at Paris nightclub, 166–67; with small group in provincial vineyard, 214–15

Francis, Panama, 138

Franklin, Aretha, 177, 253

Franklin, Joe, 228

Frazier, Joe, 164

Free and Easy (Harold Arlen's blues opera), CT's involvement with, xi, 165, 167–70, 287

Freelon, Nnenna, 244

Friedland, Hans, 242

Friedman, Don, 186, 187, 226, 244, 251, 252

Fuqua, Charlie, 131

Galilee Baptist Church, 232

gambling, 55, 56, 58, 61, 70, 74, 75, 76, 83, 85, 93, 94, 96–97, 99, 101, 114, 115, 116, 119, 146, 150, 152, 170

Gamby, Oscar, 185

Gardner, Joe, 192

Garisto, Franky, 172

Garrett, Duke, 91

Garroway, Dave, 132

Gary (CT's stepson). *See* Paris, Gary

Gastel, Carlos, 118

Gault, Billy, 193, 194

Gaviglio, Philippe, 214–16, 246

Gensel, John, 205, 229, 242

George Borders' Club, 116

Germany, Jazz at the Philharmonic tour in, 160–61

Getz, Stan, 173, 290, 292

Ghee, Gene, 192, 193, 194

Gibson, Dick, 197, 210, 219

Gibson, Mattie, 219

Gillespie, Dizzy ("Diz"), 99, 107, 140, 153, 156, 158, 161, 163, 164, 192, 218, 238, 248, 288, 289, 295

Gilliam, Donald (CT's nephew), 159, 216

Gilmore, Marcus, 248

Gisbert, Greg, 241

Glasser, Dave, 252, 300

Glen Cove, Long Island, CT's residence in, 245

Glenn, Tyree, 196

Glow, Bernie, 191

Golden, Harry (CT's brother-in-law), 251

golfing, 141

Gonsalves, Paul, 138, 143, 165, 166, 286

Gonzales, Andy, 192, 194

Gonzales, Babs, 201, 290

Gonzales, Jerry, 192, 194

Goodman, Benny, 92, 172

Gordon, John, 184, 185, 187

Gormé, Eydie, 191

Graf, Bob, 117, 118

Graham, John, 250, 251

Grammy nominations and awards, 243; CT's Lifetime Achievement Award, xi, 255–57

Grand Rapids, Michigan, CT's activity in, 58–59, 62

Granz, Greta, 228

Granz, Norman ("Smedley"), 142, 158–65, 176–77, 185, 206, 216, 219, 228, 246

Graves, Joe, 106

Gray, Wardell, 118, 284

Great Lakes Naval Training Center, CT's WWII service at, 66–69, 71, 75–76, 91, 103, 118

Great Plains Jazz Camp, 212–14, 216

Green, Bennie, 70

Green, Cyril, 192

Green, Freddie, 113, 116, 118, 123, 124, 126, 173
Green, Madeline, 92
Green, Urbie, 173
Greene, Frank, 248, 251
Greenwood, Lil, 138
Greer, Sonny, 138, 157
Grey, Al ("Fab"), 73, 163, 224, 229, 231–32, 235, 240, 241, 242, 244
Griffin, Johnny, 91, 288, 289
Griot Museum (St. Louis), 254
Grissom, Jimmy, 81, 138
Growe, Ames, 242
Guerra, Steve, 247, 248
Guillaume, Robert, 168
Gut, Stjepko, 248, 251
Gwen (CT's current wife). *See* Terry, Gwen
"Gym." *See* Jim and Andy's bar and restaurant

Haas, Fred, 231
Hackett, Bobby, 80, 214
Haggart, Bobby, 172
Hall, Jim, 53–54, 173
Hamilton, Jimmy, 137, 138, 141, 143, 166, 167, 285, 289
Hamilton, Johnny "Bugs," 21
Hamilton, Melissa, 231
Hampton, Lionel, 54, 71, 79, 89, 102, 106, 108, 119, 123, 127, 198, 229, 231, 249, 292, 293; CT as performer in band of, 89–94, 135, 299
Hancock, Herbie, 204, 231
Harding, Buster, 125
Hargrove, Roy, 247, 251, 253, 256
Harlem, CT's activity in, 74, 75, 96, 182, 185; and youth band, 192–94, 227, 294
Harris, Jackie, 242
Harris, Joe, 169
Harris, Les, 231
Harry (CT's brother-in-law). *See* Golden, Harry
Hart, George, 92
Hassell, Bernice, 54
Hawk, Val, 231

Hawkins, Coleman, 74, 156, 158, 161, 291
Haworth, New Jersey, CT's residence in, xvi, 246
Hayes, Jimmy, 207
Hayes, Louis, 173
health problems, CT's, 178, 183, 186, 190, 219–20, 224–25, 226, 228, 229, 230–33, 235–40, 246, 249, 253, 254
Heard, John, 162, 163
Heath, Jimmy, 173, 177, 184, 185, 201, 209, 226, 229, 233, 241, 244, 247, 251, 253, 258, 288
Heath, Mona, 247
Heath, Texas, CT's residence in, 228, 242, 245
Hefti, Neal, 104
Helms, Johnny, 229
Henderson, Rick, 166, 184
Henderson, Skitch, 175, 182, 201
Hennessey, Jack, 106
Herbolzheimer, Peter, 254, 296
Herman, Sam, 173
Herman, Woody, 118, 157, 201
Hershorn, Tad, 247
Herwig, Conrad, 209, 248
Hiawatha (CT's son). *See* Terry, Hiawatha
Hicks, Alan, 247, 249, 252, 255, 257
Hicks, Dobbie (CT's pseudonym), 135
Hicks, John, 231, 241, 299
Hillery, Art, 162
Hines, Earl, 201
Hinton, Milt ("Judge"), 182, 188, 202, 227, 229, 231, 242, 247, 249
Hinton, Mona, 227, 242, 247
Hite, Les, 70
Hitson, Jimmy, 29, 39–41
Hixon, Dick, 173
Hodge, Derrick, 248, 256
Hodges, Johnny, 107, 137–38, 139, 141, 158, 285, 286
Hoffman, Michael, Dr., 206–7, 230, 231
Hogans, Lee, 247, 252
Holiday, Billie, 74, 111, 135–36, 284
Holland, CT's activity in, 161, 219, 230, 245

Holland, Peanuts, 105
Holley, Major, 73
Holley, R.T., 180
Holloway, Red, 177, 196, 245, 247, 251, 298, 300
Holmes and Jean, 80
Holzfeind, Frank, 153
honorary doctorates, awarded to CT, 207, 227, 248, 253
honorary high school diploma, awarded to CT, 253
Hopkins, Charles ("Chuck," CT's nephew), 257
Horn, Robert, 81
Horne, Lena, 71, 202
House, Danny, 209, 211
House, Dougal, 183, 211
House of Representatives Jazz Resolution, 219
houses owned by CT, 179–80, 206, 228, 245
Howard, Buddy, 245
Howard University Jazz Ensemble, 244
Hoyle, Arthur, 254
Hubbard, Freddie, 202, 231
Hudson, George, 75, 77–81, 83–94, 88–90, 94–96, 99, 108, 111, 124, 165, 214
Hultin, Randi, 242
Humphrey, Christopher, 231
Hunter, Lurlene, 186
Hunter, Stafford, 248, 251
Hut, Ethel, 27, 33–34, 54, 76–77, 98, 138

Ida Cox and Her Dark Town Scandals. *See* Cox, Ida
Ink Spots, 131
International Art of Jazz, 22
The Interpretation of the Jazz Language (CT's book with Phil Rizzo), 198
Irby, Fred, 244

Jabbar, Kareem Abdul, 237
Jackson, Al, 131
Jackson, Dewey, 8, 19, 42–44, 48, 51
Jackson, Michael, 256
Jackson, Milt, 247, 290, 291, 292, 296

Jackson, Peewee, 89
Jackson, Quentin ("Butter"), 130, 141–42, 167, 169
Jackson, Sandy, 247
Jacquet, Illinois, 71, 89, 95, 96, 161
James, Ray, 212
Japan, CT's activity in, 216, 218
Jazz at the Philharmonic tours (J.A.T.P.), 160–61, 219, 294, 297
jazz camps, CT's involvement with, 212–14, 216, 229
jazz festivals honoring CT, 205, 227, 229–30, 251, 253
Jazz Foundation of America, 254
Jazz Journal, 186
Jazz Mobile program, 194, 227
Jeffers, Jack, 184, 185, 187, 188, 249, 251
Jenkins, George, 91
Jennings, Carl, 192, 194
Jennings, Peter, 254
Jeter-Pillars Orchestra, 23, 89
Jim and Andy's bar and restaurant, New York, 144, 173–74, 182
jingles, commercial, 172, 186, 189, 191
Johnny Pops (CT's brother-in-law). *See* Davis, Johnny Pops
Johnson, Bill ("Frog"), 113, 116
Johnson, Buddy, 78, 91, 167–68
Johnson, Gus, 113, 116, 118, 173
Johnson, Jimmy, 138
Johnson, J.J., 173, 292, 293, 297
Johnson, Joe ("Ziggy"), 80
Johnson, Lennie, 168
Johnson, Osie, 173, 177
Johnson, Plas, 242
Jones, Eddie, 245
Jones, Etta, 231
Jones, Hank, 173, 229, 231, 293
Jones, Jimmy, 74
Jones, Philly Joe, 144–45
Jones, Quincy ("Q"), xi, xvi, 192, 193; challenges in show with, 170; CT's gets gig offer from, 165; CT gives lessons to and plays first chart of, 121; CT's help with health from, 246; CT as member of "Free and Easy"

show band of, 167–69; CT's recording date and gig with, 201; CT's surprise at Grammy award from, 256; first "Clark Terry Award" to, 258; selected discography of, 287, 290, 291, 295
Jones, Rufus, 138
Jones, Sam, 173
Jones, Thad, 247
Jones, Tim, 53, 58
Jones, Virgil, 185, 187
Jordan, Duke, 173, 186
Jordan, Louis, 88, 135
Juanita (CT's sister). *See* Terry, Juanita ("Neet") Hopkins
"Juanito." *See* Tizol, Juan
Juilliard School of Music, 145

Kato, Donya "Mama D," 247
Kauflin, Justin, 247, 249, 252
Kaufman, Cheryl, 226
Keane, Helen, 187
Kelly, Wynton, 173
Kendrick, Stantawn, 247, 249, 251, 252
Kennedy, Edward ("Ted"), 253
Kennedy, John F. (President), 202
Kennedy, Robert F., 202
Kennedy Center, 217
Kenny, Bill, 131
Kenton, Stan, 78
Kent State University, 245
Kilbert, Porter, 168, 169
Killian, Al, 105
Kimball, David, 66, 70
Kindred, Bob, 239, 247, 297
King, Martin Luther, Jr., 152, 202
Kirby, John, 141
Kisor, Ryan, 228
Klaxton, Chris, 247
Kleinsinger, Jack, 244
Klink, Al, 172
K.M.B.B.G.A. pens, 190, 191
Knepper, Jimmy, 198
Kobeem, Joseph, 210
Koeniges, Martin, 187
Koulavaris, Jim, 173–74
Krupa, Gene, 172
Kugler, Roger, 212

"Lady K." *See* Cox, Katherine
Laine, Cleo, 230, 296, 298
LaJuana (Gary's wife). *See* Paris, LaJuana
Lamond, Don, 173
Lang, Harvey, 208
Las Vegas, CT's activity in, 149–50
Lawrence, Arnie, 184, 185, 193
Leach, David, 209
Leali, Brad, 248
Lee, John, 246
Legacy (Gary's daughter). *See* Paris, Legacy
Len Bowden and His Melody Masters, 62–64
Lesczak, Vito, 231
Let's Talk Trumpet: From Legit to Jazz (CT's book with Phil Rizzo), 198
Levine, Aaron, 169, 170, 171, 175–76
Levinsky, Walt, 172
Levy, John, 74
Lew, Barzillai, 156
Lewis, Ed, 113
Lewis, Jimmy, 117, 118
Lewis, Mel, 173, 200, 297
Lieb, Dick, 172
Lillian (CT's sister). *See* Terry, Lillian
Li'l Tony (Tony's son). *See* Paris, Anthony Bruce V
Lincoln Junior High School, St. Louis, 13, 17–18
Lindberg, Jeff, 247, 254, 301
Linton, Henri, 253
Liston, Melba, 169, 184, 189–90, 252
Little, Wilbur, 186
Little Bill (cartoon television show), 257
Litwak, Bob, 229
Loftis, Keith, 242
London, England, CT's activity in, 254
London, Lucy, 39–41
Loonstijn, Annette (Hans' wife), 219, 230
Loonstijn, Hans, 219, 230
Lord, Tom, 283
Los Angeles, CT's activity in, 161, 230; with Charlie Barnet's band, 103–4;

Los Angeles, CT's activity in,
(*continued*)
with Duke Ellington's band, 134; and
Grammy Award ceremony, 255–57
Louis, Joe, 70, 124, 150
Lowe, Mundell, 173, 288
Lowenthal, Dick, 244
Lowenthal, Dr., 232
Lujan, Lilliana, 247
Lujan, Tony, 209, 247, 248, 251
Lunceford, Jimmy, 55, 68, 71, 78, 89,
153
Luty, Bryce, 212
Lynch, Jerry, 51–52, 86
Lynch, Quentin, 192, 193
lynching, 107

Mabern, Harold, 247
Mable (CT's sister). *See* Terry, Mable
MacManus, Cameron ("Cinnamon"),
247, 249, 251, 252
Madagascar Fats, 210
Madarao Jazz Festival (Japan), 218
Madison, Levi, 46
Mahogany, Kevin, 253
Malone, Russell, 247
"Mama D." *See* Kato, Donya
Mandel, Johnny, 200
Manhattan School of Music, 193, 229,
230, 244, 253
Mann, Herbie, 201, 291
Marable, Fate, 48–51, 63
marching band, CT's childhood par-
ticipation in, 14–17, 20, 66
Margueritte (CT's sister). *See* Terry,
Margueritte ("Skeety Reet") Davis
Marie Louise (CT's sister). *See* Terry,
Marie Louise
marriages, CT's: to Gwen, 242–43,
246, 247, 250–51, 255, 256; to Pau-
line, 111–13, 116–18, 122–23, 126,
145, 152–53, 159, 167, 169–70, 175,
180, 182, 205–12, 217, 221; to Sissy,
22–23, 39, 50, 51, 54, 64, 73, 74, 83,
98, 102, 221
Marsalis, Branford, 209, 210, 231, 240
Marsalis, Delfeayo, 231

Marsalis, Ellis, 231
Marsalis, Wynton, 231–32, 235
Marshall, Wendell, 166
Martin, Earl ("Siam"), 81
Matheson, Alan, 242, 255
Matteson, Rich, 213
Matthews, Big George, 79, 113, 115
Matthews, Lewellen, 193
Matthews, Miles, 193, 194
Matthews, Ronnie, 186
Mattie Lucille (CT's sister). *See* Terry,
Mattie Lucille
Mavrin, Mario, 231
Max (Tony's son). *See* Paris, Maximus
Maxwell, Jim, 172, 191, 250; confronts
racist homeowner to help CT buy
first home, 179
McBee, Cecil, 231
McConnell, Rocks, 73, 79
McCurdy, Ron, 162
McFarland, Gary, 173, 229, 290, 293
McField, Sy (CT's brother-in-law),
8, 11–14, 23, 25, 26, 37, 42, 45–47,
51, 58, 63, 90, 96, 102, 108, 127; in
Dewey Jackson's band, 3; CT goes to
Dewey Jackson's band with, 43
McGowan, Jason (CT's nephew), 257
McGowan, Odell (CT's nephew), 83,
216
McLaurine, Marcus, 226, 229, 244,
247, 249, 251, 252
McLaurine, Miyuki (Marcus' wife),
247
McLean, Jackie, 192, 198
McLean, Rene (Jackie's son), 192, 194
McLeod, Alice, 166
McMahon, Ed, 175, 205
McMurray, Cliff ("Wheels"), 229
McTomson, Checkers, 56, 57
media coverage of CT, 87, 95, 186, 191,
196–97
Mediterranean cruise, tribute to CT
on, 245
Megabow, Annie, 250, 258
Melis, José, 172, 175
Melody Maker magazine, 186
memorabilia, CT's, exhibits of, 218, 253

Meredith, Don, 212
Metronome magazine, 87, 95
Meyer, Gerd, 219
Michaels, Lloyd ("Karate Chops"), 184, 185, 187, 193
Michelle (Rudy Jr.'s daughter). *See* White, Michelle
Miles, Art, 202
Miles, Butch, 245
military service, CT's, 64–76
Millander, Lucky, 91, 94, 95
Miller, Don, 225
Miller, Dorie, 153. *See also* Dorie Miller apartment building
Miller, Eric, 92
Miller, Glenn, 80, 172
Miller, Michael ("Migueligans"), 255
Miller, Sue (Don's wife), 225
Mills Brothers, 14, 80
Mingus, Charles, 149, 198–99, 288, 291
Mitchell, Red, 214–15, 298
Mitchell, Sweetie, 242
mobsters. *See* organized crime
Molina, Charlie, 212
Monk, Gale ("T" III's wife), 233
Monk, Nellie (Thelonious Monk's wife), 233
Monk, Thelonious, 107, 168, 231, 233, 234, 235, 237, 241, 242, 248, 252, 254, 285, 286, 294, 299, 301
Monk, Thelonious ("T") III, 231, 233
monkeys, CT's truck ride with carnival, 40–41, 43
Monk Institute, 231, 233–34, 237, 241, 242, 248, 252
Monteiro, Shawnn (CT's goddaughter), 253, 257–58
Montgomery, Bob, 185, 212, 230
Montreux Jazz Festival, 164, 227, 295, 296
Moody, James, 196, 213, 229, 231, 296
Moore, Archie, 145, 199–200
Morgan, Joe, 122–23, 147
Moroni, Dado, 218, 227
Morris, Joe ("Chop Chop"), 91
mother of CT. *See* Terry, Mary
Mouse, Jack, 212

Mraz, George, 218
"Mr. C." *See* Carney, Bill
Mulligan, Gerry, 200–201, 230, 288, 290
"Mumbles" (CT's composition), 176–77, 178, 223, 225, 248, 257, 293
Mumbles newsletter, 241
Mundy, Jimmy, 125
Murlene (CT's niece). *See* Davis, Murlene
Murphy, Mark, 172, 189, 191
Murray, Ray, 192

NAACP, 109, 178
Nance, Ray, 129, 130, 137, 138, 140, 196
Nash, Lewis ("One"), 244
National Association of Jazz Educators, 196, 197
National Visionary Leadership Project, 254
navy, U.S., CT's service in, 64–76
NBC television network, 174, 176, 178, 179, 180, 182, 185, 191, 198–202, 204–5; CT becomes first Negro on staff at, 170–71; CT called to join staff of, 169; CT helps to recruit Snooky Young for, 175; CT joins roster of first-call musicians for product commercials, 172–73; other musicians on staff at, 172
Neal, Marvin, 192
Neiman, David, 221
Neiman, Peter (CT's playson), 221
Nelson, Kariyma (Jo Ann), 247
Nelson, Oliver, 173, 291, 292, 293
New England Conservatory, 253
New Jersey Public Library, 244
Newman, David ("Fathead"), 244
Newman, Joe, 173
New Orleans Jazz Festival, 242
Newport Jazz Festival, 201, 287, 299
New School, New York City, 229
Newsom, Tommy, 172
New York City, CT's activity in: Apollo Theater, 92, 96, 133, 145, 149, 192; and Beacons of Jazz Award, 229; with Big Bad Band, 184–91; with Bob

New York City, CT's activity in
(continued)
Litwak's band, 229; with Charles
Mingus's band, 199; with Charlie
Barnet's band, 108; and Christmas
production at St. Bartholomew, 239–
40; with Count Basie's band, 108–9,
119, 124–26; with Duke Ellington's
band, 134, 144, 234; and Etoile Music
Productions, 188–91; with George
Hudson's band, 96; as jazz educator,
191–93; at Joe Franklin's television
show, 228; with Lionel Hampton's
band, 92; with MSM Jazz Orches-
tra, 244; at NBC television network,
171–74; and recording sessions for
albums, 226, 230–31; at Tonight
Show, 173–76, 178, 179, 180, 182,
185, 191, 198–202, 204–5; with Mel
Tormé, 229; and tribute to Gary
McFarland, 229; during WWII,
73–75; with Young Titans, 249
New York University, 244
Nice Jazz Festival, 201, 225, 230
Nicholas, Harold, 168
Nielson, Anja, 247
Nikki (Tony's daughter). See Paris,
Nicole
Nimo, Koo, 210
Noble, Ray, 103
Noonan, Jerry, 212
Northern Illinois University, 253
Norton, Larry, Dr., 246
Nottingham, Jimmy, 106, 185
Nugent, Pete ("Public Tapper #1"), 80

Obama, Barack (President), 254
Odessa (CT's sister). See Terry, Odessa
Odrich, Ron, 185
Olatunji, Babatunde, 202
Oldham, Lloyd, 138
Olds Company, 155
Olivia (Tony's wife). See Paris, Olivia
O'Neal, Hank ("Hankles"), 233, 243,
245, 246
O'Neal, Milton, 192
"O.P." See Peterson, Oscar

Orange, John, 81
organized crime, 81–83
Otis (CT's cousin). See Berry, Otis
Otter, Ned, 209
Outlaw, Richard, 52–53
Owens, Jimmy, 185
Oxenhorn, Wendy, 254

Paar, Jack, and Tonight television
show (NBC), 171, 175
Pablo Records, 159–60
Pace University, tribute to CT at, 244
Page, Dave, 91, 93
painting, acrylic, CT's practice of, 245
Palmer, Beaver, 58–62
Palmer, Singleton ("Cocky"), 81, 83,
87, 90
Paradise Jazz Party, Scottsdale, Ari-
zona, 225
Paris, Anthony Bruce ("Tony") IV
(CT's stepson), 221, 250
Paris, Anthony Bruce V (Tony's son),
251
Paris, France, CT's activity in: with
blues-opera band, 169–70; with
small group at nightclub, 166–67
Paris, Gary (CT's stepson), 221, 241,
249, 250, 251, 257
Paris, Gwen. See Terry, Gwen
Paris, LaJuana (Gary's wife), 249, 250,
251
Paris, Legacy (Gary's daughter), 249,
251
Paris, Maximus (Tony's son), 251
Paris, Nicole ("Nikki," Tony's daugh-
ter), 251
Paris, Olivia (Tony's wife), 251
Parker, Bunky, 81
Parker, Chan, 169
Parker, Charlie ("Yardbird"), 107, 143–
44, 156, 290
Parker, J. Allen, 111
Parker, Willie ("Weasel"), 81, 96, 111,
242
Parlan, Horace, 214–15
Pass, Joe, 163, 206
Pastel Music publishing company, 189

Paterson, Pork Chop, 131–32
Patterson and Jackson, 80, 128
Pauline (CT's second wife). *See* Terry, Pauline
Payne, Cecil, 173, 289, 290
Payne, Ves, 88
Payton, Nicholas, 231, 243–44, 247
Peale, Norman Vincent, 183
Pearl Harbor, Japanese attack on, 58
Pedersen, Niels, 164
Pender, Gotch, 53
Penn, George, 192
Penque, Romeo, 174
pens, K.M.B.B.G.A., 190, 191
Peoria, CT's activity in, 54–58
Perriman, Gus, 42–44, 47–48, 49–50, 176
Perry, Dick, 172
Persip, Charlie, 173
Persson, Åke, 169
Peter (CT's playson). *See* Neiman, Peter
Petersen, Jack, 212
Peterson, Kelly (wife of Oscar), 228
Peterson, Oscar, 158, 159, 164, 176–77, 228, 249, 290, 292, 295, 296, 297, 300
Petrović, Boško, 219, 229, 231, 246, 295
Petrucciani, Michel, 215
Pettiford, Oscar, 148, 149, 166
Pettiway, Bernard, 192, 193
Philadelphia, CT's activity in, 110, 244
Phillips, Anne, 172, 238, 239
Picasso, Pablo, 159–60, 185, 245
Pichon, Fats, 48
Pickens, Willie ("The Picker"), 245
Pine Bluff, Arkansas, xvi, xvii, 85, 222, 250–53
Pitts, Trudy, 244
Pizzarelli, Bucky, 172
Plater, Bobby, 91
Playboy Jazz Festival, 201
Pleasantville, New Jersey, CT's summer residence in, 206
Pomeroy, Herb, 173, 228
Poole, Carl, 172
"Pop" (CT's father). *See* Terry, Clark Virgil

Pope, Lee, 88
"Pops." *See* Armstrong, Louis
Pops, Johnny, 3, 10, 11, 95
Portland, Oregon, CT's activity in, with Charlie Barnet's band, 104–6
Portnow, Neil, 255, 256, 257
Powell, Adam Clayton, 234
Powell, Richie, 134
Powell, Seldon, 173, 188
"Pretty Girl." *See* Spearman, Versie
Previn, André, 256
"Prez." *See* Young, Lester
Prince, Mason ("M.P."), 66
Princeton University, 228
Procope, Russell, 138, 141
prostitution, 54, 55, 56–57, 59–61, 93, 174
Pryor, Richard, 55
pseudonym ("Dobbie Hicks") used by CT, 135
Puente, Tito, 240
Pyles, Robbie ("Shitty"), 1, 5–7, 15, 29, 33, 84, 108, 254–55, 258

"Q." *See* Jones, Quincy
Queensboro Community College, 229
Quill, Gene, 173, 200
Quinnipiac Jazz Festival, 197; CT honored at, 205

racism, 28, 31–32, 34–35, 36, 67–68, 73, 76, 92–93, 105, 106, 109–10, 149–51, 162, 179, 202–4. *See also* civil rights movement
Ragsdale, Maxine, 225
Ramsey, Lawrence, 192
Randle, Eddie, 86
Raph, Alan, 200
rap music, 243
Raschel, Jimmy, 54
recordings, of CT's compositions: "Marina Bay Rednecks," 163; "Mumbles," 177, 178; "Out on a Limb," 71; "Phalanges," 110
recording sessions, CT's: with Charlie Barnet's band, 110; for Chesky Records, 226; with Dinah Washington,

recording sessions, CT's *(continued)*
134–35; with Duke Ellington's band,
134, 142; with Eddie "Cleanhead"
Vinson's band, 87–88, 162; with
Gerry Mulligan's band, 200; with
Lionel Hampton's band, 229, 231;
Norman Granz's production of, 162–
63; for TCB Records, 226–27; with
Thelonious Monk's band, 234–35.
See also albums, CT as performer on
Reddon, Fannie Mae (CT's mother-in-
law), 98, 100–103, 111, 127
Reddon, Henry (CT's father-in-law),
98, 101, 102, 103, 111, 127
Redman, Joshua, 241, 244
Reed, Benny, 86
Reese, Della, 138
Reeves, Dianne, 252, 257, 300, 301
Rehak, Frank, 173
Reid, Irene, 229
Reid, Rufus, 247
Reider, Jim, 200
Rentschler, Steve, 209
Reuben and Cherry Carnival, 23–32,
67, 95, 141, 190
Ricci, Paul, 172
Richardson, Jerome, 168
Rizzo, Phil, 198
Roach, Max, 134, 234–35, 241, 301
Robbins College, Florida, 244
Robert, George, 227, 242, 246, 298, 299
Robert, Joan, 242
Roberts, Bugs, 96
Robinson, Jackie, 151–52
Robinson, Janice, 186
Robinson, Mayola ("Sissy"; CT's first
wife), 22–23, 39, 50, 51, 54, 64, 73–
74, 83, 98, 102, 221
Roche, Betty, 138
Rockefeller, John D., 171, 174
Rodriguez, Willie, 173
Rogers, Kenny, 192, 194
Rogers, Shorty, 154
Rollins, Sonny, 234, 286
Rollins, William, 81
Roosevelt, Franklin D., 75
Rosengarden, Bobby, 172

Royal, Ernie, 79, 173, 185
Royal, Marshal, 79, 118, 120, 196
Rudy (Pauline's son), 98, 100, 101,
102, 103, 111, 127, 182, 208, 211
Rushing, Jimmy, 113, 114, 116, 153,
294
Russell, Randy, 209
Rutgers University, 228

Sanders, John, 166
Sandoval, Arturo, 247
Sargent, Gray, 227, 245
Savitt, Jan, 6
Saxton, Bill, 192, 194
Schifrin, Lalo, 201, 292, 293
Schildkraut, David, 134
Schlinger, Sol, 173
Schmidlin, Peter, 227
Schneider, Chuck, 212
Schroeder, Adam, 248, 251
Scott, Allen, 197, 225
Scott, Billy (CT's cousin), 7, 13, 46, 74,
102, 108
Scott, Buster (Abdul Hameed), 91,
92–93
Scott, Clyde (CT's cousin), 13–14
Scott, Gertrude (CT's maternal aunt),
2–3, 7, 13, 23, 33, 84, 102, 108, 112
Scott, Hazel, 71
Scott, James ("Short Stop"), 192, 194
Scott, Shirley, 201
Scott, Tony, 75, 150, 285
Seals, William, 81
Seattle, CT's activity in: with Count
Basie's band, 120–21; with Duke
Ellington's band, 134
Seiler, Dave, 227, 239, 245
Selmer Instrument Company, 153–55
seventieth birthday celebration, CT's,
227–28
Severino, Frank, 206
Severinsen, Doc, 105–6, 172, 182, 191,
204–5, 294
Shanahan, Dick, 107
Shank, Bud, 107, 299
Shantz, Andy, 247
Shaughnessy, Ed, 138, 196

Shavers, Charlie, 95, 158
Shaw, Woody, 184
Shertzer, Hymie, 172
Shihab, Sahib, 166, 168
Shire, Shelly ("Muscles"), 233, 246
"Shitty" (CT's childhood friend). *See* Pyles, Robbie
Shorter, Wayne, 233
"Shorts" (CT's brother). *See* Terry, Charles Edward
Shorty Mac, 23–24, 26, 39, 190
Shpak, Josh, 255
Shpak, Noah, 255
Simon, George, 87, 95
Simon, John ("Faithful"), 231, 232, 235, 246, 247
Sims, Zoot, 158, 161, 173, 185, 257
Singleton, Annette, 71–72
Singleton, Willie, 185
Sissy (CT's first wife). *See* Robinson, Mayola
Skinner, Billy, 192
"Skoonje." *See* Bellson, Louie
Slaten, Whitney, 248, 251
Slater, Steve, 212
Slonaker, David, 209
Small, Leonard, 25, 66
Smith, Carrie, 229
Smith, George ("Harmonica"), 162
Smith, Stuff, 74
Smith, Sykes, 71, 153, 154
Smith, Willie, 73, 79, 89
Sneed, Ann, 242
Snodgrass, C.L., 212
Snodgrass, Henry, 120, 126
softball, CT as player of, 100–101, 166, 182–83
Soladar, Rosalie, 224, 232, 235, 242
Sollenberger, Jay, 212
Soloff, Lew, 184, 185, 187, 244
Sommerville, Reverend ("Rev"), 4, 18, 25, 30–31, 105
Soph, Ed, 186
Sousa, John Philip, 20
South Carolina Jazz Festival, 229
Southeast Missouri State University, 253

Spearman, Versie (CT's mother-in-law), 251
Speert, Arnie, 248
Sproles, Victor, 186, 187, 210
Stametz, Della, 244
Stamm, Marvin, 185
Standifer, Floyd, 168–69
Stewart, Rex, 129, 136, 137, 196
Sting, 194, 217
St. Louis, CT's activity in: and Blueberry Hill Walk of Fame star honoring CT, 254; in childhood, 1–21, 33, 43–45, 46–47, 133; with Eddie "Cleanhead" Vinson's band, 77–90, 94–96; with Ellington's band, 1–2, 117, 128–32; with Fate Marable's band, 48–51; and George Border's club gig, 116–17; with George Hudson's band, 77–84, 88–90, 94, 95–96, 99; and Griot Museum wax figure of CT, 254; and Hawaiian Club jam sessions, 87, 100; and J.A.T.P. performance, 161; with Len Bowden's band, 62–64; and Lincoln Inn gig, 42–43, 47–48, 176; with Lucky Millander's band, 94, 95; with Pauline's family, 101–3, 110–11, 126–28; post-WWII return to, 76–77; and visit with Gwen, 243
Stone, Basil, 81
Stoner, Cyrus, 81
Stratton, Don, xv, 193
Strayhorn, Billy ("Strays"), 146–48, 153, 185, 201, 209, 247, 286, 293
Stripling, Byron, 209
Studd, Tony, 173, 186
Students Targeting Adult Responsibility (STAR), 220–21, 242, 256
Stump and Stumpy, 128, 131
Sumner High School Swingsters, 25, 66
Sumney, Harold, 244
Sung, Helen, 248, 251, 252–53
Sunol, Jordi, 246
Swartz, Bob, 187
Swartz, Charles, 207
Sweden, CT's activity in, 244–45

Switzerland, CT's activity in, 161, 164, 208, 218, 219, 227, 230, 248–49, 297

Tarrant, Merrell, 66
Tate, Buddy, 113, 116, 229, 231, 288
Tate, Dennis, 192
Tate, Grady, 184, 186, 229, 231, 241
taxation, 190
Taylor, Billy, 194, 196, 202, 286, 289, 292; CT's first flugelhorn recording with, 154
TCB Records, 226
teaching activity, CT's, xv–xvii, 2, 191–98, 205, 206, 217–18, 227, 233, 240, 242, 245, 247–48, 250–52, 257–58; and jazz camp, 212–14, 216. *See also* youth bands, organized by CT
techniques, musical, practiced by CT, 12, 30, 44–45, 50, 68, 73, 84, 141, 153, 168, 178, 195–96
Temperley, Joe, 185, 187
Terrence (Rudy Jr.'s son). *See* White, Terrence
Terry, Ada Mae McField (CT's sister), 3, 11–13, 17, 23, 26, 32, 42–46, 50–51, 62, 67–68, 72, 78, 90–91, 95–96, 102, 159, 212
Terry, Charles Edward ("Shorts" or "Ed,"CT's brother), 3, 6, 9, 94, 108, 159, 212
Terry, Clark Virgil ("Pop," CT's father), 2–6, 8–13, 17, 22, 24, 33, 39, 43, 54, 62–63, 68–73, 95, 101, 109, 110, 127, 181, 207, 212, 216
Terry, Gwen (formerly Paris, nee Jones; CT's current wife), xi, xvi, 220–33, 235–38, 240–41; in marriage with CT, 242–43, 245–47, 250–51, 255–56
Terry, Hiawatha (CT's son), 51, 64, 74, 83, 98, 100–102, 127, 145, 159, 181, 206, 216, 221, 240, 243
Terry, Juanita ("Neet") Hopkins (CT's sister), 3, 159, 212, 216
Terry, Lesa (CT's cousin), 244, 257
Terry, Lillian ("Lil," CT's sister), 3, 145, 159, 212

Terry, Mable ("Sugar Lump," CT's sister), 3
Terry, Margueritte ("Skeety Reet") Davis (CT's sister), 3–4, 10–11, 62, 68–69, 72, 94, 102, 111, 127, 159, 207, 212, 216–17, 236–38, 243, 251
Terry, Marie Louise (CT's sister), 3, 95, 97, 102, 159, 212
Terry, Mary (CT's mother), 3, 108, 212, 223
Terry, Mattie Lucille (CT's sister), 3, 159, 212, 216
Terry, Mona (CT's cousin), 257
Terry, Odessa ("Dessie," CT's sister), 3, 11, 159, 212, 216
Terry, Pauline (nee Reddon; CT's second wife), 96–103, 106, 107, 110, 217, 221; death of, 211–12; in marriage with CT, 111–13, 116–18, 122–23, 126, 145, 152–53, 159, 167, 169–70, 175, 180, 182, 205–12
Terry, Teri (CT's cousin), 255, 257
Terry, Virgil Otto ("Bus," CT's brother), 3, 63, 95, 108, 159, 212
Terry, Zela (CT's cousin), 257
Terry Tunes (compilation of CT's compositions), 110
Thielmans, Toots, 230
Thigpen, Ed, 177, 214–15, 218, 293
Thimes, Denise, 253
Thomas, Joe, 89
Thomas, Stanley, 66
Timmons, Bobby, 173
Tizol, Juan, 141, 143, 149
TOBA (Theater Owners Booking Association), 89, 95, 113, 133
Tom Powell Post #77 Drum and Bugle Corps, 14–17, 26, 66, 97
Tonight Show, 173–74, 176, 178, 179, 180, 198, 202, 204–5, 225, 228, 231, 240, 250; CT considered for band leader of, 182–83, 185; CT debuts "Mumbles" on, 175; CT introduced to jazz education while with, 191; CT performs with Archie Moore on, 199–200; CT's recordings while working with, 201

Tony (CT's stepson). *See* Paris, Tony
Torain, Roy, 66
Tormé, Mel, 229
Torres, Crystal, 247, 248, 251, 256
Tosti, Don, 107
Travis, Nick, 200
Trent, Ricky, 172
trumpets played by CT: Buescher, 63; in childhood, 1, 7–8, 10, 12, 21; Olds Company "CT Model," 155; Wurlitzer ("Gray Ghost"), 21, 25, 26
Tucker, Dion, 248
Tunnell, Bon Bon, 6
Turk. *See* Austin, Willie
Turk's band, CT as member of. *See* Austin, Willie
Turney, Norris, 245
Tyrell, Steve, 246, 300, 301

University of Arkansas at Pine Bluff, xvii, 250, 251, 253
University of Central Oklahoma, 230
University of New Hampshire, xv, 207, 227–28, 233, 239, 245, 247, 248, 253
University of Pittsburgh, 218
Urban League, 109, 170, 178; campaigns for CT to be hired as first Negro staff member with NBC, 169

VanEpps, Donald, 29, 35, 37
Vashon High School, St. Louis, 17–23, 24–25, 30, 97, 98, 253
Vashon High School Swingsters, 11, 20–21, 24, 25
Vaughan, Sarah, 80, 128, 131, 132, 201, 288, 294
Vax, Mike, 185, 300
Veiled Prophet Parade, in St. Louis, 97
Verrette, Paul ("Pablo"), 227, 245
Vienna Conservatory Band, 245
Village Vanguard (New York), 200, 252, 288
Vinson, Eddie ("Cleanhead"), 87–88, 162
Vitous, Miroslav, 204

Waller, Fats, 21, 210
Wallin, Bengt-Arne, 242, 244–45, 295
Walton, Alphonso Stack, 70, 79
Warren, Earl ("Smiley"), 113, 116, 118, 173
Washington, D.C., CT's activity in, 114–15, 197, 217, 244
Washington, Dinah, 92, 134–35, 202, 284, 285, 286, 289
Washington, Jack ("Sergeant"), 113, 116
Washington, Kenny, 226
Wasserman, Ed, 173
Watkins, Julius, 169, 173
Watson, Deek, 131
Waukegan, CT's activity in, 70
Wayne, Fred, 192
Webb, Chick, 87
Webster, Ben, 74, 137, 138, 149, 150, 196
Webster, Freddie, 89
Webster, Paul, 89
Weidler Brothers, 106
Wein, George, 201–2, 225, 230, 232, 246
Wein, Joyce (George's wife), 201–2, 246
Wells, Dicky, 113, 115
Wess, Frank ("Magic"), 184, 187, 188, 193, 196, 209, 212, 229, 299
Whaley, Tom, 138
White, Betty (Rudy Jr.'s wife), 182, 208
White, Michelle (Rudy Jr.'s daughter), 182, 206; song for Michelle, 293
White, Rudy, Jr. (CT's stepson) 111, 127, 182, 208, 211
White, Rudy III (Rudy Jr.'s son), 182, 206
White, Terrence (Rudy Jr.'s son), 182, 206–7
White, Woodie, 70
White House, CT's performances at, 196, 294
Whitney Museum, 207
Wichita Jazz Festival, 252, 295
Wilder, Alec, 173
Wiley, Georgette (CT's sister-in-law), 251
Wilkins, Cynthia (Jimmy's wife), 242
Wilkins, Ernie, 25, 66, 71, 124–25, 168,

Wilkins, Ernie *(continued)*
183–84, 185, 187, 188, 193, 205, 209, 246, 288
Wilkins, Jenny, 246
Wilkins, Jimmy, 25, 66, 71, 124–25, 183, 186, 242
Wilkins, Ron, 209
William Paterson University, xv, xvi, 247, 248, 249, 250, 252
Williams, Barbara Jean (CT's niece), 97
Williams, Billy Dee, 233
Williams, Cootie, 129, 137, 146
Williams, Irene, 168
Williams, Irv ("Shithouse Shorty from Local #40"), 81
Williams, James, 227, 247, 299
Williams, Joe, 100–101, 103, 124, 125, 183, 201, 210, 225, 291, 292
Williams, Richard, 185
Williamson, Claude, 107
Wilson, Clarence Haydn, 19–21, 24–25, 60, 98, 108
Wilson, Derby, 80
Wilson, Gerald, 71, 73, 89, 100, 102, 107
Wilson, Jack, 206
Wilson, Marty, 202
Wilson, Nancy, 92
Winding, Kai, 173, 289

Winfield, Barbara, 138
Woode, Jimmy, 141, 166, 218, 245, 258, 286
Woodman, Britt, 141, 173, 198, 245
Woods, Chris, 185, 187, 210, 212
Woods, Mitchell ("Booty"), 91
Woods, Phil, 168, 169, 173, 184, 185, 187, 189, 200, 244
Woodyard, Sam, 138, 166
Wright, Austin, 80
Wright, Julius, 70
Wright, Lamar, Jr., 91
writings, CT's, 198, 225, 247
Wynters, Gail, 240

Young, Dottie, 175
Young, Lester ("Prez"), 70, 136, 142, 158, 213, 196
Young, Snooky, 89, 109, 175–76, 196, 202, 204
Young, Trummie, 89
Young Titans of Jazz, 248–49, 301
youth bands, organized by CT, 192–94, 205, 209–10, 227, 231

Zito, Freddie, 106
zoot suits, 77–78, 83
Zurbrugg, Hans, 248, 249
Zurbrugg, Marian, 249

Designer: Claudia Smelser
Text: 10.75/15 Janson
Display: Janson
Compositor: BookMatters, Berkeley
Cartographer: Bill Nelson
Printer and binder: Thomson-Shore, Inc.